THE ARMS
BAZAAR

THE
ARMS
BAZAAR

From Lebanon to Lockheed

ANTHONY
SAMPSON

THE VIKING PRESS

NEW YORK

For Barbara Wootton

This edition distributed in Canada by
Penguin Books Canada Limited

LIBRARY OF CONGRESS CATALOGING IN PUBLICATION DATA
Sampson, Anthony.
The Arms Bazaar.
Includes index.
1. Munitions.   2. World politics—20th century.
1. Title.
HD9743.A2S35   1977   338.4'7'6234   77-5753
ISBN 0-670-13263-2

Printed in the United States of America
Set in Monotype Bembo

Contents

Introduction

THIS is a book about the arms trade and its development over the last century, culminating in the contemporary boom in arms sales. It is about the companies who make the arms, and the attitudes and methods of the men who buy them and sell them, or try to control them. It does not pretend to analyse the weapons themselves, or the nature of the warfare for which they are designed. The question of arms overlaps with many other major problems—the central arms race between the superpowers, the defence of NATO, or the control of nuclear weapons—which fall outside the scope of this book. But conventional arms exports, particularly those to the Third World, have always raised special moral and diplomatic problems, many of which go back to the nineteenth century; and I have tried to show these problems as they have been seen by practitioners on both sides, at critical points in the development of the trade.

The trade of its nature is secretive, and the task of the researcher is thus difficult, but there have been brief periods when it has been illuminated with sudden flashes—in 1913, 1934 and more recently in 1975-6. The successive revelations about Lockheed and Northrop are historically important not so much for the evidence of bribery, which caused the immediate scandal, as for their detailed documentation and testimony, which gave unique insights into the day-to-day workings and attitudes of arms companies and salesmen all over the world: no previous enquiry has provided a comparable body of reliable documentation. To what extent other companies in America or other countries have behaved in a similar way cannot be so confidently known. The Dassault scandal of 1976 threw a fitful light on the French company, but with no comparable detail; the British companies

remain shrouded in secrecy, while the detailed workings of
Russian or Czech arms exports are beyond the reach of any
Western investigator. The methods of Lockheed and Northrop
thus have a special prominence in the last half of this narrative.
But while this attention may be disproportionate to their world
role, both companies are specially deserving of attention, quite
apart from their enforced visibility: Lockheed as the biggest arms
company in the world, and Northrop as the most aggressive
exporter.

In a trade involving 150 nations and hundreds of companies, I
make no apology for not trying to be comprehensive: for
statistics and details of individual countries the reader can turn to
the publications of SIPRI in Stockholm. I believe that the descrip-
tion of specific episodes, and of the personalities involved, can
help to throw a different light on the problem. In thus personalis-
ing an emotive subject there is always a danger of seeking scape-
goats, and oversimplifying the problems, which has been evident
in past outbursts against the 'Merchants of Death'. But I have tried
to show the trade from both sides, and to present the point of
view of the company salesmen and executives as fairly as I can.

I have let the characters and situations as far as possible speak
for themselves, pointing to the resemblances and contrasts. It
has been my special aim to convey the *feel* of the business, as
experienced both by the dealers and makers of arms, and by those
charged with controlling them; and I have used a journalist's
privilege of access and travel to try to show the problems as they
are seen by different people in different parts of the world.

I became interested in this subject from two directions. I had
already written two earlier studies of multinational corporations,
The Sovereign State of ITT, and *The Seven Sisters* (about the giant
oil industry): thus the arms companies, which are among the
earliest and biggest of the global companies, naturally aroused my
curiosity. At the same time my interest in oil companies had
led me into the consequences of the oil crisis of 1973, the problems
of the Middle East, and the turning of oil into arms. In visiting
Iran and talking to the Shah I was struck by the extent of the
escalation of arms sales; and the loss of control was becoming
increasingly evident in successive visits to Washington. While
preparing the book, the problem and the scandals have escalated
all round me.

In writing about a global subject, I have owed a great deal to people in different parts of the world who have been generous with their time and assistance. I owe special gratitude in Washington to Jerome Levinson, chief counsel of the Senate Subcommittee on Multinational Corporations, whose assistance and friendship have been a constant stimulation: the three volumes of hearings of this subcommittee have provided a deep mine of reliable evidence. Two other members of his staff, Karin Lissakers and Geoff Shields, have also given me invaluable advice and suggestions. In Washington I am also very grateful to the following who have given their time and suggestions: James Akins, David Calleo, Shahram Chabin, Fritzy Cohen, Thomas Corcoran, General Howard Fish, Jane Frank, Thomas Halstead, Senator Gary Hart, Thomas Hughes, Amos Jordan, Nat Kearn, Geoffrey Kemp, Priscilla Klapp, Joseph Kraft, Henry Kuss, William Lewis, Robert Mantel, Judith Miller, Richard Moose, Robert Murray, Charles Naas, Paul Nitze, James Noyes, Kermit Roosevelt Sr., George Sherman, Laurence Stern, Thomas Stern, Paul Warnke, Bob Woodward and Ardeshir Zahedi.

In New York I am grateful to George Ball, Igor Gordevitch, Michael Jensen, Guy de Jonquières, Walter Levy, Pete Oram, Jay Palmer and Emma Rothschild. And in Los Angeles I am indebted to Del Bowman, John Brizendine, Les Daly, Al Delugach, Charles Foley, Ken Hull, Michael Klare, Carl Kotchian, Matthew MacKendrick, Garry Near, Peter Nehemkis, Barney Oldfield, William Perreault, Rowena Rathbone, Brent Rushforth, Derek Shearer, Lloyd Shearer, Natalie Shiras, John Simon, Ronald Sobell, Raymond Towne and John Whittles.

In London my thanks are due to Michael Addams, Lord Armstrong, Lord Balogh, Bill Bernhardt, Christoph Bertram, Lord Briggs, Alan Brothers, Sir Raymond Brown, Alain Camu, Andrew Cockburn, Herbert Coleman, Robin Cook MP, Mike Cooley, Jim Corfield, Sam Cummings, Geoffrey Edwards, Sir Harold Evans, Bassam Freiha, Charles Glass, Sir Arnold Hall, P. A. Hearne, Michael Holroyd, Adnan Khashoggi, Nazem Kodmani, Gavin Lyall, Michael MacDonald, Sandy Merritt, Tom Mullins, Herman Nickel, William Rodgers MP, Patrick Seale, J. D. Scott, Harry Simmons, John Stanley MP, Robert Stephens, Sir Lester Suffield, Louis Turner, William Wallace, Sir Fred Warner, Andrew Wilson and Pierre Young.

In Paris I am indebted to General de Bénouville, Bernard Cassen, Eric Gerdan, Jim Hoagland, Martine Marie, Christine

Ockrent, Claude Rivière, Robin Smythe, Anthony Terry, Sam White and Gavin Young; in Bonn and Hamburg, to Nicholas Colchester, Freimut Duve, Gerhard Mertins and George Vine; in Stockholm, to Dr Frank Barnaby, Ingemar Dörfer, Per Gedin, Curt Mileikowsky, Lars Persson and Baron Ramel; in The Hague and Amsterdam, to Sue Masterman and Joop van Tijn. In Beirut, Cyprus and Athens, I have been helped by Dany Chamoun, Tony Clifton, Joseph Fitchett, Jim Muir, Ian Seymour and James Skinner; in Jerusalem, by Irwin Fraenkel, Dan Horowitz, Eric Silver and Leah van Leer. In Tokyo I am indebted to many, including the following: Hideo Aoki, Keiichi Ito, Bernard Krisher, Yoshio Murakami, Hiroshi Ota, James Phillips, Paul Rubin, Jutaro Sakimoto, Murray Sayle, Charles Smith, Richard Smith, Takasui Tachibana, Jiro Tokuyama and Yoichi Watanabe. The Japanese ambassador in London, Tadao Kato, has helped me to understand Japan's problems.

In writing a topical book, trying to catch a moving target, I have had to work at speed, and I am specially grateful to publishers, agents, and translators who have helped to take the strain. Per Gedin of Wahlstrom and Witstrand in Stockholm, Freimut Duve of Rowohlt in Hamburg, Jean Rosenthal of Laffont in Paris and my agent in Tokyo, Hideo Aoki, have all been specially helpful and encouraging. In New York I have gained much from the tactful and perceptive comments of my editor Alan Williams of Viking Penguin, and from the calm efficiency of my agent Sterling Lord. In London I am grateful as always to my long-suffering publishers, Hodder and Stoughton, including Alan Gordon Walker, Rivers Scott, Stephanie Darnill and Jane Hourston. Michael Sissons, of the A. D. Peters agency, has again spurred me on. Robert Urwin, for the sixth time, has provided an index at high speed. Bettie du Toit has given valuable advice and encouragement. The Surrey Fine Art Press has set the book with remarkable swiftness. I owe an incalculable debt to my assistant Wendy Stephenson, for her research, typing and re-typing and organisation of the whole project; and finally to my wife Sally who has read, advised and kept me going through this pursuit.

March 1977

The Toys of Death

The guns spell money's ultimate reason.
                                        Stephen Spender

We recognise arms as not a means to starting a war, but as a means
to stopping a war.
            Sir Raymond Smith (arms salesman in Venezuela), 1975[1]

FLYING into Washington one afternoon in May 1976, to investigate the problems of arms sales, I found the only available hotel
room in the capital was in one of those sprawling convention
centres which seem to belong to no place at all. The lobby was
loud with the baying and slapping of gladhanders, and each guest
was wearing a big label stretching halfway across his jacket. I
had driven in from the airport with a visiting Englishman with a
quiet professorial air who explained to me, to my surprise, that
he was an arms salesman: he had come over to Washington to
attend a helicopter convention at this same hotel, and he suggested
that I might care to join the opening shindig. I thus found myself
suddenly plunged into the ballyhoo of the business.

It was not difficult to find. At one end of the lobby a banner
emblazoned with the sign of a kingfisher proclaimed the Helicopter Association. I descended two escalators into the underworld of the lower basement, where I came upon a vision that
seemed like an overcrowded child's drawing. The cavernous,
brilliantly-lit hall was surrounded with stalls prickly with guns,
torpedoes and electronic devices, and in the middle of the hall,

[1] Interview on BBC TV Midweek programme, July 2, 1975.

shining under the bright lights, were a cluster of helicopters looking as odd and washed-up as sharks in a museum. There was a comic little Bell helicopter, a big bubble with blades above it like a dragonfly. There was a luxurious executive chopper, comfortably upholstered in two-tone to suit corporate directors. And in the centre, under the blue sign of Boeing, was a white whale of a helicopter, the Boeing LAMPS, with long rotor blades above a fat belly which looked immovable. On each side of it was a bright torpedo, and all round it the salesmen and customers were chatting and drinking, while their wives leant on the torpedoes and the children climbed in and out of the cabin.

The whole basement looked like a giant toyshop or fairground, and at the stalls of each of the chief manufacturers—Boeing, Hughes, Sikorsky or Bell—salesmen stood by tables of drinks and canapés to welcome the visitors. At the Air Force Association stall a man in a bright red jacket with a permanent smile invited guests to win a prize by guiding beans through a maze. At the Hughes stall big rotor blades turned slowly above the Hughes executives who looked like the aristocrats of the industry in well-tailored dark blazers. As the evening developed the cocktail parties filled up with guests, all wearing wide labels as if they too were exhibits. There were men from the army, navy and air force, with their wives; there were congressmen diligently escorted by lobbyists; and there were solitary and earnest-looking officers and attachés from abroad. Two stocky Iranian colonels, standing together, peered gravely at the engines and intricate hardware, and the man in the red coat with difficulty cajoled them into playing the bean-game. The Brazilian air attaché inspected the under-sides of the helicopters, and the Australian air attaché was fascinated by the Hughes' machine-guns.

The fairground atmosphere was infectious. The names of the helicopters—the Sea Knight, the Chinook, the Sea Stallion—emphasised their playfulness and the television screens at the stalls displayed their uncanny achievements. The 'Incredible Lifting Machine' could lower girders on to bridges, the 'Big Mother' could rescue troops from impossible places, and one film showed two giant helicopters dancing round each other back-wards and forwards, to ballet music, like waltzing elephants in the air. A special heroic camaraderie clearly bound together the helicopter men, and I was handed a green leaflet containing a quotation from Harry Reasoner of ABC television which explained how helicopter pilots were different:

> In generality, airplane pilots are open, clear-eyed buoyant extroverts and
> helicopter pilots are brooders, introspective anticipators of trouble. They
> know if something bad has not happened it is about to.

Certainly the sheer awkwardness and challenge of the thing,
its ability to defy gravity, to keep still, to lift people and objects,
made the helicopter seem a part of any boy's fantasy. Yet there
was no room for misunderstanding: the real point of the helicopter was to kill. To remove any doubt, at the entrance to the
hall a three-barrelled 30mm gun pointed straight at each visitor,
with a brochure of jargon explaining exactly what it was for.
It had a rate of fire growth capability up to 2,000 shots-per-
minute; it fulfilled an area attack/destroy role; it offered optimum
interface with fire control/aircraft. The Hughes stall advertised a
whole family of guns: there was a lockless light machine-gun
which weighed only 18 pounds, firing 420 rounds a minute, 'a
major advance in the field of small arms', and there was a 7.62
chain-gun which could fire 800 shots-per-minute, ensuring the
highest reliability at all rates of fire.

On the television screens the peaceful antics of the helicopters
were abruptly interrupted by outbreaks of killing. One moment
the creatures were cavorting comically in the air, the next moment
shooting off a quick burst of missiles, exploding into orange fire.
The brochures amplified the confusion of roles: the big Sikorsky
helicopter, we were told, was known as the 'dawdling drome-
dary', and in the Vietnam war it was called the 'Big Mother'
because of its humane acts, rescuing soldiers from the hands of the
enemy; but it was also 'an active killer, not just a passive hunter'.
It was the Vietnam war which marked the helicopter's triumph
in both roles: both in rescue, and in devastating attacks on the
Viet Cong. With its ability to hover, to reconnoitre and drop
bombs at short range, the helicopter was an invaluable weapon
against guerrilla warfare and rebels. Not for nothing are helicopters now specially popular with governments threatened by
internal revolt.

In the language of the trade there was little to distinguish the
peaceful and warlike uses: the same clusters of nouns—indicating
capabilities, systems or control units—described both. The very
word 'weapon' appeared to be going into disuse and some
companies, like General Nucleonics or Systems Research, gave

no indication of what their products were for. The salesmen moved without any change of tone from executive choppers to linkless ammunition feed systems providing fire growth capability. The contorted vocabulary was clearly designed to avoid any mention of killing or war or destruction. Sikorsky provided a whole booklet about the 'survivability' of their helicopter, with an official definition of survivability: 'the capability of an aircraft to avoid and withstand a man-made hostile environment without sustaining an impairment of its ability to accomplish its designed mission'.

But the only real test and challenge to helicopter capability was a war; and Vietnam had given a useful fillip to the business. 'It's been well blooded', an electronics salesman assured me, about his system which had been used in helicopters over Vietnam, and the words 'combat proven in South East Asia' were important in any sales pitch. The antics, the sudden take-offs and spectacular liftings on the television screens were all very well, but it was the sudden bursts of fire-power, the rain of bombs and the swoosh of torpedoes, which provided the real climax for the customers.

Since there was no current American war, the helicopter salesmen were inevitably looking more actively for business abroad; foreign clients provided not only extra profits, but extra experience, and an additional challenge. Of course by far the most important customers were still the US navy, army and air force; their brochures tactfully proclaimed their close, happy associations ('A History of Achievement: US Navy and Sikorsky Aircraft . . .'). But the Iranians, Brazilians or Peruvians offered exciting alternative prospects, and Iran was the salesmen's dream. Bell Helicopters delivered the first three hundred sixteen-seat helicopters to Iran in 1975, which three days later set up a new record for maximum altitude. The Shah of Iran was the kind of patron that salesmen dream of—a war-lord who understands the same shoptalk, as fascinated by the gadgets as they are.

Coming up from this carefree underworld, the bright images lingered in my mind over the next days, between discussions about arms sales in the Pentagon and the State Department. The arms industry, I realised, had a verve and drive which made their own logic beyond any arguments about strategy and diplomacy, and it refused to accept that it was different in kind from other industries: it was only more adventurous and inventive. This was, after all, just another salesmen's convention.

A SMALL WAR

A few months later, following the trail of the arms trade to the Middle East, I visited the city of Beirut, just before the end of the eighteen-months' Lebanese civil war, when it was still raging at its height. It was a very minor war in terms of the total international arms trade: it did not involve aircraft or missiles, and it was scarcely worth the attention of the major arms dealers. It was a second-hand war fought with small arms and artillery. But it showed what was meant by fire-power and kill-capability. The scale of destruction had gradually increased, from rifles to machine-guns to mortars to heavy artillery, so that by the end the whole city-centre was devastated, and between 40,000 and 60,000 lives were lost—more than in all four Arab-Israeli wars. The great city of Beirut, which had been the hub of Middle Eastern commerce, had become a ruined shell, its gutted skyscrapers staring out, with blank holes instead of windows, across the desolate port. It had become a lethal laboratory of the world arms trade. Beirut was always unique in the Middle East for its cosmopolitanism and free trade: it was the city where everything was for sale. It was appropriate that it should become the centre for the free trade in weapons, flowing in from all corners of the world. Money could be quickly transmuted into guns; and the most prosperous city in the Middle East had become the most deadly.

In February 1975, just before war had broken out, Beirut was at the height of its prosperity and sophistication, enriched with the flood of oil money from its Arab neighbours, with the skyscraper hotels bustling with tourists and businessmen. The city tingled with the awareness of the world markets: at the souk the money-changers in their tiny stalls could accept currencies that London banks had not even heard of. Compared with the bleak oil towns of the Persian Gulf, with their rich but isolated communities, Beirut seemed more miraculous than ever. Its old Levantine role, as the entrepôt between the Arab hinterland and the West, now seemed all the more important in its capacity to absorb the Middle Eastern wealth: the fulcrum of the Arab world was Beirut airport, congested with planes from all corners of the globe, with stetsons, yashmaks and burnouses all jostling each other.

Eighteen months later the journey itself was a reminder of how fragile are the life-lines of any modern city. Before it had taken four hours from London: now it meant a flight to Cyprus, then a long wait for a boat and a twelve-hour voyage at exorbitant cost to Junieh, ten miles north of Beirut; then a tense car-ride at dawn across the desolate no-man's-land between East and West Beirut—swerving through the zig-zag barricades, the ruins of the neo-classical public buildings hardly distinguishable from the Roman ruins—and thus at last into the centre of Beirut. It was beyond recognition, like all other wrecked cities—like Portsmouth in England in 1944, like Hamburg in 1946, like Port Said in 1956. Along the main shopping street, the Hamra, there were only a few stalls on the pavement selling whisky and cigarettes, which—together with guns—alone remained in constant supply. The skyscrapers looked solid from a distance but turned out to be like Chirico buildings, with only blackness inside. Beirut was running its history backwards, back to the religious wars of the Middle Ages. The cheery slogans and shiny shop signs carried a gloomy irony in a city isolated from the outside world. The old film posters with bright blazing guns were stuck over with austere Palestinian recruiting posters showing more guns.

Everywhere there were guns. That great Beirut bazaar now seemed to have narrowed down to one commodity—guns of all shapes, sizes and nationalities, from pistols, rifles and machine-guns, to mortars, bazookas and heavy artillery. At a roadblock the militia waved their American M16 rifles in the air in one hand, in the same cocky style as the film posters, while they sipped Pepsi with the other. In a bar a group of middle-aged businessmen carried big pistols hanging uneasily beside their paunches, while the young men displayed fancy pistols shiny with chromium-plate, with Texan-style patterned holsters. The troops drove round in trucks swivelling the big Russian machine-guns, the Dushkas or 'little darlings', pointing into the sky. The trading genius of the Beirutis had quickly adjusted itself to the weapons market, and everyone knew the current price of a Kalashnikov rifle or a Browning pistol, which fluctuated each week with the state of supplies or the prospects of peace. The sound of gunfire had taken over from hooting and shouting as the normal noise of the city, with cracks, thuds, whoomphs, yows and booms punctuating the conversation.

On one day I was there, a hundred people were killed on both sides—nearly all of them civilians. At the street-corners plain posters were stuck on the walls with photographs of dead youths or children. It was, everyone explained, a cowards' war: only between five or ten percent of the dead were soldiers.

The Lebanese, with their separate religious and tribal loyalties, had long had a special addiction to personal weapons. In the nineteenth century they would buy elaborately decorated pistols from Smyrna, which were proudly displayed in their homes, and it was the custom to fire shots in the air at weddings and other celebrations. Their private armouries had developed with each new challenge. The crisis in 1958, when American marines landed in the Lebanon, brought a new load of weapons, and many Lebanese later acquired American M16 guns which they kept ready at home. The delicate balance between Christians and Moslems had been upset by the inrush of Moslem Palestinian refugees who built up their own armouries, and by the militant reaction of the Christians, who made up much of the prosperous bourgeoisie. Each Arab-Israeli conflagration increased the tension and the Christians' fear was still greater after the civil war next door in Jordan in 1970, where Palestinians nearly subverted the regime of King Hussein. In the following five years the Christians were already arming themselves rapidly, smuggling in M16 rifles, Czech M58 rifles and any other small arms they could fire, and spending their evenings in arms-drill. But though there were weapons accumulating on all sides, and sporadic outbursts of fighting from the Palestinian camps, few Lebanese expected a real civil war.

Even in April 1975 it seemed at first a very limited skirmish. The Christians and Palestinians began fighting in a suburb with rifles and machine-guns, and the rest of Beirut continued much as usual. Then the shooting suddenly spread to the city-centre: the Christian Falangists captured the Holiday Inn, and for five months snipers waged war between the high-rise hotels. Machine-guns were followed by mortars, which wrecked the skyscrapers and made the whole area uninhabitable. Bigger field weapons appeared on the scene, providing steady and indiscriminate bombardments through the heart of the city, while massacres on both sides heightened the fury. The battle-lines were formalised, and the city partitioned, with the no-man's-land of wrecked buildings separating East from West. The airport was bombarded, burning a pilot to death, and was then closed, and Beirut, cut off from its life-line, became a desolate outpost, with only yachts and small boats to take the Lebanese to the safety of Cyprus.

After the destruction from weapons came the opportunity of the looters and vandals: the guns prepared the way for anarchy, and bank vaults, warehouses, stores and antique shops in the rich heart of the city provided a haul whose value was later estimated at a billion dollars: at one British bank alone the Christians were reported to have taken a hundred million dollars. Much of the spoils went to individual looters who built up quick fortunes with jewellery or cash; but part of it was used by the right-wing leaders to buy more arms, so that the treasure of Beirut was constantly being recycled into guns.[1]

But whatever the scale of the looting, it was not enough to pay for the war, the financing of which was the central mystery. It was clearly beyond the resources of private individuals, or of the Lebanon itself: it could only come from foreign governments. The Palestinians' support was fairly open, for they had their own armouries inside their camps, provided by the radical Arab regimes in Syria, Iraq and Libya. The high price of oil had given Libya and Iraq, particularly Libya, huge scope to buy and resell arms, while in the background the richest of all the oil states, Saudi Arabia, was financing the Syrians who in turn provided arms for the Palestinians. Most of the Palestinian arms originated in Russia or Eastern Europe, arriving through their left-wing Arab allies; their standard weapon, the Kalashnikov automatic rifle, the AK47, had taken the place of the rifle or the pistol as the personal weapon of the soldiers. If they were not supplied with them they could buy them through dealers on the open market, at a price fluctuating according to supply and demand. The Palestinian weapons from Syria could come across the common frontier, while the ports of Sidon and Tyre unloaded big ship-ments from Libya and further afield. Their rifles and machine-guns were augmented with rifle-propelled grenades, mortars, bazookas, Dushka heavy machine-guns, Katusha rockets, and a new explosive device called a Grad. They received Russian-made scout cars and anti-aircraft guns which they fired against tanks and troops; when the Lebanese army split up, they obtained a new arsenal of heavy artillery. The bullets turned to shells, fired with the same abandon.

It was on the Christian side that the problem of arms supply was more difficult, for the Christians had no land frontier with a

[1] See *International Herald Tribune*, November 29, 1976.

friendly country, and they needed quickly to find weapons abroad and import them by sea. It was a challenge to the international arms trade. The Christian military leaders, faced with the Palestinian victories, flew to London, Paris, Teheran and Washington, to arrange for rapid purchases of arms: one of their first orders was by itself worth ten million dollars. They had the advantage of a large and scattered expatriate population; there were five million Lebanese abroad, compared to only two million in the Lebanon, many of whom were glad to help on the Christian side. At the Maronite Church of Our Lady of Mount Lebanon at Beverly Hills, the priest asked his congregation to contribute to the Lebanese Christian cause.

At the tourist resort of Aquamarina, near the Christian stronghold of Junieh, there was a small cove where ships could come in at night unobserved. Six months after the beginning of the war, in September 1975, a boat of unknown nationality was observed at Aquamarina, with a crew who were thought to be speaking Turkish, and unloaded crates full of Kalashnikov rifles. The rifles turned out to have been bought from the Bulgarian state trading agency, called Texim, which was known to be specially anxious to earn foreign currency. The Bulgarians (if they knew the destination) were not deterred by the fact that Soviet arms were supporting the Palestinians.

Beirut became the magnet for small-arms dealers from all over the world. The West German Günther Leinhäuser, who was said to have supplied weapons to Congolese, Biafrans and Kurds, was reported to have brought 300 tons of weapons from Morocco, including Spanish machine-guns and American and Russian mortars. A Lebanese Armenian, Sarkis Soghanalian, based in New York, came back to Beirut representing several American arms companies including Colt; his sales included 3,000 chromium-plated pistols, and he gave a press conference publicised by the American embassy. Even the preposterous 'Colonel' Hubert Julian, 'the Black Eagle of Harlem', arrived in Beirut: a veteran and unsuccessful arms dealer of seventy-eight, he had worked for the Emperor of Ethiopia, had bought arms for Guatemala, and had been 'ambassador at large' for Moise Tshombe in Katanga; he announced that he had come to sell sugar but was also investigating arms deals. The arms trade in Beirut became a substitute for all the other trades that had been destroyed; the price of a Kalashnikov or an M16 took over from the stock market as the index of trade. Pistols of all shapes and sizes poured out on to the market, often more as showpieces than as serious weapons, and when the first Arab peace-keeping force arrived in Beirut, the pistol market enjoyed a new boom from the visiting soldiers.

The journeys of the weapons on their way to the Lebanon were circuitous and often hazardous, but they revealed all the old internationalism and greed of the arms trade. The traders and sailors of the Eastern Mediterranean, who had been expert in arms smuggling since the crusades, reasserted their old skills; and Greek shipowners made small fortunes from running risks, as they had done in the Napoleonic wars. At the port of Halkida, north of Athens, the SS *Destiny* was found to have 1,800 Mauser rifles on board; at Piraeus sixty cases of Belgian automatic rifles were collected by a Lebanese sea captain; at Athens airport two Lebanese Christians were found on their way to Cyprus having left suitcases in the transit lounge, containing six sub-machine-guns and thirteen revolvers. But more often the weapons were trans-shipped on the open sea, to make their landing at night: many were first carried in oil tankers, where the extra metal content could be concealed from detection by the American sixth fleet, and then transferred to small boats; specially useful were the ex-RAF rescue launches, with Packard engines, which could race to the Lebanese coast at 45 knots. Some weapons came through Morocco, some through Spain, some through Marseilles, some (I was told by a Falangist agent at Junieh) even came from the Mafia, transferred in Italy. One important source of arms was West Africa, which has many Lebanese expatriates in countries which are glad to sell weapons at a profit. Ghana had a stock of Kalashnikovs bought from Nigeria which had previously been bought by the Biafran army from Israel, which had captured them from the Egyptians and Syrians in the 1967 war. Ghana was now glad to sell them off profitably to the Lebanese Christians, and thus they returned to the Middle East.

Dany Chamoun was one of the chief arms buyers on the Christian side; a clean-limbed young man with the style of an old-fashioned English public schoolboy, he was the son of the right-wing ex-president Camille Chamoun, and the commander of the 'Tiger' militia. At the Hotel Montemar, overlooking the port of Junieh, he talked with boyish enthusiasm about buying weapons as if he were describing a supermarket. He had been given his first machine-gun, he said, at the age of five, and had learnt how to strip and assemble it: 'I appreciate what a gun can do.' It was natural, he explained, that Beirut should offer great scope for buying arms: 'It was always the place where anyone could get anything; that's why all you people loved it—its charm was its lawlessness. The Lebanese love to buy guns. They buy guns to impress each other, and they take pride in their guns, more than in their nation. People here will never give up their personal weapons—it's like losing their wife.'

There was never much difficulty in getting the weapons you wanted, he went on, provided you had the money. At the beginning the Christians even bought Russian guns from the Palestinians, who had got them from the Syrians: the soldiers sold them privately when they needed the money. 'Then we bought more Russian guns from Bulgaria, which we fixed up through Western Europe. We could buy German G3s with no difficulty—they're made under licence in lots of countries. And we could buy Israeli weapons through Europe. With tanks, we were offered M41s and M48s, but eventually we chose Shermans, because they used the same ammunition as the French AMX tanks. We bought French fuses through Libya. Of course most of the weapons came from governments, not from private dealers; the idea that private dealers can arrange a war is really Victorian.'

Was there no difficulty with the export controls from the producing countries, I asked. He laughed and explained that it was very easy to buy an 'end-use certificate'—the guarantee signed by a purchasing government undertaking not to re-export the arms. 'All we do is to go to a friendly country, and ask them to order arms, which are then sent on to us. It's all in Thayer's book.' (He gave the impression that he had used George Thayer's classic book on the small-arms trade, *The War Business*, as his guide to arms-buying.[1]) 'But,' he added, 'you must always obey the eleventh commandment: Thou shalt not be found out.'

Chamoun, like others, was reticent on the question of where all the money came from. The estimates of the total cost of arms and ammunition bought by the Christians varied from $200 million to $600 million—and even though many Lebanese Christians were rich, they could not have raised even the lower figure by themselves. Rumours about the sources of funds were rife—that they came from looted banks, from the CIA, from the Israelis, from West German financiers, from the Vatican, from Iran.

[1] George Thayer: *The War Business*, London, Weidenfeld & Nicolson, 1970.

There was even evidence from Paris that some of the two million dollars, which had been stolen from the Dassault company by their accountant, de Vathaire, had been paid to the Lebanese Christians via the eccentric mercenary Jean Kay.[1] Some or all of these funds may have contributed to the Christian arsenal; but much had also come from Saudi Arabians, who had also financed the Palestinians. It was not a defined policy of the Saudi government to play off both sides, but the Saudis, as conservative Moslems, were inevitably confused: as Moslems they tended towards the Palestinians, while as conservatives they looked to the Christians. While some of the princes were supporting the Palestinians, others were worried by the danger of a Palestinian victory, and were secretly financing the Christians. The great surplus of oil money, swilling around Saudi Arabia in search of outlets and power, could transform itself quickly into the currency of arms. Thus oil turned to bullets on both sides.

The weapons had confused origins from the beginning; but, after a year's fighting, when the Palestinians were showing signs of defeating the Christians, the alliances spectacularly changed, bringing greater confusion. The Syrian regime, which had originally armed the Palestinians, now dreaded an all-out Palestinian victory which could undermine their own domestic stability, as did the Saudis and Kuwaitis—each with their own discontented Palestinian minorities. The Syrian army thus changed allegiances and moved into the Lebanon in force, to support the Christians with tanks and heavy artillery: the Syrian soldiers found themselves fighting their former allies, against weapons from their own arsenal.

Soon afterwards came evidence of another source of weapons. Already early in 1976 an arms dealer in Britain had been surprised to receive a request from the Christians for ammunition for Russian mortars; for he knew that the mortars could only have come from Israel. Then in May 1976 there were signs of unusual activity at the cove at Aquamarina, with big barges as well as small boats landing at the ports. Christian soldiers were soon showing themselves with all kinds of new weaponry, including Belgian FAL rifles, Dushka machine-guns, and even super-Sherman tanks which had only been supplied to Israel. Then the new alliance was revealed[2]: the Israelis were supplying the

[1] See chapter 16.
[2] See Joseph Fitchett in *The Observer*, July 18, 1976.

Christians with weapons shipped directly to Junieh, protected
by Israeli patrol-boats; while on the southern border of Lebanon
the Israelis were offering military protection to the Christians.
The Israelis were arming the Christians with all kinds of weapons
from their 'grocery store', many of them captured from the
Egyptians and Syrians in the 1973 war. And each new shipment
soon showed itself in a new Christian offensive.

The Palestinians now had little prospect of victory; and the
Saudis, who had helped to arm both sides, now saw the dangers of
a real massacre. By October 1976, a summit of Arab leaders
had been convened by the Saudis in Riyadh, and had agreed on
a cease-fire, to be supervised by an Arab peace-keeping force. The
war was theoretically over, but the killing still continued
sporadically.

All through the carnage and the shifting alliances, the two great
Mediterranean fleets of the Americans and Russians, each with
about sixty ships, kept their distance. The Palestinians implored
the Russians to help them get their arms through the blockade,
or to show their support by landing at Sidon; the Russians
observed and monitored, but never intervened. The American
fleet, which eighteen years earlier had landed marines in the
Lebanon, now refrained from even showing itself along the coast.

The war, like all wars, was a very special case, caught in the
cross-fire between so many other rivalries outside its frontiers, and
with private armies in its midst. But it provided a ghastly demonstration of how easily weapons can get out of control and establish
their own anarchy. The arms that major powers had originally
supplied to one country for one purpose were used by another
country for an opposite purpose; guns and countries changed
sides in a few months, while the super-powers would not or
could not intervene. The flow of new riches into the area, with
such constructive potential, had served to finance the destruction
of its most civilised city, with the tradition of *laissez faire* turning
into an acceptance of *laissez détruire*. And this small-arms war
provided a specially ominous warning, for it was waged in a
corner of the world which, as we will see, was receiving an
unprecedented build-up of big arms from all the major powers.
The war was over. The shooting still continued sporadically, but
the flow of arms abated. Soon afterwards, a European arms dealer
was offered a consignment of arms from Bulgaria which had
been en route for the Lebanon. 'There was some lovable material,'

the dealer told me, 'but the price was far too high: the Lebanon war had made them too greedy.'

THE DOG BENEATH THE SKIN

It is the small arms which have been the instruments of most of the hundred wars since the Second World War, from Lebanon to Biafra, from the Yemen to Katanga; and which have been the cause of most loss of life. And it is the trade in rifles, machine-guns or mortars which reveals the cold heart of a business in which diplomacy and wars are translated into orders, balance-sheets and profits. It is here that the day-to-day juxtaposition of death and commerce seems most casual, and the sale of guns looks as banal as any other business. To get the feel of the trade, I set out to visit its uncrowned king, and found him in a surprising setting.

Near the centre of Manchester, in the middle of Victorian industrial Britain, is an unpretentious brick warehouse, alongside the ship canal and adjoining a fine Gothic church. The warehouse was built after the First World War, originally as a newsprint store for the London *Sunday Times*, and its only distinguishing marks are a heavy stainless-steel door, and big letters across the top of the building saying INTERARMS. But it is difficult to enter: the steel door has a spy-hole and two entry-phones, and a television camera looks down from the outside wall. There is a long wait before the door opens. Once inside, the reason becomes clear, for this is the biggest private arsenal in Europe. It is the British headquarters of the most successful of all the small-arms dealers, Sam Cummings, the chairman and principal shareholder in the Interarms Company. Six storeys of the warehouse contain no fewer than 300,000 weapons, stacked as densely as wine bottles in a cellar, waiting to be shipped to whatever government or company may want them. There is a rifle range inside the building for testing the weapons: occasionally a sharp crack disturbs the peace of the artisans re-assembling the guns.

Upstairs is a row of cheerful offices, with a small exhibition of machine-guns on the floor by the entrance; and it is here that Sam Cummings himself comes over once a month from Monte Carlo to take stock of his empire. He is a relaxed chubby-faced man, who looks much younger than his forty-nine years: his style is genial and innocent, with a beatific smile, like a boy who has been a gun-freak, and has suddenly found all his wishes come true—which is, more or less, what he is. He loves publicity: his walls are decorated with photographs of celebrities handling his guns or with newspaper articles about himself, and he presents a well-rehearsed personality. He talks quietly and courteously and dresses in a clerical black suit, with a white shirt and cautious tie, like an old-fashioned solicitor. He does not smoke or drink, and travels as little as possible, economy class. He and his manager, Mr Spence, both in their dark suits, lunch at a nearby Manchester pub, where they are both so immaculate, so elaborately polite, that an observer might perhaps guess there was something odd about their business.

Cummings talks about his trade with such loving attention to detail and technicalities that he succeeds, like all good arms dealers, in making it sound as boring as machine tools or camshafts. But he also offers himself as the philosopher of the business, like a Greek chorus who has sadly discovered the secrets of human motivation, and he likes to provide aphorisms to make his points. 'The arms business,' Cummings told me, as he had told senators and congressmen, 'is founded on human folly. That is why its depths will never be plumbed, and why it will go on forever. 'All weapons,' he says, 'are defensive, and all spare parts are non-lethal.' The policy of balancing supplies to the Middle East, he has explained, has been a total mirage and illusion: 'the more the Americans try to keep the balance, the more the Russians put their thumb on the balance, to throw it out of kilter.' As for the attempts to control arms exports, he says, 'the plainest print cannot be read through a gold sovereign (or a rouble or golden eagle).'

He remains essentially a trader in guns, and a connoisseur of their infinite variations. Above his desk hangs an ugly-looking weapon, a rifle-propelled grenade called the RPG 7, which specially interests him. It was captured in Northern Ireland, one of a hundred which were imported from Libya by the IRA, with instructions in Arabic: they did not know how to use it, it was said, until the BBC explained on television. But the war in Northern Ireland, Cummings stresses, was very petty in terms of the arms business: 'just a few misguided nuts in America, and a few guns from Libya; thank God Gadaffi didn't really support them seriously.' Northern Ireland reinforces the point that, for urban guerrillas, a few guns can go a very long way.

For his company Cummings has adopted the classical-sounding slogan: The Arms of Man. And for his motto, he takes the motto of his own American private school, the Episcopal Academy in Philadelphia: *Esse Quam Videri*—to be, rather than to seem. The motto sums up well enough the recurring attitude of arms dealers from Sir Basil Zaharoff onwards. Others may talk about peace and disarmament, but they, the arms merchants, know that human nature is based on aggression and violence, and that will never change. They have seen the dog beneath the skin.

Cummings' own adventurous career provides a kind of pocket history of the small-arms trade over the last quarter-century. He was brought up in Philadelphia, the son of a prosperous father who had lost his fortune in the great crash. He was fascinated by guns since he acquired an old German Maxim gun at the age of five, and, when he was drafted into the army after the war, at Fort Lee in Virginia, he became a weapons instructor and made money on the side by selling old German helmets. After university he toured Europe and was astonished to discover the piles of old weapons still left abandoned on the battlefields of the Western front: he then resolved to become an arms salesman. For a time he was employed by the CIA to help identify captured weapons in the Korean war—which reinforced his expertise, and gave him useful links with intelligence. He joined a Californian arms company called Western Arms, which made handsome profits out of selling surplus arms both to the American public and to the CIA for its clandestine operations.

By the time he was twenty-six, he had set up his own company with the high-sounding title of International Armament Corporation, and began buying a hoard of surplus weapons, to sell either as converted sports guns or as arms for foreign armies. His initiative was timely: on the one hand there was a huge surplus from the Second World War, now constantly being augmented by the cold-war re-arming. On the other hand there was a succession of coups, small wars and rebellions which urgently needed second-hand arms. Cummings soon found himself the master-broker. He was always restricted by the government licences which he needed to export his weapons; but governments often had their own political motives, as well as financial reasons, for allowing exports.

Cummings established his first private arsenal in Alexandria, outside Washington, and found customers for his wares among the regimes of Latin America. After the right-wing revolution in Guatemala in 1954, he supplied the new government of Castillo-Armas with American Garand rifles which he bought in Britain. In the Dominican Republic, he became friendly with the dictator, Trujillo, and supplied him first with machine-guns, then (in one of his most remarkable deals) with Vampire jet fighters which he bought in Sweden. In Costa Rica in 1955, when exiles tried to invade their homeland, both sides were armed with machine-guns bought from Cummings. In Cuba he was believed to have supplied the Castro forces before the revolution, and also some of the anti-Castro invaders for the Bay of Pigs fiasco. In the meantime he was able to replenish his growing private arsenal with huge quantities of surplus from Europe and the Middle East. After the Suez war of 1956, for instance, he bought 2,000 Russian small arms captured by the Israelis from the Egyptians. In the late 'fifties he bought nearly a million Lee-Enfield rifles from the British government, which kept him in stocks for some years: most of them were sold to Americans as sports guns, others were sold to Kenya and Pakistan.

In all his exports, whether from Britain or from America, Cummings has been controlled by the licensing systems of the governments, which allow weapons to be sold only to friendly countries for legitimate security, when they are not actively preparing for war. He is on good terms with governments; he finds the British Defence Sales Organisation, in Soho Square, rather easier to deal with than their American counterparts in Washington, because they have more definite policy instructions. The controls and 'end-use certificates' are quite strict, and he carefully abides by them. But there is never much certainty, as we have seen in the Lebanon, about where the weapons will eventually end up.

His underlying relationship with Western governments, particularly with Washington, remains shrouded. In the past he has fostered elaborate mystery about his connections with the CIA: he has talked cryptically about intelligence, and even named one of his companies (Cummings Investment Associates) with the same initials. He was also able to build up his own intelligence system, which was useful to Washington. But nowadays he keeps his distance, and maintains that he has nothing to do with the CIA. 'I was never a wild fanatic for the spook business,' he told me: 'I'm glad to be out of it, and I prefer more humdrum deals. They'll throw you on the chopping block well before they throw themselves, and in the end they're just as dumb as you and I.' In fact most arms dealers agree that the CIA is now much less active in arms deals than it was in the 'fifties and early 'sixties. 'The CIA stopped selling arms since Vietnam and Cambodia,' I was told by the West German arms dealer Gerhard Mertins, a former associate of Cummings who worked with German intelligence. 'Cummings always boasted about the CIA, but that was really his idea of showbiz. You can keep a hundred rifles secret, but you can't keep a thousand secret, let alone submarines or armoured cars. In this business everybody knows what everybody else is doing. We're one big family.'

By the end of the 'fifties, Cummings was established as the world's leading private arms dealer. 'Perhaps it was a combination of luck and serendipity,' he says; 'we have no monopoly of brains.' But he soon had the advantage of sheer size, and he is now reckoned to have ninety percent of the small-arms trade. He has built up huge stocks in the United States and Britain—now augmented by another arsenal in Singapore—from which he can quickly supply customers throughout the world, and he has agents and offices in every major capital. He has a personal fortune, and runs his companies from his large flat in Monte Carlo, where he now lives with his Swiss wife. In 1968 his American business faced a crisis, when Congress passed the new Gun Control law—which was designed, not so much to control guns, as to protect the American gun-makers, led by Remington and Winchester, from cheap overseas competition. Cummings' American business, particularly in sports guns, remains very profitable: he still has a big arsenal in Alexandria, and he has recently opened a factory in Midland, Virginia, to make handguns for the American market. But since the new law Cummings has operated more from Britain: his Manchester arsenal is now the biggest, and he only visits America once every few years. From Manchester, only about twenty percent of his exports are sporting guns, and the remaining eighty percent go to foreign governments and armies: his recent lucrative customers include Israel, Kenya and the Philippines.

Cummings' total world sales, as he insists, are still tiny compared to the big aerospace companies: he has never exceeded an annual turnover of $100 million, which is less than the cost of a squadron of fighters. But he remains, as an individual entrepreneur, a kind of weather-cock of the arms trade. He is much more aware and more sensitive to the world scene than the bureaucrats in the big companies, and he can manoeuvre and take advantage, buying and selling, more quickly. His thirty years in the business have given him a unique experience, and as he walks round his Manchester arsenal he can portray the history of the world in terms of the much-travelled weapons, which provide a melancholy museum of warfare.

Here, he points out, is a stack of American Garand rifles which were first exported to Germany in the 'fifties for the first German re-armament. When Germany got more advanced weapons they were transported to Jordan in the late 'sixties, and when Jordan got more advanced weapons they were bought by Cummings and shipped to Manchester. From there many of them were shipped to the Philippines, to help fight Moslem rebels financed by Libya, while a few remain in Manchester waiting for customers. Here, just next door to the Garands, are some British Enfield rifles which were captured by the Japanese in Indo-China, then taken over by the Americans and used in Vietnam, before they were bought by Cummings. Here are some Springfield rifles which were first supplied to the French in Indo-China in the 'fifties. Here are Mausers which were brought over to Taiwan by General Chiang Kai-shek when he left the mainland in 1949. Over there are German ME42 guns which were left by Hitler's troops in Greece, Swedish guns made under licence in Egypt and captured by the Israelis, British Sten guns dropped by parachute during the Second World War for the French Maquis, American Brownings from the Dominican Republic, Belgian Mausers from Venezuela, American M16s from the Chilean army.

Cummings knows that his arsenals depend for their stocks on the aftermath of wars. Small arms have a much greater longevity than aircraft or missiles, and he is still making profits out of the residue of the Second World War, which marks the age-limit for most ordinary arms sales. Each new conflagration in the Middle East, each new re-arming, provides a new surplus, much of which is likely eventually to find its way into his arsenals.

But there remains, he says, one huge exception which is still an enigma to the arms business: what happened to the vast stocks of American arms left in South Vietnam? The total value has been reckoned at five billion dollars, and they included 800,000 M16 rifles, six hundred M48 tanks, a hundred self-propelled guns

worth a million dollars each, 73 Northrop Tiger fighters,[1] some
of which had been packed in crates a month before the evacuation
in April 1975. There was even an IBM computer, with Vietnamese trained to use it, to provide a complete inventory. But
none of them has come on to the international arms market;
and some of them by now must have been ruined and rusted in
the tropical climate.

'It's very odd, it really doesn't make sense,' says Cummings:
'the North Vietnamese already had enough to win the war, and
the American stuff is non-standard for them.' There has been
no comparable lost opportunity since Chiang Kai-shek left China,
when the Chinese communists never sold off the weapons he
left behind, except for 10,000 Garand rifles which were bought by
Indonesia. The Vietnam residue was a far richer haul. Could it
conceivably, I speculated, be some question of principle? I
thought I detected a quiet shudder from Cummings, but he
replied with his maxim: 'the plainest print cannot be read
through a solid gold sovereign.'

Cummings likes to portray his arsenals as an index of the
world's folly; their stocks go up and down according to the
state of war or peace. To him, the Lebanon is only one small
outlet in the total world market (he was approached, he explained,
by Dany Chamoun to provide arms for the Christians, but the
British government would not permit it). 'Of course I'd like to
see this building filled up with arms,' he said. 'World peace would
give me the chance to build up my inventory. But people are
always ordering more arms, which run down the stocks again. I
don't see any prospect of that changing. There are huge new
markets opening up; soon there will be re-arming of China,
which everyone in the business knows will happen; that will bring
the story round to full circle since Chiang Kai-shek left twenty-
five years ago. And then Russia. And then Europe again. There's
never any end to it.'

Yet the trade of Sam Cummings, as he is the first to point out,
is only a small fraction of the total world's arms trade, and in
economic terms almost negligible. Such private arms dealers,
supplying only small arms, account for less than five percent of
the total arms exports; and the cost of the arms supplies in the
whole Lebanese war, even at the highest estimate of a billion

---

[1] Cummings' account was later confirmed by the official Pentagon report released on
November 10, 1976.

dollars, amounts to only one-twentieth of the estimated arms exports from the West in 1975. The factories that make machine-guns, rifles and ammunition are of minor importance in terms of their nations' economies compared to the giant plants of Lock-heed, Dassault and the aerospace companies with which much of this book is concerned.

The important arms salesmen of today, as we shall see, are government servants, honoured or knighted for their services to exports: the major arms exports to the Middle East are achieved not by gun-running or by quick bargains in Manchester or Paris, but by long drawn-out negotiations between civil servants in Washington or London, endorsed by presidents and cabinets. The setting for a modern arms deal is not an old hulk unloading crates at night at a deserted wharf, but an Arab prince being welcomed in London or Paris by a guard of honour and by the Minister of Defence. And it is such dignified deals that have been responsible for the unprecedented scale of the arms race in the Middle East which marks the climax in the narrative that follows.

But the small-arms trade still has its relevance to the bigger traffic. The public mind has been accustomed to make a kind of class distinction between the small-arms wars, with their confused local battles and second-hand supply routes, and the build-up of elaborate defence systems and sophisticated aircraft, each one of which costs more than a shipload of machine-guns for a whole war. Western politicians are apt to depict the sophisticated weaponry (the very words sound attractive and harmless) as the delicate weights and counterweights in the intricate balances of diplomacy, and to view the machine gun with a moral repug-nance not accorded to the air-superiority aircraft. The sense of abstraction in big arms may be scarcely surprising in an age when fighters or missiles can be developed at the cost of billions and become obsolete without ever being tested in war. And the separation of attitudes goes back at least to the nineteenth century when successive wars were fought with rifles on the frontiers of India or Africa, while the European powers built up majestic fleets of battleships and arsenals of howitzers, to provide deter-rents never likely to be used. But the battleships failed to deter the great powers from nearly destroying each other, and the machine-guns designed for use against savages became the weapons for slaughtering Europeans. The local wars of today, which themselves so easily escalate from one calibre to the next, each carry their warning of how quickly a deterrent can turn first into provocation, then into catastrophe.

In the following chapters I begin by briefly tracing the changing attitudes to the sales of industrial arms since their origins a century ago, as revealed by the attitudes of the first arms magnates, the 'merchants of death', and their critics. I then pass to the problems of Western arms sales since the Second World War, with the growing responsibilities of governments, culminating in the sudden boom in the trade and the arms race over the past four years. I illustrate the methods of arms salesmen and the problems of control in more detail by providing case histories of Lockheed, Northrop and other companies, supported by recent investigations and amplified by my own interviews: I thus try to show both the bare bones, and the flesh-and-blood, of the arms trade. I conclude by discussing the situation under President Carter's administration, and the prospects of effective control. In the course of the past century, the scale and technology of the industry has been transformed, and much of the responsibility has shifted from private companies to government officials; but the underlying problems and attitudes have remained, like an ancient curse.

2

The Faith of the Armourer

I should like to invent a substance or a machine with such terrible
power of mass destruction that war would thereby be made impossible
for ever.

Alfred Nobel to Berthe von Suttner, 1876.[1]

IT WAS in the mid-nineteenth century, in the wake of the first
industrial revolution, that the modern armaments industry began
to take shape, inspired and pressed forward by a handful of
inventive entrepreneurs who developed the science of explosives
and guns. These singular men, who in a few years built up huge
companies based on unparalleled means of destruction, provide
many insights into the character of the thrusting new industry,
and they cast long shadows into the future. Two characteristics
were very striking from the start. Firstly, the development of
armaments was regarded as inseparable from the whole movement of industrial progress. Secondly, it was of all industries the
most global.

Of the driven men who presided over this new industry, none
was so isolated and tormented as Alfred Nobel, the inventor of
dynamite and founder of the annual peace prize. His life had a
legendary quality, as though he were a reincarnation of Dr
Faustus or of Alberich, the Nibelung who renounced love for
the sake of power. His view of the world showed a continuous
dichotomy. On the one side he was a poetic idealist, a pacifist, a

[1] See Erik Bergenren: *Alfred Nobel*, London, Thomas Nelson, 1962, p. 189.

passionate admirer of Shelley; on the other a ruthless financier, obsessed with the science of explosives. And that duality lived on after him, in the disputes over the awards of his peace prize and in the ambivalence of Sweden itself, which is still both an inventive manufacturer of arms and a persistent campaigner for world peace.

From his beginnings, young Alfred Nobel seemed to belong to no country or place. He was born in Stockholm in 1833, when Swedes were beginning to carry their inventiveness through the world; and at the age of eight his father moved the family to St Petersburg, where he set up a torpedo works. The four Nobel sons were all imbued with ambition, and two of them, Robert and Ludwig, were destined to play a historic role in developing Russian oil and exporting it to Europe. But Alfred was the most brilliant and cosmopolitan, and at seventeen he went to live in America for two years, before returning to Russia and Sweden. He worked with his father, who was experimenting with new explosives, but young Alfred, a trained scientist, was soon outdoing his amateur father, and became especially interested in the deadly new explosive called nitro-glycerine. By 1862, at the age of twenty-nine, he first succeeded in making nitro-glycerine explode, and the next year he received his first patent for the product. He and his brother Emil set up a small factory in Stockholm, and there in September occurred the disaster which was always to haunt him. The nitro-glycerine exploded, blowing up the factory and killing five men, including Alfred's brother. His father never recovered, the citizens of Stockholm were outraged, and Nobel had to continue his experiments on a pontoon moored outside Stockholm.[1]

The explosive liquid was already becoming invaluable for blasting rock, particularly in pioneering territories like California, but as nitro-glycerine was transported abroad there were a succession of further disasters. Like nuclear energy a century later, it had a wonderful potential, but terrifying dangers. In New York a German traveller left a flask in a box in a hotel, a waiter noticed a red vapour coming out of it, and carried it into the street, where a moment later it exploded, wrecking the fronts of the houses and blasting a four-foot hole in the street. In Panama a steamer carrying nitro-glycerine exploded and sank, with the loss of seventy-four lives. In San Francisco the Wells Fargo warehouse exploded,

[1] H. Schück and R. Sohlman: *The Life of Alfred Nobel*, London, Heinemann, 1929, p. 86.

killing fourteen. Every country was now terrified of the stuff, and several forbade the possession of it. But Nobel, in spite of his domestic catastrophe, persisted in experimenting, and eventually discovered a method of mixing nitro-glycerine with a kind of clay, called Kieselguhr, which made it both much more practical, and less dangerous. By 1867 he had patented a new invention called 'dynamite', or 'Nobel's safety powder'.

The amazing new substance was soon the basis of an international industry, and of a huge fortune for Nobel. Gradually each country overcame its fears about the explosive, and realised its peaceful benefits—for instance in piercing the Rocky mountains or the Alps. Nobel travelled the world, setting up local joint ventures to make dynamite, bitterly litigating on behalf of his patents, and establishing his own firm control over the industry. In its monopoly and complexity, Nobel's empire had some resemblance to John D. Rockefeller's Standard Oil Trust, which was also set up at this time.[1]

Nobel was often unfairly accused of endangering the world, for his dynamite was essentially for peaceful purposes, and was far safer than the old nitro-glycerine. But he never lost his interest in developing further explosives. He became the father of the new industry, and Sweden became known as 'the classic country for explosives'. He went on to discover a form of cordite for guns called ballistite, and he even bought, at the age of sixty, the Swedish gun company Bofors, and set himself up in the old manor house belonging to the firm. He liked to explain that his interest in explosives was essentially technical: 'you know, it is rather fiendish things we are working on'—he explained to his friend Ragnar Sohlman—'but they are so interesting as purely theoretical problems, and so completely technical, as well as so clear of all financial and commercial considerations, that they are doubly fascinating.'[2]

But in the meantime Nobel felt himself pursued, as he put it, by 'the spirits of Niflheim'—the cold dark world of the dead, in Norse mythology. He had frequent attacks of migraine and periods of melancholia: he never married, never allowed anyone to come close to him. He once wrote to his sister-in-law, Ludwig's wife: 'I drift about without rudder or compass, a wreck on the sea

[1] Bergenren, p. 86. See also W. J. Reader: *Imperial Chemical Industries, a History* Vol. I, London, Oxford University Press, 1970.

[2] H. Schück, etc, *Nobel, The Man and his Prizes*, Amsterdam, Elsevier, 1962, p. 36.

of life.' He never lived in one place for more than a few months: when his early laboratory in Paris was closed down by the French authorities he moved to San Remo, thereafter he was constantly moving, between Italy, Sweden, Britain and America. 'My homeland is where I am working,' he said, 'and I work everywhere.'[1] His letters betrayed his misogyny and misanthropy—numerous friends, he wrote, were only to be found among dogs: women were the 'fair, but usually repulsive sex'. 'If there is one piece of advice that I would give to my friends, it is never to do a good turn. Every time I have yielded to this lamentable propensity, I have made another enemy'. His company was apt to be disconcerting; he moved jerkily, with a mincing walk and very changeable face round his deep-set eyes, and his conversation was disjointed and often macabre. One of his favourite projects, was to set up a 'suicide institute' on the Riviera, with beautiful views and a first-class orchestra, where prospective suicides could prepare for their departure with dignity. Yet Nobel persisted in seeing himself as an idealist, a social democrat, even a Bolshevist; and he enjoyed writing poetry, much of it in English, in the style of Shelley, expressing his own lonely Faustian striving. As a boy of eighteen he had described his boyhood:

> With an imagination made to scale
> The utmost heights to which the mind can soar
> I had no judgment then to check its flights
> Or trace its drawbacks to its golden dreams.[2]

Shelley had helped to inspire Nobel with an interest in pacifism which he retained throughout his explosive researches. As he became more involved in military inventions, so his interest in pacifism increased. It was further stimulated by his acquaintance with an Austrian aristocrat, Berthe von Suttner, who applied to be his private secretary in 1876, and later became famous as an authoress and influential pacifist. He wrote letters to her, expressing a qualified interest in the peace movement, and briefly visited the meeting of the Peace Congress in Berne in 1892, at which she was prominent. But when she visited him afterwards, he explained to her with poignant optimism: 'my factories may end war sooner than your Congresses. The day when two army corps will be able to destroy each other in one second, all civilised nations will

[1] Bergenren, p. 71.
[2] Ibid., p. 9.

recoil from war in horror, and disband their armies.' He recognised that before this age of world peace was reached, there would be an intermediate stage, which he wryly called 'the peace of the cemetery'. But it was a recurring theme for Nobel that war would soon become too terrible to wage, and no doubt it provided a justification for his fascination with explosives. 'Let the sword of Damocles hang over every head, gentlemen, and you will witness a miracle,' he told a meeting in Paris in 1890; 'all war will stop short instantly, if the weapon is bacteriology.'[1]

Nobel did not agree with most of the 'gasbags' at the 1892 conference, who put their faith in arbitration; but he did believe that nations could guarantee each other against aggression, and thus make wars impossible. The year after the Peace Congress, he first mentioned his proposal, to Berthe von Suttner, to devote part of his fortune to a peace prize. Two years later he signed the famous will which provided for annual prizes, including one 'for the person who shall have done the most effective work for promoting friendly relations between the peoples, for the abolition or reduction of standing armies, and for the formation and increase of peace congresses'. Two years later Nobel died at San Remo, in the circumstances he had always dreaded, without friends or relations around him, only servants.

Thus this tormented and misanthropic man bequeathed the most famous of the world's peace prizes. The awards themselves, chosen by a committee appointed by the Norwegian parliament, were soon to reflect some of the confused attitudes of their founder. On the one hand they were awarded to high-minded pacifists who were uncompromising in their condemnation of war, like Henri Dunant, the Swiss founder of the Red Cross, or Berthe von Suttner. On the other hand they were also granted to some of the most ruthless and worldly practitioners of world power politics, like Theodore Roosevelt, Austen Chamberlain or Henry Kissinger. Thirteen years after the peace prize was first awarded, the war broke out which disproved Nobel's belief that civilised nations would recoil from war in horror. The Nobel Trust was torn apart, with its factories making explosives to use against each other: and the only Nobel prizewinner in five years was the Red Cross.[2]

[1] Ibid., p. 194.
[2] Ibid., p. 89.

MAJOR BARBARA

Four years after the Nobel Peace Prize had first been awarded, George Bernard Shaw's play *Major Barbara* appeared in London in 1905. The play reflected the contemporary anxiety about a world that was coming to depend increasingly on armaments. Its central character was an armaments manufacturer, Andrew Undershaft, whose motto was Unashamed, and who had built up the vast business of Undershaft and Lazarus, based on destruction: the Undershaft torpedo, the Undershaft quick firers, the Undershaft submarine. He proclaimed without shame the 'faith of an armourer'—'to give arms to all men who offer an honest price for them, without respect of persons or principles'—and he boasted of his supragovernmental power: 'The government of your country!' he exclaims to his patriotic son Stephen: 'I am the government of your country: I and Lazarus. Do you suppose that you and half a dozen amateurs like you, sitting in that foolish gabble shop, can govern Undershaft and Lazarus? No, my friend; you will do what pays us. You will make war when it suits us, and keep peace when it doesn't.'

Undershaft argues with his pacifist daughter, Major Barbara of the Salvation Army, and the idealist Professor of Greek, Adolphus Cusins. Eventually the two idealists inspect the model town and factory of Undershaft's business, and are overcome by the welfare and contentment of the workers: 'It's all horribly, frightfully, immorally, unanswerably perfect.'

There have been many theories as to the model for Undershaft; and Shaw himself, while recording that Gilbert Murray was the model for the Professor, gave no clue. It has been confidently stated that Undershaft was based on Alfred Krupp[1], and on Sir Basil Zaharoff[2]: certainly with his overwhelming paternalism and his ability to override governments Undershaft shows characteristics of both. But a more likely candidate for the model was Alfred Nobel whose peace prize had recently stirred up a great deal of controversy, and whose rationalisation of his own career showed some resemblance to Undershaft's. Nobel's boast to Berthe von Suttner, that 'my factories may end war sooner than your Congresses', has a very Shavian ring, and Nobel's inter-

[1] William Manchester: *The Arms of Krupp*, London, Michael Joseph, 1969, p. 282.
[2] J. D. Scott: *Vickers, A History,* London, Weidenfeld & Nicolson, 1962, p. 80.

nationalism and homelessness were very similar to Undershaft's.[1] But Undershaft explicitly rejects Nobel's theory that arms factories will achieve a balance of terror: his son-in-law Charles Lomax says, 'Well, the more destructive war becomes, the sooner it will be abolished, eh?' To which Undershaft replies, 'Not at all. The more destructive war becomes the more fascinating we find it. No, Mr Lomax, I am obliged to you for making the usual excuse for my trade, but I am not ashamed of it. I am not one of those men who keep their morals and their business in watertight compartments.'

Major Barbara was to be quoted often over the following seventy years, in recurring arguments about the arms business: for it broached the central problem that the prosperity of the world was coming to depend on the manufacture of the means of destruction. The problem went way beyond the existence of a few multi-millionaires, like Krupp, Armstrong or Nobel, who had exploited the new opportunity: for whole communities were growing up, on the Ruhr, the Tees or the Allegheny, which had become dependent on this thriving export industry for their survival. The industry, of its nature, was constantly developing new technologies and new opportunities, and the arms business, dynamic, innovative and expansive, was threatening to become the spearhead of the advance of industrialisation.

KRUPP V. ARMSTRONG

At the first great international industrial exhibition, at the Crystal Palace in London in 1851, there were only a few hints of the new importance of the arms business in the industrial age. The great majority of the exhibits under the great glass roof in Hyde Park—the machinery, statues, textiles and fashions—were luxuriously peaceful. But there were a few exceptions, including two remarkable exhibits from the remote state of Prussia which provided a foretaste of a promising new industry. One was a solid ingot weighing 4,300 pounds, the biggest 'monster ingot' ever cast. The other was an elegant, highly-polished six-pounder cannon, displayed under a canopy topped with the royal Prussian flag. It

[1] Louis Crompton: *Shaw the Dramatist*, London, Allen & Unwin, 1971, p. 115. He points out that in the manuscript draft of *Major Barbara*, Undershaft boasts of selling a new rifle to the Swedish, Italian and German governments—just as Nobel sold his patents. I am also indebted to Michael Holroyd, the current biographer of Shaw, for his observations on this comparison.

was admired more for its beauty than for its effectiveness: 'the exquisitely finished six-pounder steel gun, mounted on its carriage,' said *The Illustrated Exhibitor* in 1851, 'is a model of good workmanship, which has deservedly attracted much attention.'[1] Both the Prussian exhibits were under the name of the firm of Friedrich Krupp, of Essen, and they represented the first major venture abroad of the young head of the firm, Alfred Krupp.

So much has been written about the Krupp family as the armourers of the Second and Third Reich, as the industrial partners of the Kaisers and Hitler, that it is important to recall that the origins of the vast company were almost the opposite— as the exporters of steel to the rest of Europe, with their own country Prussia as one of their minor clients, and with guns as a sideshow to their chief business of steel and railway tyres. The first success of Alfred Krupp, the great 'Cannon King' who built up the firm, was an international success, and only by selling his goods abroad could he impress his own government. The letters of this restless steelmaster, written through the fifty years of the making of modern Germany,[2] reveal a fanatic obsession with his metal and a dictatorial control over his firm, with all the anguish of a businessman searching for secure markets and self-sufficiency. But only with the coming of Bismarck and the victory of 1870 did his interests begin to merge with those of the state.

The young Alfred Krupp, as a tall lean youth of fourteen, had inherited the almost bankrupt concern from his father, with only six workers in Essen, on the Ruhr. He was fired with determination to vindicate his family and outdo the English who dominated the steel market. The Customs Union in 1834 gave him new opportunities, and he was soon getting orders from Paris, Flanders and Switzerland; but Prussia was too conservative and too poor, and refused to give him protection against English steel. Krupp travelled to Sheffield to try to find the secrets of the English success, and achieved his first real triumph at the 1851 exhibition, followed by others in Munich and Paris. He began selling a few guns, and even obtained an order from the Khedive of Egypt, but the Prussian army still scorned him, and by 1857 he was complaining that the Prussian State Railways had given him less business during their whole existence than France had given

---

[1] *The Illustrated Exhibitor*, London, John Cassell, 1851, p. 480.
[2] *The Letters of Alfred Krupp 1826-1887*, edited by William Berdrow, London, Gollancz, 1930.

in one month. His gun business was small and unprofitable, and in one revealing letter in 1858 he describes his attitudes to guns and other products:

> Alongside these appliances of peaceful intercourse, those of war—guns—are also provided for. The ideal is the highest degree of indestructibility; in the former case, for furthering the safety and property of human lives, in the latter for increasing the capacity for destruction. The former assumes the leading position, and must provide our living. The latter I cultivate at great sacrifice, in the interests of progress, and this work will not achieve a value in my eyes until I can serve my fatherland with it in time of need. For the blessings of peace, however, I gladly renounce such an opportunity for proving what a home industry can do, as well as my pride therein ... I have had to seek the means for the employment and nourishment of my people, for the most part abroad among the natural enemies of my industry.[1]

By the next year he had received his first big Prussian order, for 300 rifled six-pounders; in 1861 his factory was visited by the King, and the next year Krupp had a brilliant success at the new London Exhibition with his breech-loading gun. The English were much more impressed than the Prussians, who continued buying British ships and muzzle-loading guns; and the Russians gave a huge order for big guns which helped Krupp to develop his technology. Krupp often lamented that he was forced to sell guns to countries which might become the enemies of Prussia, and used this threat to persuade Prussia to buy his guns. But the Prussian government in peacetime could still not by itself place enough orders to provide the expansion that Krupp wanted. By 1865 Krupp was in serious difficulties, and Bismarck refused to lend him money or increase his orders; so that he had to obtain a loan from the French banker, Seillière, who had thirty years earlier helped to establish the French armaments company of Schneider, at Le Creusot. In April 1866 Krupp insisted, against the express request of Bismarck, on exporting a consignment of guns to Austria, and Krupp's guns fired on both sides in the Austro-Prussian war. In the following years Krupp succeeded in raising a further loan from the King of Prussia, but this did not prevent him also trying to export his guns to France; and only the complacency of the French generals stood in his way.

It was the Prussian victory over France in 1870, achieved with the help of Krupp's guns, which consolidated the relationship between the company and the state: it was the first industrialised

---

[1] Alfred Krupp to Alexander von Humboldt, 1858. *Letters*, p. 164.

war for Europe, as the civil war had been for America, and it
established Krupp's reputation throughout the world as the
Cannon King. He continued to export with huge success to
anyone who would buy, in spite of another financial crisis in
1873. But the German government was now a major customer,
and the great boom of the 1870s transformed the company: the
small town of Essen expanded into one of the great industrial
centres of Europe. In his sixties Krupp, determined to undermine
the Social Democrats, had turned Essen into a model of paternal
welfare for his workers, and set a pattern for Bismarck's welfare
state. By the end of his career he was employing 20,000 workers
where he had begun with six.

As an old man, increasingly detached from the works, he
reflected about the problems of his trade: in 1881 he speculated
about the possibility of a war between Germany and Russia, and
wrote that 'evidently I could not carry on the work as Krupp in
Russia to make armaments against Germany'. Four years later
when war between Britain and Russia seemed possible, he
appeared torn between the technical interest of a war and its
dangers. 'One thing just strikes me,' he wrote in stilted English
to his London agent, 'that none of the civilised countries had at
any time a battle on the sea since the new guns. English vessels
were in the battle of Cronstadt thirty-five years ago, but they had
no fight. A war, if it exploded between England and Russia,
would be a lesson to all nations respecting the value of arms and
that would be on the side of much more important losses—the
only benefit of a war which I still hope will be suppressed.'

By the time of Alfred Krupp's death in 1887 his company was
already a national institution, and his descendants were established as a kind of industrial royal family, in their melancholy
palace, the Villa Hügel, looking over the smoke of the Ruhr. No
subsequent Krupp was to have the same fanatic zeal as Alfred; his
son became a homosexual and committed suicide, and the fortune
then passed to his granddaughter Bertha, who married a stiff
aristocrat, Gustav von Bohlen, who changed his name to Krupp
and took over the firm. But the company had acquired its own
momentum, and the family came to be regarded, particularly by
the British, as representing the very spirit of German militarism.
Certainly Krupp's enjoyed special relationships with the Second
Reich, and became, more than any other steel company, indispensable to its military preparations.

Yet Krupp's remained essentially an international company, prepared to do business with any other government unless formally prevented: and half their guns were sold abroad, through a network of agents who were usually nationals of their own country. In 1909 they had actually offered to build eight warships a year for the British navy, before the Kaiser vetoed it. Krupp's international network of agents had already acquired the characteristics of a separate diplomatic service, as one American pacifist correspondent described it in 1911: 'King Krupp of Essen has ambassadors of his own in every great capital of the world, from Tokyo to Constantinople, and from St Petersburg to Buenos Aires. He has even in Sofia a representative who knows more about local politics and has a larger acquaintance with politicians than all the legations put together.'[1]

The relationship between Krupp's and the German government was an uneasy one, and it reached a crisis in 1913 when a major scandal was uncovered by the Social Democrat opposition, revealing that Krupp's had systematically bribed naval officers to give them secret details of government projects and correspondence. After the trial, several officers were cashiered and imprisoned, and one Krupp official was sent to jail. The war minister, Josias von Heeringen, defended himself in the Reichstag, shortly before he was forced to resign, with a caustic reply to his Social Democrat critic, Karl Liebknecht. He pointed out that the government were dependent on private industry in order to ensure the great quantities of weapons that might be needed in a war; for a state factory could not provide the necessary expansion, whereas a private company could obtain foreign orders in the meantime, to maintain its full production. 'Who gets the advantage from that? Undoubtedly the workers who are represented by the Social Democrats, for if the foreign orders were cancelled, the factories which employ them could no longer exist.'[2]

In Britain the process of industrialisation had been much longer-established than in Germany, but the British arms companies almost equally rapidly emerged as a dominating influence. Between the ending of the Napoleonic wars in 1815 and the Crimean war of 1854 there had been virtually no improvement

[1] Francis McCullagh: *Syndicates for War*, p. 6 (World Peace Foundation Pamphlets Series 2 part 3).

[2] Reichstag debate, April 18, 1913.

in the British army's gunnery, until the obvious inadequacy of the guns in Crimea gave the generals cause for concern. The source of the improvement was accidental. While Alfred Krupp was so obsessively building up his steelworks in the Ruhr, an enterprising lawyer in Newcastle, William Armstrong, had been developing in a much more casual way a talent for engineering. In 1845 Armstrong devised a plan to make cranes for the Newcastle docks to be operated by water pressure, and he set up a small factory at Elswick, a village outside Newcastle. During the Crimean war the War Office asked him to design submarine mines to blow up Russian ships, and he and his partner, James Rendel, were so shocked by the archaic guns used in the war that they set about designing a new kind of breech-loading rifled gun with an elongated projectile instead of the old cast-iron balls. The new 'Armstrong gun' was finally perfected in 1858 and accepted by the War Office. Armstrong generously presented the patents to the nation, became a civil servant concerned with ordnance, and was knighted, while a new factory was set up at Elswick to meet the government orders.

But the Elswick company soon ran into attacks from the Royal Ordnance Factory, which claimed that it had been overcharging, while naval officers distrusted the new-fangled gun. By 1862 the contracts were terminated, and the army returned to muzzle-loading guns, made by the government factory. As for the Elswick company, as Armstrong said afterwards, it 'had no alternative but to commence a new career, based on foreign support, and it was by that support—and not by government patronage—that the Elswick Ordnance Works was established'. It was a momentous decision. As Vickers' historian succinctly records it: 'In this way, by a negative decision taken purely in reference to internal politics, the British government set up a rival to Krupps and thus created the competitive international armaments industry.'[1]

The moral and patriotic problems of selling arms to foreigners were evident to Armstrong from the start. He had been knighted by his government, and been well paid by them: he told his partner's brother Stuart Rendel (later Lord Rendel), 'he could not possibly, so soon as he had left office, start upon the supply of guns to foreign powers.' Rendel replied with arguments that were to re-echo through the armaments business over the next

[1] Scott, p. 31.

hundred years. He told Armstrong that 'his first patriotic duty was to maintain prestige of the system he had induced the Government to adopt and in which he still believed; that the manufacture of arms for foreign powers was far from an unpatriotic act, for the country was benefited to the extent to which its experience and power of production were increased, whereas foreign countries were disadvantaged to the extent to which they were dependent on us for their munitions of war.'[1]

Armstrong, according to Rendel, 'still looked at the matter with much indifference', but he agreed to let Rendel try to sell his guns abroad, and offered him five percent commission on all orders he brought in: thus casually was Stuart Rendel launched as the first great British arms salesman. The new company was soon very successful in exporting arms, much encouraged by the American civil war which was then raging; one of their first foreign orders came from Charles Francis Adams, the Minister for the United States in London, and was swiftly followed by orders from the South.[2] Rendel, though a radical liberal, had no compunction in selling to both sides. He was soon selling guns in every direction: he sold them to Italy through his friend the naval attaché, Captain Albini (who later became an admiral and still later head of Armstrong's in Rome). He sold them to the Khedive of Egypt through his friend Lord Goschen, who had negotiated the first Egyptian loan. He sold them to Turkey, and Chile. In Russia and Austria he found the Krupp interest too strongly installed,[3] but he obtained a provisional order for arming one of the first Prussian ironclads until 'the order fell through under Krupp influence'.

Through the 1860s, Armstrong's company, like Krupp's, depended primarily on foreign orders for their arms business: their average orders from the British government amounted to only £1,654 a year for their first fifteen years. In 1870 they became agents for the American Gatling machine-gun, which was adopted by the Royal Navy and made useful profits for Armstrong's until it was superseded by the Maxim gun. Rendel himself was making so much money out of his five percent commissions that he had to be made a partner in the firm: later, fortified by his fortune, he became a Liberal MP and intimate

[1] *The Personal Papers of Lord Rendel*, edited by F. E. Hamer, London, Benn, 1931, p. 277.
[2] Ibid., p. 277.
[3] Ibid., p. 280.

friend of Mr Gladstone. By 1883 Armstrong's had become a
public company, with a nominal capital of two million pounds,
established as second only to Krupp as a world exporter of arms.

Krupp and Armstrong dominated the armaments world: 'our
business leaves little or no room for other gunmakers,' wrote
Rendel. Krupp, he explained, 'can be the only person besides
ourselves who deals with any European power'. The rivalry had
spurred both sides to sell their arms further afield, while both in
London and Berlin the governments used the foreign competitor
to play off against the home company. The British government
approached Krupp in 1863 to supply guns in place of Armstrong,
though later deciding against it, and Krupp commented to Crown
Prince Friedrich, 'why should England not obtain the material
from her friends abroad, until her own industries can make it?'
The Admiralty in London maintained a lofty disdain towards
Armstrong, as is indicated by a stately exchange of letters in
1870. Sir William Armstrong wrote humbly in the third person
to the First Lord of the Admiralty, Hugh Childers, suggesting he
might care to visit the Elswick works, whose operations 'make it
inexpedient from a public point of view that its practice should be
overlooked in any important decision on artillery'. The First
Lord agreed to see Armstrong in London, but wrote frostily
that he could only find time to deal with questions 'such as may
be necessary to discuss in reference to the current business of this
department'. The Admiralty sent the letter to the wrong address
and failed to keep a copy, so the meeting was abortive.[1] It was
not exactly a military-industrial complex.

But Armstrong could survive without British orders, and by
the 1880s the village of Elswick had become a city of forges,
factories and steelworks, 'an arsenal in itself'. The Elswick works
were regarded not so much as the manufacturers of lethal
weapons, as the leaders of British engineering. Lord Armstrong,
as he had now become, built himself a massive house, Cragside,
designed by Norman Shaw, with electric light generated from
the neighbouring stream, and an elaborate conservatory with
plants hydraulically turned to face the sun. It was a monument
hardly less extravagant, though less portentous, than Krupp's
Villa Hügel. The visitors' book at Cragside records the remarkable

[1] Unpublished letters between Sir William Armstrong and Hugh Childers, MP,
February 21–28, 1870: in the possession of the present Lord Armstrong, to whom I am
indebted.

range of foreign visitors who came to Armstrong's to buy guns and warships, including the Shah of Persia (1889) and his Grand Vizier, the King of Siam (1897), the Emir of Afghanistan (1895), and numerous delegations of naval officers from China, Japan, Norway, Turkey, the United States, Chile and Peru. Several of these clients were to be important customers for British arms eighty years later.

It was at Cragside that Lord Armstrong spent his last years, fulminating against the power of the new trades unions, and watching his yards at Elswick become the world's biggest supplier of warships. He did not betray unease about his trade, though he was clearly conscious of criticism. 'It is our province, as engineers,' he said, 'to make the forces of matter obedient to the will of man; and those who use the means we supply must be responsible for their legitimate application.' He professed to believe that war would become less murderous as hand-to-hand fighting was superseded by new inventions, which widened the distance between combatants: 'we may fairly anticipate that, the more the element of intelligence supersedes that of animal force in military struggles, the more will the barbarity of war be mitigated'. When he died in 1900, most of the obituaries were admiring, though the *Newcastle Daily Chronicle* was less certain: 'There is something that appals the imagination in the application of a cool and temperate mind like Lord Armstrong's to the science of destruction.' But the newspaper took heart in the recurring argument that war was becoming too terrible to be practised: 'The sight of means to do ill-deeds all round keeps the ill-deeds undone. In the nature of things the militarism of the time must bring its own abatement . . .'.[1]

VICKERS, MAXIM AND ZAHAROFF

Armstrong's factories and shipyards were now facing growing competition from the Vickers company, based on Sheffield. Its founder, Edward Vickers, had made his first big profits exporting steel bars to America to build railroads during the 1850s; but like other steel companies Vickers were in difficulties with the end of the railroad boom. By 1888 they were beginning to make guns for the British War Office, to rescue themselves from the falling-off of trade: but 'if the directors of Vickers felt any sense of destiny

[1] See David Dougan: *The Great Gunmaker*, Newcastle, Frank Graham, 1970, pp. 68-9.

on entering into the armaments business, they characteristically did not record it.'[1] Nine years later, faced with growing naval orders, they took a much bolder decision, to build warships complete with guns, engines and armour plate. They bought a ship-yard in Barrow-in-Furness, and in the same year they acquired a company at the opposite and more lethal end of the arms business, the Maxim-Nordenfelt company, which made machine-guns operated by their own recoil which were far more reliable than the old Gatlings.

No one in that era portrays more vividly the cheerful internationalism of the arms business than Sir Hiram Maxim, and his autobiography has such light-hearted charm that it is hard to remember that it is concerned with the most deadly machine of its time:[2] with the coming of the machine-gun it was less easy to share Armstrong's belief that engineers were making war less murderous. Maxim was a natural inventor: he was brought up as a country boy in Maine, where he invented a mousetrap. He first became famous as a pioneer of electric light, which brought him to Europe in 1881 for the Paris Exhibition. But it was not until he devised a new kind of automatic gun in Paris that he suddenly became a world figure, with kings and potentates seeking him out. This bright-eyed American with his bushy spade beard began touring the world to show off his deadly machine, to the astonishment of his spectators, who quickly foresaw its revolutionary effect. 'The Yankees beat all creation', exclaimed Lord Wolseley from the War Office, when he saw hundreds of cartridges fired: it would not be long, he surmised, before someone would turn out a machine that would manufacture fully-grown men and women.

Maxim considered his gun as specially useful 'in stopping the mad rush of savages',[3] and its advantages were soon shown in the colonial wars, where it was commemorated by Hilaire Belloc:

> Whatever happens we have got
> The Maxim gun, and they have not.[4]

At the battle of Omdurman in 1898 the British troops were armed

[1] Scott, p. 41.

[2] Sir Hiram S. Maxim: *My Life*, London, Methuen, 1915. See also Hiram Percy Maxim: *A Genius in the Family*, New York, Harper's, 1936.

[3] Maxim, p. 182.

[4] Hilaire Belloc: *The Modern Traveller*, 1898.

with Maxim guns against the Sudanese, and in the words of a famous newspaper report 'a visible wave of death swept over the advancing host'. Maxim gaily records how Sir Edwin Arnold later described the battle: 'In most of our wars it has been the dash, the skill, and the bravery of our officers and men that have won the day, but in this case the battle was won by a quiet scientific gentleman living down in Kent.'[1]

Throughout the world Maxim found eager customers for his gun: the Russians were particularly keen buyers, and after the Russo-Japanese war Maxim was told that 'half of the Japanese killed in the late war were killed with the little Maxim gun'.[2] In selling his invention Maxim became a citizen of the world; he dined with the Tsar, was congratulated by the German Emperor, collaborated with Nobel. He was loaded with honours from grateful nations, and in England, where he settled down, he was knighted. He showed no signs of guilt about the nature of his invention, writing about it with the same affectionate pride as about his first mousetrap, and he was photographed showing it off to his grandson in his garden. But he did wryly observe: 'It is astonishing to note how quickly this invention put me on the very pinnacle of fame. Had it been anything else but a killing machine very little would have been said of it.'[3]

By buying the Maxim-Nordenfelt machine-gun business in 1897, the Vickers company had also bought the services of the most celebrated of all the international arms salesmen, Basil Zaharoff, who was later to be depicted as the archetypal 'merchant of death'. In the story of Zaharoff the legend is difficult to separate from fact. A mass of literature has grown up around him with very little evidence, and he left no personal record behind him: his methods and reputation, which he carefully cultivated, depended on his being 'the mystery man of Europe'. But behind all his self-dramatisation Zaharoff was a figure of historical importance; for he was not merely a master of salesmanship and bribery, but an operator who understood the connections between arms and diplomacy, between arms and intelligence, and who could serve as both salesman and spy. In his person he represented all the mixed loyalties of the burgeoning arms business: 'I sold armaments to anyone who would buy them. I was a Russian

[1] Maxim, p. 258.
[2] Ibid., p. 213.
[3] Ibid., p. 313.

when in Russia, a Greek in Greece, a Frenchman in Paris.'[1]

His career began in the Balkans, where his origins were obscure: he was born, perhaps in Constantinople, between 1849 and 1851, and was brought up both in Turkey and Greece. According to his own account, he sailed his own boats from Athens to the coasts of Africa, and made his first hundreds gun-running for savages. 'I made wars so that I could sell arms to both sides. I must have sold more arms than anyone else in the world.'[2] His first major job was in 1877 as salesman in Athens for the Swedish company, Nordenfelt, which was then selling not only machine-guns, but a new kind of submarine. Zaharoff sold submarines both to Greeks and Turks, and had considerable success in the militant atmosphere of the Balkans; but in selling further afield he came under serious competition from other guns, notably Maxim's. When Maxim came to Vienna to demonstrate his gun to the Austrian army, Maxim (according to his own account) observed that Zaharoff was watching the performance with the newspaper reporters. Maxim showed off the gun, by cutting out the initials of the emperor, F J, on a new target; but after the tests Zaharoff quickly explained to the reporters that the gun being tested was actually the Nordenfelt gun. Maxim nevertheless got an order for 160 guns for Austria, and he evidently later forgave Zaharoff's trickery, and became quite friendly with 'Mr Zed Zed'.

By 1888 Maxim and Nordenfelt had merged, with Zaharoff as their salesman, playing an increasingly important role in the company: by 1895 he was collecting a commission of one percent on all continental sales. Then in 1897 Vickers bought Maxim-Nordenfelt, and Zaharoff became agent for the whole Vickers group, with a commission of nine-tenths of one percent of the profits of the combined company, together with expense allowances which included £1,000 a year towards the cost of his magnificent house in Paris, which he had made his headquarters. Zaharoff 'brought in a vast amount of business',[3] and before long his commissions were making him a rich man: in 1902 he was paid £34,000, in 1903 £35,000, in 1904 £40,000 and in 1905 £86,000.[4] Exactly how important he was in the decisions of

---

[1] Interview with Rosita Forbes: London *Sunday Chronicle*, November 29, 1936.
[2] Ibid.
[3] Royal Commission, 1935-6, Minutes, p. 360, Q 1994.
[4] Scott: p. 80.

Vickers remains obscure; he was never on the board, but he was probably the most valuable and highly paid member of the company, and according to *The Times* obituary in 1936, 'he may almost be said to have been Vickers'.[1] In an industry which depended so heavily on exports he was the indispensable link with their markets.

In the scramble to sell arms at the turn of the century, Zaharoff was the master-salesman, competing across Europe and Latin America with Krupps, Schneider and his British rivals, Armstrong, selling anything from battleships to machine-guns. His contacts were regal. In Russia, which was hectically re-arming itself after its defeat by the Japanese, Zaharoff was well-placed through his background, and he successfully outmanoeuvred the French company, Schneider. In Spain he had high-level aristocratic connections, and he was later to marry the Duchess of Villafranca. In Paris he bought a newspaper, the *Excelsior*, and was sufficiently close to French governments to be rewarded with the Légion d'Honneur. In the Balkans he was uniquely placed to exploit the political divisions. His own cosmopolitan connections symbolised the internationalism of the industry: in one company, a French torpedo subsidiary (Société Française de Torpille Whitehead) he was a partner together with 'an English minister, the wife of a German minister, a French rear-admiral, the wife of an Austrian naval officer, a member of the "pan-German" family of Reventlow—and the widow of Herbert von Bismarck, daughter-in-law of the Iron Chancellor.'[2]

Stories proliferated in the European capitals of Zaharoff's corruption and deviousness—leaving wallets stuffed with notes on ministers' desks, travelling between opposing Balkan states to escalate orders on both sides. The actual proof of such bribes is never likely to emerge, for Zaharoff destroyed all his diaries and papers three years before his death. But his telegrams to Vickers show him 'greasing the wheels' in Russia in 1900, 'doing the needful' in Portugal in 1906, and in the same year 'administering doses of Vickers to Spanish friends'.[3] And Vickers' historian

---

[1] *The Times*, London, November 28, 1936.

[2] Robert Neumann: *Zaharoff: the Armaments King*, London, Allen & Unwin, 1938, p. 158.

[3] Clive Trebilcock: *The British Armaments Industry 1890–1914*, from Geoffrey Best and Andrew Wheatcroft: *War, Economy and the Military Mind*, London, Croom Helm, 1976, p. 93.

gives his own assessment:

> It would be naive to imagine that the standards of business ethics in the Balkans and in South America in the 'Seventies and 'Eighties were the standards of Whitehall or the Bank of England. Bribery was not accidental or occasional, but essential and systematic in every field of commerce. It would be equally naive, however, to imagine that when Zaharoff paid bribes, the money paid appeared under a ledger entry of 'Bribes' in the books in London. The evidence, what there is of it, is quite of another kind, of inferences from notes of expenses, of guarded phrases in private letters. About Zaharoff's activities before the amalgamation of 1897 there are not even hints. After that date there is evidence that on two or three occasions in Serbia in 1898, in Russia later, and probably in Turkey, Zaharoff paid secrecy commissions, or bribes, of sums running from about £100 to possibly several thousand pounds. There is no evidence about whom they were paid to and what they were paid for, but the likeliest thing is that they went to forestall German and other rivals.[1]

Bribery was doubtless prevalent in many industries, but there were several reasons why it was specially rife in the arms business. The great majority of orders were from governments, where the decision could well depend on one or two individuals, whose support was therefore essential. The advantages of buying one warship or gun, as opposed to another, were often uncertain, and arguments could thus easily be swayed. The orders were often very large, so that a single decision was more critical for an arms company. And the sales were usually conducted in secrecy, for reasons of national security. Moreover as the commission increased, officials might well favour bigger orders, beyond the capacity or needs of their country, to ensure that their share would be greater. The story was told of an English salesman who went out to a European country to arrange a contract for a cruiser with a European government: he paid a succession of 'commissions' to officials concerned with the contract, until one official made such an exorbitant demand that the Englishman exclaimed, 'How can I build the cruiser?' The official replied, 'What does that matter, so long as you get paid and we get paid?'[2]

One major Vickers bribe (apparently not involving Zaharoff) came to light in 1914 in Japan, after a scandal which had some similarities with the Japanese Lockheed scandal sixty years later. Vickers, like Armstrong's, had been big suppliers to the Japanese navy, and with their agents, Mitsui, were said to handle a quarter

[1] Scott, p. 81.
[2] F. W. Hirst: *The Political Economy of the War*, Dent, London, 1915, p. 98.

of all Japanese foreign trade. In 1910 Vickers were bidding against Armstrong to build the battleship *Kongo* for Japan, and they took the precaution of arranging to pay large sums of money to the Japanese Rear-Admiral Fujii, who was advising on the estimates. Vickers got the contract, worth £2.4 million, but when the *Kongo* was delivered three years later an enquiry revealed a web of bribery, including not only the Rear-Admiral but the agents Mitsui, who bribed a friend in the naval stores department. Trials followed, the Rear-Admiral went to jail, and the Prime Minister, Yamamoto, resigned (to become premier again nine years later).[1] The *Kongo* case, reverberating in Britain and coming so soon after the revelations about Krupp's bribes, revived fears that the arms companies were setting their own secret foreign policy.

How far bribery was specially prevalent in the arms industry has been much debated. Certainly arms salesmen were not uniquely venal. In Japan there was evidence of large scale bribery in other businesses, and in China a Foreign Office correspondent noted that 'no concession has been obtained without large sums spent in bribing the high officials in Pekin'.[2] But the connection between arms and bribes was specially ominous, not only because of the danger of the product, but because of the scope for expanding the whole market. The Vickers company and others contended that the aggressive selling of arms did not increase the total sum spent on armaments; it merely deprived other companies of that share of the market. But other evidence, then and later, has suggested that arms bribes were able to stimulate orders which might otherwise never have been made.[3]

Already, before 1914, Zaharoff's name had begun to represent the seamy side of the arms business, particularly in the years of the Boer war and after, when arms companies were under fire from Liberals led by Lloyd George. Yet he emerged from the end of the world war as Sir Basil, a Knight of the Bath, an honour conferred by Lloyd George. A favourite photograph shows him at his installation at Westminster Abbey in 1924, resplendent with his white handlebar moustache and goatee beard, enveloped in a satin cloak, and topped with the tricorn hat and white plume of the order—the very picture of the illustrious grandee.

---

[1] Royal Commission, 1935-6, Minutes, p. 155. Also *Japan Times Weekly*, July 10, 1976.

[2] Trebilcock, p. 94.

[3] Royal Commission, 1935-6, Minutes, p. 388, Q 2347 and Report, Command 5292, 1936, p. 36. See also Lockheed evidence, specially chapter 10.

The explanation of this remarkable transmogrification may well lie not only in Sir Basil's ability to purchase honours, but also in some services to intelligence; but it is here that Zaharoff's career, like other arms dealers' since, goes deep underground. He loved to suggest that his arms dealings were really part of his patriotic effort. Thus he wrote to Sir Vincent Caillard of Vickers that his associations in Germany were:

> really an attempt to establish an intelligence organisation in that country. This way I was able to tell the Allies far more about the enemy than could their own espionage services . . . I would not, and I did not, hesitate to sell arms to Germany's potential allies, or to make deals with German arms firms, despite the fact that Germany was the potential enemy. I maintain that this knowledge we acquired of the enemy's potential was of the utmost importance to the Allies when war came.[1]

Zaharoff told extravagant stories about his wartime missions on behalf of the allied governments. He described to the novelist Rosita Forbes, in an apparently authentic interview, how he had been sent to Germany during the war 'to discover certain things that Lloyd George wanted to know', in the uniform of a Bulgarian doctor. 'I paid heavily for that uniform and the man who sold it died.' When he returned, he said, he was greeted by Clemenceau in the railway station, and by Lloyd George in London, with the Grand Cross of the Bath in his pocket: 'They say that the information I brought ended the war.'[2] Most of the wartime stories about Zaharoff's exploits can be discounted, but there is no doubt that he emerged as the confidant of Lloyd George, the old scourge of the arms companies. The friendship continued after Lloyd George lost power, and in 1928 Zaharoff was visited by Lloyd George in Monte Carlo. 'He was a very remarkable man and a great admirer of LG,' wrote Lloyd George's secretary, A. J. Sylvester, describing the visit, 'the care and attention he showed to my chief touched me deeply.'[3]

How deeply Zaharoff was involved in war policy; how far he ran his own intelligence system; how much, if at all, he was consulted by war leaders, all this remains cloaked. After the war Zaharoff continued to work for Vickers, specially concerned with Spanish contracts, until at least 1925, when he was seventy-five; but he spent most of his time at Monte Carlo, or at the Château

---

[1] Donald McCormick: *Pedlar of Death*, London, McDonald, 1965, p. 87.

[2] Forbes interview, November 29, 1936.

[3] A. J. Sylvester: *The Real Lloyd George*, London, Cassell & Co., 1947, p. 170.

de Balincourt, near Pontoise, surrounded by a wooded park and a stone wall with high wire fences, where, in November 1936, his funeral was held in strict secrecy. The London *Times* obituary recorded that: 'in the closing years of his life Sir Basil's admiration for politicians waned, and with regretful philosophy he observed that sooner or later they nearly all suffered from an exaggerated idea of their importance.'[1] It was a sentiment which echoed Andrew Undershaft's contempt for the 'foolish gabble shop' of parliament.

Sir Basil offered the perennial political justification for arms sales: that they provide the connections and intelligence that enable the major powers to extend their influence and keep links with their clients, even if they become their enemies. As Zaharoff is said to have explained to Lloyd George, in justifying his position in wartime: 'the sale of arms is part of national prosperity, and the nation which sells to other nations understands best the real military and naval position inside those countries to which it sells.'[2] Zaharoff saw arms as the ultimate currency, and in this he was the archetype of all arms dealers since, who see themselves as the realists in a world of idealists, from Khashoggi to Sam Cummings (who lives, as he likes to note, not far from Zaharoff's old home in Monte Carlo). There are no memorials now to commemorate Zaharoff's career, beyond some second-empire furniture at the top of Vickers' skyscraper on the Thames, and a Zaharoff Chair of Aviation at the Imperial College of Science and Technology; but his ghost still flits through the ministries of defence, and his philosophy still has its followers.

[1] *The Times*, London, November 28, 1936.
[2] McCormick, p. 122.

3

The Great International

Articles against peace are written with pens made of the same steel as cannons and shells.

Aristide Briand

By the early years of the century the arms business had become the most international industry in the world, with a web of inter-connections between the continents. Vickers forged close links with foreign companies with the help of their financial expert Siegmund Loewe, who had reached an agreement in 1900 with a lively American company called Electric Boat, which had just been set up by an American lawyer, Isaac Rice (and which was to be the parent of the modern General Dynamics). Electric Boat had acquired patents for a new kind of submarine driven by electric batteries, whose licences Vickers acquired to build throughout Europe: Vickers were soon lending large sums of money to Electric Boat, until they were eventually supported by contracts for the US navy. Loewe also made agreements with the French company Le Nickel, which through its deposits in New Caledonia had a monopoly of the nickel that was essential for strengthening steel, which in its turn led to the formation in 1901 of the Nickel Syndicate. Loewe also made a licensing agreement between Vickers and the Deutsche Waffen company in Germany, in which the Loewe family had an interest, giving them exclusive rights to sell automatic guns in Germany.[1] And the next year Vickers obtained from Krupp's the licences to make all Krupp's time fuses for shells—which was to become the most notorious of all licensing arrangements.

The most remarkable world agreements were in the business of armour-plate, which was crucial to the new naval warfare. By 1893 Krupp had devised a special hardened steel which could withstand shells much more effectively, which he licensed to his rivals, in return for a fat royalty of £9 a ton; by 1897 all the main British steel firms were using the Krupp steel. In America in the meantime Hayward August Harvey had devised a new kind of armour-plate, which he too patented through the world; and by 1894 the ten main producers of armour-plate, including Vickers, Krupp and Carnegie, formed the Harvey Syndicate, to control prices and share out foreign orders for the Harvey steel. For the next seventeen years this syndicate, together with the rival Krupp patents, controlled the sales of armour-plate, until the patents for both expired in 1911.

The internationalism of the arms companies was a constant incentive to innovation and experiment, often against the conservative instincts of their home governments and the admirals and generals who preferred the more elegant traditions of the old warfare. In Britain foreign orders could often provide more interesting challenges to the shipyards than the British navy. In 1899 Sir William White, the Director of Naval Construction, bitterly complained that British warships had been delayed because of an order to build a Japanese battleship; and in 1902 Vickers and Armstrong's built two battleships for Chile which performed so well that the British navy eventually insisted on buying them. South America provided a kind of testing-ground for the great powers, as it would often do later, and the expansion of the Japanese navy provided a special challenge to Armstrong's yard at Elswick. The Japanese wars with China (1894) and Russia (1904) provided new trials of naval technology, and, in the words of a Newcastle historian, the victories of Japan were 'in a measure the victories of Elswick.'[2] After the Japanese victory over the

---

[1] Sir Charles Craven, the Managing Director of Vickers in 1936, testified to the Royal Commission on the Private Manufacture of Arms, that Loewe 'was still a director of the Deutsche Waffen company, and of another company the name of which I cannot read, in Germany, while he was with Vickers' (Minutes, p. 377, Q 2234).

[2] F. Harrison: *A History of Newcastle upon Tyne*, Hewitt & Ridge (Whitley Bay), 1913, pp. 230, 264.

Russian navy at Vladivostock in 1905, the Armstrong workers took a day's holiday to celebrate.

In the first years of the century the arms race in battleships reached a new intensity with the technical breakthrough achieved by the *Dreadnought*, the British battleship with big guns and heavy armour which immediately made all older warships out of date. It was an early example of arms technology upsetting the governments' nice calculations of the balance of power: thereafter the world's navies turned to the new battleships, making the huge earlier British navy obsolete; and the shipyards of Vickers and Armstrong in Britain faced more serious technical competition from Krupp's in Germany (who had bought the Germania shipyards in Hamburg).

The global development of the arms industry was rapid, and the pioneers of the trade, like Maxim, Nobel or Zaharoff, were at home in all the Western capitals. The Nobel dynamite trust was probably the most highly-organised of them all: with its far-flung explosives factories held together by two central companies, with international boards representing the interests of all the subsidiaries, it was the forerunner of the modern multinationals. The most destructive trade was also the most global; as one later critic observed: 'the Great International, which political idealists and labour strategists have sought for so long, was actually taking shape in the armament industry.'[1]

There was no evidence that these world-minded companies wanted to provoke a European war, as was often later alleged: such a result would obviously put their whole future at risk. But their salesmen were naturally eager to emphasise and exaggerate the build-up on the other side. A notorious case was that of Mr Mulliner, a director of the Coventry Ordnance works, who wrote to the War Office in 1906, after the first *Dreadnought* had been launched, to warn them of the 'enormous expenditure now going on at Krupp's' for making very large naval guns quickly. He repeated his warnings and in 1909 he was invited to address the Cabinet, when he stressed Germany's superiority. Soon afterwards the question of Germany's increased naval building became a contentious political issue, with the Conservative opposition demanding a doubling of Britain's own battleship programme:

'we want eight and we won't wait'. Mulliner's role in stimulating this new arms race, when it came to light, caused a furore among Liberals. In fact Mulliner's role was only part of the pressure on the government,[1] but the Mulliner affair, on top of the Krupp scandal, only revealed what was already apparent: that the arms companies stood to gain from each new alarm, and did their best to encourage it.

CARNEGIE AND PEACE

In this global market-place, the American arms industry was now becoming a factor. While European steel companies had long been dependent on exporting arms for their profits, the American companies were at first preoccupied with the vast internal market, making railways, bridges or machinery. They were able to regard themselves as aloof from the bellicose Europeans, though without any defined moral attitude. The most active American arms company, du Pont, had sold gunpowder both to Spain and to the Latin American republics fighting against Spain; and they had supplied both Russia and Britain in the Crimean war. But during and after the American civil war— when they resisted the temptation to sell to the Southern states— du Pont were kept fully employed supplying Federal needs, and emerged with a powerful monopoly position, later consolidated by the great Powder Trust. The magnates of the period were engrossed in expanding their home market and overcoming their rivals, and the battle for the commercial domination of the continent was itself a kind of substitute for war. It was not till the end of the century, as the railway boom receded and successive governments became more imperialistic, that American steel companies were more dependent on government contracts for arms, and on exporting arms abroad.

In this turning from railroads to armaments, from a peaceful ideology to imperialism, a special interest attaches to the career and the attitudes of Andrew Carnegie, who built up the biggest steelworks in the United States. For Carnegie, like Nobel but with far greater extroversion, combined commercial ambition with idealism; and as his steelworks were turning to armaments,

[1] Royal Commission, 1935–6, Minutes, pp. 724–5, 748–51. Evidence of Sir Maurice Hankey and Admiralty note.

he was proclaiming more ardently his devotion to pacifism. As a young boy in Scotland, Carnegie had been invested with a moral confidence which helped to drive him forward, and with a deep distrust of the monarchical and autocratic systems of Europe. The son of a hand-loom weaver, brought up in the town of Dunfermline surrounded by poverty, he had been inspired by the peaceful idealism of the People's Charter of 1838, which asked for universal manhood suffrage. Arriving in the States at the age of twelve, and achieving his first success as a telegraph-operator at fourteen, he corresponded with his cousin Dod, back in Dunfermline, explaining the splendours of American democracy, the freedom from poverty, and the lack of standing armies, compared with the immense army and police system of Britain.

From the beginning, Carnegie's pacifism was confused, like that of many young Americans at that time; for he was also a militant supporter of American aggrandisement, and he made his first profits as a young capitalist out of the civil war. He built up Carnegie Steel in Pittsburgh with the same ruthlessness as the other great monopolists of the time, but he maintained a pacifist position on any debate concerning war, and praised the United States government for maintaining an obsolete navy. 'It is one of the chief glories of the Republic,' he wrote in 1896, in his book *Triumphant Democracy*, 'that she spends her money for better ends and has nothing worthy to rank as a ship of war.'

His first real test of business morality came when President Arthur attained office after Garfield's assassination in 1881. Arthur asked for four modern steel warships which Congress reluctantly approved—a programme which constituted 'the first tentative moves towards the creation of that industrial-military complex of the mid-twentieth century'.[1] This offered further exciting prospects for the steel industry, as the navy expanded under President Cleveland; but Carnegie at first was adamant, and in 1886 told Cleveland's Secretary of the Navy, W. C. Whitney, that he would make no bids for armour plates. But by the end of the same year he had already changed his mind under pressure from his partners, and was telling Whitney, 'you need not be afraid that you will have to go abroad for armour-plate'; while he reassured himself that armour, unlike guns, was essentially

[1] Joseph Frazier Wall: *Andrew Carnegie*, New York, Oxford University Press, 1970, p. 645.

defensive. By 1889, under Harrison's Republican administration, the navy was expanding still further, and Carnegie was now enthusing, 'there may be millions for us in armour'.

The next year Carnegie's company signed a contract for six thousand tons of armour-plate, and he was also soon able to get profitable orders for the Russian navy, with the help of US naval officers who secretly provided him with advance information about Russian specifications. One of them, Lieutenant C. A. Stone, rationalised his indiscretion with the habitual justification: 'it would be to the advantage of the US that we keep running on the armour manufacture for others, if the US cannot keep us employed. We improve by continued manufacture, while a stoppage would prevent such continued improvement.'[1] The profitability of arms exports was soon assured when Carnegie reached an agreement with his only American rival, Bethlehem, that they would remove competition by sharing orders between them. Carnegie's profits from armour-plate have since been estimated at about 300 percent, and the high costs eventually attracted the interest of the US navy. In 1893 the secretary of the navy brought charges against Carnegie for concealing the bubbles or 'blowholes' in armour-plate, and for giving special treatment to the plates selected for testing; eventually Carnegie had to pay a penalty of ten percent of the price of the plates.

The orders for armour-plate were specially welcome to Carnegie because the demand for other steel products was falling off, with the end of the railway boom. Carnegie had now abandoned his principles against making guns, and was recommending his partners that they make gun forgings. this time it was the partners who objected, not because the guns were too deadly, but because the profits were too small, and projectiles would pay better, because 'guns fire many times their own weight in projectiles'.

Yet Carnegie was proud to be an advocate of peace in foreign policy, even though his company would benefit from war. He records a lively argument with President Harrison when he was threatening war with Chile: 'You're a New Yorker, and think nothing but business and dollars,' said Harrison (who came from Ohio). 'That is the way with New Yorkers; they care nothing for the dignity and honour of the Republic.' 'Mr President,' replied Carnegie, 'I am one of the men in the United States who

[1] Wall, p. 648.

would profit most by war; it might throw millions into my pockets as the largest manufacturer of steel.'[1] In the Spanish-American war of 1898 Carnegie took up a strong anti-Imperialist position, and even offered to buy the Philippines for $20 million, to give them their independence. But his pacifism came into conflict with his jingoism. In the boundary dispute between Britain and Venezuela in 1896 he bitterly attacked Britain for refusing to allow American arbitration, and came close to advocating war. And he was militant over the question of Canada, whose loyalty to the British monarchy exasperated him, and which he regarded as the natural stamping-ground for American business.[2]

By the end of the century, however, Carnegie had moved into more active pacifism, and by 1901 he had sold his steel company— which became part of United States Steel—and devoted himself to philanthropy. He had befriended a group of high-minded pacifists on both sides of the Atlantic who believed that wars could be avoided by setting up machinery for arbitration: they included Nicholas Murray Butler at Columbia University; David Starr Jordan at Stanford University; Elihu Root, later secretary of state; W. T. Stead and Norman Angell in London; and Berthe von Suttner, the authoress who had been Nobel's private secretary. Carnegie's naive views about peace, punctuated with warlike outbursts against Canada, often embarrassed the purer pacifists; but they needed each other, and between 1903 and 1914 Carnegie gave away $25 million in the cause of international peace. His monuments include the 'Palace of Peace' at The Hague, to house the international court; the Pan-American Union building in Washington; and the Carnegie Endowment for International Peace, which he instructed 'to hasten the abolition of war'. Carnegie was so confident of achieving that aim that he stipulated that when the establishment of universal peace was attained, the money should be spent on banishing the 'next most degrading evil or evils'.[3]

But Carnegie remained torn and confused between the two worlds of pacifism and power, and two of his heroes were the Kaiser and Theodore Roosevelt. After Roosevelt became president in 1901 Carnegie was in close correspondence; Roosevelt needed Carnegie's money for the Republican party, and

[1] *Autobiography of Andrew Carnegie*, London, Constable, 1920, p. 351.
[2] Ibid., p. 898.
[3] Ibid., p. 928.

Carnegie needed Roosevelt as his instrument. In 1907 he failed
to persuade Roosevelt to accept the idea of an international peace
force (borrowed from Berthe von Suttner) and arbitration treaties,
and he was shocked by Roosevelt's determination to increase the
US navy in response to the Japanese threat; but he remained
loyal to Roosevelt. The president on his side accepted Carnegie's
support with distaste, as he wrote to Whitelaw Reid in 1905:

> I have tried hard to like Carnegie, but it is pretty difficult. There is no type
> of man for whom I feel a more contemptuous abhorrence than for the one
> who makes a God of mere money-making and at the same time is always
> yelling out that kind of utterly stupid condemnation of war which in almost
> every case springs from a combination of defective physical courage, of
> manly shrinking from pain and effort, and of hopelessly twisted ideals. All
> the suffering from the Spanish war comes far short of the suffering, prevent-
> able and non-preventable, among the operators of the Carnegie steelworks,
> and among the small investors, during the time that Carnegie was making
> his fortune.[1]

But Roosevelt was quite prepared to tolerate Carnegie's friendship, even after he had ceased to be president in 1909; and it was
then that Carnegie planned his boldest peace move—a meeting
between Roosevelt and the Kaiser. He had become convinced
that the Germans had been unjustly accused by Britain of warmongering, and the Kaiser had been glad to receive Carnegie's
praise. While Roosevelt was big-game hunting in Africa after
he had ceased to be president, Carnegie made preparations for
him to meet the Kaiser in Berlin. The meeting took place in 1910,
somewhat overshadowed by the death of King Edward VII, and
the two leaders agreed that war between Britain and Germany
would be madness.

Carnegie maintained a pathetic faith in the efficacy of money,
buildings and institutions; he even offered to increase the salaries
of the judges of the international court, to speed up the peace-
making process. He was confident, like many of his pacifist
friends, that peace could be achieved through arbitration between
the civilised leaders of the world, ignoring the pressures of mass
democracy. He was also convinced that there should be a race
alliance between the 'Teutonic nations'—Britain, Germany and
the United States.

By 1913 Carnegie had reached a new peak of optimism about
world peace, and he went to Berlin in June to present the Kaiser

[1] Ibid., p. 928.

with a memorial, signed by seventy officials of leading American societies, thanking him 'as the foremost apostle of peace in our time'. He was oblivious of the danger-signs of growing popular nationalism and hectic competition in armaments, and he maintained his high hopes when he came to stay at Skibo, his castle in Scotland, in the summer of 1914. There he set about finishing his autobiography, concluding with a chapter called 'The Kaiser and World Peace', which described his meeting in Berlin the year before. The Kaiser, he recorded, had welcomed him with outstretched arms: 'Carnegie, twenty-five years of peace, and we hope for many more.' And Carnegie had replied, 'And in this noblest of all missions you are our chief ally.'

As he wrote the last words of his book, Carnegie heard that war had broken out. He added a paragraph, beginning: 'As I read this today, what a change! The world convulsed by a war as never before! Men slaying each other like wild beasts.' He ended the paragraph with a hopeful injunction to 'watch President Wilson!'—but the manuscript ended abruptly. His optimism never recovered; and though he lived five years longer, his wife— as she recorded in the introduction to his autobiography— believed that the world disaster had broken his heart.[1]

WAR

In the First World War the arms industry, which had been the very spearhead of free trade, the core of the Great International, showed itself as the means of its wholesale destruction. The Faith of the Armourer, which Andrew Undershaft had expounded, and which Nobel, Krupp and Zaharoff had enthusiastically embraced, 'to give arms to all men who offer an honest price for them', was taken to its absurd extreme, and the weapons which the German, British and French had been selling round the world were turned against their own armies. British guns, sold to Turkey, were fired against British soldiers at the Dardanelles.[2] The Maxim gun which Sir Hiram had sold to Germans, Austrians and Italians, was the forerunner of the machine-guns which fired

---

[1] *Autobiography of Andrew Carnegie*, p. v.

[2] In fact, according to the evidence of Sir Maurice Hankey in 1936, only 13 of the 234 Turkish guns were British and Hankey suggested that if Britain had supplied more, Turkey might have been on the British side (see Royal Commission, 1935-36, Minutes, p. 618). But the presence of British guns on the Turkish side made a powerful political impact. See next chapter.

from all sides on the Western front. The French had sold 75mm guns to Bulgaria, which were now used against French troops. Krupp's more than anyone had served to arm their nation's enemies; in Russia, Krupp guns were mounted against the German soldiers; the Belgian army had been armed by Krupp's; and nearly all the major navies had armour-plate and shells made by Krupp patents. At the Battle of Jutland both sides fired shells with Krupp fuses; and this profitable monopoly emerged publicly after the war, when Krupp's successfully sued Vickers for payments of royalties on its shells.

The arms merchants quickly became the object of public hate and suspicion. While the British and French companies had been supplying the rest of the world, they failed to fulfil their promises in supplying their own armies; and having concentrated on naval armaments they were unprepared for the massive development of land battles. The British companies' profits, though controlled, were enormous; while the American companies, led by US Steel and du Pont, were transformed by war orders. US Steel, which had absorbed Carnegie's old steel company, had made average annual profits in the four pre-war years of $105 million, while in the four war years they were $240 million; and du Pont's average profit went up from $6 million to $58 million. The Federal Trade Commission accused the companies of 'inordinate greed and barefaced fraud', and the cost of the weapons was a cause of great bitterness to the Allies. But on the other hand, the access to this private-enterprise arsenal was a crucial advantage to the Allies against Germany. 'We owe our national existence and our liberty today partly to foreign private manufacture,' said the Secretary to the Committee of Imperial Defence, Sir Maurice Hankey, twenty years later; 'without it our sea power would have lost half its value, and we should have succumbed to a better-prepared enemy.'[1]

Certainly the arms companies had become much richer through the war, and there were widespread suspicions that they were actually trying to prolong it. Sir Basil Zaharoff was quoted as believing that war should be waged to the bitter end. But in terms of the Armourer's Faith in free trade, they had encompassed their own downfall. The retreat into nationalism and protection, the desolation of post-war Europe and the Russian

[1] Royal Commission, 1935–6, Minutes, p. 596, Q 4335.

revolution, had all put up new barriers against trade. It was not
for another twenty-five years that the world would begin to
offer the armourers comparable global opportunities.

Looking back on the pre-war armourers in the knowledge of
the catastrophe that followed, it is easy to exaggerate the contemporary awareness of the evils of the trade, and it is important
to see them in the light of the times. One recent historian, Clive
Trebilcock, insists that, ignoring that posthumous taint, they
must be seen simply as businessmen among businessmen, who saw
their products essentially as deterrents, wishing for peace.

> Only after the holocaust of 1914–18 did it become clear that the new arma-
> ments could imply an horrific and unacceptable kind of conflict. But for
> the Edwardian armourers, their trade was much like any other heavy
> manufacture, and possessed no especially distasteful associations. They could
> believe that the armaments industry was an essential adjunct to the stability
> and security of an era. They were proved wrong, but not warmongers.

And the arms companies, Trebilcock suggests, provided an
unusual amount of technical innovation which spurred other
industries: 'no less than with the modern aerospace industry, and
conceivably rather more so, government defence equipments
proved capable of stimulating innovations which could be transferred by a process of "spin-off" from the military to the civilian
sectors of the economy.'[1]

No doubt the arms companies did make important contributions to industrial progress: the Birmingham Small Arms company
turned from rifles to motorcycles and Daimler cars, and Vickers
made ocean liners as well as battleships. Yet many of the magnates
showed some signs of concern about their consequences; and the
more articulate of them, like Nobel and Carnegie, became more
determined to work for peace as they saw their destructive power
become greater. Satirists like Shaw and Belloc made their powerful points long before the First World War, and the armourers'
insistence on the deterrent effect could not be altogether confident
after, say, the casualties of the Russo-Japanese war when 'half
the Japanese were killed by the little Maxim gun'.[2] Many contemporaries reflected the agonised bewilderment at seeing
industry turning to destruction. In the words of the Newcastle
Daily Chronicle, on the death of Lord Armstrong: 'on the one

[1] Trebilcock, pp. 89–105.
[2] Maxim: p. 213.

hand we have the most wonderful machinery of production that has ever been known; on the other, we have the most tremendous machinery of murder. . . . Nothing could have been more unexpected by the earlier prophets of democracy than the apparent return of militarism with a vengeance at the end of a liberal and humanitarian century.'[1]

[1] Dougan, p. 69.

4

The Faith of the Pacifist

We certainly are in a hell of a business when a fellow has to wish for
trouble so as to make a living.

> Frank S. Jonas (agent for Remington)

THE HORRORS of the First World War induced a surge of indignation against the armourers which built up in the following
decade, with a curious delayed action, into a crescendo of indiscriminate public disgust. Already in the first years of peace,
returning soldiers were resentful of the war profiteers and of
workers who had earned high wages in the factories, and many
serving officers believed that the arms companies had been a
contributory cause of the war. In Britain Lord Wester Wemyss,
who was First Sea Lord during the war, advocated the nationalisation of the arms industry, and a notable Admiralty memorandum in 1919 was later published and repeatedly quoted:

> The interrelation between foreign and home trade in armaments is one of the
> most subtle and dangerous features of the present private system of pro-
> duction. The evil is intensified by the existence of international armaments
> rings, the members of which notoriously play into each other's hands. So
> long as this subterranean conspiracy against peace is allowed to continue,
> the possibility of any serious concerted reduction of armaments will be
> remote.[1]

[1] Royal Commission on the Private Manufacture of and Trading In Arms, 1935–6,
Annexe III, p. 742. Also *Life and Letters of Lord Wester Wemyss*, London, Eyre & Spottis-
woode, 1935, pp. 405–8. The Admiralty later contended that the memorandum was not
endorsed by Lord Wester, but his widow was emphatic.

Lord Grey of Falloden, the British Foreign Secretary at the out-break of the war who had declared, 'The lamps are going out all over Europe', later wrote in his memoirs: 'Armaments were intended to produce a sense of security in each nation—that was the justification put forward in defence of them. What they really did was to produce fear in everybody.'[1] The discovery that Vickers and Armstrong's had helped to arm Britain's enemies heightened the indignation. 'I shall never forget,' recalled Ramsay MacDonald in 1934, 'when I went down the Dardanelles immediately after the peace, we saw the guns that had been owned and operated by the Turks lying broken in their escarpments pointing towards that shore where our men landed and hung on to so long by their eyebrows. On those guns was a brass label bearing the name of a British armaments firm.'

When the victorious powers gathered in Paris for the peace treaty, the Allied leaders were glad to blame the arms companies. As Lloyd George recalled: 'There was a feeling, to begin with, that Krupp's in Germany had had a very pernicious influence upon the war spirit in Germany, and had stirred it up a good deal for their own ends. . . . There was not one there who did not agree that if you wanted to preserve peace in the world you must eliminate the idea of profit of great and powerful interests in the manufacture of armaments.'[2] The French prime minister Georges Clemenceau was indignant about the interlocking interests of the Schneider company and their influence on the press. The most influential critic was Woodrow Wilson, fired with his zeal for the League of Nations. It was he who inspired the historic para-graph of the Covenant of the League which stated: 'The Members of the League agree that the manufacture by private enterprise of munitions and implements of war is open to grave objections.'

Exactly how the British and French delegations came to agree on this drastic condemnation was later much debated, but the 'grave objections' stood enshrined in the Covenant. In the same paragraph the members of the League committed themselves to disarmament, which led to the setting up of a 'Temporary Mixed Commission' to make proposals for reducing armaments, which in turn established a special sub-committee. They produced a report in 1921, spelling out the 'grave objections' mentioned in

[1] Lord Grey: *Twenty-Five Years 1892-1916*, London, Hodder and Stoughton, 1925, p. 52.

[2] Royal Commission 1935-6, Minutes, p. 544, Q 3989.

the Covenant, in the form of six points. The points were put together, it transpired, with remarkable casualness and without any real investigation; but they, like the Covenant, were to become part of the faith of the pacifists. They were:

1. That the armament firms have been active in fomenting war-scares and in persuading their own countries to adopt warlike policies and to increase their armaments.
2. That armament firms have attempted to bribe government officials, both at home and abroad.
3. That armament firms have disseminated false reports concerning the military and naval programmes of various countries, in order to stimulate armament expenditure.
4. That armament firms have sought to influence public opinion through the control of newspapers in their own and foreign countries.
5. That armament firms have organised international armament rings through which the armament race has been accentuated by playing off one country against another.
6. That armament firms have organised international armament trusts which have increased the price of armaments sold to governments.

They provided a devastating indictment of arms companies. But for the next ten years little was done about them, while all attempts by the League to achieve disarmament were frustrated. The export of arms continued, and Britain was the leader in the trade. The scale of production, it was true, was much lower than in the pre-war years, and a British system of licensing exports, introduced at the beginning of the war, was still enforced. But there were never more than seven refusals of licences in one year, out of four hundred applications,[1] and the newest instrument of warfare, the aeroplane, was exempt from licensing. British diplomats (the Foreign Office later insisted) did not canvass for arms orders; but once a foreign national announced its intention to buy arms abroad, the foreign service 'naturally does its best to secure that the British firms should get a proper opportunity'.[2] And the incentive to encourage exports was now greater than ever, for the arms industry was facing an unparalleled slump.

THE SLUMP IN ARMS

The two leading British arms companies, Vickers and Armstrong's, were bewildered by the problems of peace. In 1919

---

[1] Royal Commission 1935–6, Minutes, p. 340, Annexe H.
[2] Sir John Simon in the House of Commons, November 8, 1934.

Vickers had confidently predicted that shipbuilding would assure them of work for ten years, but the expected boom in merchant shipping never happened and orders were suspended or cancelled. In 1920, for the first time in its history, Vickers declared no dividend, and did not do so for four of the next six years. Barrow workers were laid off in thousands: many were to migrate down to Coventry, the new boom-town of the motor-car, but many remained, and Barrow became one of the worst centres of unemployment. The great shipyards were forsaken, and birds nested in the cranes.[1]

Vickers had planned to move quickly into other products, and a Peace Products Committee proposed a whole range of new lines from railway engines to toys. They had plans for mass-produced Wolseley cars to undercut the American companies, for washing machines, sewing machines and gas meters: and they bought the Metropolitan Company, which had a growing electrical business in Manchester. But none of these ventures came up to expectations. Vickers faced the difficulties of so many arms companies since, in trying to turn swords into ploughshares: they had depended on big government orders which demanded high quality and accuracy and they had no training for the commercial market-place.

Vickers hoped to make new profits from the air, which promised to revolutionise travel. They soon predicted that airships were more promising than 'heavier-than-air machines', and in 1923 they began the construction of two monsters, 700 feet long, the R100 and R101, to provide regular fast travel within the British empire. In 1930 the R101 set out on its flight to India, and sailed slowly and unsteadily across France, until above Beauvais it went down in flames, and with it Vickers' dream of the future. With aircraft they were more successful, and in 1928 they bought an enterprising little company called Supermarine, which was devising fast new monoplanes. But the British market for aircraft was still tiny, and the air force, reduced to a tenth of its wartime strength, gave very few orders. Both for aircraft and ships, Vickers once more looked abroad to make up their profits. By 1926 the slump had produced a financial crisis for the company: the shares were written down to a third, the board was reconstructed, and the last family chairman, Douglas Vickers, resigned. A new managing director was appointed, Commander

[1] J. D. Scott: *Vickers, A History*, London, Weidenfeld and Nicolson, 1962, p. 144.

Charles Craven, a shrewd ex-naval officer who was soon to become the dominant personality in the British arms trade.

Armstrong's, in the meantime, were in much more serious straits, a classic case of a Victorian company which had lost the founder's dynamism. Lord Armstrong's successor, Sir Andrew Noble, had in turn bequeathed a dictatorship without a dictator, and the next chairman, who took over in the First World War, was one of the most unlikely of all the arms salesmen that crop up in this book. John Meade Falkner was an antiquary who had begun his career as tutor to Sir Andrew's sons, and who then moved into the company with an eccentric style of his own. He travelled through Europe and South America selling arms: 'Everywhere he went this tall gaunt voluble charming man made friends by his command of languages, his dignity, his seeming irrelevance, and his patience.'[1] But his real interests were in medieval liturgy, in bicycling round Oxfordshire churches, and in writing novels and ghost stories including *The Lost Stradivarius*. As chairman of Armstrong's he was a disaster.[2] Already during the war the company was in confusion, and when Falkner retired in 1920 he was succeeded by a much more determined businessman, Sir Glyn West, who however had no financial expertise and little judgment: he committed Armstrong's to an extravagant scheme in Newfoundland, to develop forests and a huge paper mill, which was disastrously ill-organised. By the end of 1924 Armstrong's was virtually bankrupt.

The British government, like other governments since, could not countenance the collapse of a major arms company, but did not wish to nationalise it. So the Bank of England discreetly moved in, and eventually brought pressure to force a merger with Vickers, using the Sun Insurance Company as their front to guarantee the new company, now called Vickers-Armstrong. It was a condition of the rescue that the new company would undertake to restrict themselves to the trade they knew most about. They were thus back with the business of shipbuilding and heavy engineering—and predominantly armaments. From 1930 to 1934 fifty-six percent of the company's turnover, excluding the aviation companies, was devoted to arms.[3] The vision of their

---

[1] Sir William Haley: *John Meade Falkner*. In Transactions of the Royal Society of Literature Vol. 30 (New Series), London, Oxford University Press, 1960.

[2] Or as Haley puts it: 'there are hints that he was not the most outstanding of chairmen.'

[3] Scott, p. 189.

future as wide-ranging merchants of peace had dissolved, and their prosperity depended once more on the re-arming of nations. 'It is no good disguising the fact,' said the chairman Sir Herbert Lawrence at the 1927 annual meeting, 'that we are an armament firm depending on armament orders. If there is to be a further limitation of armaments the future of the armaments business of Vickers, like that of any other armament firm in the country, may become difficult.'[1]

With the lack of British orders, the arms business depended as much as ever on exports. In 1930 and 1931 Britain was still by far the biggest exporter of arms in the world, responsible for nineteen percent of world exports in 1930 and twenty-eight per-cent in 1931 (even excluding her exports to dominions and colonies).[2] Vickers, it was true, was no longer the centre of an international network of companies: its scope had been restricted by the rise of economic nationalism, the revolution in Russia and the world depression. The main surviving Vickers holdings abroad were their Spanish company, making warships for the new Spanish navy, in which Sir Basil Zaharoff was still very active; and the Japanese steelworks, the Wanishi company, which they shared with Mitsui. Both investments ran into troubles with nationalist policies, and were sold off in the 'thirties. But Vickers were still very well organised for exporting from Britain, with their network of agents and salesmen (including at least two who were also correspondents for *The Times*)[3], and there were still wars in Asia and South America to provide new markets.

In 1931 the Japanese invaded Manchuria in China, in the face of condemnation from the League of Nations including Britain. The war produced a new boom in British exports both to Japan and China, where arms were later used to support Chiang Kai-shek against the Chinese communists. For a short time the British government imposed an embargo, but without any effect. As the Financial Secretary to the War Office, Duff Cooper, described it: 'In a fortnight we took off the embargo, but during those weeks we lost a great many orders. China and Japan did not get less munitions because of our embargo, but the men in this

---

[1] Royal Commission 1935–6, Minutes, p. 66, Q 542.

[2] By 1932 France had overtaken Britain as chief exporter, with twenty-nine percent against Britain's twenty-two percent; but if Britain's exports to the empire are included, she remained at the top, with thirty percent in 1932. (See Royal Commission, 1935–6, Hankey Memorandum, p. 648; and League of Nations Statistical Year Book, 1934.)

[3] Royal Commission 1935–6, Minutes, p. 360, Q 2001–2006.

country got less work, less food, less employment.' It was to be
the recurring argument against embargoes. In South America
there was new scope for arms exports when the Chaco war broke
out in 1932 between Bolivia and Paraguay: British exports to
Bolivia jumped from £27,000 in 1932 to £331,700 in 1933.
Eventually President Roosevelt embargoed all American munitions to Paraguay, but Britain did not follow, and when du Pont
were asked to quote for explosives they passed the enquiry on to
their British associates, ICI.[1]

As the League of Nations continued to seek agreement on disarmament, it was hardly surprising if some arms companies
were apprehensive of the results of a permanent peace. In 1926 an
ebullient American lobbyist, William G. Shearer, was employed
by three companies engaged in naval shipbuilding—Bethlehem
Corporation, Newport News and the American Brown Boveri
Company. Shearer went to Geneva for disarmament conferences
and lectured and lobbied through America to encourage the
building of warships; with the typical hyperbole of a lobbyist he
reported to Bethlehem that 'as a result of my activities during the
69th Congress, eight 10,000-ton cruisers are now under construction'. At the Geneva conference held in 1927 he was paid
$27,000 for six weeks' propaganda, to try to prevent agreement on
restricting warships: he wrote articles and press releases stirring
up suspicions of British intentions, and canvassed delegates and
journalists. The conference was probably doomed in any case,
but there is no doubt that Shearer helped to poison the atmosphere. As one of the British delegates, Lord Cecil of Chelwood,
recalled afterwards: 'I cannot help feeling that it would have been
a decided advantage if Mr Shearer had not been present at
Geneva.'[2]

The companies' dread of disarmament was of course taken up
by communist parties as evidence of the fundamental evils of the
capitalist system. As Harry Pollitt of the British Communist
party put it: 'War is inseparable from capitalism. . . . War is not
only terrible, but is a terribly profitable thing. . . . We do not
believe that the problems associated with the armaments industry
can be abolished until the present system is abolished.'[3] After the

[1] ICI maintained they did not take advantage of it. See Royal Commission 1935–6,
Minutes, p. 451, Q 2687.

[2] Ibid., p. 5, Q 2. See also Philip Noel-Baker: *The Private Manufacture of Armaments*,
London, Gollancz, 1936, p. 363.

[3] Royal Commission 1935–6 Minutes, p. 67, Q 548.

great crash of 1929 and the soaring unemployment the most depressed areas, including Barrow and Newcastle, were often those that depended most heavily on armaments, and by 1932, the worst year of the depression, Vickers were employing only 16,000 workers. The empty slipways and derelict cranes provided a vivid illustration of the dependence of workers on the arms trade.

In the midst of the slump, in March 1931, the *New Statesman* published an article by Emil Davies, half-comic, half-serious, called 'The Return to Prosperity or the Pretended War'. It foresaw a possible outcome in four years' time, with half the population out of work. The prime ministers of the world devised a system whereby all nations would stage a pretended war, against an unknown enemy; the unemployed were put into uniform, shipyards worked day and night, food and clothing industries revived to supply the troops; and when too many warships had been built, they were sunk in the English Channel to provide the foundations of a bridge between Dover and Calais. Once the wartime prosperity had been established, the politicians realised that they could not afford to allow peace.[1]

THE ROAD TO ISOLATIONISM

In the meantime the lobbying of William Shearer was to set off a chain reaction which led to an unprecedented crusade against the arms companies. He took the rash step of filing a suit against the three shipbuilding companies led by Bethlehem that had employed him, suing them for $258,000 in lobbying fees which they had not paid. The whole nature of his employment and the arms companies' opposition to disarmament thus became public.

In the previous decade the American public had been apathetic towards the whole question of arms control; the six points and the 'grave objections' of the League of Nations, on which Woodrow Wilson had been so insistent, had been ignored and forgotten, and the United States had never joined the League. But the Shearer revelations coincided with a growing wave of pacifism and an underlying distrust of big corporations made more intense by the Great Crash of 1929, and the indiscretions of a single salesman became the passionate concern of the nation.

The Shearer case provided just the documentary detail which

[1] *New Statesman*, March 7, 1931, p. 55.

was needed by the peace organisations and religious bodies who
had been patiently campaigning against the arms traffic, and
among them was the Women's International League for Peace,
whose secretary was an inexhaustible crusader called Dorothy
Detzer. She was now determined to initiate a full enquiry into
the munitions business, and after lobbying several senators she
eventually, at the end of 1933, achieved the support of the junior
senator from North Dakota, Gerald P. Nye. He was a Progressive
Republican, a handsome and eloquent man of forty-two, who,
as one observer remarked, was chiefly distinguished by 'a high-
water hair cut and yellow shoes'.[1] He was not an intellectual, but
he had a resonant voice and a high moralising style and he
embraced the campaign against the arms trade with rhetorical
fervour: 'Was ever a more insane racket conceived in depraved
minds or tolerated by an enlightened people?' By April 1934 the
Senate had passed Nye's motion calling for an investigation, and
a committee was established with Nye as chairman and six other
members, including Senator Vandenberg from Michigan.

The press acclaimed the campaign. In the spring of 1934
Fortune magazine published a vituperative article on 'Arms and
the Men', which calculated that in the First World War it had
cost $25,000 to kill a soldier, 'of which a great part went into the
pocket of the armament maker'. A polemical book, *The Merchants
of Death*, by Helmuth C. Engelbrecht and Frank C. Hanighen,
became a best-seller and Book-of-the-Month selection in April
1934. John Gunther described in one article how two hundred
firms were earning 'cold cash profits on smashed brains or
smothered legs'.[2] President Roosevelt and his Secretary of State,
Cordell Hull, at first appeared to welcome the proposal for an
investigation, but Hull was horrified when Nye, 'an isolationist
of the deepest dye', was appointed to lead it. 'It is doubtful,' he
recorded in his memoirs, 'that any congressional committee has
ever had a more unfortunate effect on our foreign relations. . . .'[3]

The Nye Committee had an eager young staff of investigators,
including a legal assistant called Alger Hiss, and they set about
issuing subpoenas to fifty companies and collecting a mass of
documents from their files. By September 1934 the hearings

[1] John E. Wiltz: *In Search of Peace*, The Senate Munitions Inquiry 1934–6, Louisiana State University Press, 1963, p. 29.

[2] *Chicago Daily News*, August 3–5, 1933.

[3] *The Memoirs of Cordell Hull*, London, Hodder and Stoughton, 1948, Vol. I, p. 398.

began, with evidence from the Electric Boat company, the submarine manufacturers who for the past thirty years had worked closely with Vickers, and the three top men of the company appeared for questioning: the president, Henry R. Carse and two vice-presidents, Lawrence Y. Spear and Henry R. Sutpher.

The committee staff had uncovered a series of letters between Carse and his British counterpart, Charles Craven of Vickers, which seemed to confirm the worst suspicions about the cynical greed of the arms makers and their international conspiracies. In one letter, Spear wrote to Craven complaining: 'It is too bad that the pernicious activities of our State Department have put the brake on armament orders from Peru by forcing the resumption of formal diplomatic relations with Chile.' In another, Craven told Spear: 'I am trying to ginger-up the Chileans to take three more boats.' In another, Craven said: 'I wonder whether you have heard that our friend Percy Addison is now the Director of Dockyards. I helped him all I could to get the job. . . .' Another letter referred to contracts from the British Admiralty to both Vickers and Armstrong's, 'who have agreed to put whatever price I tell them'. Another from Craven referred contemptuously to 'Geneva or any other fancy convention'.

The Craven letters furnished examples of all six of the 'grave objections' to private armaments which the League of Nations had described ten years earlier, and particularly the objection that arms sales encouraged bribery. 'We all know that the real foundation of all South American business is graft,' said Spear to Craven: 'I would not be too modest about the price and would cover it into a substantial amount in excess of the ten percent above referred to, my own experience being that at the last minute something extra is always needed to grease the ways.'

The directors of Electric Boat were followed by executives of other companies, who provided further incriminating correspondence. Frank S. Jonas, an agent of the Remington company who was selling tear-gas in Latin America, described how 'the unsettled conditions of South America have been a great thing for me.' He confessed that, in selling arms to both sides, 'it would be a terrible state of affairs for my conscience to start bothering me now.' Clarence Webster of the Curtiss-Wright aircraft company was asked what he meant by a commission: 'In fact it would be bribery, would it not?' 'It would. It is rather a harsh

word, but it would, strictly speaking.' The testimony from company representatives did little to dispel the sinister impression from
their correspondence, and Spear confirmed that he regarded
his government's peace-making diplomacy as pernicious.

Successive arms salesmen made clear that they saw no basic
distinction between selling arms and selling anything else: 'It is
no different than any other business,' said Henry Carse to Senator
Clark. The salesmen's complaints about their rival companies
provided a rich field of abuse. An agent for an American company, Driggs Ordnance, in Turkey, described how 'the Vickers
crowd are the dirtiest opponents here, they have almost an entire
embassy in number working for them and use women of doubtful character freely.' And a Polish agent for Driggs even complained that King George V had lobbied the Polish ambassador
in London to prevent Driggs selling weapons to Poland.

The Nye Committee failed to uncover any serious evidence
of an international armaments ring. But they did reveal very
vividly the constant tendency towards bribery, and the playing
off of one country against another to sell arms. It became clear
that the arms salesmen were frequently supported by the American embassies: 'It makes one wonder,' commented Senator Nye,
'whether the army or the navy are just organisations of salesmen
for private industry, paid for by the American government.'

The fact that the aggressive arms sales were condoned by the
government raised again the fundamental issue of the control of
arms exports, and provoked anxious discussions between the
White House and the State Department. The basic dilemma of the
government was summed up in a trenchant memorandum
written by President Roosevelt's adviser, Bernard Baruch, and
sent by the State Department to the president in February 1935.
Baruch outlined the problem of how the United States could
maintain in peacetime its capacity to produce armaments in an
emergency, and went on:

> The only expedient yet used is for the governments of industrial countries
> at least not to discourage (and I fear almost universally to encourage) the
> manufacture of lethal weapons for *exportation* to belligerent countries
> actively preparing for war, but which have an insufficient munitions
> industry or none at all. Without specific evidence I still conjecture that the
> Nye investigation will disclose that our Government has not operated on a
> different policy. To put it bluntly, this is a method of providing a laboratory
> to test killing implements and a nucleus for a wartime munitions industry

by maintaining an export market for instruments of death. Of course, it is absolutely indefensible and we could not be put in a position of excusing it.[1]

Thus candidly and brutally did Baruch assess his government's underlying policy. Roosevelt's comments are not recorded, but Baruch's analysis was difficult to contradict, and the concept of the export market as a military laboratory continued to be plausible in the following decades.

In its early stages the Nye Committee had uncovered some valuable evidence and drawn attention to the real dangers of uncontrolled arms sales. But in the meantime the isolationist mood of the country was growing, and the sympathetic members of the committee, including Nye and Vandenberg, were exploiting it vigorously. The objection to any kind of foreign involvement or responsibility grew louder as Mussolini prepared for war against Ethiopia; and the views of most of the committee became increasingly at variance with the policies of Roosevelt and Cordell Hull. 'The majority of the Committee,' recorded Hull, 'in effect dug the ground out from under those of us who had the international viewpoint and who argued that, if the peace of the world was to be maintained, the United States had to take its share in the effort.'[2]

Riding on the isolationist wave, the Nye Committee moved on from the arms traffic to investigate war profits during the First World War, and the circumstances by which the United States entered the war. They produced evidence about how New York bankers, led by Morgan, had supported the Allies in the early years of the war, while the United States was supposed to be bound to strict neutrality; and the committee showed itself increasingly sympathetic to the German viewpoint, and critical of the whole American involvement in the war. They insisted on revealing secret wartime correspondence with Britain and France, generating bitter reactions in London and Paris and a major row with the State Department.

Congress became more determined to detach America from the world's problems and more insistent on passing a Neutrality Bill which would limit overseas involvement. Roosevelt was considering a much less prescriptive definition of neutrality, but he found himself overwhelmed by the national revulsion. By

[1] Wiltz, p. 93.
[2] *Hull Memoirs*, Vol. I, p. 399.

August 1935, encouraged by the Nye Committee, Congress passed a Neutrality Bill which compelled the president, in the event of any war between foreign countries, to apply an arms embargo. The president and Cordell Hull, who had stood out for allowing presidential discretion, now reluctantly accepted the Bill, bowing to the wind of isolationism while Mussolini was preparing for war in Africa.[1]

The Bill did contain one feature that was welcomed by the president: the setting up of a national Munitions Control Board to supervise American exports of arms. It was the first American move to limit the free trade in arms. It did not give the government the power to prohibit arms deals in peacetime, but it did prepare the way for a possible world agreement. And, as Cordell Hull hopefully said: 'It gave us more control over our own foreign policy.' But the movement for controlling the arms companies, which had begun three years earlier with Shearer's revelations, had now extended far beyond its original purpose and had culminated in a resolution for withdrawal from the rest of the world. Three months after the Neutrality Bill was passed Mussolini invaded Ethiopia, and Hitler was now openly re-arming.

THE ROYAL COMMISSION

The Washington hearings had provoked protests and investigations about arms companies all over the world, particularly in Latin America and Europe: and the failure of the first Disarmament Conference at Geneva in 1932 had encouraged the belief that peace was being sabotaged by vested interests. A succession of lurid books and articles denouncing the companies had appeared in many countries, with each title echoing the last: the attack on the arms industry had become itself a minor industry. Lehmann-Russbuldt wrote *Die Blutige Internationale* in 1930; H. C. Engelbrecht wrote articles on 'The Bloody International' (1931) and 'The Secret International' (1932) before his best-seller *The Merchants of Death* (1934). The Union of Democratic Control in Britain produced *The Secret International* in 1932; Fenner Brockway published *The Bloody Traffic* in 1933, and in the

---

[1] In fact the administration now realised that an embargo would damage Italy much more than Ethiopia, who had no money to buy arms abroad, anyway. See Hull, p. 414. The concern for Ethiopia was less deep than it appeared.

same year Beverley Nichols wrote *Cry Havoc!* Sir Basil Zaharoff,
by now living a secluded life in France, was the subject of several
books, and featured in the Lanny Budd novels by Upton Sinclair.
The demonology of the arms business was now established, with
the same morality-tales repeated each time.

Many of the attacks on the Western arms-mongers came
from communist sympathisers who saw in the Soviet Union an
ideal society freed from warlike pressures: and Moscow encouraged their faith by pressing persistently for international
disarmament. Only a few visitors to Russia, like Barbara
Wootton, pointed out that the Russians despised pacifists, and
were preparing vigorously for war.[1] But the criticisms of the
arms companies came not only from socialists and communists,
and the mood of pacifism was very broad-based. The League of
Nations in December 1933 passed a resolution 'that it is contrary
to the public interest that the manufacture and sale of armaments
should be carried out for private profit'; and in 1935 the League
of Nations Union organised a ballot in Britain, posing the
question, among others: 'Should the manufacture and sale of
armaments for private profit be prohibited by international
agreement?'. Over ninety percent said Yes.

The British Labour party, provoked by the revelations from
Washington, demanded the prohibition of private manufacture
of arms, and in November 1934 their leader Clement Attlee
opened a debate in the House of Commons, with copious
quotations from the Nye hearings, comparing the arms trade to
prostitution and slavery. The foreign secretary, Sir John Simon,
replied to Attlee in scathing terms: because brothels and slavery
were evil, should they therefore be nationalised?[2] Simon's reply,
though well-argued, was contemptuous and only stirred up the
public resentment. But two weeks later Simon uncharacter-
istically changed his tack and agreed to a British inquiry into the
private manufacture of arms. By February 1935 a Royal Commission had been appointed, whose members included the

[1] 'While many a gentle-hearted pacifist in England or France, Germany or America,
often proclaiming himself a sincere admirer of the Russian Communist experiment, seeks
to mitigate the horrors of warfare by prohibition of the use of poisonous gases or aerial
bombing, the three United Russian societies—the Society to Aid in Defence, the Friends
of Aviation and Chemistry, and the Friends of the Air Fleet—claim five million members,
amongst whom they seek to spread knowledge of aeronautics and chemical warfare, as
well as practical proficiency in handling rifles and gas masks.' Barbara Wootton: *Plan
or No Plan*, London, Gollancz, 1934, p. 234.

[2] House of Commons, November 8, 1934.

historian, J. A. Spender, the former war correspondent, Sir Philip
Gibbs, and a League of Nations official, Dame Rachel Crowdy.
The inquiry began its hearings in May, taking evidence in public
—a rare procedure in Britain—and continued with long gaps for
a whole year. It was clearly inspired by the American hearings,
though with much more cautious terms of reference, and it
remains one of the most revealing of all British inquiries. The
heavy folio volume of testimony, a thousand pages of small type,
conjures up all the bitterness of the argument about arms and
profit.

The inquiry began with broadsides from every political
direction. It started with the most prestigious of all the critics,
Lord Hugh Cecil, son of the former prime minister Lord Salis-
bury, who gave evidence on behalf of the League of Nations
Union, and continued with pacifists, communists and high-
minded liberals. Dr Christopher Addison, who was a wartime
minister of munitions, attacked the arms companies for failing to
deliver the shells they had promised in 1914. Philip Noel-Baker,
the Labour MP who had been a delegate to the post-war Peace
Conference, produced a massive memorandum on the evils of
private manufacture. And Lloyd George himself gave fiery
evidence: 'I think the less you leave to private manufacture, the
less is the incentive to promoting agitation for war.'[1]

The climax of the hearings came with the testimony of Vickers,
beginning with their chairman, Sir Herbert Lawrence, a former
general and banker. The private export of arms, he maintained,
was a constant incentive to efficiency and innovation: only
recently Vickers' development of an efficient new anti-aircraft
gun had depended, not at all on British orders, but on demand
from abroad. And he summed up the importance of free enterprise:

> State manufacture is traditionally unenterprising, and there will always be
> a tendency to be satisfied with conditions which may be expected to 'last
> my time'. In private manufacture there is the restless activity which derives
> from competition, and from the fear of being left behind in the race for
> employment.[2]

'I do not think,' Lawrence said, 'that any of the great inventions
of the last hundred years would have been heard of if you had
had a purely national system or a system which depended purely

[1] Royal Commission 1935–6, Minutes, p. 536, Q 3866.
[2] Ibid., p. 347, Q 1843.

on a democratic vote.'[1] When Sir Philip Gibbs questioned him about Vickers' effects on world peace, he was forthright: 'Quite obviously I do not deny the fact for a minute that Vickers' principal interest is in making armaments and instruments of war; but to infer from that that the Board of Vickers is anxious to use them in war, is I think carrying it too far.' But is it not inevitable, suggested Sir Philip, that armaments firms will dislike, or even attempt to prevent, anything like a reduction in arms? Sir Herbert refused to draw that inference: 'If the world is to be at peace, it might be, quite obviously, that the business of Vickers Limited will disappear. That may be a consummation to be wished for.'[2]

But it was Sir Charles Craven, the managing director, who was the star Vickers' witness, and he had already become famous through the publication of his correspondence with the Electric Boat company. Immaculate, unflappable and articulate, he provided the very model of a modern arms manufacturer: as a former naval officer, with all the confidence of the quarterdeck, he only added to the public's resentment, and made no concessions to his critics. He knew that he carried his company with him, and that thousands of jobs depended on him: he had battled to keep the Barrow shipyards busy, and he was a kind of hero to the workers; he had even made political speeches urging them to vote Tory. Craven, like his American counterparts, refused to concede that armaments were intrinsically more dangerous than any other industry. In a classic exchange with Sir Philip Gibbs (who was both journalist and novelist), he returned each salvo with another:

SIR PHILIP GIBBS: You do not think, for instance that your wares are any more dangerous or noxious than, we will say, boxes of chocolates, or sugar candy?
SIR CHARLES CRAVEN: Or novels, no.
SIR PHILIP GIBBS: Well, we will say not more dangerous than pig iron that is to be turned into ploughs and harvesters.
SIR CHARLES CRAVEN: If the business is honestly managed, and properly managed, and properly controlled by the home country, no.
SIR PHILIP GIBBS: You do not think, for instance, that any of these fancy things which you export to these other countries are likely to be more dangerous than children's Christmas crackers?

[1] Ibid., p. 362, Q 2030.
[2] Ibid., p. 358, Q 1958-1962.

SIR CHARLES CRAVEN: Is that really a question that is intelligent, or requires an intelligent answer, sir?
CHAIRMAN: If you can answer it, you had better answer.
SIR CHARLES CRAVEN: I once nearly lost an eye with a Christmas cracker, and I have never lost one with a gun.
SIR PHILIP GIBBS: That seems to be rather reassuring to the peoples of Europe; but these questions, which seem rather trivial, and which I have put in a light way, really go rather deep into the question we have to consider; because I want to put it to you that the continual expansion of arms by your export trade abroad might have very unpleasant effects in the world. Do you agree with that at all?
SIR CHARLES CRAVEN: I do not consider that by so exporting arms we are increasing the consumption of arms at all.
SIR PHILIP GIBBS: You do not?
SIR CHARLES CRAVEN: No.[1]

Sir Philip returned to the attack at the end of his questioning, referring to the letters published in America. Was it not true, asked Sir Philip, that throughout the correspondence 'you show a certain levity of mind with regard to the business that you are doing; that is to say, that all through those letters the general tone is that you think the more munitions in the world the merrier for the world, and that it is a jolly good thing, really, for all countries to buy munitions of war, and that you personally really regard with some contempt all methods to restrict armaments and all peaceful associations which have the idea of the limitation of arms? Is that a fair expression of the rather jocular tone of your letter?' Craven simply replied: 'Most unfair.'[2]

The Vickers case was supported by a succession of government witnesses arguing for private manufacture. One of the most confident was Admiral Sir Reginald Bacon, a former director of Naval Ordnance, who insisted that there was no danger in increasing armaments:

SIR PHILIP GIBBS: You talk about the loss of trade to the country if the export of arms were stopped, and you say that it would work out practically to this: that it would deprive about 100,000 men of their work and wages?
SIR REGINALD BACON: Yes.
SIR PHILIP GIBBS: But may I suggest to you that the increase of armaments might lead to a war, which would deprive millions of men of their work and wages?
SIR REGINALD BACON: No, sir: the increase in armaments will stop war.
SIR PHILIP GIBBS: It did not do so in 1914.[3]

[1] Ibid., p. 392, Q 2435–2440.
[2] Ibid., p. 395, Q 2494.
[3] Ibid., p. 322, Q 1670–1672.

But in the meantime the defence of the companies was also being carefully prepared by the most formidable of all British civil servants. Colonel Sir Maurice Hankey (later Lord Hankey) had been Secretary to the Committee of Imperial Defence for the past twenty-four years, and Secretary to the Cabinet—the first to hold the office—for nearly twenty years. He had seen six prime ministers come and go, and had been present at most of the crucial conferences in war and peace. Incisive, tireless and logical, he was appalled by the emotionalism and woolliness of the attack on the companies, and determined, with the connivance of Stanley Baldwin, the prime minister, to demolish them: 'I have a perfect terror,' he told the Commission, 'of the abolition of the industry.'[1]

Hankey summed up his case in three sentences: 'First, prohibition of private manufacture would be disastrous to Imperial Defence; second, in any case, it is out of the question when we are in the throes of a great programme of re-conditioning our forces; and third, the case for prohibition has not been established.'[2] In two long memoranda he insisted that no convincing evidence had been found by historians to prove that arms companies had fomented the First World War; and he denounced as absurd the suggestion that arms manufacturers, because their profits depend on war, will deplore the reduction of armaments. 'Doctors, pharmaceutical chemists and nurses depend for their profit on ill health and disease. It would be outrageous to suggest that for that reason they try to encourage epidemic disease or are lukewarm in the promotion of public health.'[3]

Hankey insisted that private manufacture was essential to national defence. It was incomparably more elastic than government factories, 'owing to commercial orders and foreign armaments orders'; it provided much greater prospects for invention, research and development; and its indispensability had been shown in the First World War, when Britain had been saved by supplies from American private industry. 'Even if the alleged evil effects had been made out, it would be out of the question to abolish private manufacture today when we are actually engaged in a heavy re-conditioning of our forces.'

Hankey's testimony about national defence was triumphant, and Sir Philip and Dame Rachel were apparently convinced. But

[1] Ibid., p. 703, Q 4899.
[2] Ibid., p. 688, Q 4854.
[3] Ibid., p. 723, para. 59.

on larger moral questions of exporting arms, and the responsibilities of governments, he was silent. One of the commissioners, Sir Thomas Allen, suggested that private manufacture was really 'the shifting of an obligation which is a proper function of government', and he asked Hankey: 'You would not agree with that—shifting the burden on to other shoulders which the government should undertake itself, at whatever risk and at any cost?'. Hankey replied with rare modesty: 'I do not think my opinion would be valuable.'[1]

The Commissioners, presenting their report five months later, were much influenced by Hankey. The report was not altogether a whitewash, and it was much more sensitive to the public concern than Hankey or the Vickers directors. It described how modern armaments had intensified the fears, suspicions and jealousies of nations: 'Montesquieu said that kings should so make war as to have done one another the least possible damage when peace was restored; modern governments seek to arm themselves with weapons which inflict the maximum of loss and suffering upon their opponents.' The commissioners did not accept that the arms industry was no more dangerous than others: 'It is always necessary to bear in mind that competition between armament firms differs from all ordinary commercial competition in that the success of one firm does not mean the failure of another, but rather increases its chances of doing business.'[2]

They criticised the 'frivolous and cynical language' of some company directors in their correspondence and they commented: 'In so far as it is supposed that armament firms are unaware of or blind to the special dangers of the trade they are pursuing, they themselves are largely responsible for it.' They had reservations about the uncontrolled employment of ex-army or naval officers by arms companies. But they did not accept that the companies had fomented war scares or influenced the press; and they concluded unanimously that 'the reasons for maintaining the private industry outweigh those for its abolition.' They insisted that the only effective remedy against the dangers of the arms trade lay in international agreement.

---

[1] Ibid., p. 713, Q 5010.
[2] Royal Commission Report 1936, Command 5292, p. 36.

THE VINDICATION OF VICKERS

The prospects of any such agreement were now increasingly remote, and during the eighteen months that the Royal Commission was sitting, the public attitude towards armaments was already changing. In October 1935 Mussolini invaded Abyssinia; in March 1936 Hitler invaded the Rhineland; in July 1936 the Spanish civil war began. The mood of pacifism which had reached a peak three years earlier had waned, and in Churchill's words: 'Far from being excluded from lawful thought, the use of force gradually became a decisive point in the minds of a vast mass of peace-loving people, and even of many who had been proud to be called pacifists.'[1] In the light of what we now know (and of what many like Churchill perceived at the time) to put so much blame on the private arms companies for provoking war seems naive. Whatever the prospects for disarmament may have been in the 'twenties, Hitler's determination to arm Germany in the 'thirties could hardly be blamed on Vickers.

The re-arming of Germany, though concealed, was already very visible; and the house of Krupp was re-emerging as a powerful engine of war. The head of the firm, Gustav Krupp von Halbach, had suffered successive humiliations since the First World War: he had been declared a war criminal, had watched his factories being invaded by the French, and had been imprisoned when his workers resisted. But directly after 1926, when the Allies finally left Essen, Krupp's began their recovery, specialising in high-grade steels (Krupp steel was used for the top of the Chrysler building in New York). Gustav Krupp, like other German captains of industry, was at first shocked by Hitler's crudity; but after he came to power in 1933 Krupp soon came to terms with Hitler and with some reluctance turned over most of his factories to making weapons, including the pocket-battle ships and a secret arsenal of tanks. By the mid-'thirties Essen was again a boom town, with the Krupp family reaping huge profits. The company was no longer at the centre of an international nexus, and as Hitler became more demanding, Krupp had to abandon his exports to concentrate on German production. He became increasingly subservient to the dictator, and indispensable to the Nazi system as its most important supplier.

[1] Sir Winston Churchill: *The Second World War*, Vol. I, *The Gathering Storm*, London, Cassell and Co., 1948, p. 169.

By the autumn of 1934 the British government had initiated a programme of re-armament against the menace of Hitler, and the British companies were soon out of their slump. In fact Vickers-Armstrong had already in that year turned the corner into profit, and paid a dividend of six percent; but the flood of new orders soon ensured their future and doubled their profits. The shipyards at Barrow and Elswick were again filled with warships and submarines, and the unemployed were back to work. The aircraft factories became the focus of Britain's defences. The suspicions of private companies were forgotten or buried except by communists and committed pacifists. The concern over the export of arms became less relevant as Britain's home require-ments became greater, and exports were soon more strictly con-trolled to avoid interfering with Britain's own re-armament. The air ministry had acrimonious disputes with Vickers and other companies over late and inadequate deliveries; they had to look to Lockheed in America to provide enough bombers,[1] and British aircraft were supplied with guns from abroad. But the Spitfire fighter and the Wellington bomber, both produced by Vickers, were triumphs of private enterprise and stubborn independence.

With the outbreak of war in 1939 and the Battle of Britain the next year, the image of Vickers was now totally reversed. There were no scandals about shortages comparable to those of the First World War: the government was involved from the beginning in expanding and financing production, and excess profits were more strictly controlled. The shipyards which had been attacked as the exporters of death were now the scenes of heroic endeavour, and the aircraft factories which produced the Spitfires were part of the nation's mythology: the Spitfire obliterated the memories of Zaharoff.

The spectre of unemployment had vanished, and the advantages of a 'Pretended War' which the *New Statesman* had imagined a decade earlier were now achieved with a real war. But as victory came within sight, the economists were again worried about the problem of maintaining full employment and production in peacetime. In August 1943 the *New Statesman* reprinted the old article in full and its editor commented: 'Some economists are now writing to prove that the nation can comfortably stand the financial burden of the war. One wonders what they would have written before 1939, if a Labour government had proposed to

[1] See next chapter.

spend on the distressed areas one-thousandth part of the cost of the war, and which sort of "prosperity" will be aimed at after the war?'[1]

The vindication of Vickers coincided with the peak of the British company's role. By the end of the war the battleship, which had been Vickers' special pride for the past fifty years, was already obsolete; and the war in the air was becoming so complex that it was beyond the scope of a single British company. As Vickers' historian puts it:

> The nineteenth-century revolution in armaments had been a revolution in favour of heavy industry. The change that occurred during the Second World War with the advent of radar, the birth of homing devices, rocketry and atomic warfare, was a change in the direction of an alliance of pure science and light industry. In the birth of this new warfare Vickers played very little part.[2]

The new arms industry, with its vast research costs and long development programmes, involved governments much more deeply in finance and decision. The atomic bomb was beyond the resources of any private company. And in the course of the war the centre of the world's armaments industry had moved decisively away from Britain or Germany to the great Russian factories in the East, and to a booming El Dorado of arms in the Far West of America.

[1] *New Statesman*, August 7, 1943.
[2] Scott, p. 297.

5

The Making of a Complex

Under the spur of profit potential, powerful lobbies spring up to argue for even larger munitions expenditures. And the web of special interest grows.

Dwight D. Eisenhower, (1961)[1]

UP TILL the Second World War, the American arms companies had an even more uncertain existence than the Europeans. The First World War had made huge profits for the steel companies, and had transformed du Pont into a major corporation. But disarmament had been more thorough and lasting than in Europe, and the isolationist movement which Senator Nye had encouraged increased the public determination to avoid armaments, and to hold to Thomas Jefferson's principle that the United States had no need for a standing army. The tank factories or shipyards were converted or closed down. The Electric Boat company, which had made its profits from submarines in the war years, had been reduced to desperately soliciting orders in Latin America to keep its yards at Groton open, and during the Depression was glad to be repairing hair curlers for beauty parlours.

The infant American aviation industry which had blossomed in the First World War was badly hit by the outbreak of peace, when contracts were cancelled and hundreds of surplus planes sold off cheaply. But flying had such an exciting potential in peacetime that a few pioneers persisted with their vulnerable

[1] Dwight D. Eisenhower: *Waging Peace*, New York, Doubleday, 1965, p. 615.

little companies, and their precarious history and character have a very special historical importance; for they were eventually to become the biggest arms corporations of all.

Their origins were bound up with the development of the West Coast, and particularly of California. The very first aviators, developing their machines from the bicycle, flew their planes in France or in the Eastern States, where there was capital and engineering skills: Glen Curtiss set up his company in Buffalo, New York, which became the chief producer of aircraft in the First World War. But after that war the centre of the industry was already beginning to move to California, attracted by the forests of spruce, the clear skies and the cheap non-unionised labour. In the open fields round Los Angeles, aircraft and motion-pictures grew up together, and both industries thrived on stunts, risks and glamour: film stars took to the air in helmets and goggles, and pretty aviatrixes looked for parts in the movies. (There were strong associations between flying and sex: 'wait till you get them up in the air, boys,' said one popular song, 'you can make them hug and squeeze you, too').

The two industries, aviation and movies, shared the same kind of hazards and some of the same entrepreneurs. Cecil B. De Mille learnt to fly in 1917 and bought eight war-surplus planes, setting up his own De Mille field in Hollywood; he became the biggest operator in the area until 1922 when, losing money, he sold his planes and turned to movies. Syd Chaplin came to Hollywood in 1919 as manager of his brother Charlie; he was fascinated by aviation, and set up an airfield along Wilshire Boulevard, organising regular trips to Catalina Island until he closed the business in 1920.[1] One entrepreneur combined a lasting interest in both industries. Howard Hughes, as a dashing millionaire of twenty-one, came to Hollywood to make movies: his second film was an epic about airmen in the First World War, for which he bought fifty planes, hired a hundred pilots and spent $350,000. The making of *Hell's Angels* gave Hughes an obsession with aviation; he became a pilot, and later set up his own aircraft company and bought control of Trans World Airlines, while keeping the RKO film studios. Hughes Aircraft was eventually to become one of the major suppliers of electronics and satellites, and is still

[1] David D. Hartfield: *Los Angeles Aeronautics, 1920–29.* Northrop Institute of Technology, 1973, pp. 11–19, 32–4.

today a private company controlled by the Hughes Medical Trust.

While the young aviation industry shared some of the wild optimism of the movies, it soon faced even harsher financial problems: and the companies, to survive, had to obtain solid orders from commercial airlines, or contracts from the armed services in Washington. Donald Douglas, the son of a bank cashier in Brooklyn, came to Los Angeles in 1915 with a degree from the Massachusetts Institute of Technology: by 1922 he had established a factory in an abandoned motion-picture studio in Santa Monica, where he built torpedo planes for the US navy; two years later he had signed his first export order, to Norway. It was military contracts that established the Douglas company, until it gained its first commercial orders in 1933 for forty DC2 air transports for the new Trans World Airlines.

Further north Bill Boeing had set up a small plant beside his shipyard in Seattle. The son of a German businessman, he had taken an engineering degree at Yale, and came to Seattle to buy timber. He saw the opportunities for aviation in the war and sold planes to the navy, but with peace he converted his plant to making furniture. It was not till Boeing produced a pursuit plane for the navy in 1923 that he became securely established in aviation with the first of a long line of navy planes, followed by a contract for the post office. For a short time Boeing had its own airline, United; but in 1934 a law was passed separating airmail contracts from construction companies, and the Boeing plant at Seattle was left on its own in the midst of a slump, with employment down from 1,700 to 600. Bill Boeing left in bitterness, and for its recovery the company again looked to military aircraft, to a four-engined bomber called the Flying Fortress. Already by 1937 the Boeing plant and much of the town of Seattle were dependent on military orders.[1]

No company had a more chequered beginning than the Lockheed Corporation, whose troubles over the next sixty years will run through this book like an elephant's track. Lockheed originated in 1912, when Allan and Malcolm Loughead, the sons of a woman novelist, began building a seaplane in San Francisco: by 1916 they had established the Loughead Company in Santa Barbara (they could not decide how to spell their name). With

<hr />

[1] Harold Mansfield: *Vision, the Story of Boeing*, New York, Popular Library, 1966, pp. 20–59.

the help of a brilliant young designer, Jack Northrop, they put together a new plane called the F1; but it was turned down by the navy, and ended up being much used by movie companies for filming aeronautic adventures. The company languished: by 1919 Malcolm left it to market a new invention, a hydraulic brake system for cars (which soon made him a huge fortune); and in 1923 Northrop left to take a job with Donald Douglas, and later to found his own corporation.

Allan Lockheed (as he now called himself) at last found new capital and formed the Lockheed Aircraft Corporation in 1926. For a time Lockheed prospered: it became famous as the maker of the record-breaking Vega monoplane, designed by Jack Northrop, in which Amelia Earhart flew solo across the Atlantic. Orders boomed, and the Lockheed company moved to a bigger building at Burbank, north of Hollywood, surrounded by the vineyards and walnut orchards of the San Fernando Valley. Then in 1929 Lockheed merged with the Detroit Aircraft Corporation which had ambitions to be the General Motors of the air; but after the Great Crash the Detroit company went bankrupt in 1931, and with it Lockheed. Allan Lockheed, after other adventures with aircraft enterprises, turned to selling real estate around Burbank.[1]

The next year the company was resurrected and the derelict Burbank property was bought by a syndicate of young investors, led by a thirty-five-year-old Boston banker, Robert Gross, who was to play a leading and controversial role in the aircraft industry. Gross was a stocky, well-groomed Harvard graduate with a smooth centre parting; he had begun his career in the investment house of Lee, Higginson, which became interested in aviation investments after Lindbergh's famous flight across the Atlantic in 1927. After several shaky ventures, Gross learnt about the potential of the bankrupt Lockheed, and in the depths of the slump he was able to raise $50,000 to buy it. Aviation, as it turned out, was one of the few industries which expanded during the depression. Gross and his partners pinned their hopes on producing a twin-engined passenger plane, the Electra, which soon became a winner: by 1935 Lockheed was making a profit, and by the end of 1936 it was employing 1,200 people. Lockheed, unlike Boeing and Douglas, was firmly concentrating on com-

---

[1] *Of Men and Stars: A History of the Lockheed Aircraft Corporation*, Burbank, March 1957–January 1958.

mercial planes: 'the one market that will never fail us,' said Gross, 'is the American public.'

But by April 1938 Lockheed suddenly faced an irresistible opportunity for military exports. It came from Britain, just after Hitler's invasion of Austria, when the need for American aircraft was urgent, and a British purchasing mission arrived in California. Lockheed's only order at the time was for a few transports for Japan: before the British arrived the Lockheed engineers rapidly converted their latest plane, the Super-Electra, into a mock-up of a reconnaissance bomber, and mounted a high-pressure sales drive for the purchasing mission. Two months later the British air ministry ordered two hundred of the bombers, which they christened Hudsons. Overnight the order put Lockheed into the big league: it was the largest single order ever received by any American aircraft manufacturer. Lockheed bought more land in Burbank and doubled their workforce. By 1939 they were making a profit of $3 million and delivering 356 planes of which 329 were military.[1] From now on Lockheed too were dependent on arms sales.

The outbreak of war in Europe transformed the whole aircraft industry. The Army Air Corps was rapidly expanding, and by May 1940 Roosevelt was announcing his target of 50,000 planes a year. In Seattle the Boeing Flying Fortress went into production, and in Long Beach, south of Los Angeles, Douglas set up a new plant for bombers and fighters. For Lockheed, Britain was now the overriding customer. The orders for Hudson bombers had gone up to 1,700 by the end of 1941, and Lockheed now employed 50,000 people, more than any other aircraft company in the world.

After the attack on Pearl Harbor in December 1941, California became the chief arsenal of America. The war in the Pacific turned the harbours of San Francisco, Los Angeles and San Diego into crowded bases and embarkation points, and the shipyards of Henry J. Kaiser sprang up along the coast to turn out mass-produced 'Liberty Ships' in a few days. Aircraft became the biggest single industry in the United States and the economic mainspring of California, which produced nearly half the American planes. The plants which had been struggling for orders two years earlier were now flooded with them, and small companies founded just before the war became giant manufacturers. North

[1] *Of Men and Stars*, Chapter IV, June 1957.

American Aviation had been formed by 'Dutch' Kindelberger in 1935 in a small shed just south of Los Angeles; seven years later it was one of the biggest of all aircraft companies.

Boeing, which had still made a loss in 1939, became the world's biggest producer of bombers: the orders for Flying Fortresses were so large that they could only be produced by a consortium of Boeing, Lockheed and Douglas. The war boom spread out to feeder plants up and down the coast, and into the Mid-West and the South. In St Louis Jim McDonnell, 'Mr Mac', founded his own company in 1939, and saw it grow in three years into the chief industry of the city. The expansion of the defence industries and the armed services transformed the pattern of employment throughout the United States. In 1939 defence spending had accounted for 1.5 percent of the Gross National Product, and unemployment was running at seventeen percent: by 1944 defence was forty-five percent of the GNP, and unemployment was only 1.2 percent.[1] But in California, which had suffered acutely from pre-war unemployment, the change was more dramatic than anywhere.

North of Hollywood, the Lockheed factories were now dwarfing the movie studios all around them: by June 1943 Lockheed was employing 94,000 people. The San Fernando Valley and Burbank filled up with shacks, pasteboard houses and camps for migrant workers attracted by the high wages: the refugees from Oklahoma and Arkansas, the Okies and Arkies who had been destitute before the war, flocked into the Lockheed plants along with housewives, schoolboys and out-of-work actors. Lockheed was no longer an interloper into the exotic world of Los Angeles, but the centre of its industrial complex. Robert Gross was the president of a major corporation, wielding his power jointly with his brother Courtlandt, the vice-president. Young engineers and executives, many in their twenties, found themselves managers of an incongruous workforce, constantly improvising and innovating to keep their production targets: 'I worked twelve hours a day for two years,' one of them recalled to me, 'with only two days off, both of them Christmas Day.' Lockheed was a proud isolated community with its own legends and heroes, much more earthy and puritanical than Hollywood, and more certain that they were indispensable for winning the war.

But the price of this expansion and prosperity, everyone knew,

[1] Economic Report of the President, 1960.

was a dependence on a temporary wartime economy, and on the decisions and indecisions of Washington. The Gross brothers were no longer independent pioneers selling on a free market: their whole future depended on the great five-sided fortress that had gone up on the Potomac, whose largesse could not continue. By the middle of 1943, eighteen months after Pearl Harbor, Lockheed had already passed its peak of employment. All through 1944 the Pentagon were cancelling orders, and by the end of the year jobs at Lockheed were down to 60,000, and by the summer of 1945 they were down to 35,000—fewer than in 1939.

Then on August 6, 1945, a Boeing Super Fortress flew over the city of Hiroshima and dropped the atomic bomb; and with it transformed the whole perspective of the arms business. The political decision had been taken by the Americans and British without moral worries, except from some scientists. ('The historic fact remains,' recorded Churchill, 'that the decision whether or not to use the atomic bomb to compel the surrender of Japan was never an issue.')[1] But once it had been used, and its first object achieved, the horrors and the opportunities were both soon evident. 'If we can't work out some sort of organisation of great powers,' wrote Dean Acheson on the day of Hiroshima, 'we shall be gone geese for fair.'[2] The plan subsequently worked out by Acheson and Lilienthal, and presented in 1946 as the Baruch Plan, seemed to promise the kind of peace through terror of which Nobel had dreamed half-a-century earlier: atomic development would be banned to all nations, and would only be undertaken by an international authority with a staff of expert scientists, with large powers of inspection and control. But the Russians were already hectically trying to develop their own bomb, which exploded four years later; and they flatly turned down the Baruch Plan. The hopes for controlled peace were followed by a balance of terror more uncertain and fearful than anything Nobel had imagined.

In the first months after the atom bomb had exploded, it seemed to many ordinary people in the peace that followed that, whatever its horrors, it would quickly make the old warfare of guns, fighters and ships obsolete. (I recall doing gun drill in the British navy when the news of Hiroshima was announced: the

---

[1] Winston Churchill: *The Second World War*, Vol. 6, *Triumph and Tragedy*, London, Cassell, 1954, p. 553.

[2] Dean Acheson: *Present at the Creation*, New York, Signet (Paperback) 1970, p. 163.

gun seemed suddenly totally pointless.) For four years the United States alone had the atom bomb, which gave a new sense of security, and the opportunity to convert rapidly to peacetime industries. The combination of peace and the bomb precipitated a surge of economic activity in most parts of America, but it heightened the crisis in the aircraft industry.

The air force declared ten billions worth of property surplus, and by 1946 total aircraft production in the United States was down to half of one percent of its wartime peak. The upstart aircraft cities, like Burbank, Seattle or St Louis, were threatened with massive unemployment. The Boeing Super Fortress which had dropped the A-bomb had hastened the decline of the company which made it. In Seattle Bill Allen, who had been Bill Boeing's lawyer, took over as chairman, and his first act was to shut down the plant making Super Fortresses, with no prospect of anything in their place.[1] At Santa Monica the Douglas company, which had made 29,000 aircraft during the war, produced 127 in 1946, and Donald Douglas remarked: 'The future is as dark as the inside of a boot.'[2]

Of all the big companies Lockheed showed the most promise for peacetime: for they not only had the first jet fighter in production, the P-80 Shooting Star, but also the Constellation, a transport adapted for the army which could be rapidly converted into an airliner, which put them ahead in the race for the expected air travel boom. Their chairman Robert Gross was now the wonderman of the industry, with a style and perspective that the rugged engineers lacked. He lived in a big pink house in Bel Air with four servants. He collected Braques and Kandinskys which, he explained, gave him the same kind of aesthetic satisfaction as his planes. He played Wagner on the piano and had movie stars including Walter Pidgeon among his friends. The engineers and salesmen were devoted to him: he was always asking about their families and home lives, and disliked talking about money. He knew nothing about aerodynamics, but he knew how to sell planes. In January 1946 he was depicted on the cover of *Time* magazine, together with the Constellation airliner: 'In Burbank, California, one day last week, a big shark-bodied plane rose from the Lockheed air terminal, circled out across the San Fernando Valley, and headed east over the mountains.'

[1] Mansfield, p. 152.

[2] *Flight Plan for Tomorrow*, Santa Monica, Douglas Aircraft Company, 1966, p. 49.

But for all aircraft companies the years 1946 and 1947 were terrible times: and for Robert Gross they were the hardest he could remember. By 1946 Lockheed were again experiencing losses, and by April 1948 their employment was down to 13,800. While other industries—cars, houses, televisions and consumer goods—were booming, aviation still slumped. The dreams of mass-production of light planes, of 'a hangar in every home', were soon shattered, and all the big companies had problems with new airliners, including the Constellation. Never were the companies more conscious of their 'roller-coaster existence'.

In 1948 the companies received some succour from the Finletter Commission which produced for the government a report on 'Survival in the Air Age', stressing the need for a bigger air force and a financially viable industry; and a few months afterwards the need for air transports was dramatically demonstrated by the Berlin Air Lift. By the end of 1948 the companies were over the worst: Lockheed was once more making a profit, again depending on military aircraft. Boeing received a new boost from its new jet bomber, the B47 Stratojet. Douglas was now selling eighty-seven percent of its production to the services.

But the industry and the regions which depended on it were still precarious, particularly on the West Coast. Between 1940 and 1950 California had experienced an inrush of people without precedent, even for that accommodating state: the population had gone up by over fifty percent to 10.6 million. It was one of the 'greatest migrations of history', but its basis in terms of jobs and resources was dangerously flimsy. By March 1949 half a million people were unemployed in California, equivalent to fourteen percent, or twice the national average: and the population was expected to increase by another ten million in the next quarter-century. To accommodate such an increase Governor Earl Warren warned that there must be drastic planning of resources, particularly energy and water.[1] But Californians in the course of their war-change had also lost a good deal of their independence. However much they looked to right-wing politicians like Richard Nixon to express their rugged self-reliance, they also looked to Washington for their basic support—especially for continued defence contracts.

[1] Carey McWilliams: *California, the Great Exception*, Santa Barbara, Peregrine Smith, 1976, p. 344.

Then in June 1950 came the Korean war, and with it a sudden new up-swing on the roller-coaster—a swing which this time would never again turn abruptly down. The notion that the atom bomb would make land warfare obsolete was now thoroughly disproved; instead, according to the subsequent ruthless analysis of Walt Rostow, the Korean war was held to show that 'industrial capital could, to an important degree, be successfully substituted for manpower against an Asian land army'.[1] The effect on industrial capital in California was electric. The air force had found itself desperately short of fighters and bombers, and Korea was soon the laboratory for the new jet fighters, now tested against the Russian MiGs. Douglas supplied their new Skynights, and won big orders for their transport, the C124. But Korea was, above all, a Lockheed war. The Lockheed jet fighters, the Shooting Stars, flew forty percent of the combat missions, and shot down the first MiG jets; while the navy ordered the Lockheed transports, the Super Constellations, to carry troops across the Pacific.

At the end of 1950 Lockheed took over the huge plant at Marietta in Georgia, the biggest integrated aircraft plant in the world, which had lain idle since the Second World War, and used it to assemble more Boeing B47 bombers. By 1951 the plant employed 10,000 workers, and the expansion into Georgia 'marked a turning point in Lockheed's growth'.[2] It provided new capacity and ambition to the company: its general manager was a young accountant from Alabama, Dan Haughton, who had an almost evangelical zeal to make and sell aircraft. And Georgia also gave Lockheed (its rivals sourly noticed) a political advantage, making connections with Southern senators with influence over defence contracts, and particularly with Senator Richard Russell of Georgia, the chairman of the Armed Services Committee. Robert Gross knew that his whole company's future depended on Washington, and his Georgia extension gave him new clout on Capitol Hill.

With the Korean war the Pentagon's spending on the aerospace industry shot up from $2.6 billion in 1950 to $10.6 billion in 1954. When the fighting ended there were cutbacks in orders, but the continuing cold war ensured that defence spending would

[1] W. W. Rostow: *The United States in the World Arena*, New York, Harper, 1960, p. 232.
[2] *Of Men and Stars*, Chapter IX, January 1958.

be maintained. The explosion of the hydrogen bomb in 1952 at first brought new worries to the aerospace industry, that it might reduce the need for 'conventional' arms. (The word was first recorded in its new meaning in the *New York Herald Tribune*, just after the bomb was exploded: 'we must decide whether the new fire package will permit a reduction of our more conventional military weapons'.[1]) But that choice was never resolved, and the familiar weapons continued to be produced, together with a growing range of new missiles and warheads, providing new momentum for research and development, so that project and counter-project could make inventions obsolete in a few years. Douglas had been developing successive Nike missiles for the army since 1945. Lockheed formed a separate missile division in 1954. Boeing was well-placed both to produce bombers and to shoot them down, and while they went ahead with the B52 bomber, they also developed an unmanned missile, the Bomarc. As Boeing put it, 'we know how to build a strategic bomber: why shouldn't we be the ones to build a defence against it?'[2]

From now on defence contracts for aerospace companies never went below $10 billion in one year. Airlines were providing much more business as air travel at last became more popular, but the Pentagon now accounted for ninety percent of the companies' spending, and they were all once again dependent on military budgets. The Pentagon began cutting back on aircraft in 1957, but the missile industry faced a new challenge with the launching of the first Sputnik, 'the Pearl Harbor of the technological war'. Intercontinental missiles became the top priority, and Boeing achieved a new role as the chief contractors for the Minuteman.

For the ageing pioneers of the industry, who had seen it grow from its independent origins, the success was somewhat hollow. Bill Allen of Boeing had always wanted to be primarily a builder of civil planes, as in the early years with Bill Boeing. By the end of the 'fifties Boeing was indeed established as the world's leading producer of airliners, with a succession of efficient and economic planes beginning with the Boeing 707. But Allen's satisfaction 'had its sense of emptiness, even of alarm';[3] for the commercial aircraft still could not be viable on their own, and the military pro-

[1] *A Supplement to the Oxford English Dictionary*, Vol. 1, Oxford, 1972, p. 626.

[2] Mansfield, p. 206.

[3] Ibid., p. 282.

grammes were carrying the commercial on their shoulders. And defence orders, though often lucrative, were increasingly demanding and competitive; the long runs of big bombers were giving way to short runs of much more sophisticated weapons, employing fewer people.

The relationships between these companies and their giant patron were now intricate and tense. In 1960 four aerospace companies obtained defence contracts worth a billion dollars or more: three of them (Lockheed, Boeing and North American) were based on the West Coast, and one of them (General Dynamics) in Missouri. All four were to maintain that position, on and off, for the next decade, with some fluctuations in their fortunes. They were in many respects helplessly dependent on the Pentagon, which was the monopoly buyer, in the position of monopsony. They had nowhere else—or almost nowhere else—to go. The Pentagon could set them against each other, make them undercut each other, bankrupt them, merge them, or rescue them.

But the companies had their own counter-weapons. The Pentagon had to maintain a viable defence industry, and the air force, army and navy each had their own claims and their own favourite suppliers. The companies each brought their own political pressures to bear on Washington, through their influence with senators and congressmen and their huge employment of labour. General Dynamics could usually rely on the support of Stuart Symington, Senator for Missouri; Boeing had the solid backing of Henry Jackson, the 'Senator for Boeing'; and Lockheed was now an indispensable employer both in California and Georgia, where it could count on Senator Russell.

As the Pentagon contracts became bigger and fewer and the companies more precarious, the relationship was hard to recognise as any traditional kind of free enterprise: 'Pentagon capitalism' was a system all of its own. The Pentagon now appeared increasingly to be taking turns in its awards, balancing out the demands of the three services and of the major aerospace companies so that plants could be kept open, and politicians satisfied. When one project came to an end, or when a company was in serious difficulties, a new project would be awarded, in keeping with 'the follow-on imperative' or 'the bail-out imperative'. Some of the more extravagant projects, with the least obvious strategic justification, could be explained by the need to keep the aerospace companies viable.[1]

The future of the companies thus depended on a complicated interplay of forces: from the strategists at the Pentagon; from the three services; from the senators and congressmen; from the labour unions; and from the managers themselves. Much of the skill of running the companies lay in manoeuvring the other elements and playing them against each other to secure the maximum orders and profits. The more difficult this juggling act, the more important became the single personality of the man at the top. Bill Allen of Boeing, Robert Gross of Lockheed, or Jim Kindelberger of North American, all had to be predators in the Washington jungle. For all their apparent dependence, they still had very strong cards to play: for whenever seriously threatened they could present themselves publicly not only as the guardians of the nation's defence, but as the keystones of the prosperity of their states, and as the guarantors of jobs. And they still had loose money whose presence could make itself felt in crucial quarters.

It was appropriate that the first serious warning about the 'military-industrial complex' should be made by President Eisenhower, who had presided over its formation and who well understood the workings of the military mind. 'We have been compelled to create a permanent armaments industry of vast proportions,' he explained in his famous farewell speech in January 1961: 'this conjunction of an immense military establishment and a large arms industry is new in the American experience. The total influence—economic, political, even spiritual—is felt in every city, every state house, every office of the federal government. . . . In the councils of government we must guard against the acquisition of unwarranted influence, whether sought or unsought, by the military-industrial complex. The potential for the disastrous rise of misplaced power exists and will persist.'[2]

This sensational warning was ascribed to Eisenhower's speech writer, Malcolm Moos (later president of the University of Minnesota) who had been disturbed by the numbers of serving officers who had moved into the arms companies.[3] But Eisenhower himself firmly stood by this speech, and during his presidency, as he described it: 'I began to feel more and more

---

[1] James R. Kurth: *Why We Buy the Weapons We Do*, Foreign Policy Magazine, Summer, 1973.

[2] *Waging Peace*, p. 616.

[3] Bernard Brodie: *War and Politics*, New York, Macmillan, 1973, pp. 290–296.

uneasiness about the effect on the nation of tremendous peace-time military expenditures. . . . In the long run, the combinations of pressures for growth can create an almost overpowering influence. Unjustified military spending is nothing more than a distorted use of the nation's resources.'[1]

Eisenhower's warnings were to seem much more urgent in the following years, when under a Democratic administration the words 'military-industrial complex' became part of every radical's vocabulary of protest against the Vietnam war. But the problems of misplaced power and the distortion of resources were to be more lasting and widespread than Vietnam, and showed themselves on a global scale as the arms companies looked abroad for their profits.

BRITAIN IN RETREAT

The dropping of the atom bombs in 1945, as the climax to the war in the Pacific, marked the final conclusion of European supremacy in arms. In the words of Professor Michael Howard, 'they marked the end of that era of European world dominance which the voyages of Columbus and Vasco da Gama had opened nearly five hundred years earlier.'[2] The United States had emerged as by far the largest arms producer in the Western world, and the scale of spending gave American companies an immense advantage both in developing their own technology and in exporting to others. But the European companies had traditionally depended much more heavily on export for their survival, and some of them retained very important areas of influence. The European colonies, as they emerged into independence, still kept their links with their former masters; and Britain and France, while taking back seats in the major arms contest, were all the more determined to hold their own and compete with other weapons. Britain had very high hopes that she could become a major exporter of commercial airliners to the rest of the world. The dashing of those hopes was not only a national tragedy, but a factor in the world arms trade; for the less the civil opportunities, the more the British companies looked towards military orders.

At the end of the war the British arms companies were cut down almost as drastically as the Americans. Aircraft production

---

[1] *Waging Peace*, p. 615.
[2] Michael Howard: *War in European History*, Oxford University Press, 1976, p. 135.

went down to a tenth of its peak, and Vickers—still the biggest
arms company—again faced the problems of changing to peacetime products. They again made some bold attempts at con-
version, and even tried to break into the American tractor
monopoly, turning from tanks to tractors. But the tractors were
an extravagant fiasco, and Vickers experienced once more the
difficulties of adjusting from a single government-customer to a
consumer market. In commercial aircraft, however, Vickers'
prospects at first looked exciting: by 1948 they were flying the
first of the Viscount turbo-prop airliners, of which four hundred
were sold over the next ten years across the world, including
America. At the same time the de Havilland company developed
the world's first jet airliner, the Comet, whose success caused
serious alarm to the American companies, particularly Boeing.
But these two triumphs proved short-lived: the Comet had a
succession of crashes, and it was over four years before the metal
fatigue had been rectified, by which time it had lost all its lead
over the Americans. And the Viscount turned out to be Vickers'
only major success: its turbo-prop successor the Vanguard was
overtaken by the pure jets, and the V.1000, a jet airliner to compete with the Boeing 707, was abandoned when the government
withdrew its support in 1955.[1] From then onwards, the British
airlines became increasingly dependent on American companies,
and the British plane-makers became more desperate for orders.

With military aircraft, the British experience was even more
demoralising. In the first years after the war two jet planes, the
Gloster Meteor and the de Havilland Vampire, had a spectacular
success: over seven thousand were produced, of which two
thousand were for export. The Korean war produced a demand
for two new planes, the Hawker Hunter and the English Electric
Canberra, which were also widely exported. But then British air
policy became thoroughly confused, with the development of
the H-bomb and the preoccupation with the nuclear deterrent.
The Defence White Paper of 1957 proposed to concentrate on
rockets and guided missiles; new aircraft projects were cancelled,
and the industry undermined. Great hopes were now put in the
British rocket, Blue Streak, but by 1960 it was aborted in favour
of the American Skybolt, which itself was later cancelled.
Another white hope was the TSR2 bomber (or tactical strike

[1] For an account of Vickers' post-war problems see J. D. Scott: *Vickers, A History.*
pp. 301–52.

reconnaissance weapon) which was being built jointly by Vickers and English Electric; but that too became far too expensive, and was cancelled in favour of an American plane, the FIII.[1] And in the meantime the concentration on the nuclear deterrent itself became outdated, with new policies and with the surge of guerrilla warfare in the developing world, which brought a new demand for manned aircraft.

Many of Britain's aircraft fiascos could be blamed on the indecisions and confusions of governments, and the disorganisation of an industry with too many companies:[2] compared with the French or the Swedes, the sheer wastefulness of the British resources was extravagant. No European power could now afford indecision, for the cost of new aircraft and systems was multiplying with each new generation: the Spitfire which had cost £10,000 in the Battle of Britain had given way in 1960 to the Lightning which cost £500,000; and far more costly projects were to come. The old liberal system of competing companies could not cope with such costs, and by 1959 the British government insisted that the plane-makers should be merged into two: Hawker-Siddeley and the new British Aircraft Corporation, made up of the combined aviation interests of English Electric and Vickers. Rolls-Royce, as the critical makers of engines for both groups, now enjoyed benign government support. But even these bigger companies could not compete with the giants of America, with their regular billion-a-year in defence contracts.

Behind all the governments' confusions lay the basic indecision about Britain's world role, which always raised the question: what were the weapons *for*? So long as Britain tried to defend areas in the Far East, the Middle East or Africa, the problems of producing a neat rationalised industry were multiplied. The multiplying costs of each project put a growing burden on Britain, who still insisted on her freedom of action. The only solution to reducing the costs of her defence industries was the traditional one: to export arms wherever she could.

The first post-war decade was a boom time for British arms sales. The great stock of unwanted armaments, which was left over as the detritus of the Second World War, provided an

[1] See Chapter 8.

[2] See the Plowden Report on the British Aircraft Industry: London, HMSO, 1965, Command 2853.

overflowing second-hand arsenal. Much was sold as scrap, and much was dumped into the North Sea or allowed to rust into disuse. But much could be sold off to foreign governments, either directly or through private dealers like Sam Cummings; and even today the wartime Lee-Enfield rifles are used by troops in Africa or Asia, while old British motor-launches and mine-sweepers can be seen in the Mediterranean ports. With aircraft, the process of obsolescence was becoming much faster, and the development of jets soon outdated the old piston-fighters, which added to the stocks waiting for export. Old planes, like second-hand clothes, could be sold off to poor relations.

The British government always of course stressed its diplomatic responsibilities: a white paper in January 1956 emphasised that 'the general policy of HM government in the sale of arms is primarily governed by political and strategic considerations: only when these have been satisfied are economic considerations, i.e. the contribution of arms sales to export earnings, taken into account.' But the economic considerations were increasingly important now that exports were desperately needed, and the commercial pressures to export arms were almost as great on the government as they were on the companies.

In the first ten years after the war the arms trade was virtually an Anglo-American monopoly, with Britain as the greatest beneficiary. In the years of austerity and retreat from the Empire the selling of arms was a godsend, and as the Empire diminished, the numbers of nations and clients multiplied, each looking for arms as their source of independence, or status. Between 1945 and 1955 Britain sold over two billion dollars' worth of arms to private traders, and $1.7 billion's worth to foreign governments, excluding warships. The warships still provided an important trade to the developing countries, but jet aircraft were becoming a more valuable export. The trade could not compare with the great old days when Vickers and Armstrong armed half the world. But Vickers were again receiving orders from familiar nineteenth-century clients, including the Chileans and Peruvians; and the foreign orders were once again welcome not only for the profits, but for the opportunity to escape from the stifling home influence of the British government. Between 1945 and 1955 Britain provided ten warships for the Middle East, twenty-six to Asia and Australia, six to South America, five to Africa; while she delivered 194 jet aircraft to the Middle East, 402 to Asia and

Australia, and 205 to South America.[1]

It was a golden age for British arms exports, whether to the developing world or to Europe; the formation of NATO and the flow of American aid to Europe provided extra opportunities. The Americans, under their policy of 'offshore procurement', bought equipment from Britain for the continent. In the long term, this easy boom was a doubtful advantage: it encouraged British arms companies in an arrogant attitude of take-it-or-leave-it,[2] and it distracted British attention from the more important export battles to come, in electronics, cars or consumer goods. But in the short term, few people were inclined to reject this bonanza.

Looking back on this period, the aftermath of the most destructive war in the history of mankind, it might seem surprising that there was not more public concern about the rush of arms sales. Certainly the problems of disarmament were discussed as never before, with a growing body of experts engaged in increasingly complex debate. But it was nuclear disarmament which understandably dominated the arguments and conferences; and compared to the new danger of a nuclear holocaust, the old problem of the export of conventional arms seemed relatively harmless, and inevitable as a by-product of the extending cold war.

And in that first decade, the competition to sell arms was restricted by the nature of the Anglo-American monopoly. The United States exports were governed more by diplomatic than commercial expediency: while Britain earned cash for most of her exports, America gave most of them away, as part of her expanding programme of military aid. New acts of Congress, in 1949 and 1954, authorised the providing of arms to friendly countries on the 'principle of self-help and mutual aid'. Britain and the United States still worked closely together, and by obeying unwritten understandings about areas of influence they could avoid any drastic competition to sell arms or to stimulate an arms race.[3]

But the Anglo-American monopoly, and the British success,

---

[1] John L. Sutton and Geoffrey Kemp: *Arms to Developing Countries 1945–65*, London, Institute for Strategic Studies 1966, Graphs 1 and 2.

[2] 'Some British salesmen thought that their products were God's gift to lesser humans, and unfortunately in their dealings with customers this attitude showed.' Richard Worcester: *Roots of British Air Policy*, London, Hodder and Stoughton, 1966, p. 20.

[3] Sutton and Kemp, pp. 29–30.

were very short-lived. As the cold war extended and British influence diminished, so the Americans moved into traditional British areas, in response to Soviet threats. The Middle East ceased to be a British preserve, and became a frontier of the central confrontation. In India and Pakistan the Americans and Russians began supplying the rival components of the old British empire, and in South-East Asia the United States became the biggest source of arms. The Latin Americans turned towards the North, and only in Africa could Britain remain the major arms supplier— which was soon to present huge moral problems. By the early 'sixties, the United States was by far the biggest exporter of arms, forcing Britain to compete more desperately for her markets abroad.

ENTER DASSAULT

And any remaining restraint was now being challenged by the re-emergence of France as a major manufacturer of arms, and particularly of aircraft. The French had a long proud tradition of inventiveness in aviation, commemorated in the vocabulary of the industry by such words as fuselage, aileron and aeroplane itself. The Wright brothers had begun their experiments in France, and the flight of Louis Blériot across the English channel in 1909 was a landmark in aviation. After the humiliations of the Second World War and the Nazi occupation, successive French governments were determined to catch up with the industry in Britain and America, as an assertion of national independence, supported by the full patronage of the state. And as the instrument of the recovery they put much of their faith in a single man who came to represent the ruthless spirit of the industry.

No individual has spanned so completely the aviation era, none embodied so vividly its political problems, as the French manufacturer Marcel Dassault, and his story is a large part of the story of the French aircraft industry. The son of a Jewish doctor, Adolph Bloch, he was brought up in Paris at the end of the nineteenth century. At the age of seventeen, in 1909, he was inspired by the pioneer flights of Blériot and the Wrights to enrol in the new College of Aeronautics, and during the First World War he set up his own company to make planes which he began mass producing just as the war ended.

With the post-war collapse of the industry he turned to real estate in Paris to make money, and it was not until the 'thirties that he again had a chance to design aircraft: first for the French post office, then for the French air ministry who needed a bomber in response to Hitler's re-arming. He was now well-established as an aircraft designer, while his brother Paul was a distinguished soldier: the Popular Front government nationalised Dassault together with the rest of the French armaments industry, but having paid him his compensation the government still needed him to run the company; he was now already well aware of his value to France. When the British and French prime ministers both flew to Munich in 1938 to see Hitler, Mr Chamberlain flew in a Lockheed plane but M. Daladier flew in a Dassault plane.[1]

With the Second World War he became a national hero. After the fall of France in 1940 he was interned with other French aircraft designers, and refused to work for the Nazis in return for his freedom. In 1944 he was transported to Buchenwald, where he still refused to co-operate and was sentenced to death, to be saved only by the arrival of the Allied armies. He emerged a frail-looking man of fifty-two, partly deaf with weak eyesight, but still burning with ambition to build aircraft, and with a twinkle in his fading eyes. He had all the lustre of the Resistance, and he and the post-war president, de Gaulle, were natural allies. His brother Paul as a Resistance fighter had adopted the name of *Char d'Assault*, or assault tank; and after the war the brothers changed their names from Bloch to Dassault.

Marcel Dassault set about rebuilding the French aircraft industry after devastation of the war. He bought some land at Mérignac, alongside an airfield outside Bordeaux in the heart of the claret country (the aircraft industry, as in California, encouraged the migration towards the sun). The French engineers were backward in the technology of the new jet engines, and like the Americans and Russians they were determined to acquire the expertise of the defeated Germans. They made contact with Herman Oestrich, the chief designer of the German BMW aircraft factory, and smuggled him out of the American occupation zone into the French zone and then into France itself, giving him every technical support in return for his skills. Oestrich was soon the key component of the French nationalised aero-engine company, SNECMA, and by 1948 he produced his first jet engine, the Atar: from then onwards successive Atar engines provided the

[1] Marcel Dassault: *Le Talisman*, Paris, Edition 'Jours de France', 1973.

thrust for Dassault's aircraft. It was a fact of which the Germans became very conscious: that the French success story was originally dependent on a German technical team.

But Dassault was the master-mind behind the French recovery. His company owed much to American aid, through the Marshall Plan which put it on its feet, but it soon asserted its independence and remained (unlike SNECMA) a private company. With his technical mastery and his political power, Dassault was able to build up a team of designers in his own mould, training them and dominating them, creating a much more compact and decisive organisation than the Anglo-Saxons.[1] He prided himself on knowing every detail of his planes, making his teams interdependent, avoiding the sub-divisions and sectionalising of American companies. He had learned caution from his earlier mistakes, evolving his planes gradually, never putting a new engine into a new airframe, playing a 'subtle game of Meccano'.

From his first jet fighter, the Ouragan, he developed a faster fighter, the Mystère, which evolved in 1955 into the supersonic Super-Mystère: and from this Dassault gradually developed his most famous plane, with a Delta wing and optional rocket booster, the Mirage III: like a mirage in the desert, he explained, the enemy could never catch up with it.[2] It first flew in November 1956 during the Suez war and two years later reached twice the speed of sound—at almost the same time as the British Lightning. In a period of French humiliations in Algeria and at Suez, the Mirage was not only an aeronautical achievement but a glamorous symbol of French power, and the feats of the plane, flown by much-publicised test pilots, became part of French folk-lore. It was soon adopted by the French air force, primarily as a strike aircraft, but it could also be used for intercepting, ground attack or reconnaissance. Dassault did not at first expect to sell the Mirage abroad, but it soon turned out to be one of the most phenomenal of all French exports. More important, it was regarded as a diplomatic as well as a military weapon, and in the following decade the Mirage, as will be seen, became a major counter in French foreign policy.[3]

Since the Second World War, Dassault had been committed

---

[1] Robert Perry: *A Dassault Dossier*, Santa Monica, Rand Corporation, 1973.

[2] 'Aussi invulnérable aux coups de l'adversaire que le mirage est insaisissable pour le voyageur du désert', *Le Talisman*, p. 94.

[3] For an account of the twists in Dassault's foreign relations see Jack Gee: *Mirage—Warplane for the World*, London, Macdonald, 1971.

to the support of de Gaulle through all his tribulations and he depicted his activities as part of his service to the General and to France. When in 1951 Dassault founded the weekly magazine *Jours de France* he appointed his right-hand-man, General de Bénouville, as its editor-in-chief, using it as a vehicle for Gaullist policies until de Gaulle was returned to power. Thereafter, as Dassault explained, it was a magazine dedicated to romance and fashions, carefully avoiding mention of any catastrophes and presenting *la vie en rose*—a formula also followed by his cinemas. Just before de Gaulle came up for re-election in 1965, Dassault produced a daily paper called *24 Heures*, likewise dedicated to optimism and entertainment, which lasted for a year. Born in the same decade, Dassault shared de Gaulle's longing for France's former glory; photographed alongside the towering general, he looked like a twinkling imp. De Gaulle gave him a copy of his memoirs with the inscription: 'To Marcel Dassault, in memory of our struggle and of the part he has played in giving stature to France.'

By the time de Gaulle returned to power in 1958 Dassault's position in French politics had become almost institutionalised as a kind of one-man embodiment of the military-industrial complex. He was one of the richest men in France. He owned ninety-eight percent of the shares of the aircraft company, and he had extended into all kinds of other businesses, including real estate, cinemas and a bank: he ran his companies from a magnificent Second Empire mansion on the Champs-Elysées, filled with fine furniture and impressionist paintings, with all the panoply of an independent state. His companies were run by his trusted lieutenants, and his son Serge, who had graduated at the Polytechnic and at the College of Aeronautics, took command of Dassault electronics.

In 1951 Dassault had been elected as deputy for the Oise district, which he has represented ever since, leading a formidable lobby of deputies supporting defence interests. He infrequently visited his district, but he poured money into it, for swimming pools, tennis courts, playgrounds, and a local newspaper, which kept his electors content, and he subsidised newspapers for his allies in parliament. He recruited ex-air force officers into his company, led by General Gallois, the most eloquent exponent of the French *force de frappe*, the nuclear strike force, who became Dassault's adviser on combat aircraft. During de Gaulle's ten years as president, Dassault and his planes became an essential part of France's independent foreign policy.

For the British and Americans the extent of the private political power of Dassault was mind-boggling, making the American attacks on their military-industrial complex seem trivial. No American plane-maker, not even Lockheed, could muster this kind of influence, protected by the government, and immune to public criticism. The Dassault executives looked with pity on their British competitors, divided and frustrated by each reversal of government policy. 'How could the British government have squandered all that magnificent tradition?' one of them asked me. 'It's not for the ministry to decide, it's for the industry: the British government turned its back on reality.'

But for French governments, whatever their political complexion, the privileged situation of Dassault made perfect sense, in the old French *étatist* tradition. The support of a private entrepreneur as the centrepiece of the arms industry provided the dynamic that the state needed, both to develop arms for itself and to extend itself abroad, operating with much greater freedom than the government, but always serving its ultimate needs. It was the kind of relationship that Krupp had reached with the Kaiser's government before the First World War, the relationship which the war minister von Heeringen had so lamented when he resigned.[1] Such a private empire might be dislikeable, and a constraint on democracy, but it seemed a small price to pay for the contribution to national security and foreign influence. In the course of the 'sixties, Dassault was soon able to show the British and American industries just how effective that formula could be; and the combination of de Gaulle's ruthless foreign policy and Dassault's technological drive reduced any remaining prospect of the international control of arms sales.

But neither the British nor the French, for all their determination to sell arms, could effectively compete in the long term with the growing American exports. Their search for markets was more desperate than the Americans', for neither of them had a big enough home market to sustain their industry; and while the American companies became more aggressive with mounting competition, the Europeans were driven by the rivalries between countries. As the superpowers set a more hectic pace for innovation and new systems, which only their continents could afford,

[1] See Chapter 2.

so the Europeans lagged further behind; and even France, behind her patriotic bravado, was critically dependent on advanced American technology.

For this Western European predicament there might seem an obvious solution—to pool their resources to create a continental defence industry. But this begged all the questions of European defence policy. Through the two post-war decades, Britain still looked across the Atlantic for her security and first loyalties, and France remained deeply suspicious of this Anglo-Saxon connection; while both Britain and France shared a deep distrust of Germany, without whom no European defence force could make sense. All Western Europe thus looked to America for their ultimate protection, and in this situation the American arms companies had an obvious advantage. The commercial dependence could not be separated from the political, but the Europeans were reluctant to face up to it, and their weakness was reflected in corruption and in increasingly 'Latin American' attitudes. The Americans found Europe an easy prey for their products, but the Europeans were determined to extract what they could in return. In the seedy dealings which follow, it is hard to judge which side behaved worst.

6

Lockheed and the Battle for Europe

Corruption is going to do more to bring down democracies around the world than almost anything else.

Senator Percy, May, 1976.[1]

IT WAS characteristic of the post-war age that the archetypal arms salesman should now appear not as a frenetic inventor, like Maxim or Krupp, nor as a relentless capitalist, like Craven or Carse, but as a genial bureaucrat working loyally for his government and preoccupied by technicalities and logistics. Henry Kuss, who became the Pentagon's chief arms salesman for most of the 'sixties, saw himself originally as the organiser, not of arms sales, but of rationalisation and co-ordination: a big rubbery man, with a wide chin and an easy smile, he was a salesman of the most disarming kind, with the sort of open face that might appear on television to sell biscuits. A church-going Lutheran, he was dedicated to making a decent, free world; he had been a naval officer in the war and then became an expert on logistics, dealing with the intricacies of supplying Western Europe with arms.

As the Europeans recovered from the war, they could afford to buy their arms, and Kuss soon became a critical figure as the co-ordinator of arms purchases from America. It was not he who was a super-salesman, he insists, but others who were super-buyers: it was a natural development from Europe's capacity to

¹ Multinational Hearings, Part 14, p. 380.

buy, and the insistence of Congress on reducing free arms. 'It's an awful boring story—who's going to read that?' But the elevation of Henry Kuss was in fact to have huge repercussions on the attitude of all Western nations to arms sales, and to set in play forces which were not easily checked. 'I thought I was doing a good job turning government aid into sales,' Kuss reflects. 'It's the world that has changed. . . . But how can I have moral repugnance when the world is full of armies and navies?'

Already in the late 'fifties the Pentagon had promoted Henry Kuss to take charge of a new division called Military Assistance Planning, to ensure that free arms only went to countries that could not afford to pay for them. But Western Europe, which was much the biggest market, was still very short of dollars; and the Europeans wanted anyway to build up their own arms industry. So the Pentagon reached a compromise, that they would encourage 'co-production' agreements, by which American arms would be made in Europe under licence. European countries, particularly Germany, would thus have the benefit of the employment and high technology, while American companies would still make their profits, and the US Treasury would spend less on foreign aid. Thus European companies soon became deeply involved in manufacturing American weapons, and by 1959 the most spectacular of all the new planes, the Lockheed Starfighter, was licensed to Germany and others. The American companies were beginning to join a long European boom.

Then came the Kennedy administration in 1961, when the Pentagon was swiftly penetrated by the personality of the new secretary of defence, Robert McNamara. With his Ford Motor background, he was determined that the Pentagon must be run on business-like lines, in selling arms as in every other department, and there were pressing reasons for reform. In the first place there was a lamentable lack of standardisation of weapons within the countries of NATO, whose armies in 1961 employed fourteen different types of small-arms ammunition, while the Russians only used one. Whether with aircraft, missiles or guns, each European country was pursuing its own research and production in a chaos of non-collaboration, and the dangers became more evident in the Berlin crisis of 1961. The system, McNamara insisted, had to be unified; and since American arms were the most advanced, with much the biggest home market, the first step lay in vigorously promoting American sales. It was a kind of updating of Henry Ford's slogan: you can have any arms you like, provided they're all the same.

In the second place the Kennedy administration was deeply worried about the deficit in the balance of payments, which was running at $3 billion—a figure which now seems trivial, but then seemed a grave threat to the dollar: 'At that time we took the floating exchange much more seriously,' recalled Paul Nitze, the former banker who was then secretary of the navy: 'the stability of the reserve currency seemed essential for the whole international system.'[1] In this crisis the giving away of arms at the rate of $1.5 billion a year seemed all the more profligate. At the beginning of his presidency, Kennedy told the NATO allies that they must now pay for their arms. During 1961 a task force headed by McGeorge Bundy and Paul Nitze investigated the problem, assisted by Henry Kuss and other Pentagon specialists, and decided to set up a special group inside the Pentagon. It was given a name which was a masterpiece of Pentagon newspeak: International Logistics Negotiations. But the ILN was really unashamedly an organisation for selling arms.[2]

At the head of this office was appointed Henry Kuss himself, who left little doubt about his purpose. He soon became a legend in Washington and the European capitals with his bulldozing methods, his big shape and bonhomie, and his missionary style. Like all the great salesmen, like Zaharoff, Craven or Krupp, he saw no basic difference between weapons and any other goods; but from his authority in government he elevated arms sales into a special crusade, so that *not* to sell arms was almost a crime: 'This tendency of American companies, to refrain from entering into the international arms market, is a serious one,' he explained. 'From the political point of view international trade is the "staff of life" of a peaceful world. With it comes understanding; the lack of it eliminates communications and creates misunderstandings.'[3]

It was now the government that was urging companies to sell. Kuss, with his own staff of forty, set up four teams, Red, White, Blue and Grey, which divided the world market between them, to persuade foreign governments of the need to buy arms, and

[1] Interview with the author, May 18, 1976.

[2] For a lively account of the setting up of ILN and Henry Kuss see George Thayer: *The War Business*, Paladin (paperback), London 1970, pp. 152-7.

[3] Speech to American Ordnance Association, October 20, 1966.

the American companies of the need to sell them. They soon produced results: from 1962 onwards Kuss could boast that the
United States was selling an average of $2 billion in arms each
year—more than twice the value of the arms given away in
grant aid.[1]

This great wave of arms sales at first evoked few vociferous
reactions, whether in Congress or elsewhere. The cold war was
raging, and most of the arms went to the industrialised countries
of NATO and Japan who could afford them and needed them.
The Europeans, after all, could stand up to salesmanship; and if
they were forced to standardise their equipment, so much the
better. Only a fraction of the sales went to the developing world,
and this market was kept in check, partly by the control system
within Washington, and partly by the sheer poverty of the clients.

The system for licensing arms exports was, in theory, quite
formidable. The State Department held the power to forbid sales,
and to decide which countries should be allowed weapons; and
at the same time that Kuss was appointed, a new body called the
Arms Control and Disarmament Agency was set up within the
State Department. But ACDA was largely preoccupied with the
problems of nuclear weapons, and in policy-making it remained
subservient to the secretary of state. In the words of a staff report
of the Foreign Relations Committee in January 1967: 'ACDA,
despite its charter, does not sit at the high table when decisions
on the sale of arms are made.' The basic decisions were made in
the cabinet, where Dean Rusk was a much less dominating figure
than McNamara from the Pentagon. McNamara gave his complete backing to Kuss, and at a press conference in 1965 he
explained his concern that developing countries should not
divert too many resources to arms. But the mounting salesmanship was already defying that concern.

The new involvement of governments helped to muffle any
public concern about arms sales. For governments not only conferred a new respectability on the business; they also appeared
to take over the moral responsibilities. Any conflicts between
commercial and moral interests were now resolved in the privacy
of the Pentagon and the State Department, and company salesmen
no longer needed to have qualms, as did Frank S. Jonas of
Remington in the 'thirties ('we certainly are in one hell of a

business'). The pressure to export was now stronger, and governments were as mindful of the needs of full employment, or of
the balance of payments, as any private company. A labour
unionist making his point to a congressman was as effective a
lobbyist as any captain of industry, and governments could now
be prodded into exports from three separate directions—from the
Treasury to earn foreign currency, from the separate states to
maintain employment, and from the armed forces, to reduce
costs by increasing production. To politicians and civil servants
arms exports were now a component of the whole national
balance sheet, like any other trade figure, and the consequences
could be lost among the statistics. But behind this dry respectability, a major change was occurring: for the arms salesmen
were now again being unleashed, with all their traditional lack
of scruple, to romp around the world.

THE LOCKHEED-BERNHARD NETWORK

   While the Pentagon was thus putting its full weight behind the
selling of arms the biggest American aircraft companies had
already been crossing the Atlantic in the 'fifties to expand their
market. The more intense the competition inside the United
States, the more the companies looked towards the less developed
territory of Europe, where only Britain and France had effective
aircraft industries. Teams of salesmen came over from California
or Seattle, knowing little of the language and subtleties of the
continent, but desperate to establish their close contacts and
relationships. As planes became more expensive and orders less
frequent the process of selling took on still more the character of
a war; a battle of a few days could affect a decade to come. 'You
can't imagine the tension of the business,' one aircraft salesman
said to me: 'you might find salesmen from different companies,
all trying to sell to the same customer, all staying in the same hotel.
They may even have dinner together in the evening; but each of
them knows that the others must have *someone* inside the airline
or government who really desperately wants the sale to go
through. We'll do anything to find out who it is—reading their
cables, paying the porter, getting telephones tapped—because
our jobs and the jobs of thousands depend on it.'
   In this invasion of Europe, Lockheed was to play a dominant
role as an arms company determined to establish a global market.

How far Lockheed's methods and ruthlessness were unusual, how far they were typical of the business, may never be fully known; for it was only successive accidents that revealed Lockheed's secrets, and the subsequent evidence provided a more detailed picture of the nature of workings of arms deals than anything in the previous century of the secretive trade. But other evidence suggests that Lockheed was very far from unique; and the narrative that follows, with the shadowy figures suddenly lit up by the spotlight of investigation, belongs to the authentic tradition of Zaharoff, with the timeless characteristics of the arms trade: the desperate need for a single big order; the small cast of greedy characters; the interplay of diplomacy and commercial pressure; and the bribery concealed by diplomatic security.

Robert Gross, the chairman of Lockheed, always saw himself as an internationalist, with a more cultivated style than the other aircraft tycoons; but he still remained a tough financier and salesman and he had (as one of his ex-colleagues recalls) 'some very cheap friends'. He committed the company to a growth of ten percent every year, and he offered his salesmen abroad commissions on sales which ensured their enthusiasm. It was often very difficult, in fact, to know who had really achieved a sale; in the aircraft business it was specially true that 'success has a thousand fathers but failure is an orphan'. Commissions were often paid to people who had done nothing, and Gross was very susceptible to people with titles, or high-sounding friends. And behind the commissions lay much more that was unspoken: above all the assumption that every big contract calls for a payoff.

To support the Lockheed invasion of Europe, Bob Gross set about organising a network of agents who could open the doors. One of the most important of them was a shrewd and articulate Dutchman, Fred Meuser, who had been running the KLM office in New York, where he had frequent contacts with Lockheed. Meuser had had a very cosmopolitan career: he had been at college in Switzerland, where he became a keen sportsman and skier, and he spoke several languages effortlessly. During the war he flew with the British Royal Air Force and after the war joined the new Dutch airline KLM, who had sent him to New York. American aircraft executives found him genial, though inscrutable, and for Gross he seemed a natural choice. He joined Lockheed, became a naturalised American citizen, and in 1954 was transferred to Geneva, to be Lockheed's director for Europe,

Africa and the Near East. He soon built up a network of what he called 'top-of-the-top contacts'.

To help him Meuser chose an old Swiss college friend, Hubert Weisbrod, an expert skier and amateur pilot who had practised international law in Zürich. Weisbrod was an invaluable ally. Much of Lockheed's subsequent success (Meuser boasted later in a characteristically high-flown letter) 'was in no small measure due to his expert counselling and behind-the-scenes pulling of strings. Hardly ever did Hubert appear in the open for the support of Lockheed's interests; practically all his constructive work was done discreetly, indirectly.'[1] What this meant, in plain language, was that Weisbrod was an ideal conduit for secret funds. As a lawyer Weisbrod had a special advantage, for in Switzerland lawyers like bankers are protected from investigation, and Weisbrod in spite of his travels remained 'a solid Swiss citizen'. Meuser and Weisbrod, with their discreet Swiss bank accounts, were soon at the hub of a Lockheed web extending from Geneva to Jakarta to Johannesburg. Swiss secrecy was to be critical for the whole system of Lockheed corruption.

Meuser also recruited an influential Dutch friend and old colleague from KLM to help in Lockheed's sales effort, a Resistance hero named Teengs Gerritsen. As a young man, Gerritsen had been a famous sportsman, an Olympic skier who also played soccer for Holland. In the Second World War he had stayed in Holland under the Nazi occupation, working as a British agent until he was captured, tortured, and nearly killed; his body was used in medical experiments that affected his health. After the war, in the twilight years when a new Holland was taking shape, he was very active in a club of ex-Resistance members, many of whom were now important in Dutch politics. On Fred Meuser's advice, Gerritsen was secretly hired as Lockheed's special consultant at a salary of $18,000 a year. Gerritsen knew little about airlines, except what he had picked up from KLM, and he never visited the Lockheed plant in California. The Americans came to him, as he later explained, because he had good contacts.[2]

Meuser and Gerritsen undoubtedly had many useful contacts, and Gerritsen had old friends in The Hague in the ministry of economics. But both of them had one contact who overshadowed all the rest, Prince Bernhard of the Netherlands. Gerritsen had

[1] Northrop Papers: Meuser to Tom Jones, August 10, 1974.
[2] *Vrij Nederland* interview by J. van Tijn, January 24, 1976.

first met the Prince before the war at an ice-hockey match, and after the war the Prince had sought him out as a Resistance hero, and befriended him. Fred Meuser was still closer; he had been a childhood playmate of Princess Juliana, who married Bernhard in 1937 and became Queen in 1948, and through Juliana he had also become the close confidant of the Prince. After the war the Prince spent holidays with Meuser and stayed with him in New York.

It was through Meuser that Robert Gross became acquainted in the early 'fifties with Prince Bernhard. The extrovert business-man-prince was already a world figure, with his wide smile, his white carnation and his perpetual business activities: in Holland he was not only director of the national airline, KLM, and scores of other companies, he was also Inspector-General of the Forces, and a kind of ambassador-at-large. His mixture of royal and commercial activities was welcomed by the Dutch; for he seemed to symbolise the marriage of the traditional House of Orange with dynamic commerce, and he was given a free rein by parliament to take on lucrative directorships.

The strains or conflicts of interest that might lie behind this dual role were not much discussed, for he was well trusted. It was true that he had grown up in Germany, as the son of an impoverished princeling; he had worked for the IG Farben chemical combine and had actually been a probationary member of the SS before the war. But that memory had been obliterated by his wartime career in Britain, where he was not only a pilot in one of the RAF's Dutch squadrons, but commander-in-chief of the Dutch forces abroad. It was in this grand capacity that he returned to Holland and received the German surrender; his mother-in-law Queen Wilhelmina wished him to remain as commander-in-chief, but was overruled by the parliament. The Prince remained a national symbol, associated with the Resistance and giving a new panache to the royal house. With his dashing style he was a natural salesman, whether for his country or for exporting companies, and he personified the Dutch commercial recovery: even some Britons, complaining about their own stuffy monarchy, envied the Dutch their queen's commercialised consort.

Bernhard was also very active in international organisations dedicated to the reconciliation of business and statesmanship. In 1954 he presided over a gathering of international businessmen and politicians at the rococo Bilderberg hotel outside Arnhem, to discuss global problems; and the subsequent annual Bilderberg conferences, held in different parts of the world under the Prince's chairmanship, soon acquired a special mystique as the meeting-place for bankers, statesmen and industrialists. Bilderberg conferences soon became a bogey for the left, for the participants were secretive and predominantly conservative: but they had no special policy, and were quite prepared to invite social democrats like Helmut Schmidt and Denis Healey. In 1961 Bernhard founded another high-flying organisation, the World Wildlife Fund, with support from international grandees and tycoons including Courtlandt Gross of Lockheed (Robert Gross's brother), Tom Jones of Northrop and his friend Fred Meuser; and as the protector of the world's animals the Prince appeared still more benign.

Behind these and other global get-togethers there was nothing very sinister; only the premise that what was good for the free world was good for international business, and vice-versa. They provided a prestigious setting in which tycoons could casually encounter politicians, and in this arena the Prince was in his element: he had the talent of the sophisticated public relations man, for bringing people together and putting them at their ease, with the added splendour and reassurance of his grand title.

The Prince had married into one of the richest families in Europe—a fact that helped to allay any worries among Dutchmen that he might be using his commercial activities for personal gain. But in fact he was kept on a short rein both by his wife, and by parliament, who allowed him up to $300,000 a year and a staff of only one male secretary—a meagre arrangement compared for instance with that of Prince Philip in Britain (likewise a prince without much money, married into a very rich family) who was allowed a personal staff of eight. Bernhard complained mildly about his position in an article for *Colliers* magazine in June 1953: 'We princes have financial problems of our own. Like many people these days, most of us have trouble in making ends meet. Some people think that kings and queens are still as rich as fabled King Midas. It isn't so.' His financial problems and ambitions were not much noticed by the Dutch, but they were soon well appreciated by Lockheed.

In fact Prince Bernhard was always having trouble making ends meet, for reasons that were not revealed to the Dutch public. To some ministers and newspaper editors it was well known that for many years the Prince's marriage to the Queen had had some difficulties, and that his extramarital activities had been extensive. Occasionally news of a girl-friend leaked out, and it became known much later that in the early 'sixties he had a mistress in Paris, Poupette, who had a young daughter; but the editors and the politicians were not inclined to pursue such stories at the time. With such discretion, few people were seriously worried by the Prince's private life; nor would it be relevant to the politics of Holland or Lockheed were it not for the fact that it was very expensive. The Prince looked after his friends and their children generously, and he could hardly ask the Queen for extra financial support. In the Prince's vulnerability, and the sham of his public morality, lay the opportunity for Lockheed and others; for what the state could not supply publicly, the Lockheed network could supply secretly. To well-placed businessmen in the 'sixties (a Lockheed executive assured me) 'it was common knowledge that the Prince was on the take'. If so, it was common knowledge well concealed from common people.

At the time the Lockheed network in Europe seemed to represent the very essence of the Atlanticist spirit, with agents who were both respectable and heroic; and while some of them were secret, they were secret in a grand cause. Lockheed at the time had a special aura, as the biggest defence company, with close links with intelligence: it had built the spectacular U2 spy plane at the special behest of Allen Dulles, the director of the CIA in the 'fifties, and the plane achieved sudden fame when it was shot down by the Russians in 1960, interrupting the summit conference. There were some suspicions that Lockheed's links with the CIA might go much deeper, into their operations and agents abroad; but this remained speculation.

The Lockheed agents made up a proud club, many of them with brave war records. In Belgium Lockheed hired another wartime RAF pilot, Jean-Pierre Bonsang. In London they hired Commander Michael Parker, the Australian naval officer who had been Prince Philip's private secretary and who now became an enthusiastic Lockheedian and a close colleague of Gerritsen. In the cold-war climate of that time, with Berlin still threatened, the selling of aircraft was part of the security of the West. The Lockheed people were helping to unify the West by standardising their aircraft, and for anyone inside the military-industrial complex, the business was a crusade.

THE STARFIGHTER

In the first post-war years the chief business of Lockheed in
Europe, as of Douglas and Boeing, had been selling commercial
airliners; and the Lockheed Constellations and Super-Constel-
lations had considerable success. But the formation of NATO and
the admission of West Germany into the alliance in 1955 soon
created a military export market without precedent in the history
of the industry. From the beginning NATO had agreed that new
weapons should wherever possible be standardised, which would
greatly increase the stakes of each contest. The prospect of common arms for a community of 200 million, on the same scale as
the United States and the Soviet Union, was a dazzling one—most
of all the prospect of a NATO fighter, which emerged after 1955.
In this contest Germany was the chief prize, for whereas first
Britain and later France had their own aircraft industries,
Germany had none; and whichever plane Germany chose was
likely to be followed by Holland, Belgium, Italy and others. The
German choice would thus affect the balance of the whole
Western aircraft industry.

By 1957 the three major Western aircraft-producing countries
were limbering up for the contest. Britain's fighters (to quote
Harold Macmillan) were 'in a sad state of confusion', and the
only likely British plane was a Saunders Roe fighter which only
existed as a mock-up on the Isle of Wight. But in France Dassault
had already developed his Mirage III, which had shown promise
in the Suez war. And the United States had several contenders:
the Super Tiger, made by the Grumman company on Long Island
(see chapter 14): the Northrop plane, the N-156F, the prototype
of the later Tiger (see next chapter) and the Starfighter, or F104,
which had been developed by Lockheed.

The Starfighter was the most spectacular candidate. It had been
designed by Lockheed's chief designer Kelly Johnson with a
pencil-thin fuselage and tiny wings only $7\frac{1}{2}$ feet long, and it was
called 'the missile with a man in it'. It could shoot up like a rocket
and fly at twice the speed of sound. Experienced pilots were
fascinated by it, but it was an unforgiving plane: it needed meti-
culous handling, and many Starfighters crashed during its
development. The United States air force after ordering a few

found them too unreliable, and sent their remaining planes to Taiwan and Pakistan. But Lockheed were all the more determined to sell the Starfighter to Europe, where they prepared an unprecedented foreign sales campaign. Their determination was intensified by their troubles at home. In 1957 they had suffered heavily from the cutbacks in defence spending in America which lost them $150 million in cancelled contracts in five months. Soon afterwards they faced another crisis when a succession of their new Electra airliners crashed from the skies; the wings had to be strengthened at huge cost, and Lockheed in the meantime lost out in the airliner race. Once again they looked to defence exports to rescue them.

To this financial incentive was added the zeal of a new leader who was soon to dominate the whole company. Daniel Jeremiah Haughton had already become a legendary name in Lockheed: he had run the Marietta plant in Georgia with a combination of cost-efficiency and tireless salesmanship. A country boy from Alabama, a coal-miner's son, he had emigrated to California in the depression, and in 1939 joined Lockheed as a systems analyst when few people knew what that meant. But he soon breathed the very spirit of aeronautic adventure; with his passionate evangelical style, he seemed almost to equate aircraft with universal salvation. Even in London, addressing hard-boiled civil servants, he had been observed to bring tears to their eyes: 'I had an alarming feeling,' said one normally sceptical Rolls-Royce executive, 'that if he told us to march out of the window, we would follow him.'

In 1956 Haughton became Lockheed's executive vice-president, with Robert Gross as chairman and his brother Courtlandt as president; but it was soon clear that Haughton was the driving force. He impregnated the whole corporation with his drive and devotion. He got up at four in the morning, and worked so hard that he needed two teams of secretaries and assistants working in shifts to keep up with him. At home he was devoted to his invalid wife, who suffered from multiple sclerosis. His style was hard-driving but disarming: he liked to wear his hat on the back of his head, and to mix gin rummy with business. In the industry his domination evoked both worship and bitter resentment. But the aviation industry depends on huge gambles and aggressive salesmanship, and tends to encourage autocracy.

Haughton inspired his Lockheedians to go abroad and sell their planes, and his drive and impatience pressed them to use whatever hard-selling methods they could employ. The Lockheed salesmen were in any case 'goal-orientated', convinced that the future of the corporation depended on them, and the instinct of the team quickly responded to the whip of the leader. But Haughton liked to insist that each man knew his precise responsibility: 'find me the man,' he would say, 'who thinks he'll be fired if he doesn't get the contract.'

By far the most important market for the Starfighter was Germany, on whose choice other countries' would very likely depend, and it was there Lockheed concentrated their first offensive. They had already established a well-connected agent called Günther Frank-Fahle, who before the war had worked, like Prince Bernhard, for the IG Farben combine, of which he had become a director. After the war Franke-Fahle had set up his own company, Deutsche Commerz, and in the mid-'fifties Lockheed took him on as their representative: he soon succeeded in selling Super Constellations to Lufthansa, the new German airline, against sharp competition from Douglas.

But to sell the Starfighter Lockheed also mounted a special invasion from California, and a team of twenty salesmen descended on the Kaiserhof hotel in Bonn to begin a long siege. For weeks they relentlessly lobbied the members of the Bundestag, gave parties, made speeches and presentations, and waited and waited in their long watch on the Rhine.

Bonn at that time was still a sleepy city with a modest life-style: the German economic miracle was only just beginning, and this Lockheed bandwagon, with its pressure and extravagance, appeared like a delegation from Eldorado. No other aircraft delegation could compare with it. The Grumman people were still very unfamiliar with Europe. The Dassault *équipe* enjoyed close support from the French embassy, but were prepared to make few concessions to the Germans. And the British maintained a take-it-or-leave-it attitude, showing reluctance to disclose too much about their chief candidate, the Saunders-Roe fighter. The man from Rolls-Royce (who would make the engines) drove around in his Rolls-Royce car and made stately statements: to the watching journalists he seemed not so much a salesman as the ambassador from Derby. After the first lobbying was over, there were soon only two serious contenders, Dassault and Lockheed.

Their ultimate target was the minister of defence, Franz-Josef

Strauss, who had taken office in 1956 determined to build up Germany's forces into a powerful component of NATO. This outspoken Bavarian, with his bullying, knockabout style, expressed all the released energy of Germany re-armed, but his foreign policy was ambiguous. In the past he had been an American protégé; he was let out of a prison camp in the American zone to become an interpreter and later district commissioner, and he had many American friends. But Strauss also wanted to build up a strong Paris-Bonn axis within the new European Common Market; and he was constantly torn between Washington and Paris. (When I later asked him which he would choose, he replied: 'Do you choose between your shirt and your underpants?')

The choice of a fighter would be a critical watershed. Strauss's Francophile mood inclined him towards Dassault, as the foundation of a Franco-German technological alliance; but he was also obsessed with American technology, and wanted to make Germany part of a nuclear strike force. And the very complexity and danger of the Starfighter was a challenge to the revived German Luftwaffe. In the words of Strauss himself: 'Forbidden to fly military aircraft for eleven years after World War Two, we had to call on a brave, young generation to literally plunge into a new and complex equipment, instruction and weapon systems in one long, all-encompassing jump'.[1] Just how brave, was not apparent till later.

By the fall of 1958 Strauss had decided to choose the Starfighter. By December the Bundestag had ratified his decision, and in March 1959 the contract was signed for the first 96 planes. In the next two years other countries followed: Holland, Belgium, Italy, Canada, Japan. It was a triumph both for Lockheed, and for standardisation. The planes were all produced in Europe, through co-production agreements which gave work to European factories and helped to provide a base for European aircraft technology; in Germany the famous pre-war companies Messerschmitt and Heinkel led a consortium to make the Starfighters outside Munich. But while the factories were in Europe the technological future lay more than ever across the Atlantic. For Lockheed it was a victory not only against the French, but against their Ameri-

---

[1] Franz-Josef Strauss: *The decision to go with the Starfighter*. From *Those Wonderful Men in the Cactus Starfighter Squadron*, Los Angeles: Litton Industries, 1976, p. 15.

can rivals. In the next fifteen years over three thousand Starfighters were to be built.

It is tempting to speculate how different might have been the
subsequent development of Europe if the French plane had been
chosen instead of the American; a common European fighter
might have brought much else in its flight path, in terms of technical and political collaboration, providing the basis for a much
more competitive industry independent of America. As it was,
the French and British companies were to be left on their own,
and increasingly out-distanced by the Americans.

But the Europeans' reasons for choosing the Starfighter seemed
logical enough. Whatever the technical arguments, the American
connection still loomed large in the mind of Germany and
Strauss. Once Germany had chosen, the smaller countries had
pressing reasons to follow, and they always feared that if they did
not buy American, the Americans would lose interest in defending
them. The American embassies were rooting strongly for Lockheed; and when the Dutch government were faced with the
choice they were told that 'if a European machine was procured,
there was no need to count on American support'.[1] But at the
same time Lockheed had been operating in the shadows, in order
to take no chances. There were many observers and journalists in
Bonn at the time who suspected, or assumed, that large sums of
money were changing hands; in Germany, Lockheed was clearly
desperate to get the contract, and in the climate of the time many
politicians on the make expected to be *honoriert* or 'seen right'.
Many rumours were circulating, then and later, about the flow of
money into party funds. But the account that follows restricts
itself to the evidence provided by personal testimony, company
documents and official reports.

About the same time that the Dutch government had chosen
the Starfighter, at the end of 1959, Fred Meuser from Switzerland
suggested to Lockheed that they might present his friend Prince
Bernhard with a Lockheed JetStar executive plane, then worth
about a million dollars. The suggestion, Lockheed later insisted,
was not linked to the Starfighter deal; it was inspired by the
relationship of many years' standing between Robert Gross and
the Prince, and was designed to create 'a favourable atmosphere
for the sale of Lockheed products in Holland'. The idea was

---

[1] Report of the 'Commission of Three' (Donner Report), The Hague, August 26,
1976, English translation, chapter 3, p. 9.

discussed in Burbank; Gross was in favour of it but Haughton (according to his own later account) was never sympathetic, and Lockheed eventually turned it down because the gift would be 'fraught with great tactical difficulties'.[1]

Soon afterwards, early in 1960, Fred Meuser came up with another idea: that the Prince should be given a million dollars instead. Meuser pointed out to Lockheed that Bernhard had many personal and charitable commitments, and the sum could be justified as a commission on the Starfighters that would be delivered over the following three years. Robert Gross again approved, and asked Meuser and his Swiss colleague Hubert Weisbrod to arrange it. On September 2 Gross himself met the Prince in Rome and on September 26 one of Lockheed's lawyers, Roger Bixby Smith, called at the royal palace of Soestdijk, where the Prince explained how the million dollars should be paid through Weisbrod in Switzerland.

Four days later Roger Smith met with a remarkable intermediary, at the Hotel Dolder in Zürich: he was Colonel Pantchoulidzew, a White Russian who had become very intimate with the Prince's mother, and who was even rumoured to have married her. The colonel gave Roger Smith a slip of paper with the number of a bank account; and thereafter successive sums were transferred by Lockheed into that account: first $300,000 in October 1960; then $300,000 in 1961 and then $400,000 in 1962. Exactly where the money ended up is still not proven; but there is little doubt that it was intended for Prince Bernhard or his family.

In the meantime Fred Meuser had received his own recompense in connection with the Starfighter sale, in the form of 3.6 million Deutschmark (equivalent to about $900,000 at the time) as his commission for the sale of the first ninety-six planes. Lockheed sources now maintain that Meuser's commission was simply a routine one, in his capacity as head of the Geneva office; and that he had no effect at all on the Starfighter deal, which was secured by the team from California. But Meuser, we know, was employed partly for his secret 'top of the top contacts'; and he has himself never disclosed the nature of his true services.[2]

An even more shadowy figure came into the foreground after

---

[1] Donner Report, chapter 2, p. 3.

[2] The Donner Report stressed that 'Mr Meuser, a very important witness, was not willing to open his books'. (chapter 1, p. 4.)

the Starfighter sale. In 1960 Robert Gross in California had received a letter from Strauss asking him if he could find a job for an old friend of his, Ernest Hauser, an Austro-American former intelligence officer who had given him his first job when he came out of his prison camp. Gross passed the letter to Haughton, who passed it to the German office, who threw it away: but soon afterwards Gross met Strauss in Germany. Strauss pressed him again, and Hauser was accordingly given a job in 'customer relations' in Lockheed's office in Koblenz. Hauser became quite a familiar figure in Bonn, a talkative and extravagant man, impressing journalists with his friendship with Strauss, who was his son's godfather. According to Lockheed men, Hauser was a very difficult employee, always intriguing and ultimately counter-productive: he left Lockheed after three years, and went on to sell helicopters and to be charged with forging documents, whereupon he left Germany for America. But Hauser himself, in his much later statements and his published diary, alleged among many other things that Strauss's party had been given $12 million by Lockheed. His evidence and diaries have been found very unreliable,[1] and the gift has never been substantiated. But the fact remains that Hauser provided a personal link between Lockheed and Strauss, at the time when the sales of Starfighter planes were still continuing.

The back-door role of Prince Bernhard and Fred Meuser remained undisclosed for the following fifteen years. But the public Lockheed lobbying offensive in Germany, in the wake of the first Starfighter sales, soon aroused bitter resentments. By 1962 Strauss had resigned, after the furore caused by his raid on the *Spiegel* magazine, and he was succeeded as minister of defence by Kai-Uwe von Hassel. Germany was now moving towards closer relations with France, and agreed to build a joint Franco-German transport plane, the Transall. Lockheed, however, were determined to sell the Germans their own Hercules transport, and unleashed a new lobbying offensive on the Bundestag with such relentless tactics that von Hassel publicly accused them of deliberately using false statistics, declaring that 'those Lockheed rogues will never get into my office again.'[2] Von Hassel not only persisted with the Transall project, but delayed an order for further Starfighter trainers, and demanded an apology from Courtlandt

[1] Donner Report, chapter 2, p. 13.
[2] *Time Magazine*, November 22, 1963.

Gross (who had now taken over as chairman of Lockheed on Robert's death from cancer). Gross duly apologised, but the distrust of Lockheed still remained.

For the Starfighter programme was now beginning to go very wrong, after the first fighters had been delivered in May 1961. The German Luftwaffe, in their technological zeal, had insisted on overloading it with equipment which made it much heavier and more complex than the original model; and the German pilots, even after an extensive training in Arizona, were not fully experienced. The Starfighter, in the words of General Steinhoff, then Inspector of the Luftwaffe, 'was forever jealous of the pilot's full attention. It rewarded discipline with deeds of airmanship; it could punish the dilatory or those who gave themselves to distractions. It was a marvel in capable hands, and merciless to the careless'.[1] The mercilessness soon showed itself. In the following seven years up to December 1968 ninety-one Starfighters crashed. The plane became notorious as the 'flying coffin', or the 'widow-maker', and the Starfighter widows themselves became an angry anti-Lockheed lobby. With each series of crashes the original choice of the Starfighters became more contentious, and by the time of the 1966 election the Starfighter scandal played a role in the fall of the Chancellor, Ludwig Erhard.

What role bribes or commissions may have played in clinching the Starfighter decision will never be fully known, for when Strauss left the ministry of defence all the relevant papers were destroyed. The part played by Bernhard remains also obscure. The Prince told the subsequent Donner Commission that Robert Gross had originally offered him the million-dollar plane 'because he was satisfied that Lockheed had been able to sign a contract to provide Germany with the Starfighters'.[2] But at the same time, as the next chapter shows, the Prince was active in promoting the Starfighter's American rival. The Donner Report found that in the Dutch procurement of the Starfighter there was 'no evidence of improper attempts by the aircraft industry to influence the decision-making':[3] and undoubtedly Bernhard and Meuser were both to some extent bluffing Lockheed with the magic of monarchy, pretending to more influence than they had. Later glimpses of Lockheed's tactics, whether in Europe, Japan

[1] *Those Wonderful Men*, p. 29.
[2] Donner Report, Annexe A.
[3] Donner Report, chapter 3, p. 117.

or the Middle East, will suggest a consistent gullibility and willingness to pay out money. As one Lockheed executive put it to me: 'we never knew who might be blocking us, with his foot across the road; and with such big contracts, we couldn't afford to risk being blocked.' Yet for all Lockheed's naivety, the size of the payments to Bernhard, and their continuation over the years to come, suggest solid grounds for gratitude.

But the commissions and bribes were in any case only one part of Lockheed's relentless commercial pressure, backed by a diplomatic offensive; Lockheed were able to offer Germany the co-production of sophisticated aircraft on a scale which the French could not equal. The Lockheed bandwagon, with its outriders of commission-men and agents, was only part of a great re-arming crusade dedicated to linking Europe indissolubly with America. The Europeans, unprepared effectively to unite their industries or defend themselves, were an easy target. The corruption of European politicians and officials was only part of a deeper malaise on a continent which looked towards America both for protection and spoils.

As for the effectiveness of the Starfighter in the defence of Europe, no one will ever know. It was never proved in battle, whether in Europe, Vietnam or the Middle East. By the mid-'seventies it was already being replaced, and its place in history rests less on its performance than its scandals.

FROM BRIBERY TO EXTORTION

It was not until the late 'sixties that Lockheed were again stomping through Europe with a high-pressure sales campaign. By 1967 Courtlandt Gross had retired from Lockheed to return with some relief to Philadelphia, and Dan Haughton had taken over as chairman. The patrician era was now finally closed and Haughton, with his passionate drive, was surrounded by a group of like-minded enthusiasts, many of them also imported to Burbank from the South, known to the Californians as the 'Southern Bloc'. Haughton flew constantly between California, Washington and Georgia, whipping up enthusiasm, scrutinising costs, and ensuring political support. His style was moralistic, but not scrupulous: he liked always to seek out the responsible sales-man, but he did not question too closely the way in which business was done. He knew that his company was getting more deeply involved in corruption: 'though I didn't know every detail, I knew many of them,' he said later, 'and I could have known them all.'[1]

Haughton rarely travelled abroad, except to Britain, and he was not really at ease with the snobberies of Europe ('I ordered a bottle of Château d'Yquem 1947,' complained one European Lockheed executive, 'and he put some ice in it'). He left the international business largely to the new president, Carl Kotchian. A farmer's son from North Dakota, Kotchian was a heavy, broad-shouldered man with a down-turned mouth, which turned suddenly into a surprising smile. He was regarded by most Lockheed men as Haughton's shadow; like his boss he was an accountant, who had worked diligently under him in Georgia. But Kotchian was also assertive. As one salesman put it: 'Haughton always played the country boy act—"we're only here to pay the rent"—but when you left him you had to make sure you'd still got five fingers. Kotchian always liked you to know he was clever.' Kotchian was more directly responsible for weaving the web of Lockheed agents abroad, which was eventually to entangle him. He had already some glimpse of corruption before joining Lockheed, when he had worked for an oil company which kept $100,000 available in cash for day-to-day pay-offs; and within Lockheed he had inherited Bob Gross's network. Kotchian saw bribes straightforwardly as part of the cost of doing business abroad, and he was worried only by the return on the investment. He reckoned he could smell corruption, he explained, and he smelt it in most countries, except Britain, Canada, New Zealand and a few others. In Britain, influence was more snobbish.

In his constant travels, Kotchian had found himself meeting many world figures, including Prince Bernhard, Franz-Josef Strauss and many Middle Eastern leaders—some of whom he was secretly paying. But he preserved some of the detachment of the North Dakotan. In the aerospace tradition he liked to throw big parties wherever he arrived: but he did not enjoy close friendships with foreign leaders who were indebted to him, as Bob Gross had done, or as Tom Jones of Northrop was doing (see next chapter). Kotchian met Prince Bernhard abroad, but not in Holland: he felt it somehow unclean to have a public friendship with a secret agent.

Kotchian's activities abroad were the more frenzied because,

[1] Multinational Hearings, part 12, p. 371.

after 1967, Lockheed's position at home was becoming more perilous. They were now the biggest arms company in the world; the Starfighter had made them the biggest exporters of arms technology, and the Vietnam war had brought a new boom. But their size only made them more vulnerable: they were still on the roller-coaster, and by 1967 they were having wrangles with the Pentagon over their giant transport, the Galaxy, and growing difficulties with their projected airliner, the TriStar (see chapter 12). Lockheed looked to the old world to redress the balance of the new. But the European scene too was becoming more competitive, and the Lockheed salesmen were wading deeper into the muddy waters of corruption. The mud came from both shores. While the Americans were relentless, impatient and often naive, their European agents were wily and grasping, and quite prepared to rob both the company and their own governments. It was, after all, a boom time for Europe; the aerospace band-wagons carried with them all the excitement and permissiveness of big spending and pay-offs.

It was in Italy, not surprisingly, that Lockheed found itself in the murkiest European waters: for in Rome in the mid-'sixties the Italian boom was at full pressure, and the political parties and their agents were without scruple in exacting their full tribute, particularly from foreign companies. The CIA had set a pattern of secretly financing the parties, which the companies followed, and the aircraft companies with their huge single deals provided special opportunities. To some Italians it seemed almost an act of patriotism to fleece the Americans, who did not seem to mind; but in fact they were fleecing their own people.

Lockheed moved into Italy in strength at the beginning of 1969, in an aggressive frame of mind. They had just failed to sell their Orion naval reconnaissance planes in Holland, where they had lost out to the Bréguet Atlantic plane, which they believed had won through bribery[1]—though the Atlantic had the more obvious advantage of being made by a NATO consortium, with a Dutch chairman. The Lockheed team then progressed to Rome, to try to sell their Orions there; but again they lost out to Bréguet. They now put all their hopes on selling the Italians their Hercules transports—the huge long-range cargo planes which were indispensable in the Vietnam war, but of doubtful benefit to a small country like Italy. Lockheed were specially

[1] Ibid., part 14, p. 378.

anxious to sell Hercules because they needed to keep the production-line in Georgia busy, and they were 'running out of lead time': and Kotchian himself came to Rome to lead his team's campaign.

After the failure to sell the Orion, one of the Lockheed team, Don Wilder, was approached by an Italian senator in Rome who advised him to employ a local consultant, and Kotchian accordingly took on an agent, Ovidio Lefebvre: he was a lawyer who had been an old colleague of Giovanni Leone (later president of Italy) and who ran an agency with his brother Antonio. Ovidio Lefebvre, said Kotchian, was 'one of the finest gentlemen I have run into in the world', but one day, driving in Rome, Ovidio told Kotchian: 'I'm embarrassed, and I'm just chagrined, but I'm going to have to recommend to you that you make some payments if you wish to sell airplanes in this country.'[1] The payments were, for the most part, to go to the ministry of defence, evidently for the minister's political party, the Christian Democrats. Kotchian at first was not too concerned; he thought that Lefebvre's fees were reasonable 'as consultants go' in the context of an expected sale of fourteen of the giant planes, worth $60 million; and he authorised the payments quickly, in view of the urgent need to fill the order-book for Georgia.[2] But before long the demands were increasing, as they so often did. Kotchian returned to California leaving the negotiations in the hands of Roger Bixby Smith, the lawyer who had first handled Prince Bernhard nine years earlier. Roger Smith was now working for Coudert Brothers, the law firm in Paris, where he was still retained by Lockheed: but in spite of his past high-level experience, he was surprisingly indiscreet. In March 1969 he wrote an anxious letter, from the Grand Hotel in Rome to Lockheed in Georgia, which was probably more devastating than any other single document in the Lockheed files. He explained ('please hold on to your seat-belt') that Lockheed's agent Lefebvre might now need $120,000 for each Hercules aircraft that was sold—because, he went on, he had to outbid the French and German bribes. The Italian agent, Ovidio Lefebvre, he explained, would not participate in the Hercules deal, but 'will be informed, probably by Antelope Cobbler, how much the Italian side wants'; and he then added: 'Get out your little black book—mine is dated

[1] Ibid., part 14, pp. 380–2 (Kotchian's testimony).
[2] Ibid., p. 383.

October 15, 1965'. The black book referred to the Lockheed code book, which provided the translation: Antelope meant Italy, and Cobbler meant premier.

Roger Smith wrote in his own handwriting, to avoid the danger of leakage, but it was an ironic example of Lockheed's insistence on writing everything down: an insistence that has come to embarrass so many American companies, from ITT to Exxon. 'I really should not be putting even the foregoing in writing,' Smith explained, 'but I have no choice . . . I hope you keep this letter on a very strict need-to-know basis . . .'. He realised that Lockheed was dealing with dynamite, which (as he put it in his letter) 'could blow Lockheed right out of Italy'.[1] But his bosses agreed to pay the bribe and the money was duly paid through a discreet company in Panama with the innocent-sounding name of the Temperate Zone Research Foundation[2] (one of the many fronts for Lockheed bribes which posed as charitable institutions).

The payments duly had their effect: due to Lefebvre's efforts, as Lockheed recorded, the contract for the Hercules 'progressed through the complicated Italian approval cycle in record time'. But there were still delays and complications. The minister of defence was changed, and the new one also needed payment: he was promised $50,000 when the price of the plane was put up in December 1970. A Lockheed memo early in 1971 stressed the urgency of a further payment, to get the minister to sign the contract, and Lockheed were now fearful that the government might fall: 'the last thing we want is a new government and a new set of players at this stage of the game'. As a result, a further sum of $765,000 was pushed through, and the contract was at last signed, for the fourteen planes. The total payments were reckoned at two million dollars, of which $1.7 million went to 'promotional expenses'; and a Lockheed footnote pointed out that more than eighty-five percent of that was 'for the minister's political party   past and present'.[3] But that total, according to Kotchian, was not exorbitant; for an order worth $60 million, a commission of three to four percent was quite normal;[4] and the cost of paying it had been taken into account in the price.

[1] Lockheed Papers: Smith to Valentine, March 28, 1969.
[2] Multinational Hearings, part 14, pp. 52–3.
[3] Ibid., pp. 23–27.
[4] Ibid., p. 379.

Whether either Italy or NATO really needed the planes remains very doubtful. But the deal suited the agents and it suited the ministers, and it suited Lockheed.

Lockheed's bribery was often blundering, without much guarantee of success. A comic example occurred in Germany in 1971. A Lockheed executive, Norman Orwat, described how he had just dined with Lockheed's new agent in Düsseldorf, Christian Steinrücke, who had taken over from the veteran Günther Frank-Fahle. The new agent was well-connected, related to the Adenauer family, and married to a rich wife. Orwat was very impressed: it was a magnificent mansion, Mrs Steinrücke was a 'lovely lady', and the dinner party for sixteen was as 'splendidly presented as any I have attended in Europe'. Among the guests were Dr Mommsen, a former deputy minister of defence, who was a close friend of Steinrücke's, and Vice-Admiral Kuhnle, the chief of the German navy. 'I am told—and I can believe it!' explained Orwat, 'that Germans seldom turn down a dinner invitation from the Steinrückes.'[1] But the Lockheed people were rather too dazzled. Steinrücke asked them for $8,000 to bribe political parties, in order to persuade the West German Bundesbank to buy some Lockheed JetStar executive planes. But Steinrücke (according to an official statement from the Bonn government in February 1976)[2] kept the money for himself, and the Bundesbank never bought the planes. Like other episodes from the Lockheed dossier, it raised the question: who was corrupting whom?

In Holland in the meantime Prince Bernhard was becoming increasingly involved with Lockheed by the late 'sixties. Lockheed's payments of the million dollars from 1961 had encouraged them to make further approaches to the Prince, and in 1967 they again felt in need of his help. Lockheed were trying to sell their naval reconnaissance plane, the P3 Orion, to Holland against stiff competition from their French rival, Bréguet, and Lockheed asked Bernhard to try to delay the decision until their offer could be properly presented, which Bernhard appeared to achieve. But by July 1968 the Lockheed plane had been turned down in favour of the French, and Lockheed were convinced that the French had been offering bribes.[3] The Prince expressed his regret, but

[1] Lockheed Papers: Orwat to Egan, July 9, 1973.
[2] *International Herald Tribune*, February 12, 1976.
[3] See p. 134.

promised to try to persuade Dutch members of parliament, who
still had to approve it. Kotchian then sent the invaluable Roger
Smith to Annecy in France, to call on the Prince and offer him
half a million dollars to try to reverse the decision. The Prince
said that the decision could not be changed, and refused the offer,
but Kotchian still wanted to show his appreciation. Two months
later Roger Smith met the Prince again, this time on the De Pan
golf links near Utrecht, and gave him a letter of thanks from
Kotchian, together with a new offer of $100,000 as a token. Later
a cheque for $100,000 was sent to a Swiss bank, in the name of
Victor Baarn (Baarn being the district of the Dutch royal palace):
the cheque was cashed, though the Prince denied having received
it.[1]

By the early 'seventies, when he was over sixty, Prince
Bernhard was apparently in more urgent need of money, and it
was he who was now making the approaches. By 1974 the sale
of the Orion planes was at last expected to go through, and Fred
Meuser wrote to the Prince suggesting in careful language that a
four percent commission should be paid, ostensibly for the benefit
of the World Wildlife Fund. With extraordinary rashness, the
Prince then sent two handwritten letters to Roger Smith, who
had arranged his first payments fourteen years earlier. They were
written in bad English in a crude, threatening style. In the first
he explained how 'after a hell of a lot of pushing and pulling' there
was now a good prospect of the Orion sale, and put forward the
request for a commission—which would amount, it turned out,
to between four and six million dollars. Roger Smith then met
the Prince in Paris, and explained that that was too much, to
which the Prince replied that he had only had in mind about a
million.

Then the Prince wrote a second letter, complaining bitterly
that his idea had been rejected without discussion. This would
never have happened, he said, in the days of Robert or Courtlandt
Gross. 'Since 1968 I have in good faith spent a lot of time and
effort to push things the right way in critical areas and times and
have tried to prevent wrong decisions influenced by political
considerations. I have done this based on my old friendship with
Lockheed—and based on past actions. So I do feel a little bitter.'
He would do no more to help Lockheed with the Orions, and
was planning to ring up Courtlandt Gross, now retired in

[1] Donner Report, chapter 2, pp. 13-15.

Philadelphia. This embarrassing letter was passed on to California, where it soon made an impression: Roger Smith was told to visit the Prince again at the royal palace in December 1974, where he proposed to pay him a million dollars if four aircraft were bought. The Prince quickly agreed, and proposed that the money should be paid into a special bank account in Geneva: there was now no suggestion of it going to the World Wildlife Fund. But soon afterwards the Dutch government decided once again to postpone the purchase of the planes, and in the end the payment never went through.[1]

Those two handwritten letters marked the squalid climax of the relationship between the Prince and the company. The Prince's brazen demands, and his growing appetite behind his public dignity, were not unlike those of Spiro Agnew, who had recently been caught receiving bribes as vice-president in Washington. The first offer of a plane to the Prince fourteen years earlier, had been extravagant, but it was (as the Donner Commission described it) 'a conceivable gesture'. But when the offer was translated into secret money, Lockheed immediately had a hold on the Prince, which they were able to exploit by making improper requests, while the Prince's appetites increased and the relationship changed from bribery to extortion. There was no convincing evidence, in fact, that the 'pushing and pulling' by the Prince had achieved any definite results for Lockheed, and the subsequent investigations into the Dutch procurement policies suggested that the decisive factors had been technical, reinforced by the importance of the Atlantic alliance. The Donner Report saw no indication that the Prince 'defended interests in the procurement policy which were not in line with the Netherlands' interests as he saw them'. But how, in fact, did the Prince see his country's interests? Lockheed had succeeded all too easily in their first aim to 'create a favourable atmosphere'; and the Prince's corruption revealed the ugly underside of the transatlantic boom. Behind all the panoply of the royal patronage of Bilderberg and the World Wildlife Fund, and the assumption of common interest between business and the free world, was a greedy arms dealer desperate for money.

How far the Lockheed–Bernhard connection was part of an extended pattern on both sides throughout Europe will probably never be known. Certainly the Bernhard story cannot be ex-

[1] Donner Report, chapter 2, pp. 15–17.

plained simply by the ruthlessness of a single company; it suggests rather a tree of rotten fruit, waiting to be shaken into any company's lap. And even within the arms business, the Prince was not confining his interests to Lockheed. Throughout this period, as we will see in the next chapter, he was secretly working for Lockheed's principal rivals.

7

Northrop and the
Renaissance Man

I am somewhat amazed at what might be identified as the irre-
sponsibility that exists within corporations.
Senator Clark to Thomas V. Jones, June 1975.[1]

THE Northrop Corporation on the other side of Los Angelet
from Lockheed was much smaller and less famous than its gians
rival, with no great scandals attached to it; but by the early
'sixties it was beginning to make its mark in the world as a
successful exporter of fighters. The company had first been set
up in 1939 by the brilliant engineer Jack Northrop who had been
one of the co-founders of Lockheed, and had produced some
historic planes, including the 'Black Widow' night-fighter of the
Second World War, and the 'Flying Wing', which had no body
at all. Jack Northrop had a golden reputation: he set up a technical college in Los Angeles (now Northrop University) and even
had an Antarctic outpost, Cape Northrop, named after him. But
he was not an administrator or money-man, and by the 'fifties he
had left his company in financial disarray. 'Everyone who knew
Jack Northrop,' it was said, 'could work at anything he liked.'

In 1960 this easy-going company came under the control of a
new chief executive officer, Thomas V. Jones, who was then only
forty. He was a handsome and stylish figure with a strong chin
and an easy charm. The son of a Californian accountant, he had

[1] Multinational Hearings, part 12, p. 149.

won a scholarship to Stanford University and graduated in engineering: he worked for Douglas during the war, then spent four years working in Brazil, then joined the Rand Corporation, the air force think-tank in Santa Monica. From there he joined Northrop and rose rapidly to be first planning officer, then president, then chief executive. He soon rationalised the company, concentrating on the profitable lines which Northrop, as a relatively small company, could do best. He knew the company could not compete on all fronts with the giants like Lockheed, and he turned to making specialised parts for other companies. He scrapped an expensive programme for a Mach 3 interceptor, and instead developed a cheap jet trainer. He built up a team of highly-motivated engineers, and organised them with an economy and decisiveness comparable with that of Dassault in France.

Surveying the domestic competition around him, Jones saw Northrop's special opportunity in selling for export, at a time when the Pentagon was putting its weight behind arms sales. Encouraged by Henry Kuss in the Pentagon, he pushed forward with building a small, relatively cheap fighter which he had developed from the jet trainer. The Tiger, as it was to be called, was a sharp-nosed twin-engined plane which was uniquely versatile, whether for Europe or the Third World. It took off with a sexy roar, like a thousand motorbikes; it could fly at Mach 1.4 at 35,000 feet, and then zoom down to fly just above the ground, terrifying tribesmen. More seriously, it could carry missiles on its wing-tips and 20mm guns in the fuselage nose. It was cheaper and safer than the Starfighter, and it was custom-built for the Pentagon's programme of Foreign Military Sales (FMS). For Northrop, it was the chief source of profits for fifteen years.

Tom Jones was soon acclaimed as one of the 'Renaissance Men' of the 'sixties, and a luminary of Los Angeles.[1] He had, like Bob Gross, a wide range of interests and contacts: he had married the daughter of an early movie actor, Conrad Nagel (the star of *Midsummer Madness*), and he moved into a spacious ranch-style house near Bel Air, on the edge of the mountains, which once belonged to the movie mogul King Vidor. He gave Brazilian-style barbecues, and collected modern French paintings; he was a connoisseur of French vineyards and bottled wine at his home. He became a trustee of Stanford University and a director of the

[1] See for instance *Newsweek*, November 18, 1963.

Los Angeles Times. He belonged to the World Affairs Council, and made thoughtful speeches about the communist threat. Like Bob Gross before him, he appeared as an aristocrat in an upstart industry.

But Jones was a driven man, single-minded in his pursuit of money and power. Within the company he increasingly dominated every department, concealing his dealings from his board— and with good reason. For he exerted every possible pressure, legal or illegal, in pursuit of his profits. Northrop had previously practised a 'hands-off' policy towards politics, but Jones was convinced that the keys to success lay in Washington and in the capitals of the free world. He was persuaded that his rivals, particularly Lockheed and Dassault, had their own secret leverage, and he would not be outdone. He appointed one of his colleagues, Jimmy Allen—who had once done public relations for Rand— as vice-president for public relations, which in effect meant very private relations. And with his help he gradually built up the secret Northrop network.

In 1961 Tom Jones hired (through Jimmy Allen) a French lawyer in Paris, called Bill Savy, who ran several agencies, including one called Euradvice and another called Wilco. Savy was a man of the world. He had been an intelligence officer, used for several investigations into the US aerospace industry. He had worked for European companies, including Rolls-Royce, and had arranged foreign loans for individuals and corporations. Jones met Savy, and agreed 'to enter a working relationship'. Savy's ostensible job was simply to act as a 'window' to inform Northrop about European affairs, but Northrop (according to Allen's account) was soon being hard pressed to make political contributions in Washington, and within three or four years, if not earlier, Bill Savy was acting as a 'conduit', or in plainer terms as a laundry, to provide cash to pay politicians in Washington. To this end, over the following thirteen years, Savy was paid over a million dollars in 'consulting fees' by Northrop: Savy would collect the money from his Paris bank in $100 bills, up to $40,000 a time, and would divide it between his coat pockets. Loaded with cash he would then fly to New York (about six times a year), where Jimmy Allen would pick it up, in a big manila envelope, from Savy's hotel room.[1] The cash would then be

[1] Northrop Papers: Ernst and Ernst interview with Tom Jones, June 26, 1974. Northrop Executive Committee: Special Report, July 16, 1975, p. 45.

delivered to influential Washington politicians. It was a round-about route, but it was safe: the Paris laundry was well-hidden from auditors or taxmen.

Jones was also determined to establish high-level contacts in Europe. Being a small California company, and non-commercial (he explained later), 'you had to know the industrial, political and economic policies of the country . . . you can't force an issue, but have to keep in touch and be prepared to act once the clouds open.'[1]

He already had some very useful connections in Europe, and following on the trail of Bob Gross of Lockheed he had got to know Prince Bernhard of the Netherlands; Bernhard even wrote to him to ask him to help his friend Teengs Gerritsen, who was in need of $10,000.[2] In the late 'fifties the Prince, while he was so friendly with Lockheed, was really being more helpful to Northrop, which was promoting the prototype of the Tiger—then called the N156—as a rival to the Starfighter. By 1957 Bernhard was writing at length to the American secretary for the air force, Donald A. Quarles, urging the standardisation of NATO planes and recommending a simple, cheap plane; and he suggested that the Tiger seemed an obvious choice (indeed it might well have been more sensible than the Starfighter). The Prince also advised Tom Jones about how best to approach the Dutch government, and he arranged a meeting between Northrop's man in Paris, Geoffrey Parsons, and the Dutch minister of defence, S. H. Visser. But by this time in fact, the Dutch had already turned down the Tiger.[3]

Tom Jones was able to develop his friendship with Bernhard three years later when the Dutch Fokker aircraft company, of which Bernhard was a director, was looking for an American partner. Lockheed turned down the proposal because they thought it could not be profitable; but Northrop agreed to buy a twenty percent share, which gave Jones a seat on the Fokker board, alongside Prince Bernhard. Both gregarious men, they became personal friends.

Jones was determined to play Lockheed's game with Lockheed's tricks, and in the early 'sixties he proceeded also to engage the

---

[1] Northrop Papers, June 26, 1974.

[2] *The Times*, London, September 3, 1976.

[3] Report of the 'Commission of Three' (Donner Report), The Hague, August 26, 1976, English translation, chapter 3, p. 15. The Commission wrongly describes Quarles as Defence Secretary in 1958, when he had already resigned.

services of the wily Fred Meuser in Switzerland, who was boasting that he had helped to sell the Starfighter through Europe. Meuser was recommended to Jones (Jones later explained) 'by prominent European businessmen and government officials',[1] but probably the chief proposer was Bernhard. Jones consulted Meuser about how best to sell his Tiger fighters and Meuser recommended the employment of his undercover Swiss associate, Hubert Weisbrod. Weisbrod was also working for Lockheed, but Meuser argued that the two companies were not really competing, and certainly the two agents showed no apparent loyalty to Lockheed. Meuser even showed Jones the contract that Lockheed had given Weisbrod, which Jones then used as a model for his own contract. Weisbrod was to be paid no less than $125,000 a year, and in the following years he received altogether $750,000 in Northrop funds.

Jones professed himself well pleased with Weisbrod's efforts: he helped Northrop in selling Tigers in Europe and in raising European financing for their new Cobra programme.[2] 'As a result of Dr Weisbrod's activities,' Jones explained afterwards, 'Northrop has had an unusual visibility into the highest councils of NATO, the Common Market community, and the many official and unofficial discussions in Europe. . . .' The subsequent investigation by the auditors 'could find no credible evidence that Northrop received any benefit': but in view of Weisbrod's close connections with Prince Bernhard and the Lockheed parallel, it is difficult to believe that the money remained with Weisbrod.[3]

Prince Bernhard remained a close ally of Tom Jones and he showed his usefulness in 1965, six years after the first Starfighter sale, when Northrop were trying to sell their Tiger fighters to Holland. Dutch air force officers were soon made aware that the Prince, as the Inspector-General, 'had a decided interest' in the Northrop plane: he wrote to the US air force in late 1965 to ask about the Tiger's performance in Vietnam and when the Dutch defence officials held two meetings to evaluate the plane, the Prince, contrary to his usual custom, insisted on being present. The Dutch government, on their side, were glad to make use of his contacts, and when there were arguments about the payment

---

[1] Northrop Special Report, p. 14.

[2] See chapter 15.

[3] Northrop Special Report, pp. 14–16. Northrop Papers: Tom Jones to E. R. Crim, September 1974.

of royalties, the Prince was asked to contact first McNamara at the Pentagon, and then Tom Jones, to argue the Dutch case.[1] Eventually the Tigers were bought through Canada, and the subsequent Dutch investigation found, as with Lockheed, no sign that Bernhard had influenced their procurement; but Tom Jones gave credit to Weisbrod, and his contacts with 'the highest officials', for his efforts in promoting the Tiger in Holland;[2] and there is little doubt who was meant by those highest officials.

After the Dutch had bought the Northrop planes, Tom Jones was advised to employ Prince Bernhard's friend, Teengs Gerritsen, whom the Prince had asked Jones to help earlier. Gerritsen was still actively working for Lockheed, being given regular briefings on company strategy. Tom Jones later maintained under oath that he had asked Courtlandt Gross, then chairman of Lockheed, who said he had no objection to Gerritsen's working for Northrop. But Gross denied to me that he had any contact, and Lockheed executives were certainly unaware that Gerritsen was also working for their rivals.[3]

Tom Jones was impressed, he later explained, by Gerritsen's record ('he was one of these Dutch beyond-reproach types') and he hired him for $10,000 a year as a 'trusted communications channel between the highest levels of Dutch government and the president of Northrop'. Gerritsen, like the Prince, showed no apparent worries about his conflicts of loyalties: he was able to be all-Dutch and all-American, all-Lockheed and all-Northrop, all at the same time.

The Prince and Gerritsen clearly continued to be helpful to Jones. The Northrop relationship is far less documented than Lockheed's—partly because Northrop were less intent on putting everything on paper—but there was an interesting glimpse in September 1971, when Northrop were considering taking on a new Dutch lobbyist. Northrop's man in Paris, Geoffrey Parsons, advised Tom Jones to discuss the question with Bernhard: the lobbyist's main job, Parsons explained, would be to get Northrop's new plane, the Cobra, 'past the economic and political barriers of the Dutch parliament'.[4] This might seem an

[1] Donner Report, chapter 3, p. 16.

[2] Northrop Special Report, p. 14.

[3] Letter from Courtlandt Gross to the author, September 29, 1976. See also Multi-national Hearings, part 12, p. 176.

[4] Northrop Papers: Parsons to Jones, September 27, 1971.

improper purpose for the Prince to discuss; but, as he sometimes made clear, the Prince had little respect for the Dutch parliament.

Jones also looked for an ally in France, an awkward assignment at the height of President de Gaulle's anti-Americanism. He found one in General Paul Stehlin, who had only just retired as chief of staff of the French air force, but who was also a convinced Atlanticist: he had an American wife, he had lectured at Harvard and travelled widely in America. Jones hired Stehlin in 1964 for the modest fee of $7,500, to analyse 'political and economic and military situations in Europe' and for 'alerting Northrop to business opportunities in the defence-related areas'. Stehlin wrote to Jones every two weeks, met Northrop people once a month, and visited them in Los Angeles every two years. Jones found Stehlin's advice very useful, he later explained: 'He has usually been able to spot and identify changes in national policy as they affect defence, months or even years ahead of others.'[1] Stehlin never made any secret of his belief in the Atlantic alliance and the folly of France trying to defend herself alone: he later became a deputy in the French parliament, and made frequent speeches on the subject.[2] But his Northrop payments remained secret.

It was Germany that was the key European market, and Jones was convinced that Northrop was suffering from a special lack of German political leverage. A man from the German defence department, he maintained, had advised him in 1966 that Northrop had suffered from inadequate representation in Bonn.[3] Soon afterwards Jones heard from a Northrop official in Los Angeles who said that he had a brother-in-law in Washington called Frank De Francis, a counsel for the German embassy, who might be helpful. Jones then got in touch with De Francis, who proved to be a resourceful operator: a stocky, voluble American lawyer of forty, he explained that he had grown up with the German government since the occupation days. He knew nothing about aviation: 'I don't know a damn thing about an airplane,' he said years later, 'except the nose and the tail.'[4] But he had excellent contacts in Germany, including members of the Bundestag. Jones promptly hired De Francis for an annual fee of $50,000, later going up to $100,000, but he did not tell the other members of

[1] Northrop Papers: Tom Jones to E. R. Crim, September 1974.
[2] See chapter 15.
[3] Multinational Hearings, part 12, pp. 153, 171.
[4] Ibid., p. 585.

the board. From then on Jones spoke to De Francis once a week, and often once a day.[1]

De Francis was also permitted to pay other people to work for Northrop, and to be reimbursed, if authorised by Jones: but how much he paid, and what for, remains obscure. At one point in 1972 he was paid an extra $40,000 in cash, through the 'Savy fund' in Paris, for the ostensible purpose of paying two influential Germans, Dr Eddy Hess and Dr Franz Bach; but at least part of that money was diverted to Washington.[2] What was clear was that Jones regarded De Francis from the beginning as a conduit for Northrop's secret slush fund.

De Francis was soon helping to lead Jones further into the European underworld or (as Jones put it) 'increasing Northrop's sophistication in European markets'. By 1969 Jones was disappointed by the progress of the Tiger fighter in Europe and elsewhere, and he needed financial support for his new plane, the Cobra. Jones and De Francis then planned to set up a separate organisation, named the Economic and Development Corporation, which would be a 'supplemental marketing tool'. It was to consist of 'foreign nationals of substance', who would discreetly supplement Northrop's own marketing activities, and it was, according to the insistent evidence of Jones and De Francis, modelled on a similar secret organisation set up by Lockheed. ('We were trying,' said De Francis, 'to catch up their methods of doing business abroad.')[3] In fact, according to Lockheed sources, their agent Weisbrod had tried to interest Lockheed earlier in such a scheme, but they had rejected it. Northrop's secret company, however, the EDC, was eventually set up two years later, on a singularly undefined basis: incorporated in Switzerland, it was headed by a man called Dr Andreas Froriep, an investment adviser whom Jones claims he never even met. Yet the company was advanced $700,000 over the following four years, and was promised a commission of 1½ percent on all direct sales of the Tiger fighters anywhere in the world. Jones explained that the new organisation could 'provide a wide degree of flexibility in procuring the best people': and could sell the fighter 'on the basis of confidentiality'.[4]

[1] Ibid., p. 154.

[2] Northrop Special Report, p. 7.

[3] Multinational Hearings, part 12, p. 594. Special Report, p. 9. Lockheed have vigorously denied any resemblance. See *Washington Post*, June 10, 1975.

[4] Multinational Hearings, part 12, p. 625. Northrop Special Report, pp. 9–11.

Exactly what the EDC really achieved, and how, remains buried in Swiss banks: in the subsequent investigation, the EDC principals refused to give any information about the recipients of payments. The investigation concluded that Jones and De Francis had both shown poor judgment in setting up the EDC with no control over it, and 'could not conclusively rebut the appearance of impropriety'. But De Francis had no doubts about the effectiveness of the EDC in selling the fighters: 'Just look at the success of the programme,' he said in 1974, 'you cannot directly measure it, nor do you want to. The success is there.'[1] The EDC in fact looked suspiciously like the kind of shadow company that is sometimes set up to make murky payments that cannot be traced.

Frank De Francis was not only now the chief link with the European underworld, he also had influential friends on Capitol Hill: and it was in Washington that Tom Jones saw the master-keys to his commercial future. A 'very dear friend' of De Francis was Congressman Mendel Rivers from South Carolina, who was chairman of the House Armed Services Committee—a position of central importance to any arms company. Like Senator Russell from Georgia, Rivers was assiduous in getting business for his own state, and his election slogan was 'Rivers Delivers'. One day early in 1969 Frank De Francis and Tom Jones called on Mendel Rivers to propose that the Pentagon should finance a re-tooling of the assembly line for the Tiger, to increase its range and thus improve its sales overseas. Soon afterwards Rivers put the proposal to the Armed Services Committee, and in the next eighteen months, just when Congress was trying to cut down defence spending, Rivers succeeded in persuading first the Pentagon, then the House, and finally the House-Senate Conference Committee, that the Pentagon should pay $28 million as 'seed money' to re-tool the Northrop Tiger. It was a striking exercise of personal power by Rivers and his chief counsel, Russel Blandford, a former general from the Marine Corps. But it was also a triumph for De Francis: for he had only recently signed his secret contract with Tom Jones, which would allow him a commission of $\frac{1}{2}$ to $1\frac{1}{2}$ percent on all direct sales of Tigers to foreign governments. With the go-ahead for re-tooling, De Francis stood to make a small fortune from foreign sales.

Tom Jones continued to show his appreciation of De Francis's

[1] Multinational Hearings, part 12, p. 597.

services. In August 1971 the Northrop chief counsel, George
Gore, sent a memo recording a conversation with Tom Jones. It
said:

> Tom telephoned me today and asked if I had sent the $50,000 check to De
> Francis. I said it had been sent last week, the same day he spoke to me, which
> was July 29. Tom then told me that he wanted me to understand that the
> services of de Francis in connection with our securing the F-5-21 contract
> were invaluable and that we would not have gotten the contract without de
> Francis' contribution. He then wanted it thoroughly understood that if
> anything should ever happen to him, he wanted all our agreements with de
> Francis honoured.[1]

General Blandford was also looked after by Northrop, and
when he retired from the Armed Services Committee in 1972
Tom Jones discussed with De Francis how he could best be
employed. Blandford was already being retained by one of
Northrop's rivals, so they decided that he should be given a
consulting agreement with an air charter company, called United
Governmental Services, which was wholly owned by De Francis:
in this capacity Blandford was paid no less than $1,000 a month for
five years. When later questioned, General Blandford agreed that
'a fair interpretation of his employment by UGS might be that
he was retained to provide some services to Northrop . . .'[2]

Northrop's Washington office in the meantime was weaving
its own web of contracts, giving parties, lending planes or offering
free trips to influential congressmen and Pentagon officials. In
1971 Northrop began renting a duck-hunting lodge in Maryland,
near the shores of Chesapeake Bay, two hours' drive from
Washington, to which they invited hand-picked guests for week-
ends in the duck-hunting season. The first weekend in October
1971, which was fairly typical, included Senator Howard Cannon,
Congressman Bill Minsall, two admirals and four generals—a kind
of cameo of the military-industrial complex—and over the next
three years there were 144 such occasions, costing Northrop
$37,000. There was plenty of liquor, dinner at the Tidewater Inn,
and the game was cleaned by a local firm in Easton.[3] Northrop
was certainly not unique in this form of entertainment: James
Schlesinger, who was then secretary for defence, described the

---

[1] See the account by Joseph P. Albright in the *New York Times Magazine*, February 8,
1976.

[2] Northrop Special Report, p. 8.

[3] Multinational Hearings, part 12, pp. 199–238. Special Report, p. 36.

Northrop case as 'only the tip of the iceberg', and Rockwell for instance also had a hunting lodge on Wye Island in Chesapeake Bay, with very influential guests. But Northrop was a smaller and more single-minded company. Tom Jones insisted that 'it was totally done in the spirit of close relationship', and many of the visitors later insisted that they had been invited as old personal friends: but as Schlesinger observed, 'these old personal friendships seem to have generated with remarkable rapidity.'[1] The subsequent Northrop investigators, looking at the whole range of sponsored hospitality suites, officers wives' clubs, dinner parties, football games etc., noticed a consistent 'pattern of secretiveness', while the Pentagon later admonished their officers for their lack of judgment.[2]

In Paris meanwhile, Bill Savy's slush fund had been swelling over the years, but with some curious fluctuations. The payments were always bigger in election years, and in 1969 there was suddenly much more slush. The first big jump came just after the House had passed the bill to pay for re-tooling Northrop; the second came just when the House-Senate conference had agreed on the $28 million for Northrop.[3] By 1970 Savy's payments had reached $180,000; the same next year; and by 1972 no less than $240,000. The ultimate destination of much of this cash is still unknown, but the purpose of part of it later became clear. Jimmy Allen, who looked after Northrop's undercover activities, kept a list of requests for political contributions: when cash from Savy arrived he disbursed it to useful friends, including a Republican fund-raiser, Holmes Tuttle, a Democrat fund-raiser, Gene Wyman, and Senator Russell of Georgia,[4] who was also the close ally of Lockheed.

In February 1972 Jones authorised a special payment of $120,000 to Savy. He needed it to contribute to President Nixon's re-election campaign, and the money, having been laundered through Savy, duly came back to Jones in $100 notes. Then in August 1972 Tom Jones was visited in his office in Century City by Herbert Kalmbach, the fund-raiser for Nixon's campaign. They talked for fifteen minutes, and Tom Jones then took a package from his desk, and gave it to Kalmbach: inside was

[1] *New York Times*, January 24, 1976.
[2] Northrop Special Report, p. 50.
[3] *New York Times Magazine*, February 8, 1976. Multinational Hearings, part 12, p. 466.
[4] Ibid., pp. 511, 495.

$75,000 in hundred dollar bills. Tom Jones (according to Kalmbach) assumed it was money for Nixon's re-election campaign;[1] in fact it was for the secret fund for the defence of the Watergate burglars. It was this undercover gift, when it came to light a year later, which was to provide the first clue in the long trail to all Northrop's other undercover activities.

TIGER, TIGER

For Tom Jones, the Pentagon support for his new Tiger, which de Francis had helped to obtain, was the beginning of a new export boom. The Tiger II or F-5E, as it was called, was more manoeuvrable, with more powerful engines than its predecessor, and in November 1970 it was formally chosen by the US government as the International Fighter. The first programme was for 325 planes, but by mid-1975 the total orders were up to 700, with eventual orders reckoned at 1,500. The Tiger had already gone to twenty-two countries, beginning with Iran in 1965, and including Taiwan, Greece, South Korea, the Philippines, Turkey, Ethiopia, Morocco, Norway, Thailand, Vietnam, and Libya. In Washington it was regarded as a key instrument of foreign policy, through the military assistance programme, providing the nations of the Third World with their links with the West. As McNamara's doctrine spread, of selling rather than giving, so the Tiger became one of the most popular of all arms sales, with its potential against insurgents as well as external enemies. By 1975 Tom Jones could boast that the Tiger programme was contributing $2 billion to the US balance of payments: the network of foreign agents, he maintained, was an essential ingredient of Northrop's success. Forty percent of Northrop's business was now exports, and it was a model for other companies with its efficiency and cost-consciousness; it was never late with delivery. Nor had Northrop, Tom Jones insisted, ever sold any plane 'in the absence of official assurance that it would serve the Nation's interests'.[2]

Northrop executives, explaining to me later how their company had become involved in bribes and corruption, stressed insistently that their company's experience was quite different from Lockheed's: they had been led into a temporary trans-

[1] Ervin Committee Hearings, 1974, p. 2108.
[2] Multinational Hearings, part 12, pp. 150–1.

gression by mistake, through Lockheed's example, but while bribes were part of Lockheed's way of life, they were quite unnecessary for Northrop, whose plane was unique and could sell on its merits. But this advantage, it seems to me, only makes the Northrop behaviour the more discreditable, whether in Europe or (as will be seen later) in the Third World. Tom Jones certainly had less financial worries than those that afflicted Bob Gross or Dan Haughton; but there was little sign that he was reluctant to set up his corrupt system, which went further than theirs. Jones' incentive was not to rescue the company, but to reap still greater profits and power.

In the meantime Jones had succeeded in forging a close relationship between his company and the Pentagon of which both sides were proud: for Northrop had never, like Lockheed, incurred public unpopularity through huge overruns on extravagant projects. The Tiger had become one of the symbols of the free world, and newly independent states looked to it as the badge of their manhood and sovereignty. The Pentagon and the State Department were only too glad to combine good business with sound diplomacy. But this association with the dynamism of Northrop and its relentless salesmanship was bound to raise the question: was this arms trade really being controlled? Once the apparatus of bribes, leverage and 'windows' had been brought into play, could it not distort the whole process of deciding what arms a nation should have? Was it primarily for the benefit of the State Department, or of Northrop?

8

The British Dilemma

The hottest places in hell are reserved for those who are neutral in a
moral crisis.

Harold Wilson, December 21, 1965

THE HIGH pressure arms selling of Henry Kuss at the Pentagon
re-echoed through Europe, making every country aware of the
need to push their own arms. The Europeans felt threatened both
as buyers and sellers: the more they turned to America for their
advanced weapons, like the Starfighter or the Tiger, the more
they felt the need to recoup their costs by selling elsewhere. But
there, too, they were challenged by the Americans, and the
predicament brought a new edge to the competition to arm the
Third World.

Nowhere was the predicament more evident than in Britain,
which faced a new defence crisis just when the Labour government under Harold Wilson was coming to power in 1964: as in
Washington, it was the party of apparent compassion that was to
prove the more determined to sell arms. The new minister of
defence, Denis Healey, saw himself as a British McNamara,
knocking the armed services into shape: he was combative and
aggressive, with the special anti-communist zeal of the ex-com-
munist. In opposition Healey was eloquent about Britain's moral
purpose, but in office he was a pragmatist who was prone to lose
sight of the ends in pursuing the means. The Labour government

was fired with the idea of 'the white-hot technological revolution'; and in the ministry of aviation (under Roy Jenkins) was a
dynamic young Labour politician who seemed to breathe the
new fire. John Stonehouse had made his first reputation as a
crusader in Africa, where he was declared a prohibited immigrant
to Rhodesia; but he was now emerging as a tough negotiator and
salesman; with his tall frame, firm jaw and cold eyes, he was a
symbol of the new businesslike Britain.

The Labour politicians and their civil servants surveyed a
gloomy prospect for the British defence industry. By the early
'sixties the British aircraft companies were far less prosperous than
in the first decade after the war: Britain's share of world aircraft
exports had fallen from thirty-three percent in 1959 to fourteen
percent in 1964, and the new aircraft had nearly all been export
failures. At the end of 1964 Harold Wilson appointed a committee
headed by Lord Plowden to investigate the aircraft industry,
which reported a year later with a bleak assessment: Plowden
recognised that British skills and technology were well-suited for
making advanced aircraft, but in spite of the mergers the two main
companies, BAC and Hawker-Siddeley, needed far bigger
markets than Britain could provide. The only solution, Plowden
concluded, lay in collaborating with other countries, particularly
with Europe—and in higher exports. He urged that the government become much more closely involved in military sales,
with the help of military attachés serving as salesmen, and with
easy loans to foreign buyers. It was notable that in the whole
Plowden report, chaired by a high-minded public servant, no
reference was made to possible moral objections that might attend
the more vigorous selling of arms.[1]

While Plowden was still investigating, the Labour government
were realising that all the pet projects of the British industry
would have to be cancelled, and replaced by American aircraft.
The transport, HS 681, was replaced by Lockheed Hercules
planes (which the Germans had resisted). The fighter P1154
was replaced by McDonnell Phantoms; and the most expensive
collapse of all was that of the TSR2, the advanced fighter-bomber
which had been the great hope of the industry. Its costs were now
so vast that Healey was forced to cancel it, and to look to America,
where McNamara was pressing vigorously for his favourite
project, the F111 fighter-bomber developed by General

[1] Command 2853, London, HMSO, 1965.

Dynamics. It was a spectacular swing-wing plane, still unproved; it would be cheaper than developing the TSR2, but it would have to be paid for in dollars. As in America four years earlier, it was the need for foreign currency that precipitated Britain's stepping-up of arms sales: the critical decision was taken with no great debate, as a by-product of the national defence problem.

Henry Kuss had already become something of a bogey to all the Europeans, and was provoking them to establish or reinforce their own arms sales organisations. The British, with their huge bills for American weapons, now felt impelled to sell arms much more seriously, and in July 1965 Denis Healey asked Donald Stokes, the head of Leyland Motors, to advise on arms exports: he was appointed, as one minister told me later, 'like most government committees, to shove us into doing what we had to do anyway'. Stokes, like McNamara and many subsequent arms salesmen, came from the world of cars, and was then regarded as Britain's master salesman. He duly recommended that the government should set up its own organisation for defence sales, on much the same lines as Kuss's outfit in Washington.

In January 1966 Healey told parliament that he would appoint an arms salesman, justifying it in pragmatic terms with the need to win back foreign currency, and with a classic state-ment of ambivalence:

> While the Government attach the highest importance to making progress in the field of arms control and disarmament, we must also take what practical steps we can to ensure that this country does not fail to secure its rightful share of this valuable commercial market.

There were protests from left-wing members: Frank Allaun said: 'We do not want this gentleman to turn into another Krupp or Zaharoff', and Emrys Hughes complained that it would intensify the arms race, by encouraging economic conflict with America.[1] But Healey insisted that arms sales must be conducted as efficiently as possible, and four months later he announced a new post in the ministry of defence, the Head of Defence Sales, who would ensure that Britain would 'gain the advantage of full participation in the market'.[2]

The first holder of the job, Raymond Brown, was not a pro-fessional civil servant like Kuss, but a self-made businessman.

[1] House of Commons: January 25, 1966.
[2] Ibid., May 19, 1966.

Brown was an unusual intruder into the world of Whitehall, like a guided missile in a sky full of helicopters. A jolly, round-faced man with bright eyes and a neat triangular moustache, he had been co-founder of an electronics company called Racal (the first syllable came from his Christian name), which had achieved a spectacular success in the American market; Brown had advised the government, back in 1956, to co-ordinate an export drive for electronics. He now moved into the ministry of defence with cheerful energy, assisted by a general, a wing-commander, a brigadier and a major. He set up a 'surgery' each morning, to advise arms salesmen on specifications, co-ordination, and export markets. He urged the generals and admirals to provide training and support for arms sales, and cajoled the civil servants into sales-manship. (Never suggest changing the system, he was warned: talk about 'bending the rules'.) He was the kind of forthright tycoon that reassures politicians, and he got on well with Healey, and with Tony Benn at the ministry of technology. Compared with the pedants of Whitehall he was like a breath of fresh air.

Brown was not a man to see any fundamental distinction be-tween weapons and anything else: 'as for the moral question,' he told me, 'I just put it out of my mind.' But he was hurt when left-wingers compared him to Zaharoff, or when Jewish friends at the golf course jokingly called him a Merchant of Death. He tried to persuade Healey to change the name of his group, the Defence Sales Organisation, into something more innocent-sounding, like Kuss's ILN, and he suggested Export International Relations: but the government kept the name ('just like the British: always too bloody honest'). Brown saw himself essentially as a promoter of British technology, and one of his achievements was the publication of a huge illustrated volume, like a bound mail-order catalogue, of all the defence equipment that Britain has to offer: he signed the first copy. It describes all the tanks, guns and mortars in matter-of-fact language as if they were household gadgets. 'The range, mobility and fire power of this advanced light and robust equipment' (says a recent edition of the 105mm gun) 'makes it ideal for use in tough limited war conditions any-where from the Arctic to the tropics.'

Brown did not have to face many moral problems, for most of his time was devoted to other Western countries who could look after their own morality. In Europe his salesmanship did not have great scope, for the British aircraft could not compete with the Lockheed Starfighters or Hercules, or the Northrop Tigers. He tried to sell tanks to Holland, and personally lobbied Prince Bernhard, as Inspector-General of the Forces: but the British were turned down in favour of the German Leopard tanks (Brown still wonders why). In America, after the deal with the General Dynamics FIII, Brown could insist that sales must be a two-way street; he struck up an easy relationship over martinis with Henry Kuss, and they decided that there was plenty of room for both. Brown's first target was $300 million, but in the next four years he managed to sell $1,300 million in military equipment.

The developing countries formed only a minor part of Brown's market, for their capacity to buy arms was still very limited. Brown stopped once in Iran, to make a sales pitch for British tanks, which later bore fruit in the huge orders for Chieftains. He also helped to set up a new organisation to arrange government-to-government deals with the Third World, called Millbank Technical Services, which was later (as we will see) to become a powerful commercial force. But the resources of most of the Third World were still small, compared to the rich markets of America and Europe.

THE SAUDI DEAL

There was one part of the Third World which was already beginning to emerge as an important arms market, before Raymond Brown had taken up his job. The oil-producing states of the Middle East were all beginning to have extra money to spend; but the richest of them, Saudi Arabia, was now offering a special opportunity. In the mid-'sixties the British clinched a huge arms deal with the Saudis which provided a foretaste of prospects to come. The more Europeans bought from America, the more they had to sell down the line; and while the companies were in the forefront of the battle, the governments were working out their own bargains.

The prospect of a deal with the Saudis had opened up in the early 'sixties, when the Egyptians under Nasser were fighting the royalists in the Yemen, and thus threatening the Saudi regime. The Saudis became concerned with their air defence, and Western arms companies, including Lockheed, Northrop, the British Aircraft Corporation and Dassault, all moved in to try to sell to them. With oil revenues already mounting and little to spend them on, the empty and defenceless kingdom offered limitless prospects.

One man who was specially aware of the scope was Geoffrey Edwards, a rugged Yorkshire businessman with a commanding voice, big chin and leonine head: and Edwards' adventures offer an unusual insight into the operations of a big-arms dealer. He had first gone out to Saudi Arabia in 1960 to investigate prospects in civil construction. He soon realised that there were better prospects in arms, and he contacted British companies to make a bid for the Saudis' air defences. Associated Electrical Industries (AEI) would provide an early-warning radar system, the British Aircraft Corporation would provide Lightning fighters, and a service company called Airwork would provide training. A consortium was formed with Edwards as their agent, to be paid on a commission basis, and Edwards embarked on a long process of negotiation.

He bought a house in Jeddah, flew constantly between Jeddah and London, and (he claims) spent £180,000 of his own and borrowed money. He soon established a close relationship with Prince Sultan, King Feisal's half-brother, who had just become minister of defence, and took the shrewd precaution of appointing as agent Prince Sultan's brother, Prince Abdul Rahman, to whom he promised half the commission from AEI. He also consulted a prominent Saudi financier, Gaith Pharaon (to whom he eventually paid £80,000)[1], whose father was one of the King's closest advisers. Thus assured of open doors, Edwards patiently pressed the claims of his clients.

But there were now other serious contenders. The Dassault salesmen were trying to sell Mirages, with some language difficulties, but offering attractive terms. Lockheed, in the wake of their European successes, were promoting the Starfighter, and Northrop were offering the Tiger, supported by their new and well-connected agent, Kim Roosevelt,[2] and by several Saudi agents. The Americans had some diplomatic advantage, for the British Foreign Office were reluctant to give much support to the British bid: they took the view that Saudi Arabia was basically an American preserve (as Kuwait was a British one), and that a British arms deal could disturb a delicate balance.

[1] Edwards: interview with the author, July 7, 1976.
[2] See chapter 14.

In the midst of this contest the Labour government came to power in October 1964, immediately faced with its first economic crisis: and Edwards, though himself very right-wing, quickly saw a chance of closer government support. The day after the election he visited an old Labour friend, Fred Mulley, who quickly put him in touch with Roy Jenkins, then minister of aviation: and Edwards explained the economic consequences of the Saudi deal.[1] The Labour cabinet were very receptive, and as a result a surprising salesman appeared on the Saudi scene in the shape of John Stonehouse, who was Roy Jenkins' parliamentary secretary. Stonehouse soon became a zealous promoter of all arms sales, but particularly of the Saudi sale, to the dismay of many British diplomats. He later described how he told the leaders of the aircraft industry: 'the old idea that ministers and civil servants should keep at arm's length from the squalid commercial world is a nonsense . . . you must regard all of us in the ministry as an extension of your own selling organisation.'[2]

Stonehouse flew out to Jeddah and stayed with Edwards, with whom he established a cordial relationship. 'Most people in government frowned upon Geoffrey Edwards as an arms salesman grasping after his fat commission,' he wrote later. But Stonehouse appreciated that bribes had to be paid: 'what was the point of adopting a "holier-than-thou" attitude when Britain's factories sorely needed the business . . .?'[3] This Saudi experience, Stonehouse claimed later (when defending himself against charges of fraud), made him realise the extent of corruption in the world of big business.[4] Exactly how Stonehouse contributed to influencing the Saudis is still unclear: but he certainly took some trouble to re-assure them, promising that the British government would not withhold spare parts in the event of a future conflict.

By the autumn of 1965 the competition between the British, the Americans and French was becoming tense and tangled. Each company was establishing its own group of agents, with one agent often representing several rival companies, while each company accused the others of bribery. The Northrop men were very energetic: Prince Mohammed, who was one of them, gave the King details of the bribes that Lockheed had paid to his

[1] Edwards' interview.
[2] John Stonehouse: *Death of an Idealist*, London, W. H. Allen, 1975, pp. 48, 49.
[3] Ibid., p. 50.
[4] *The Times*, London, July 2, 1976.

officials, while Kim Roosevelt made the most of his intelligence contacts: 'my friends in the CIA are also keeping an eye on things,' he promised Northrop.[1] But Lockheed were confident that the Saudis would choose the Starfighter, which McNamara himself had recommended as part of a total system for Saudi defence. And Lockheed had now taken the precaution of appointing a young well-connected local agent, Adnan Khashoggi, who (as we will note later) cultivated closer links with Prince Sultan than were available to Geoffrey Edwards. The Americans had the impression, as Roosevelt reported, that 'the Saudi government would be very reluctant to settle for either the French or British offers'.[2]

But behind the scenes there was now high-level diplomatic activity between London and Washington, as a result of Britain's balance of payments crisis, worsened by the likelihood of having to buy the American FIII. Donald Stokes, still advising on arms exports, visited McNamara in Washington, and discussed whether Britain could find new markets abroad to pay for the planes. Denis Healey was already planning to set up Britain's Defence Sales Organisation, as we have seen, to help pay for the costs: but that could not recover the whole sum, and the extra earnings from the Saudis could make up the difference. McNamara and Henry Kuss realised that the British political situation was tense: they desperately needed an export triumph to make up for their industry's disastrous setbacks—and Saudi Arabia was a convenient consolation prize.

For both Healey and McNamara, this provided a neat solution, and they put all their weight behind it. John Stonehouse and Geoffrey Edwards both flew over to Washington to see Henry Kuss, to propose that the British and Americans now put forward a joint bid, combining British Lightning fighters with American Hawk missiles. Henry Kuss explained that his department could not 'just automatically' withdraw the offers by Lockheed and Northrop, but that if King Feisal agreed to the joint bid, the Pentagon would be glad to support it.[3] It was a delicate proposition: as Stonehouse put it, 'If the American companies competing for the sale, who knew they had it in the bag, thought their own

[1] Multinational Hearings, part 12, pp. 693, 697.

[2] Ibid., p. 691.

[3] US Senate Foreign Relations Committee, 1967: Arms Sales to Near East and South Asian Countries, p. 10.

defence secretary was making it easy for the Limeys all hell would be let loose and our chances would be lost in a welter of recrimination'.[1] But steps were soon taken to make sure that Feisal *would* agree: both the British and American ambassadors pressed the merits of the deal, and in November 1965 Stonehouse went again to Saudi Arabia. But the decisive factor was the fact, as Kuss put it to me, that the American government had 'called off the dogs'. 'We could not have made the offer', explained Healey, 'never mind won the contract, without American co-operation.'[2]

But the arms salesmen continued as if nothing had happened: Lockheed sent out an army of senior executives, offering a reduced price for their Starfighters; they even had with them David Rockefeller, of the Chase Manhattan bank, to discuss the financing. Geoffrey Edwards was as active as ever, and a delegation of British MPs were impressed by the 'fierce American competition': even Healey later emphasised that 'competition from Lockheed persisted to the very last moment and was very stiff indeed'. But in fact the competition was only extravagant shadow-boxing, for without diplomatic support the companies could get nowhere. After Lockheed lost, Courtlandt Gross paid an angry visit to Kuss, who tried to pacify him by reminding him that Lockheed had recently sold Hercules to Britain.

In December 1965 John Stonehouse proudly announced that the Saudis had accepted the joint offer, which included on Britain's side $154 million for BAC's planes and missiles, $70 million for AEI's radar system, and $61.6 million for Airwork's training teams. It was proclaimed as the biggest export deal that Britain had ever achieved. The British government knew quite well that they had fixed it, but they were glad to let Geoffrey Edwards take the credit and money: both Stonehouse and Prince Sultan paid tribute to his role, and he was now a millionaire with his commissions. Edwards soon had some difficulties with his fellow-agents: he was sued by three of them, including Sultan's brother, and he himself sued AEI, who refused to pay him after having paid a very shady agent called Antoine Kamouh (who was later murdered in Paris).[3] But Edwards still made a clear two million pounds—a payment so spectacular at the time that the

[1] Stonehouse: p. 53.

[2] House of Commons: May 11, 1966.

[3] See chapter 17.

Saudis soon decreed that henceforth only their citizens could act as agents. Edwards retired to Jersey and later became briefly an agent for Lockheed: he supported several right-wing organisations, and eventually set up his own company dealing with the Middle East.

The British gains from the Saudi deal at first seemed tangible enough. At the British Aircraft Corporation works at Warton, outside Preston—whose two marginal constituencies loomed large in the Labour mind—the order for Lightnings assured hundreds of jobs for the next few years. Soon the American Raytheon company could not produce Hawk missiles quickly enough for the Saudis, for their defence against the Yemen, and the British were asked to fly out Hunter and Lightning jets and Thunderbird missiles in an emergency airlift called 'Operation Magic Carpet', which provided still more business.

But there were growing complications. The training and the maintenance of the planes proved beyond the resources of Airwork, who had first won the contract, and the British ministry of defence had to become more deeply involved. Ex-RAF pilots were recruited to fly the planes, who became in effect sponsored mercenaries to the Saudis; and eventually the British government had to set up its own organisation in Riyadh, jointly with the Saudis, to supervise the programme. What began as an apparently simple commercial sale ended up, like many future arms deals, as a major government commitment: and the cost of providing the aircraft and services had escalated so far that the real profit was very doubtful. The Saudis on their side were dissatisfied with the Lightnings, which were originally designed for the short-range defence of the British Isles, and were not obviously appropriate to a huge desert country. They looked less favourably on British firms after the 1967 Arab-Israeli war, and the following year turned down the offer of British Saladin armoured cars in favour of French Panhards.

By the 'seventies the British had recovered some of their position, and gained big new maintenance contracts. But the American companies were now becoming increasingly dominant, as the mounting oil revenues gave the Saudis greater scope for spending. The original British contract and the commissions of Edwards were soon to be dwarfed—as chapter 11 shows—by the contracts with Lockheed and Northrop, and the colossal commissions of Adnan Khashoggi. As for John Stonehouse, who

pushed the deal through, his later career was thoroughly unreal:
he rose higher in the government but soon began speculating in
private ventures which led him into debt; he disappeared off the
beach at Miami, was discovered under an assumed name in
Australia, and was eventually convicted in 1976 of fraud and
forgery.

The real interest of the British deal with the Saudis lay not so
much in its size, as in its trade-off. Two months after Stonehouse
first announced the deal, the British government revealed in
February 1966 that it would buy fifty F111s from General
Dynamics, which would cost $725 million in dollar costs over ten
years; but it was not until two months later that Denis Healey
revealed that some of the dollars would be offset by the Saudi
Arabian deal, from which the Americans had agreed to stand off;
and he still insisted, in a contorted statement, that this carried no
obligation to buy F111 planes.[1] But it was only by being allowed
to sell to the Saudis that Britain could afford to buy from the
Americans; the Saudis were only the pawns in the Western
currency game. As it turned out eighteen months later, the
British could not afford to buy the fifty F111s anyway: they were
cancelled by Denis Healey after the subsequent economic crisis
and devaluation of the pound in November 1967, along with the
speedier withdrawal of British forces from East of Suez. The
Saudis in the end had been persuaded to buy British planes that
they did not want, to allow Britain to pay for American planes
that they could not afford.

ARMING APARTHEID

The old British concern about the Merchants of Death was not
entirely dormant, and throughout the 'sixties one country was the
focus of the moral dilemma about arms sales. South Africa was
a very tempting market, by far the biggest arms buyer in Africa,
and with close historic links with Britain: but South African arms
were impossible to separate from the policy of *apartheid*, which
became the object of greater world indignation during the 'sixties
as the black states in the north achieved their independence. To
weigh the solid economic advantages of selling arms against the
moral benefits of refraining, became more painful as Britain's
economic position worsened.

[1] House of Commons: May 11, 1966.

During the 'fifties South Africa imported most of its arms from Britain, including Saracen and Centurion tanks, submarines and destroyers. British investments were helping to build up the internal South African arms industry, and the British company ICI were the half-owners of African Explosives and Chemical Industries, the most important local source of ammunition. When Hawker produced the Buccaneer strike aircraft in 1955 for the Royal Navy the only other customer was South Africa, who ordered sixteen. But as the South African government became more repressive, the British Labour opposition became more opposed to supplying arms. The massacre at Sharpeville in 1961, where Saracen tanks were brought in to control the black crowds, suggested that external defence was now inseparable from internal repression, and as South Africa's minister of defence tactlessly explained: 'The first task of the defence forces is to help the police maintain law and order'.

In August 1963 the United Nations called on all states to cease forthwith the sale of arms and ammunition to South Africa, and a year later the resolution was widened to include equipment for making arms. The British Conservative government abstained both times, but when the Labour party came to power in October 1964 Harold Wilson announced a full embargo of arms to South Africa. The embargo, like most embargoes, was not as total as it looked: existing orders, including the sixteen Buccaneers, could go through; spare parts (it later transpired) were supplied to jet aircraft; and electronic equipment was provided which could be crucial for defence. The great underground radar network centred on Devon, in the Transvaal, was thoroughly equipped by Marconi. But the embargo still represented a real sacrifice of British exports, estimated at $240 million over the following three years. And the Americans joined in the British restraint.

The embargo was soon frustrated. The South African government looked for other arms suppliers and found them in France: in the following decade, South Africa bought 64 Mirage fighters, 75 helicopters and much other French equipment. The French connection became precious to South Africa and profitable to France. By 1968 South Africa was France's third biggest customer for arms sales, next to Israel and Belgium, and the French were able to use arms as the bait for big civil orders. Still more annoying, the French succeeded in avoiding heavy criticism from their

African clients further north: they insisted (implausibly) that their arms to South Africa were not suitable for internal repression, and explained that French aid to black Africa depended on high exports elsewhere. De Gaulle even managed to appear as the special champion of the Third World through his vocal opposition to the Vietnam war. For the British, it seemed black ingratitude.

But the South Africans were still anxious to buy more British arms—not only for their practical usefulness, but as tokens of a broader British commitment. By November 1967 they saw a new chance to tempt the British government: after the economic crisis and devaluation (which had brought about the cancellation of F111s) Britain was now more desperate to increase exports, and the South Africans could dangle a 'shopping list' (in the cosy language of the trade) in front of the Labour cabinet. The list included more Buccaneer planes, Westland helicopters, frigates and anti-aircraft missiles, all reckoned to be worth about $450 million in exports.

It was a dazzling temptation to an impoverished government, and it soon split the cabinet, lighting up their moral differences like a hung jury. The foreign secretary, the rumbustious George Brown, was sympathetic: he detested apartheid (he later explained), but he was convinced of South Africa's importance for Western defence, and he did not believe that these weapons would really jeopardise the position of black South Africans.[1] Brown was supported by Denis Healey, who was always vocal against apartheid in opposition, but as minister of defence was now anxious to boost arms exports. The left-wing members of the cabinet then leaked the proposal; there was a tense cabinet meeting, and Harold Wilson, who had earlier been very ambiguous, now came out with full moral fervour against the 'arms lobby', to the fury of Brown.[2]

There followed a classic parliamentary debate, reviving the old moral arguments. Stephen Hastings, a Conservative MP, asked the prime minister: 'Does he rate the conscience of the Labour party in the balance of payments?'. John Boyd-Carpenter noted that the Labour government were quite prepared to sell arms to Saudi Arabia or to the Sultan of Oman and Muscat,

---

[1] George Brown: *In My Way*, London, Gollancz, 1971, p. 171.

[2] Ibid., p. 174. See also Harold Wilson: *The Labour Government: 1964-1970*, London, Weidenfeld and Nicolson, pp. 470-6.

who maintained a medieval tyranny. Alex Lyon, on the Labour side, compared the embargo to the cotton workers of Lancashire in the nineteenth century, who went without jobs to assist those who were fighting for the freedom of slaves in the United States. Ben Whitaker, the high-minded Labour member for Hampstead, recalled that the campaigners against the slave trade were told constantly that Britain could not afford to end it.

The leader of the Conservatives, Ted Heath, pointed out that South Africa was Britain's third biggest overseas customer, and that South Africa was a critical part of South Atlantic defence. But Michael Stewart, the most effective keeper of the cabinet's conscience, and former foreign secretary, insisted that trading in arms must always be different from any other trade: 'I believe with all my strength that on every issue—morality, ultimate wisdom, and the truest expediency in the long run for this country—our policy was right three years ago and is right now.'[1]

The British thus continued, in theory, to respect the embargo; but the position was never quite as it appeared. As one defence salesman described it to me: 'We were able to sell them some helicopters because they were half-French: and they're of course the deadliest machines against natives. When the South Africans came through with an order for patrol boats we told them to redraft the order to make it look as if they're for civilian use: ("surely you must have some *black* fishing boats that need protecting?") The South Africans could get most of the ammunition they wanted through the Simonstown defence agreement. What stopped the orders was mainly that they ran out of money.'

The South Africans saw another chance to tempt the British in 1970, when the Conservatives came back to power. Their leader, Ted Heath, was pledged to resume arms sales, and he persisted in his policy in spite of a furore from the black Commonwealth and objections from Washington and his own cabinet. But it soon emerged that the South Africans did not want to buy very much: they were now much more self-sufficient, and for foreign arms they needed to be sure of continuity of supply. All they wanted from Britain was a few navy helicopters. Harold Wilson now led the attack, mocking Ted Heath for having suggested a 'glittering Eldorado' of arms orders, which turned out to be worth less than a million pounds. What the South Africans wanted, he said, was not so much the arms as the

[1] House of Commons: December 19, 1967.

'certificate of respectability' which should not be given. 'What does it profit a man—or a government—to gain control, through three or four helicopters, of a few more square miles of Indian Ocean—it is no more than that—and to lose the battle for hundreds of millions of hearts and minds on the continents washed by the ocean?'[1]

In the following years, as South Africa continued on its collision course, with black states and guerrilla movements emerging all round it, the distinctions between military and civil equipment, or between external and internal defence, became all the more impossible. As the black townships turned to rebellion, policing was indistinguishable from military defence: when in June 1976 black children began rioting in the slum-city of Soweto outside Johannesburg, leading to two hundred deaths, it was the French Alouette helicopters that were used to drop tear-gas on the crowds. In the use of electronics the line between civil and military was always blurred, and the arms salesmen blurred it further. In 1975 the South Africans ordered a computer-controlled communications network called the Tropospheric Scatter System from the British Marconi company, worth $20 million, which was typical of the 'grey area' between military and civilian equipment. It was not capable in itself of killing anyone; but it was indispensable to computer-controlled warfare and the electronic battlefield. In any advanced police state, sophisticated communications were now inseparable from means of repression.[2]

The British embargo continued to be rather less rigorous than it appeared; one defence salesman boasted to me that he had actually exported more arms equipment under the Labour government, after 1974, than under the Conservatives. In 1976 it emerged that the South Africans had succeeded in importing a million pounds worth of spare parts for Centurion tanks through a Jersey company which had given a fraudulent order, and in Jersey the company was fined a mere £1,600: but what puzzled the Defence Sales Organisation was not that the consignment had slipped through, but that the South Africans needed this subterfuge, since they could probably have got the spare parts officially, anyway. But the Anglo-American embargo of planes, tanks and guns was maintained.

---

[1] House of Commons: March 3, 1971.

[2] See Anti-Apartheid Movement: *Marconi Arms Apartheid*, April 1976, p. 2.

White South Africa was now becoming an armed camp supplied by many countries eager for their money, in which British policies made little difference. The South Africans could make their own small arms and ammunition: the French or Italians were still glad to supply heavier equipment, while the Israelis were now establishing closer links, and trying to sell Kfir fighters (see chapter 17). Even Russian and Czech shotguns and handguns were flooding into this booming market, where nearly every white household had its gun: while communists were proscribed and jailed, half the new handguns were coming from communist countries and one of the most popular shotguns selling in South Africa in 1976 was the 12-bore Russian Baikal, freely distributed in Johannesburg. 'Eastern Europe badly needs foreign exchange,' explained one local dealer, 'they don't care where their agents sell the guns as long as they are paid promptly.'[1]

Observing this outcome, there were many British Conservatives and others who maintained that the embargo had been a fatuous and expensive gesture, which had forfeited British influence in South Africa and let in all kinds of others. The insistent argument of all arms dealers had been once again vindicated: 'if we don't sell, someone else will'. But the lesson was not, I believe, quite so simple: for in such an explosive situation the supplying or withholding of arms has an importance far transcending the hardware. The Anglo-American restraint, for all its limitations and loopholes, was part of a long process of separation from white South African policies. If the embargo had never been enforced, the British and Americans would have found themselves far more deeply committed to support of white South Africa, with all the dangers of a total clash with the black states in the north, backed by China and Russia. Like the anti-slavery movement of a century earlier, the embargo was part of a wider perspective: the blockade of the slave trade was also constantly frustrated and broken over a period of fifty years, but it eventually won.

The South African embargo and the Saudi arms deal, and scores of arms deals through the Middle East, Africa and Asia, were all part of the inheritance of the disintegrating British Empire. The countries which had for decades been a closed preserve of British arms, subject to British control, were now emerging as young nations determined to assert their independence and freedom of

[1] *Johannesburg Star*, December 13, 1976.

choice. Most of them were very poor, but they looked to the symbols of power that the West had taught them, with arms in the forefront; and the West were glad to oblige. The nations of this new Third World, largely made up of former European colonies, were now becoming counters in the power struggle of the cold war, provided with arms by both sides to enlist their support; and a few of them were rich enough customers to pay for them. But the role of Britain within her former dependencies was rapidly diminishing in the face of this global contest, and the new moral dilemmas and problems of control would increasingly centre upon Washington.

9

Israelis v. Arabs

It is almost a perpetual motion machine. We all agree that the arms race is a disaster, and we all agree that it could lead to an ultimate conflict which would more or less destroy the civilised world as we know it. The old problem is, who is going to take the first move to really pull back?

Sam Cummings, April 1967[1]

OF ALL the legacies of British imperial rule, the most explosive was the position of the new state of Israel, surrounded by hostile Arab states: for the conflict was not only local, but represented deep divisions within each of the major powers, and rivalries between them. As British influence retreated the region became a cockpit for all four major powers, first France, then Russia, then the United States, who poured in arms on both sides in a succession of balances and counter-balances, like a croupier's table, each time raising the stakes and making arms control more difficult. The central arms race between Israel and Egypt was spurred on by other rivalries—between America and Russia, between Arab states, between Arabs and Iranians, or between political factions within the major powers.

As the stakes were raised the commercial pressures to sell arms increased, and the region became far the biggest market for the arms industry, setting a faster pace for other regions in the world, and producing dangerous by-products, like the Lebanese civil war. The successive stages of the Arab-Israel arms race, and the

---

[1] Testimony to the Senate Foreign Relations Committee (Near East and South Asia sub-committee), April 13, 1967.

four wars over twenty-five years, made both superpowers more worried about the world dangers, and the need for international control. But they revealed all the weakness of the concept of regional balance and local deterrence, as each time the balance was tipped or destroyed.

In the first stage the scale of the arms was relatively tiny, with both sides restrained by lack of money and by the Anglo-American monopoly. In the first Arab-Israel war of 1948–9 both sides had acquired what they could from the surplus of war. The Israelis, with the help of American donations, had put together a motley arsenal of British weapons bought from the scrap-heaps of Europe and reconditioned in Israel, and they had also picked up weapons through Czechoslovakia, including Mauser rifles, Avia fighters and modified Messerschmitts. The state that was to be the Soviets' bugbear was first armed by the East. At the end of that first war, with the frontiers still unsettled, the major Western powers, Britain, France and the United States, agreed on the necessity for arms control, and signed the Tripartite Declaration of 1951. This declared opposition to an arms race between Arabs and Israelis, and laid down that there should be a rough balance between the three principal states, Egypt, Iraq and Israel, to be enforced by a special Near Eastern Arms Co-ordinating Committee. The agreement was incomplete, and did not try to control the flow of arms from other countries; the Belgians sold small arms to both sides, Spain sold machine-guns to Egypt, and Israel bought Sherman tanks from British and European arms dealers. But it remained a remarkably effective restraint compared with what was to come: and the three major powers held a monopoly of the heavy arms in the area. The British were then supplying ninety-five percent of the jet fighters to the Middle East; the Americans were much preoccupied with Korea, and the French were still rebuilding their arms industry.

But by 1953 the French were already disturbing the balance, and the productions of Marcel Dassault gave them the opportunity to exercise their influence, using arms sales as part of a much broader diplomatic game. While Britain was refusing to supply Meteor fighters to Israel, France stepped in by offering twenty-four of Dassault's Ouragan fighters, supplemented the next year with Mystères. The French foreign ministry was seriously divided, but the intensification of the Algerian war hardened the anti-Arab attitudes. Ostensibly the French were independent operators, but the Ouragan plane deal had been financed by an American subsidy, and Washington was relieved to see Israel supplied with modern fighters to balance the sales to Egypt. The United States was playing its own intricate balancing act, supporting the Arabs with arms and the Israelis with money, and using the Europeans as the front-men for Israeli supplies. After three years, the Tripartite Declaration was virtually discredited.

In both Egypt and Israel the governments were heavily influenced by military élites, but with very different characters. In Egypt the long domination of the British army had led Nasser and his revolutionary colleagues to equate military strength with national independence, and the buying of arms was associated with the rhetoric of sovereignty. In Israel the guerrilla leaders who had helped found the nation gave the military a special political prestige, and the industrial skills of the country could be brilliantly adapted to military technology.

The cold war was now rapidly complicating the balance. The British and Americans were trying to establish a 'Northern Tier' of nations as a defence system against Russia, in which they wanted to include Egypt: but after President Nasser came to power in 1954 the Egyptians were more determined to avoid alignment, and when the Baghdad Pact of pro-Western nations was signed in 1955, Egypt kept out of it. Nasser, feeling himself threatened militarily by Israel's arms deals and politically by his Arab rivals, now looked for arms elsewhere. He tried Britain and America without success. Then, on September 27, 1955, he announced an arms deal in which Czechoslovakia would supply Egypt with Soviet arms, including fighters, bombers, tanks, anti-aircraft guns and bazookas, in return for cotton and dried dates. It was a historic development in the history of arms sales; for though Czechoslovakia was the ostensible provider, the arms clearly marked the Soviet entry into Egypt. It was the first time that Russia had sent major arms outside its own area of influence, and it was to be the first of many such incursions. The sale marked a contradiction of Russia's position of seven years before, as one of the first to recognise the state of Israel; but it was part of the broader strategy of the cold war, with Russia trying to break into the Anglo-American tier. From now on the arms race between Israel and the Arabs was to become complicated by the central arms race of the superpowers, and by the rivalries within the West.

The separate interests of the Western powers now prevented any agreement effectively to balance the Soviet intervention. The British and Americans at first did not want to antagonise the Arabs who were essential for their oil and defence system, and were reluctant to arm Israel against Egypt; Britain tried to enforce the Tripartite agreement, but the French, embroiled in war with Algeria who was supported by Egypt, now saw Israel as their indispensable ally and provided large supplies of tanks and fighters, first with American permission, then secretly. The flow of arms to the Middle East was now running at about $200 million a year, compared to about $40 million in the early 'fifties.[1] When Nasser nationalised the Suez canal company in 1956 a new flashpoint had come: the British abruptly joined forces with Israel and France to knock out Nasser, and so began the second Arab-Israel war, which was essentially initiated by Britain and France. So far from maintaining a balance, the European powers had sought to break it, and were only frustrated by the opposition of America. This second war represented a huge escalation from the first, and provided a testing-ground for Western and Soviet arms in which their reputations were at stake. On the Egyptian side, a hundred MiG 15 fighters were destroyed on the ground, while on the Israeli side the Dassault Mystères showed their superiority in dog-fights with the Egyptian MiGs: the achievement of Dassault was now advertised through the world.

The experience and destruction of the war produced a new rush of orders. On the Egyptian side the Russians quickly supplied MiG 17 fighters, bombers and submarines, so that within a year Egypt claimed to be better armed than before: and after a brief rift of relations in 1959, the Russians resumed their supplies with MiG 18s and MiG 21s. On the Israeli side Britain and America refused to sell their most modern supersonic fighters, the Lockheed Starfighters and the BAC Lightnings. But the French were soon producing the Dassault Mirage III as a match for the Russian MiG 21s, and de Gaulle, when he came to power in 1958, still embroiled with Algeria, was determined to reinforce the Israelis. By 1961 the first Mirage had secretly arrived in Israel, bringing with it a new confidence and daring to the Israeli air force; by 1963 the Israelis had captured a MiG 21 and discovered its weak points which they could then transmit back to the Dassault

[1] *The Arms Trade and the Third World*, Stockholm, SIPRI, 1971, p. 506.

designers for new modifications: Israel had become the 'branch office of the French air force', and the chief testing-ground for the Dassault factories.[1] By 1964 the Mirage III had its first real test: four Syrian MiGs swept into Israel and met two Israeli Mirages, which shot down one and put the rest to flight.

The Americans, while still ostensibly refusing to supply the Israelis in order to avoid offending Arab friends, were in fact pressing their allies to do so through back-door routes, and they made special use of West Germany, who felt morally committed to give help to Israel. The Germans dutifully pretended that this was their own initiative, and in 1964 they sent a large consignment including two hundred surplus American tanks to Israel. But the shipment was revealed and the State Department had to admit that it had supported the German aid. In the resulting furore, Nasser invited the East German leader Walter Ulbricht to Cairo, and the West Germans then stopped aid to Israel; the Americans were now forced to begin to supply Israel direct, though still at first secretly. The devious shipments through allies, in the meantime, had increased Arab fears and uncertainty about any real balance.

The Russians were now arming not only Egypt, but also other Arab clients who had moved away from the West, including Syria, Iraq and Algeria: the old British and French alliances and rivalries were giving way to the contest between the superpowers. But neither side wished to destroy the rough balance between Israel and the Arabs, or to encourage a war which could threaten world peace. The Western powers, though divided in their aims, all dreaded a conflagration that might either obliterate Israel or cut off their oil supplies, while the Soviets knew that the United States could not see Israel faced with destruction without going to war. All the major powers put their support behind the UN peace-keeping force which served as a trip-wire. But the balance was desperately delicate: with each new stage of the build-up the fear and insecurity on both sides increased, and the Palestinian guerrillas were determined to exert their influence on Arab governments. By 1965, with the Algerian war ended, de Gaulle was beginning to turn away from his support of Israel, and the next year France sold some Mirages to Lebanon, which gave Israel a new sense of insecurity about her future arms supplies. And even if the balance appeared roughly equal, the modern

[1] Jack Gee: *Mirage—Warplane for the World*, London, Macdonald, 1971, p. 109.

weapons now gave a huge advantage to a pre-emptive strike, which could destroy it overnight.

By early 1967 the fears on both sides had again reached flash-point: the Egyptians and Syrians were warned by the Russians that Israel would attack; Nasser responded by ejecting the peace-keeping force and blockading the Straits of Tiran; and the Israelis felt compelled to fight for survival. On June 5, 1967, a wave of Mirages swept low across the Nile Valley below the radar curtain, and dropped their bombs, once again, on the MiGs parked on the Egyptian airfields: by the end of the day the Israeli planes had destroyed three hundred Egyptian planes and nineteen air bases, and could occupy the Sinai desert, the West bank and the Golan heights. It had been a joint victory for Israel and Dassault, and the technical feats of the Mirages and their pilots, televised through the world, altered the whole picture of modern warfare. The pre-emptive strike of this Six-Day War, the third Arab-Israel war, had made nonsense of the concept of balance; and the only guarantee of peace now seemed to be the obvious superiority of the Israelis.

But a new build-up and new alliances soon followed. France now changed allegiances more emphatically, as she became more worried about her oil supplies. Forty new Mirages were being built for the Israelis by Dassault at Mérignac, but de Gaulle now embargoed their delivery, and after Pompidou came to power in 1969 he authorised a drastic new deployment of arms sales as a weapon of diplomacy. In Libya the young colonels had seized power, renouncing the old British arms agreements, and they looked to France to provide their arms—particularly the Mirages still waiting at Mérignac. The temptation for Pompidou was irresistible: France could offset the growing cost of importing oil, and move into an oil region where the British and Americans were now unpopular. French diplomats explained that the young colonels only wanted the Mirages as expensive toys; but the Libyans could clearly, if they wished, lend some of the Mirages to Egypt, which they eventually did. When Pompidou visited America in February 1970, under heavy criticism from Jews, he justified the sales to Libya with the time-honoured argument of arms dealers: 'Politics and France are like nature: they abhor a vacuum. There was a vacuum to fill and we thought it was in our interests and—I add—the interests of others, to fill it'. But the selling of advanced planes to this empty country with only two million people was bound to affect the balance in the whole Arab world.

With the French thus deserting Israel, the United States felt compelled to step in directly, against her traditional policy, and the arms race between Israel and Egypt now came still closer to the confrontation between the superpowers. The United States had already supplied Skyhawk fighters and Hawk missiles, but after the war the Israelis were more insistent, with their hand strengthened in election year. By November 1968 the United States agreed to allow Israel fifty Phantom fighters—by far the deadliest planes in the region. As the Egyptians continued their build-up, the Americans stepped up their aid with missiles, tanks, helicopters and more aircraft, so that most of Israel's arms were now American. The United States maintained that by supplying arms under careful regulation she could influence Israel towards a settlement; but in the meantime she was once again raising the stakes.

In Egypt the Russians again were committed to recouping their vast losses with modern equipment: and after the Six-Day War the flow of arms from both sides to the Middle East was about $600 million a year, compared to $200 million a decade earlier.[1] The technology was making its own demands. In the 'war of attrition' across the Suez canal in 1969 and in 1970 the Russians were supplying their new SAM 3 missiles, together with Soviet troops to ensure their operation: and their advanced electronic weapons needed still more Russian technicians and training. 'The sheer volume of Soviet military support for the United Arab Republic during 1970,' said the Institute of Strategic Studies, 'was without any precedent. Never before had the Soviet Union injected anything like the quantity of sophisticated military equipment into a non-communist country in such a short time.' The Russians, like the Americans, were operating a delicate balance: they did not wish to provide so many arms as to encourage a war which might drag them in, but they could not be seen to be failing their clients in the eyes of the whole Arab world. The two superpowers had a common interest in avoiding provocation, and they collaborated in negotiating a cease-fire to the 'war of attrition' in August 1970.

Now there came a new twist to the alliances. Nasser died in September 1970 and was succeeded by President Sadat, and the

[1] *Arms Trade and the Third World*, p. 506.

new leader, surveying the strength of Israel, put his hope in negotiation with America. He believed (rightly) that Russia would not back him to the point of supporting a war: Moscow was refusing to supply the most up-to-date weapons, including the MiG 23 Foxbat, and was more concerned with arming India than Egypt. In July 1972 Sadat abruptly announced that he would expel the Russians from Egypt. The break was not complete: the Soviets left behind their enormous arsenal, including 1,700 tanks, 620 combat planes and 130 SAM missile sites; Moscow was still able to strengthen its ties with Syria and Iraq; and the Russians showed some signs of being quite relieved to leave Egypt, with all its complications. But their expulsion demonstrated the fallacy of the argument that supplying arms can ensure control over the clients' policies. The ten-year Soviet arming of Egypt had left behind little diplomatic advantage.

Sadat for a time hoped that Washington could press Israel to retreat from her new frontiers; but by early 1973, watching the build-up of American Phantoms and other weapons in Israel, he resolved that Egypt must now make a pre-emptive strike to force a settlement, in alliance with Syria and with the backing of Saudi Arabia. And so, in October 1973, came the fourth war—with predominantly Russian arms on the Arab side, and American and French weapons on the Israeli side. As the Arabs pushed into Israeli-occupied territory and the Egyptians crossed the Suez canal, the war involved the superpowers more urgently than any of the previous three; the Russians airlifted supplies to Egypt, while the Americans rushed Phantoms and missiles to Israel. The desperation of both sides gave the superpowers some leverage over their clients, and eventually the cease-fire was thrashed out in Moscow between Kissinger and Brezhnev. The Israelis reckoned the cost of their side of the war, in equipment and property, at around $4 billion.

The nature of the balance now once again changed: the Russians were out of Egypt, and the Americans had much greater influence in Cairo, while also continuing to be the main suppliers to Israel. The situation was in some ways like that before 1955, before the Russians had come to Egypt, with the West holding both sides of the balance: but this time the Americans were arming the Israelis directly, and also supplying many of the Arab states, while leaving the Europeans to arm the Egyptians. There might seem to be more prospect of effective control; but this soon proved very doubtful. For Israel was now equipped, with past assistance from the French and Americans, to supply a large part of her own arms; and the huge flow of oil money into the Arab world was adding a new variable into the equation, and providing new commercial incentives to export. The Arab-Israel arms race, as we will see later, was now becoming part of a broader arms race through the whole Middle East.

While the Americans were arming both Israelis and Arabs, this did not seem to enable them to control supplies much more effectively. The arms race was now in part a race between two policies inside America: the companies wanted to export to the rich Arab nations, while Congress was determined to keep Israel ahead in the technological contest, with the help of massive aid from Washington. It was a race between California and New York: the keys to restraint lay as much in the Pentagon and Congress as in Cairo and Jerusalem.

In the quarter-century since the foundation of Israel, after four Arab-Israel wars, the record of arms control was dismal. The four major powers, changing sides and interests, had helped to provoke wars as much as to control them; and the arsenals had grown to the point where they provided an important element in the economies of the suppliers. The whole of the Middle East was now setting a breathtaking pace in its arms buying. Between 1950 and 1961 the annual rate of increase was already nearly double the world average—11.5 percent compared to 6.5 percent; but after 1961 the average rate of increase was up to twenty percent, or nearly seven times the world average (2.8 percent). By 1974 the gross national product in the Middle East was $845 per head of population, of which $135 was devoted to military spending. The only recent historical parallel to such an escalation was the arms race in Europe in the years before the Second World War.[1]

---

[1] SIPRI Year Book 1976: pp. 62–3.

10

Hanky-Panky in the
Third World

In doing business abroad you have to take into consideration the
customs of the countries.

Dan Haughton, 1975[1]

WHEN McNamara first set up his arms sales organisation in 1961,
with Henry Kuss at the Pentagon, the majority of the customers
were in the industrial world. The sales campaigns were unrelent-
ing, whether from the government or the companies, when they
sold their Hercules or Tigers to Europe or the F111 to Britain;
but these developed countries could be expected to defend their
own interests. Gradually, however, more of Kuss's sales were
going to the Third World, with a growing proportion destined
for the Middle East, and here the effects of the salesmen were
more far-reaching: for they were in a position to influence the
priorities and patterns of developing countries. In theory the
control system in the Pentagon and the State Department could
ensure that countries only bought what they really needed: in
the State Department, apart from the Arms Control and Disarmament Agency, there was the Office of Munitions Control,
to supervise the licensing of all lethal weapons. But that office
had no real authority to control the Pentagon sales; and their staff
was tiny compared to the Pentagon teams, or to the armies of
company salesmen, pushing their wares in Washington and roam-

[1] Multinational Hearings, part 12, p. 367.

ing through the capitals of the Third World. Just how ruthless and effective was their pressure would only emerge a decade later.

By the mid-'sixties, Congress was becoming more worried by the effects of arms sales in the Third World, partly as a result of the Indo-Pakistan war of 1965, where American arms (together with those of other countries) were used on both sides. Pakistanis in Patton tanks fought Indians in Sherman tanks, and both armies were flown in American transports. The United States soon embargoed the supply of arms to both sides (though later relenting to supply 'non-lethal' arms), but the American role in the war aroused sharp recrimination: 'The arms we supplied under this policy,' said J. K. Galbraith, the former Ambassador to India, '*caused* the war . . . If we had not supplied arms, Pakistan would not have sought the one thing we wanted above all to avoid: namely a military solution.'

The concern about the American role was heightened by the discovery that during the embargo Pakistan had received ninety American F86 Sabre jet fighters to reinforce their tiny air force. The planes had, it turned out, been exported by West Germany, ostensibly to Iran, but in fact for use in Pakistan.[1] The deal had been done by a German middleman, Gerhard Mertins, a bombastic arms dealer who was then an associate of Sam Cummings; but Mertins at that time had close connections with the German secret service, and it was quite clear that the sale of the planes had been permitted by the Pentagon. ('Do you imagine,' Mertins said to me later, 'that we wouldn't have American permission?') The transfer suited everyone except the Indians: the West Germans wanted to sell the planes, which were outdated by the new Starfighters; Mertins got his commission; the Pakistanis needed them urgently; and the Americans were anxious to please the Pakistanis without being seen to.

More worrying to Congress were the sales to Iran, which was already a controversial market for arms, as we will see further in chapter 14. In July 1966 Washington had agreed to sell the new McDonnell Phantom fighters to the Shah, who then, only seven months later, made a deal with Russia to buy $110 million in military equipment. The Senate Foreign Relations Committee was affronted, and the sub-committee on the Near East and South East Asia convened hearings under their chairman, Senator

---

[1] George Thayer: *The War Business*, Paladin (paperback), London, 1970, pp. 171–3.

Symington (a former secretary of the air force, who was now gradually changing his plumage from a hawk's to a dove's).

Henry Kuss testified to the senators, and insisted that most of his sales went to the seven industrialised countries; the Shah was an exception, since he had the money to buy arms, and was a reliable ally. But Senator Fulbright, the chairman of the Foreign Relations Committee, eloquently protested: 'I have been in Iran and it is a most desolate country. There are very few rich people, but the majority could easily turn to revolution. I think you are doing a great disservice to them loading them down with these arms.' Jeffrey Kitchen, from the State Department, assured the senators that they were trying to limit the amount of arms sent to the Middle East, but Senator Symington replied: 'How can you say we have been trying to limit arms sales when in five years it has grown from $300 million a year to $1.7 billion a year?' Symington concluded: 'We find that we either have been unable or unwilling to control heavy sales of arms to the very allies we have been defending and financing, which breeds continued arms races all over the world. It is difficult to understand, and our policy could have in it the seeds of World War Three.'[1]

As Congress pursued their enquiries, they discovered more about the extent of the government's pushing of arms sales to the Third World. It became clear that the military advisers in foreign capitals (the MAAGs or military assistance advisory groups) who had originally been established as part of the military aid programmes, were now acting as salesmen to assist Kuss's office (as the British and French had also been doing). It also emerged in 1967 that the Pentagon were obtaining cheap credit from the Export-Import bank to help finance arms sales: about a third of the Eximbank loans were now going to arms sales, and the *New York Times* discovered that by 1964 the Third World was paying four billion dollars a year in debt servicing alone, much of it incurred from arms sales, and equal to half the new economic aid in that year.[2]

Much of the pressure to buy arms was emanating from the Pentagon itself, encouraged by the MAAGs; but the companies, as they geared themselves increasingly to export, were becoming much more aggressive, and in the Third World they had more

[1] Senate Foreign Relations Committee: Near East and South East Asia Hearings, March 14, 1967, p. 110.
[2] See Thayer, pp. 178-182.

freedom than in Europe. As more countries achieved independence, the companies were better able to play them against each other, as Zaharoff had done fifty years earlier. The customer-governments in young nations lacked the constraints of the old industrialised countries, and the military élites were always anxious to increase their prestige and perhaps their income through new weaponry. Here the concept of the military-industrial complex had a deeper meaning: for the military could settle the pattern for a country's development, and this provided a promising territory for what arms companies called 'missionary activity', or what the State Department called 'brochuremanship' —stimulating needs and appetites through glossy salesmanship. In theory the Western governments could keep the salesmen in check. But as aid gave way to sales, so—as Henry Kuss admitted— 'it was a lot harder to sell it than it is to give away and still accomplish your objectives'.[1]

The arms companies were constantly trying to find new markets by lobbying the armies or air forces, and the Lockheed and Northrop papers provide recurring evidence of how they could thus affect national priorities. Lockheed's most profitable export during the 'sixties was the Hercules military transport, which had become an important part of the economy of Georgia. The giant Hercules had no real competitor: the Russian AN-12 and the Franco-German Transall transports were much less effective in moving troops quickly and efficiently. The army and air force officers loved this spectacular plane, but it was often very doubtful (as in Italy) whether it was really necessary for national defence; and in this situation Lockheed were sometimes in alliance with the military against civilian spending. Later I asked a Lockheed executive from Georgia why the company had to sell the plane so relentlessly, when it had a virtual monopoly; he replied, 'We're always competing with other government projects.' And the selling of the Hercules abroad was of special interest to the Pentagon who (as they admitted) wished to keep open the production line in Georgia, in case they should wish to order more Hercules for themselves.

A vivid example of the effects of this salesmanship emerged in Colombia in 1972, when Lockheed were promoting their Hercules at a time when the president had requested a reduction in the military budget. Lockheed's representative in Bogota,

[1] Near East and South Asia Hearings, 1967, p. 3.

Edwin Swartz, advised Lockheed in Georgia that 'high officers of the air force' would make a grand effort to arrange the buying of a third Hercules, in return for bribes or 'sugar' amounting to $100,000. The Bogota agent reported that he had found out that the air force would ignore the reduction in the military budget, 'IF THEY CAN JUSTIFY THEIR NECESSITY OF MORE EQUIPMENT IN ORDER TO GUARANTEE THE NATIONAL SECURITY'. 'Just between you and me,' he added, 'this is not exactly true, as you can imagine, but the important point for us is that they want sugar; and for that, they are ready to do almost anything'. The meaning was unambiguous: the point of the bribe was to sell arms, where arms were not needed.

Of all the newly-independent nations, the most emphatically military was Indonesia, the former Dutch colony which had become independent in 1949. Up till the mid-'sixties Indonesia offered great scope for arms salesmen, for under President Sukarno it was spending no less than seventy-five percent of its budget on arms; it was an example of 'an underdeveloped country preoccupied with a military build-up that is out of proportion to its economic resources'.[1] During the Sukarno regime Lockheed had employed the services of the influential Dasaad family, who had successfully negotiated the sale of Hercules and JetStar planes, until Sukarno's pro-communist policies had caused him to be embargoed by the Americans and British. As the commissions went up, Lockheed became uneasy.

In June 1965 the Indonesians wanted the price of a fourth JetStar to be increased by $100,000 so that extra commission could be paid to Dasaad. The Lockheed man involved, W. G. Myers, had worried discussions with Dan Haughton and Carl Kotchian; he explained that 'this hanky-panky had gone far enough . . . it just isn't right, and there is a limit somewhere'. Kotchian was in favour of paying the extra $100,000, but Haughton eventually refused to authorise it; and the sale of the plane nevertheless went through.[2] But the hanky-panky with the Indonesians soon went further.

In 1966 Sukarno was overthrown by President Suharto, and Lockheed hectically tried to find out whether Dasaad still kept

[1] *The Arms Trade and The Third World*, Stockholm, SIPRI, 1971, p. 461.
[2] Multinational Hearings, part 12, pp. 358, 938.

his influence. Their man Ned Ridings, the sales manager for the region, consulted the air force attaché at the American embassy Colonel Bill Slade, who promised to find out through the CIA, and he duly reported back to Ridings that Dasaad was 'in' with the new regime. 'Old Das' certainly kept up the appearance of influence: Ridings observed that a big picture of General Suharto was now occupying the place where Sukarno's picture used to be.[1] And from Geneva the far-reaching Fred Meuser intervened to stress the importance of Dasaad. But it soon transpired that Dasaad was really 'out', and Lockheed now turned instead to dealing direct with air force officers, to whom they paid bribes into a special account in Singapore, known as 'the Widows and Orphans Fund'. Lockheed wanted to interpose a new agent, as they explained in detail, to protect themselves against disclosure and to enable payments to be tax-deductible. But the Indonesians insisted on direct payments, and there was now a short cut between the two sides of the military-industrial complex.[2]

But there were still tiresome competitors, and one was the Pentagon itself, which was supplying free spare parts to the Indonesian air force. 'The Pentagon,' complained a Lockheed memo in 1970, was 'promising these people the sun and delivering it with extra.' Another competitor was a firm called Aviquipo, which was offering the Indonesians ten percent commission for spare parts, or twice what Lockheed was offering. But Aviquipo soon turned out to be a subsidiary of Lockheed itself. 'It's tough enough doing business nowadays,' complained a Lockheed executive in a memo, 'without having someone in your own house making the job more difficult.'[3] In a country already almost ruined by its previous spending on arms, Lockheed was still trying to raise the stakes, and competing with bribes against itself.

Lockheed was also contending with the Pentagon a thousand miles north, in a far less military climate, in the Philippines: it was a country where, according to the US air force commander General Gideon, the military threat was 'very small'.[4] But nevertheless in the late 'sixties twenty-two Northrop Tigers were sent to the Philippines, and in 1971 Lockheed were pressing to sell Hercules to the Philippine air force. In this case they used their

[1] Multinational Hearings, part 12, p. 958.
[2] Ibid., pp. 984–988.
[3] Ibid., p. 978.
[4] *Arms Trade and the Third World*, pp. 458–9.

agent, a public relations man called Buddy Orora, who was with
McCann Erickson and had earlier worked in the Philippine president's office. But just when the sales seemed in the bag, the Pentagon came in with an offer of twelve old C119 transports, which
had been in mothballs for years. Lockheed asked Buddy Orora to
expose this 'travesty on the Philippine people' and to stir up
'public knowledge and the resultant indignation'. Buddy duly
obliged by feeding the story to journalists and promised to follow
it up with informal contacts with the Philippine government:
'from there, things should fall into place automatically, and hopefully reach a level where the authorities will feel pressured to
"request" the US government for a review of the matter.'[1] It was
a significant glimpse of Lockheed's technique, of stirring up
foreign governments to increase their demands.

Latin America in the mid-'sixties was a subject of special
frustration to the arms companies, for this traditionally lucrative
market was being largely denied them by the Pentagon's re-
straints. There had been no war in Latin America since the Chaco
war between Bolivia and Paraguay in the 'thirties; but there were
rivalries and border disputes, such as that between Chile and Peru
(which had been so precious to Electric Boat and Vickers in the
'thirties, when they were trying to "ginger-up" Chile);[2] and
nearly every country had a military government, which made the
arms salesmen more at home. After the Second World War the
United States had emerged as the major supplier, after some
incursions by the British, but the arming was relatively restrained,
not so much as an arms race as an 'arms walk'.[3] After the Cuban
revolution in 1959, the Pentagon under McNamara tried to
encourage peaceful economic development rather than heavy
military expenditure, and concentrated on providing weapons
against revolutionaries and guerrillas. The United States, with
its leverage through economic aid, had some success in preventing
the buying of advanced weapons; they refused, for instance, to
let Chile buy Northrop Tigers, and as late as 1968 no Latin
American country possessed supersonic fighters. But the military
leaders were increasingly resentful of this restraint, and they
looked to Europe for alternative suppliers: by 1966 Chile bought

[1] Multinational Hearings, part 12, pp. 1144–8.
[2] See chapter 2.
[3] John L. Sutton and Geoffrey Kemp: *Arms to Developing Countries 1945–1965*, Institute
for Strategic Studies, London, October 1966, p. 30.

subsonic Hawker Hunters from Britain, and in 1968 the truce on arms sales was more emphatically broken when the French government agreed to sell the supersonic Mirage 5 fighters to the new military junta in Peru.

The French sale increased the resentment of the American arms companies against Washington, and what *Aviation Week* called 'the high-handed paternalistic approach' of Congress. In the four years from 1968, European countries sold arms to Latin America worth over $1.2 billion, while Americans sold only $335 millions worth. But the arms companies were working hard behind the scenes, particularly on Brazil, the fastest-growing market of all, which had both a military government and a boom economy. Northrop were in the thick of it, and they promoted their Tiger fighters in their customary way. In 1971 they engaged two agents in Brazil, who ran a company called NASA (Nacional de Servicos de Aeronautica), and who were very close to friends of General Edivio, commander of Brazil's second tactical air force: the general assured Northrop that he had complete faith in them. In the next three years, Northrop committed $2.3 million to the company in 'commissions' to achieve a sale of the fighters, and in the meantime they were lobbying relentlessly in Washington, where their network of hospitality was being carefully established.[1] The companies' efforts were handsomely rewarded. On June 5, 1973 President Nixon reversed the previous American policy to allow the Tiger fighters to be sold to Brazil, Argentina, Chile, Colombia and Peru. A new surge of sales soon followed, led by an order for forty-two Northrop Tigers, worth $120 million, from Brazil. The Northrop sales, rejoiced *Aviation Week*, were 'the opening wedges in what should be a substantial US penetration of the Latin American market'.[2]

Latin America was once again a free-for-all for arms salesmen, with the stakes rapidly increasing. Brazil was now arming herself more heavily, not only against insurgents, but against neighbours, providing a bonanza for American companies as well as the British and French: after 1973 Boeing, Lockheed, Hughes and Bell helicopters all made big sales to Brazil. The Peru-Chile rivalry was waxing stronger than ever: after Peru had been

[1] Multinational Hearings, part 14, pp. 919–932. See also Michael Jensen in the *New York Times*, July 1, 1975.

[2] See *Aviation Week*, October 8, 1973 and July 8, 1974; also Michael T. Klare in NACLA's Latin America Report, March 1975; also SIPRI: *The Arms Trade and The Third World*, pp. 685–691.

refused Tiger fighters, she accepted an offer of thirty-six Soviet fighters on much more favourable terms, and Washington felt unable to make any serious protest to Moscow in view of the extent of other American arms sales close to the Soviet frontiers, particularly in Iran.[1] Thus the Middle East build-up helped to justify the build-up elsewhere. The arms walk was now rapidly quickening into a race.

[1] Juan de Dris in the *New York Times*, October 14, 1974.

11

The Saudi Middleman

If one offers money to a government to influence it, that is corruption. But if someone receives money for services rendered afterwards, that is a commission.

Adnan Khashoggi, 1976

OF ALL the arms salesmen's provinces in the emerging Third World, it was the Middle East, from the mid-'sixties onwards, which held the most promise of profits; and it was Saudi Arabia that was developing into the richest of all their new customers, with its mounting revenues from oil. There were some legitimate Saudi fears about defence; in the mid-'sixties, as we have seen chapter 8), they were threatened by Egypt through the Yemen, and made their first big arms deal with British and American companies. But the danger from Egypt subsided after 1967, and thereafter the exact nature of the threat was always difficult to evaluate. The country was vast—one third the size of the United States, and indefensible against any serious aggressor. The Saudis were not well-versed in military technology, and the problem was (somewhat complicated by the existence of two separate defence forces, run by rival princes. The minister of defence, Prince Sultan, one of the brothers of King Feisal, regarded the conventional armed forces as his personal empire, with his brother, Prince Turki, as his deputy; while Prince Abdullah, a half-brother, presided over the National Guard, the former 'white army' of the Bedouins, which provided a rival army. Both princes competed to acquire

189

the latest weapons, and as the oil revenues mounted, so the incentive to militarise the country became greater—both for the princes and for the companies. The Saudi fears were not difficult to encourage, for their government was more fervently anti-communist than the Pentagon. It was a lucrative situation for middlemen.

As early as 1964, before the big arms deal had been consummated, Lockheed had taken on an agent, Adnan Khashoggi, who was before long to become the biggest arms dealer of them all, rivalling in his scope and fortune the great Zaharoff himself. His role was so important that his career calls for special attention. He was only twenty-six when Lockheed engaged him, and not a wealthy man, but he had an electric personality and all the mobility of a man of two worlds. Cool and immaculate, he talked quickly and incisively, changing from explosive Arabic to smooth American English. His genial style and wide laugh concealed the watchfulness in his dark eyes. His hands moved constantly, squeezing, punching, spreading over his heart, slicing the air, weaving his own world around him in eloquent mime. He epitomised the vigour of a young Arab generation determined to leave its mark on the West, to rival the international power of the Jews. But his importance in Saudi Arabia rested from the beginning on his special relationship with members of the royal family.

His father, an austere and devout doctor from Mecca, was one of the physicians to the great King ibn Saud: doctors in Arabia have traditionally wielded an influence beyond their calling. Adnan was the eldest son of the second of his father's three wives, and one of eleven children in all. He was sent to school at Victoria College in Egypt, a very British academy, where his friends included the future King Hussein of Jordan. From there, like other ambitious young Saudis, he went to college in California, first to Chico State University, north of San Francisco, then to Stanford. He never took a degree, but it was in California that he first showed an interest in business, and got to know a truck manufacturer, who later gave him the distribution rights in Saudi Arabia.

Returning to his own country, he was well placed to benefit from the expanding oil revenues. He was friendly with King Saud, the dissolute son of Ibn Saud, and among Khashoggi's princely friends two were to become very powerful in the government: Prince Fahd (who today is effectively the ruler) and Prince

Sultan, now the minister of defence—the man whom Geoffrey Edwards had already assiduously cultivated for the British arms deal, who was the crucial figure in the arms business. The young Khashoggi, with his American background, brought a worldly understanding to the constricted life of Riyadh and Jeddah, and a great capacity for enjoyment. He loved the night-life of Beirut, and he married a seventeen-year-old English girl who gave him a daughter and four sons.

Soon he was a successful businessman. He became the representative of two British firms, Rolls-Royce and Marconi. He was granted by King Saud the monopoly for developing gypsum deposits in Saudi Arabia. Three years later, with the outbreak of civil war in Yemen, he first began dealing in arms. He supplied French arms to the ruler—he was always prepared to represent different nationalities. Later he began trading in Beirut, which was in the middle of a boom in banking and real estate. And behind him were always the princes.

The financial relationship between Khashoggi and the princes was, and is, impossible to penetrate. Saudi Arabia was not only a pre-industrial society: it was essentially feudal. The chief source of private wealth was the royal family, to whom much of the oil revenues came, and the small commercial class depended largely on the patronage either of the princes or of the American companies—or, best of all, of both. The successful middlemen, like Khashoggi, were in the same kind of position as the agents and quartermasters in the European courts in the sixteenth century who made huge fortunes catering for the palaces and the armies, and charging heavily for their services.

In this context, the Western concept of corruption was virtually meaningless. If an agent charged much too much or backed the wrong man, he might suffer or be disgraced. But so long as he performed his brokerage effectively, he was indispensable to his masters. With the arrival of the American companies in Saudi Arabia, on top of the increasing price and production of oil, the middlemen—particularly those with experience of America—began to play a far greater role than before.

It was into this antiquated labyrinth that the Lockheed executives stumbled in 1964, encouraged by their successes in Europe, eager, impatient and determined to sell planes as quickly as possible. They knew very little about Saudi Arabia, except that it was becoming rich; and (as Dan Haughton later explained) they needed someone 'to teach them the customs'.[1] Khashoggi, already representing two British firms, with his convincing style and California background, was an obvious choice. By October 1964 Lockheed had signed an agreement by which Khashoggi would act as its agent for its Hercules transports, charging two percent for each aircraft sale. Exactly what the commission was *for* was left unsaid, but Khashoggi and his friends were much concerned about the continuity of the commitment. In New York in July 1965 he asked a Lockheed man, Gerald B. Juliani, to be sure that no mention of commissions be made in either Beirut or Saudi Arabia, and that all communications about commissions go through his representative in Geneva, Gérard Boissier.[2] Switzerland, once again, was the key to the network.

Through all the Lockheed correspondence with Khashoggi there looms a gap not only between different continents, but between different centuries. A highly organised modern industrial bureaucracy was confronting a resourceful representative of feudal princes: it was as if men in grey flannel suits walked into the middle of a Shakespeare play. It was never clear where the Saudi government ended and Khashoggi began. By August 1967 Khashoggi was complaining about the non-payment of $50,000 that he claimed was due to him after the sale of the fifth Hercules. Lockheed disputed its liability, whereupon Khashoggi suggested that Lockheed simply send an invoice 'through channels' to the Saudi government for the $50,000, the payment of which, he promised, would be pushed through. 'In this particular case,' wrote Gene Otsea of Lockheed in Geneva, 'he has a great interest in pushing it through, since the money will really wind up in his pocket.'[3]

By 1967 Khashoggi had formed a new and bigger company called Triad, a Liechtenstein corporation with its address in Geneva. Formally, the company was run by the three Khashoggi brothers, Adnan, Adil and Essam, but essentially Adnan was the sole boss of the expanding organisation. His relationship with the Saudi government and particularly with the ministry of defence had become more important since the Six-Day War in June, 1967. The Saudis, although not involved in the war, became more concerned about their military equipment and needed more trucks—

[1] Multinational Hearings, part 12, p. 353.
[2] Ibid., part 12, p. 1003.
[3] Lockheed Papers: Otsea to Hausman, September 4, 1967

which Khashoggi was happy to supply from California through his first agency—and as a result he was also given the contract for running the airport at Dhahran, the oil city. Khashoggi insisted that his contracts were due to his ability to deliver what the Saudis needed. The important fact remained that the minister of defence was his close friend and patron, Prince Sultan. Exactly what happened to all the money paid to Khashoggi remains concealed in bank accounts: all Dan Haughton would say was that 'we think that some of the money went someplace else'.[1]

It is important to try to see the problem from the point of view of Dan Haughton. He never actually went out to Saudi Arabia, but he knew from Lockheed salesmen that Saudi officials had demanded to be paid off; and after his experience in Europe, with the easy corruption of Prince Bernhard, he was doubtless inclined to believe all the more in the 'customs of the country'. He was convinced that the European companies, particularly the French Bréguet and Dassault, were constantly bribing; and the Pentagon had given no indication that they disapproved of Lockheed doing likewise. When he discussed payoffs and kickbacks with the Pentagon, it was not ethics that he was concerned with, but about whether the payments were allowable under Foreign Military Sales. And at the same time he was constantly hearing about the importance of exports for the balance of payments. He was always aware of his responsibilities to his 60,000 employees in California and Georgia, and the more perilous the company's domestic future, the more crucial were exports. While Lockheed were walking deeper into corruption, Haughton was being publicly acclaimed in America as a master-manager—as 'Management Man of the Year' in 1966, as 'Marketing Executive of the Year' in 1968. The bribes or kickbacks were not chargeable on Lockheed's profit and loss account: they simply added to the price paid by the customer. And in the early 'sixties the kickbacks did not seem very large; it was only by the 'seventies, when Lockheed's overseas sales were nearing the billion dollars a year, that the commissions became so large that they bred 'unfortunate side-effects'.[2]

Through all Lockheed's explanations, whether in private or public, there is the recurring impression that while others might see them as all-powerful, they saw themselves as underdogs struggling against unseen forces and cunning foreigners, paying

---

[1] Multinational Hearings, part 12, p. 353.

[2] Haughton's defence: see Multinational Hearings, part 12, pp. 347–71.

out money to curry favour wherever they could, and following the custom. But in the meantime the sums were becoming so big that they were helping to create the custom of the country itself. The commissions were turning into unprecedented private fortunes, and the very presence of the big-spending foreign companies was transforming the economy, like a luxury liner calling at a tropical island.

By the late 'sixties Khashoggi was already much more than an arms dealer; he was increasingly involved in international politics. As with Zaharoff fifty years earlier, the large-scale selling of arms had led him into the inner world of diplomacy (though like Zaharoff he was prone to exaggerate his role). Having lived in America, Khashoggi was obsessed by the influence of the Israeli lobby over American foreign policy and (like the Saudi royal family) he was determined to exert a counterpressure on Washington, more urgently after the Arab humiliation of the Six-Day War in 1967.

In the presidential election of 1968 the Arabs regarded the Democrats as the Jewish party. The Saudis pinned their hopes on a Republican victory, and Khashoggi himself had a special reason for confidence in the Republicans, since in 1967 he had become acquainted with Richard Nixon. In June of that year, just before the outbreak of the Six-Day War, Nixon visited Morocco. He was disappointed by his reception: King Hassan would not even see him. Then in Paris he was introduced to Khashoggi at the Ritz hotel by a mutual friend, a lawyer called John Pochna: they dined at the Rasputin restaurant, and Khashoggi undertook to make sure that Nixon would be received in other Arab countries in proper style. He offered to finance the rest of Nixon's tour, complete with private aircraft.

His generosity showed foresight at a time when Nixon's political future was not promising and Khashoggi himself was not very rich. He continued to see Nixon in America, and he forged another link through his business associate Bebe Rebozo, the real-estate dealer from Florida who was Nixon's close confidant in the 1968 election campaign. By the time Nixon became president in January 1969, Khashoggi was already a trusted friend; and the following month, during a two-day stay in Paris as the guest of de Gaulle, Nixon found time in his crowded schedule for a talk with him. Khashoggi mentioned his concern about his friend King Hussein who had felt himself badly treated when he had visited President Johnson, and would not come to Washington again. Nixon assured Khashoggi that he would be properly received, and a year later Hussein visited Nixon in Washington, to a much friendlier welcome.

During Nixon's presidency Khashoggi had several meetings with him, including visits to San Clemente and Key Biscayne, but it is not known what was discussed. (When Nixon finally resigned, Khashoggi wrote a letter of condolence and received a warm reply.) It was later alleged that Khashoggi had contributed $1 million to Nixon's presidential campaign in 1972 (though foreign contributions are illegal) and just before that election Mohammed Haykal, then editor of *Al Ahram* in Cairo, wrote that 'we Arabs were almost the most zealous contributors to Nixon's campaign', and that between $10 million and $12 million was paid into Nixon's election campaign fund from Arab sources.[1] Haykal's figure is thought to be a great exaggeration, but it would have been very easy for Khashoggi to contribute discreetly to Nixon's campaign. The Watergate prosecutors questioned Khashoggi, who admitted that he had paid $50,000 as a business investment, to finance a phonograph record to promote Nixon's campaign. It is possible that other money was paid through Bebe Rebozo and that other campaign contributions also partly represented Khashoggi's interests (one friend of Khashoggi's, Robert Vesco, contributed $200,000). There was one payment that some Arabs were inclined to assume represented Khashoggi and the princes: the $150,000 paid by the Northrop corporation— half of it paid personally by the chairman, Tom Jones.

While Lockheed were cementing their relationship with Khashoggi with still heavier commissions, Tom Jones was again following in the Lockheed trail as he had done in Europe, extending his secret Northrop network to sell Tiger fighters to the Middle East. The Northrop men were not facing, like Lockheed, a major financial crisis at home to spur on the exports: the Tiger had virtually no competitor, and had the thrust of the Pentagon behind it. But Northrop was just as relentless as Lockheed, and more sophisticated. Jones had already in 1965 taken on a very well-connected Middle East consultant, Kim Roosevelt, the grandson of Theodore Roosevelt and former CIA officer, who still kept some links with the Agency. Roosevelt's main role, as will be seen in chapter 14, was in Iran, where he was very close

[1] *Al Ahram*, November 3, 1972.

to the Shah. But he was also well acquainted with Saudi Arabia, and a friend of the new monarch King Feisal, who had taken over from his brother King Saud: and it was Roosevelt who suggested to Northrop in 1970 the desirability of a talk with Khashoggi. The Northrop executives accordingly met with Khashoggi in Paris and reached an agreement that he should represent them in Saudi Arabia. There was one document (as their attorney explained) that was 'open and public to justify our relationship with Khashoggi in-country'. But all other documents and agreements were secret. The fact that Khashoggi also represented Lockheed was evidently no impediment.

The Northrop men, like Lockheed before them, soon found themselves lost in the labyrinth of Saudi royal intrigue, with Khashoggi guiding them deviously through the maze. In January 1971 one of their executives, Grant Rogin, went on a five-day visit to Khashoggi in Paris, and reported his bewilderment: Khashoggi, he explained, had made it clear that there 'would be more players' before Northrop could conclude its sale of the Tigers; and one of the princes, Prince Khalid bin Abdullah, emphasised to Rogin that he would himself be indispensable for the sale. Khashoggi eventually entertained Rogin, dining in Paris at one a.m. with 'a cast of thousands', and assured him that Khalid did not really 'swing a big stick'. But Rogin returned from his visit in evident confusion: 'I'm going to have to call out who are the players . . . and soon.'[1]

By July 1971, Northrop's critical contract for twenty Tigers was ready for signing, and the Northrop team arrived in Jeddah in the blazing summer heat for the ceremony. But it was mysteriously delayed for a day, and that evening Prince Khalid came to see the Northrop team in their hotel, looking very upset. Like the wicked fairy, he was determined to spoil the party, for he had discovered that the big deal was going through on a government-to-government basis, which meant that he would get nothing out of it, while Adnan Khashoggi would get his fat commission. 'If I get nothing,' he threatened, 'then I will make sure that Adnan gets nothing.' The next day they all assembled again at the ministry of defence for the signing, and just after one o'clock the minister Prince Sultan arrived with his deputy, Prince Turki. Sultan reviewed the contract, and asked whether Northrop had an agent in Saudi Arabia. Northrop said no, and the American

[1] Northrop Papers: Rogin to Gates, January 28, 1971.

ambassador explained that, this being a government-to-government sale, there would be no middleman. Sultan then explained that usually with contracts of this size he would take months before signing, but in this case, because of his confidence in the American government and the ambassador, he would sign right away—and he did so. But Khalid was still able to have his revenge, and the Northrop team realised that Sultan's question about the agent had an ominous ring. Just after the signing Prince Turki asked to see the Northrop representatives, and then explained that he understood that there was an unfortunate disagreement with Khalid, which he hoped could be worked out to his satisfaction. Eventually Khalid had to be given one eighth of Khashoggi's commission, which amounted to between $500,000 and $1 million.[1]

The Northrop people, as they pressed for further orders for Tigers, found themselves still deeper in the business of payoffs. In October 1971 Tom Jones himself flew out to Saudi Arabia on his first visit, to see King Feisal and other leaders. On his first evening he had dinner with Khashoggi—the first time he had met him. Khashoggi told Jones that the head of the Saudi air force, General Hashim, should be given $250,000 to ensure that the orders for Tigers would go through. Jones (according to his own account) said to his colleague, Bob Gates, 'Look, this is not the kind of subject that should be brought up this way: it is very delicate, very sensitive; we have an agent to keep us from getting into these kinds of problems.' But Jones also made the emphatic statement to Khashoggi: 'Northrop meets its obligations.' Jones later explained: "The minute I heard generals, I should have said I want to see no payments made to the generals. I didn't make that statement and therefore my use of the words "Northrop meets its obligations" was misinterpreted.'[2] Soon there came the further news from Khashoggi that General Hashim was about to be kicked upstairs, and that his successor, General Zuhair, would also need to be bribed. Eventually Northrop found themselves paying $250,000 to Hashim and another $200,000 to Zuhair.

Khashoggi, explaining the incident to me, had a different account. The trouble with the American visitors, he explained, was that they were too naive. They worried because a general wasn't smiling at them that morning, not realising that he had

[1] Ibid., Macleod to Watts, July 31, 1971.
[2] Multinational Hearings, part 12, p. 181.

probably only been having trouble with his wife. They would pay people money unnecessarily because it made them feel more comfortable in a strange country. It was Northrop, Khashoggi went on, that insisted on paying General Hashim; but 'I knew that it would threaten to terminate Northrop's relationship with Saudi Arabia if it was delivered, so I stopped the cheque from reaching him.'[1]

Lockheed, in the meantime, knew that Khashoggi was also representing Northrop (whereas they never knew about Bernhard and Gerritsen in Holland). Khashoggi took care not to entertain both clients (or his other clients including the British and French) at the same time, or to let them meet on the stairs; but all parties knew that he was dealing with their rivals and regarded him as indispensable nevertheless. But both Northrop and Lockheed were by now finding that the more they paid in 'commissions', the more people demanded them. By August 1973 Lockheed found that the original two percent it had agreed to pay for the sales of the Hercules transports, whose basic price was about $2.5 million, had escalated to eight percent—an increase, Khashoggi explained, 'due to more players getting involved, and the necessity to satisfy their requirements in order to get the contracts signed'. And on top of the commissions, the company was paying up to $200,000 per aircraft for what was described as a 'marketing contingency', paid out of a special contingency fund. Most of the fund (a Lockheed memo explained on August 16) was used by Khashoggi for 'under the table compensation to Saudi officials; but we really have no way of knowing if the so-called "under the table" compensation is ever disbursed to Saudi officials, or stops at our consultant's bank account.'[2]

Already early in 1973 Northrop was having serious doubts about Khashoggi; King Feisal was known now to disapprove of him, and there was mounting resentment (one of Northrop's agents reported) against him in Saudi Arabia, so that he was now looking farther abroad—to Brazil, to the Sudan, to California— for his expansion. And both the Pentagon and Northrop were becoming more worried by the question of commissions in government-to-government contracts. As a result Kim Roosevelt recommended a showdown with Khashoggi, and a momentous meeting was eventually arranged in August 1973. It was held in

[1] Interview with author. February 16, 1976.
[2] Multinational Hearings, part 12, p. 1088.

the Pentagon, in the office of 'Dave' Alne, a former naval officer from Iowa who was then director of International Sales Negotiations (a year later he was to become international marketing consultant for several arms companies). With Alne were other defence officials—including Richard Violette, in charge of government sales, and Joe Hoenig, assistant director for sales in the Near East and South Asia. There were also representatives of the air force, including the procurement officer, General Robert F. Trimble, who had apparently become worried about the big commissions. Northrop was represented by two vice-presidents, Jim Holcombe and Manny Gonzales. Facing this array was the single Arab, Adnan Khashoggi, supported by his American lawyer, Dan Zerfas.

The record of the meeting, which was vividly reported by Gonzales of Northrop and subsequently subpoenaed,[1] gives a graphic picture both of Khashoggi's personality and of the relationship between the Pentagon and Northrop. Dave Alne began by explaining the government's worry about commissions, and hoped that Khashoggi could spread some illumination, whereupon Khashoggi enthusiastically took up his cue. He eloquently described the 'economic infrastructure' of Saudi Arabia. It was a country, he explained, where almost the entire wealth was vested in the government, which ran the welfare state for the people. The king, who believed fervently in free enterprise, wanted to build up independent businessmen, but with so little industry the only real scope was in representing foreign companies. Thus, the role of representatives was generally recognised, and it was only in the arms area—which attracted unusual publicity—that the government leaders preferred not to acknowledge them publicly.

It was a persuasive justification for big commissions as a cornerstone of free enterprise against communism, and the Americans were duly impressed. Dave Alne agreed that the US government must be very diplomatic in dealing with agents and must use 'carefully selected and artful words'. Khashoggi went on to point out that he had sold French tanks, British helicopters and Belgian ordnance with higher commissions than he had charged Northrop. He explained that his commissions were high because his office had huge overheads, and had sometimes to work ten years in obtaining a contract, with a success rate of one in five.

[1] Northrop Papers: Memo to file from Manny Gonzales, August 13, 1973.

As for giving money to the princes, it was unthinkable: 'Prince Sultan does not need Adnan Khashoggi. If he wants $10 million, all he has to do is to take it from the government. . . . Adnan Khashoggi will never offer Prince Sultan money—that is like a beggar offering riches to a king.' Even General Trimble (Gonzales noted) was impressed at this point.

Finally, Khashoggi explained the great value of the Saudi royal family as a stabilising influence (everyone nodded) and the importance of loyalty based on material values, and how for that reason the princes often asked Khashoggi to provide goods for the Bedouins: it was not 'improper influence', it was loyalty (everyone appeared to understand). As for Khashoggi's own interests, he was building a bridge between Saudi Arabia and the United States with the help of investments he made in both countries, and that, he understood, had been the object of US aid programmes.

Alne was impressed and suggested that Khashoggi was really running an 'inexpensive aid programme'. William Robinson, for the air force, had only one question: if Prince Sultan found out about the commissions, would everything blow sky high? Certainly not, replied Khashoggi, provided that the Americans, like the French, handled such questions with 'tact and diplomacy'. The meeting ended after two and a half hours in a glow of re-assurance: the Pentagon men seemed as relieved as any. Alne thanked Khashoggi warmly, saying that many people had now learned that a commission agent could be 'an honest and astute businessman rather than an influence peddler who wears horns'. After the meeting Alne said to Gonzales: 'Manny, it was a stroke of genius to invite Khashoggi here today. We couldn't arrange it, for obvious reasons . . .'

In the light of this meeting, as reported in detail by Northrop, it is difficult to remain convinced of the effectiveness of the Pentagon's control of arms sales, or the will of officials to enforce that control. Not merely were the Pentagon condoning the huge commissions for their own foreign sales, they clearly had a close community of interest with Northrop, as evinced by Alne's last remark: both were concerned to maximise arms sales, without any serious concern for the consequences. (This was the time the Northrop hospitality machine was in full swing, with a stream of Pentagon officials visiting the Northrop hunting lodge in Maryland.) Two years later Alne, when he had become consultant to arms companies, described his own view of the question of control. 'The phrase "arms sales",' he explained to Congress in a classic example of Pentagon prose, 'is an untrustworthy reference to a family of national activities so diverse, so dissimilar, so different in character that one can draw no valid conclusion at all about the entire family. Valid conclusions can be drawn only about bite-sized sub-elements of arms sales.'[1] It was another way of putting the age-old argument of arms salesmen, the argument favoured by Commander Craven, that there was nothing special about arms, that there was no fundamental difference between selling arms and selling chocolates, or novels.[2]

Moreover it is clear both from this and other evidence that the Pentagon were very actively condoning the payment of large commissions. Joe Hoenig, the assistant director of sales negotiations, who had been present at the meeting with Khashoggi, was later to spell out the Pentagon's policy on agents in the Middle East in a remarkably candid speech to the Electronic Industries Association in June 1974. He stressed the role of agents since pre-biblical times, and their usefulness in buying 'influence'—which, he explained, 'can range from normal friendships or family ties to the payments of substantial sums of money to individuals in high government positions . . . obviously the agent with the greatest margin of profit or percentage has a distinct advantage.' Hoenig warned that the French and English 'have no compunction to agreeing to excessive fees', and that even though Middle Eastern governments were favouring government-to-government deals in order to 'eliminate the influence factor', they did not necessarily mean what they said: 'this lucrative function, developed over the past two thousand years, will not evaporate easily'.[3]

After the Pentagon meeting, Khashoggi's star was again in the ascendant. He was now revealing himself more publicly to the world with the help of a PR man in Washington, and a flattering profile appeared in *Business Week*, including a quotation from the French banker Louis Dreyfus: 'Khashoggi is the only man in the Middle East you can trust.' After October 1973, with the huge increase in the price of oil and the new boom in arms, the com-

[1] House of Representatives: Committee on International Relations. Hearings on Persian Gulf, June 24, 1975.

[2] See chapter 4.

[3] Speech on 'Agents, Fees in the Middle East' by Joseph K. Hoenig, given on June 11 1974 at the Army-Navy Club, Washington DC.

missions became still more profitable. Between 1970 and 1975 Lockheed, according to their later admission, paid or committed to him no less than $106 million. And Northrop had won over a billion dollars in contracts, on which Khashoggi was due to receive about $54 million.

Khashoggi was now evolving from an arms salesman into a multinational corporation. His headquarters were divided between Paris, London, Beirut and California, in each of which his own staff awaited him. But his real home—and office—was his private airliner, first a DC9, then a Boeing 727, with its own apartment and offices, which became a symbol of the new Arab wealth. The Boeing has a 37-foot sitting room, four TV cassette sets, telephones, a Telex, and a copying machine. In the bedroom are two closets—one for Arab and one for Western clothes—so that he can emerge from the plane in either. From his airborne base he visits his enterprises on five continents, never remaining earthbound for more than a few days: Khashoggi knows that his own persuasive personality and hospitality are his greatest assets. When I talked to him in his London apartment, overlooking Big Ben, there was little sense of being in any place. The big bare rooms had an airport-lounge atmosphere; two tall young Koreans, who travel with him on the plane, acted as bodyguards, and people of all nationalities were perpetually walking through, as in a Marx Brothers' film. There was no sense of character until Khashoggi himself appeared, a portly figure walking in like a penguin with his arms swinging behind him, but generating electricity among his minions.

From his mobile base, with growing Saudi funds supporting him, Khashoggi was beginning to fulfil his dream of being the instrument of Arab financial power spreading through the globe. He saw himself as transforming the Arab world with the same boldness as that of the American tycoons who transformed the United States in the last century, whose biographies he had carefully read. 'We have the same opportunity in our countries now,' he said in 1975, 'that Rockefeller, Vanderbilt and J. P. Morgan had in putting America together.'[1]

But his real ambitions lay outside Saudi Arabia, and his greatest hopes lay in America itself. In California he bought two banks, the Security National and the Contra Costa, to provide experience for a future banking empire. In Salt Lake City he helped to

[1] Interview with Jim Hoagland, September 14, 1975.

finance a \$250-million industrial park. In Arizona he bought a share in a cattle-ranching business. He tried in 1974 to buy control of another California bank, the First National Bank of San Jose, for \$14 million, but was blocked by shareholders and retreated in some bitterness. 'I've always believed,' he said to me, 'that capital has no nationality, but I was shocked in America to discover that money had been coloured by the hate wave. It's an irony that when the Arabs, led by Sadat, were falling on their knees to the Americans, the Americans were kicking them in the ass.'

But elsewhere in the world he expanded with grandiose schemes. In the Sudan in 1972 he helped to arrange a revolving loan of \$200 million to be raised by 31 banks and guaranteed by the Saudi central bank for a giant project that originally included sugar, cattle, textiles, minerals and cement. In Brazil he helped to finance a huge meat-packing plant. In Paris, he bought a fashion house called 'Jungle Jap'. In Indonesia he went into shipping. In Lebanon he made furniture. In the Pacific he developed a chain of hotels. In Egypt he planned a \$400 million trade centre near the Giza pyramids, to include two big hotels, a tourist centre, and a brand new pyramid faced with gold mirrors, with an Egyptian exhibition inside. In Korea he became very friendly with President Park, and helped to foster the close new relationship between Korea and Saudi Arabia. It was a remarkable extension of arms dealing.

Khashoggi's own life-style became increasingly flamboyant. He never had difficulty in mixing business with pleasure. He was a tireless party-goer in Las Vegas, Paris, Cannes and Beverly Hills. In California he became friendly with the novelist Harold Robbins and his wife, Grace, who gave parties for him with Hollywood people. Then in 1974 Robbins published a fictional best-seller *The Pirate*, about a fun-loving Arab tycoon with a sumptuous private airliner.

Arms dealing remained the core of Khashoggi's business: his princely style eased his business relationships, and ensured that American companies appreciated their connection. His private yacht, the *Khalidia*, spent some time on the east coast of the United States, where he used it as a base for his entertaining. Khashoggi saw no basic distinction between business and hospitality, so that favours could be almost imperceptibly transmuted into obligations. It *looked* effortless enough. In Paris his visitors from California would find themselves caught up in his 'cast of thousands', with attentive executives and pretty, sophisticated girls who seemed fascinated to talk to middle-aged men. There would be long-drawn-out drinks, and then dinner around midnight, with the girls becoming still more affectionate. To the dazed, unsophisticated executives from Lockheed or Northrop it must have seemed almost magical, as if it really came from some genie in *The Arabian Nights.* Sometimes a private plane just happened to be at the airport to fly them to some resort; Khashoggi's yacht just happened to be waiting, and it would be doing a favour to the crew to make use of it. The style was so casual that it seemed to transcend any kind of bargain or quid pro quo. How were the executives to know, and why should they want to know, that the whole apparatus of hospitality, from the girls to the planes, was not in the least casual, and had been carefully organised at great expense with the sole object of pleasing them? And in the Arab tradition, what was wrong with that anyway—what *was* the borderline between business and hospitality?

Khashoggi always depicted himself as a bridge between two cultures and, in effect, two notions of morality: 'you cannot transplant American morality,' he insisted to me. If the Americans tried to do without him, to cut down the bridge, they would find themselves (he argued) in a far more perilous situation, dealing directly with the Saudi government, in a country on which they were so helplessly dependent for their oil supplies. Certainly the view of business on the two sides of the bridge was very different. From the Western side, Khashoggi might appear as a latter-day J. P. Morgan, but in Riyadh or Jeddah he was the friend of royal princes, whose private fortunes were hidden from any investigating committee. But the bridge carried traffic both ways: while the Western companies were transforming Saudi Arabia, the Arab attitudes with all the new wealth behind them were also influencing the Western companies—perhaps rather as the Roman Empire, having extended eastwards in the fourth century AD, was itself infected with oriental luxury. It was a poignant coincidence that after 1973, just when the United States was painfully seeking to clean up its business methods and to limit the influence of money on politics, the new Arab wealth was encouraging a much more easy-going attitude to commissions and bribes. While the Arabs were being Westernised, the West was being Arabised.

It was Khashoggi's special skill to create an atmosphere where the most abnormal deals seemed thoroughly normal and enjoyable—whether in the recesses of the Pentagon, or at late-night dinners at the Rasputin. Under his aegis neither side had much reason to question the benefits, and the build-up of arms into Saudi Arabia continued at an ever faster rate. It was good for Lockheed and Northrop, good for Khashoggi, good for the princes. The Pentagon or the State Department had little desire to get in the way.

Whether in Saudi Arabia, Indonesia or other newly-independent nations of the Third World, the energies of the arms salesmen were being unleashed, and with them the old technique of bribery and extortion. The unique nature of arms deals that encouraged bribery in the nineteenth century—the few people involved, the secrecy and magnitude of single deals—still encouraged the same methods. There were plenty of precedents for Lockheed and Northrop in the Middle East, and Lockheed doubtless had some justification for their obsession with French bribery. But the Americans, trying to outdo the Europeans at their own game, had begun to institutionalise it, substituting for 'tact and diplomacy' an elaborate organisation, with separate companies and fixed routines, so that bribery began to become a subsidiary industry itself, with its own built-in incentives. The self-contained character of the companies, with their own intelligence systems, campaigns and orders of battle, encouraged them to use bribes as if they were nations at war. Their constant worry about the other companies emerges repeatedly from the documents, while there is scarcely any reference to any perceived threat from a hostile country: the enemy is not Moscow, but Dassault—or their American rivals. The ruthless competition which the Pentagon since McNamara had so carefully stimulated was now sending out shockwaves throughout the world.

The bribes themselves, for all their magnitude, were much less important than the pressure of which they were symptoms—the hectic race to sell arms at all costs to the new nations of the world. Whatever the element of extortion, it was only made possible by the desperate haste of the arms salesmen: it took two to tango, but it was the companies which started the dance. The bribes were all the more readily given because they provided the entries into an expanding market, as many documents stress.

The appetite for arms could always be increased through fear or ambition; and it was this (as the British Royal Commission had concluded in 1936)[1] which differentiated the arms industry from all others. Among the young countries emerging from colonial status, the Western companies and governments had a special scope and special responsibility, for they were helping to form the priorities and characters of the new nations. There were plenty of rulers, like President Sukarno (or later the Shah) who needed no encouragement to arm themselves to the teeth; but in this situation the companies' eagerness to encourage the military, with such incentives as the Widows' and Orphans' Fund, was all the more depressing. The Pentagon, or the European defence ministries, were not inclined to look too closely at the companies' methods, preoccupied as they were with keeping their companies viable and competitive: the Third World was beginning to help to pay for the defence of the major powers. And by the end of the 'sixties, the companies' problems were becoming more serious—particularly in California.

---

[1] See chapter 4.

12

The California Crisis

Well, take me to the factory of death, and let me learn something more. There must be some truth or other behind all this frightful irony.

Major Barbara, 1905

IN THE fashionable suburbs of Los Angeles, in Beverly Hills or Westwood, it is not easy to remember that this city is the arms capital of the world. In that long sprawl from Los Angeles to the ocean, down Sunset or Wilshire Boulevard, the rows of villas, Gothic, Classical Spanish, Italianate, become more exotic and secluded as they reach the mountains or the sea; while the sky-scraper blocks, full of lawyers, banks or insurance companies, seem dedicated to the pursuit of abstract and rarefied money. Los Angeles still clings to its showbiz style, long after the great days of Hollywood are over. The hotels and restaurants still serve as stages, where diners can make flamboyant entrances, and the name of Hollywood still casts a faded magic over dry-cleaners or strip-joints. The shining skyscrapers of Century City, the new business centre on the site of the old Twentieth Century Fox studios, play their associations with movies for all they are worth: the Avenue of the Stars leads up to the Shubert Theatre and a surrealist hotel with porters dressed as Beefeaters. It comes as a shock to discover that one of the skyscrapers is the headquarters of the Northrop Corporation.

The entertainment business still lends a sense of unreality to

workaday suburbs: the pleasure-grounds and fun-parks—
Disneyland, the Magic Mountain or Knott's Berry farm—which
have taken over from movies as the centres of entertainment,
loom up beside the factories and freeways, defying the bleak
townscape around them, inviting their customers to escape into
nostalgia and fantasy; and all around the raised freeways the giant
signs and hoardings stick above the low shacks like exclamation
marks, so that the city hardly seems to touch ground. In such
extravagant surroundings, it seems boringly literal to discuss the
dependence of California on the arms industry, or exports of
aircraft to Saudi Arabia or Iran.

But the statistics are irrefutable. Of the total defence contracts
in the United States, California holds thirty percent—more than
any other state. About half a million people in California are
employed in the aerospace industry, which accounts for thirty
percent of all manufacturing industry in the state; and the backbone of aerospace is defence. The biggest companies in California
by sales are the oil companies, led by Standard Oil of California:
but the biggest employers are defence companies, led by Rockwell, with 40,000 workers in California, and Lockheed with
37,200. (Walt Disney, even with the armies of students employed
at peak season for Disneyland, can only provide jobs for 17,500
Californians.)[1] The prosperity of the Los Angeles region depends
primarily not on showbiz, but on oil companies and arms companies, on Lockheed, Rockwell, McDonnell Douglas or Northrop, whose great plants surround the city like an army camping
outside the walls.

Beyond the palm-tree avenues of Beverly Hills on the way to
the international airport, the single-storey houses stretch out to
the horizon, broken only by the eatery or gasoline signs, and the
tall slabs of the aerospace headquarters. At Culver City the bright
green hangars of Hughes Aircraft shine out of the wasteland: this
legacy of Howard Hughes now specialises in electronics and
satellites and makes more than ninety-five percent of its profits
from arms. At El Segundo, alongside Aviation Boulevard south
of the airport, an endless vista of plants proclaim the name of the
Rockwell B1 bomber project. Beyond it, the small town of
Hawthorne is dominated by the Northrop Corporation.

The Northrop administration building shows all the signs of a
model company—the trim row of shrubs, the car park with each

---

[1] See *Los Angeles Times* supplement, Business & Finance, Part VIII, May 16, 1976.

officer's name in descending order, the immaculate entrance hall with an oil painting of a Northrop plane on an easel, the house magazine, *Northrop News*, expounding the achievements of the Northrop 'family'. When I visited it, jovial men in bright shirts were exchanging company jokes as they waited for the company plane, and *Northrop News* was celebrating the building of the 3,000th Tiger. There was a special shed labelled Saudi Arabian operations (110 Tigers had already been ordered by the Saudis), and across the sliding doors of the biggest hangar were painted two roaring tigers, their fangs gleaming, waiting for the kill. (The companies favour names borrowed from the jungle or the zoo—Tigers, Cobras, Hawks, Eagles, Jaguars or Tomcats.)

The arms companies like to mix fantasy and reality. In the old centre of Beverly Hills, next to the Byzantine town hall and the Palladian post office, is a southern colonial mansion with pale-blue shutters and slender columns, with a cupola above the portico: in the courtyard behind, a fountain spurts out of an Italianate sculpture. Inside, the corridors are thickly carpeted, leading past large chandeliers and elegant doorways to a magnificent double staircase which is widely believed to be the original from *Gone With the Wind*.[1] It is pure Hollywood, and it was put up by Jules Stein, the former boss of MCA. But now it houses the headquarters of Litton Industries, a conglomerate whose most important business is making arms—electronics, missiles and destroyers—with mounting exports to the Middle East.

But there is nothing exotic about the real centre of the Los Angeles arms industry. On the journey northwards from Hollywood the freeway passes through the dry brown hillsides of the Santa Monica mountains, and down into the flat expanse of the San Fernando Valley. The weather is suddenly hotter and drier: the criss-cross streets, the used-car lots and thin little houses look like the outskirts of a bleak Texan town. Before the Second World War 'the Valley' was still full of walnut orchards, and its wide open spaces provided ranches for film stars and locations for Westerns. But now it has filled up with industrial workers and factories, and in the midst of the Valley, in the suburb of Burbank, loom the great sheds of Lockheed, encircling the Burbank airport, which is privately owned by Lockheed. Even here, there is an echo of the old Hollywood magic, for the airport was the

[1] **Alas**, inaccurately: it was copied from a New York town house.

setting of the famous final scene of *Casablanca* between Humphrey
Bogart and Ingrid Bergman. But there the glamour ends; inside
the Lockheed headquarters the voices are slow, mid-Western or
Southern, with no romantic dialogue or quick-fire repartee. It is
a man's world, an engineers' world, precise, self-contained and
steadily dedicated—above all to military weapons.

Lockheedians have never been much loved by the rest of Los
Angeles. More than any other company they transformed a
group of easy-going sub-tropical towns into an industrial complex with an organised army of workers: even the other aerospace
companies resent the size and arrogance of this giant, and its
special relationships with the Pentagon. Other businessmen were
conscious of a smell of corruption about Lockheed, whose buyers
insisted on exacting gifts from the subcontractors who were
dependent on them for survival, and in their deals Lockheed were
merciless in interpreting the small print. Lockheedians were an
insulated group, and many of them had grown up together over
the past twenty years. While they saw Dan Haughton as their
charismatic leader, to many outsiders his fervent southern style
seemed rather absurd: 'When I heard him talking,' said one engine
salesman, 'I felt like shouting: "Come off it, Colonel Sanders!" '
But for all Lockheed's unique arrogance, its basic problems were
bound up with its position as the world's biggest arms company.
And whatever the local feelings of hostility no Californian, in a
state with nearly ten percent unemployment, can ignore the fact
that Lockheed provides nearly forty thousand jobs. The resentment is all the greater because of the embarrassing equation: arms
means jobs.

It is hardly surprising that the arms companies should be masters
of newsspeak: that weapons should be called capabilities, deter-
rents or systems, that arms factories should be defence facilities,
exports should be transfers, preparations for wars should be
logistics, and wars themselves should be conflicts. What could be
more harmless, even laudable, than defence exports? The end-
purpose of the weapons is easily lost in the fascination with the
means, the name of the game and the state of the art. There was
little sign of concern among the men at the top, so far as I could
detect, about the nature of their business; the salesmen would
quickly be carried away by their enthusiasm in describing the
prospects for arming the world. Only once did an executive, the
president of a big arms company, break out of the conventional

neutralised language: talking about defence exports he suddenly stopped short and said: 'I wish to God we could stop the whole business of arms sales.'

ARMS AND JOBS

It is on the other side of the mountains, in the great Californian desert to the east, that the arms industry finds its fulfilment, at Edwards Air Base, where the planes are tested and flown by the air force. It is an eerie transition: as one flies across the mountain range, the whole landscape goes brown, except for a few squares of green where alfalfa is grown in irrigated sections, as bright and symmetrical as card tables. The planes land on a huge dried-up lake which forms a natural airfield; the empty desert, with the temperature at 120 degrees and with the only shade coming from planes flying overhead, provides the lonely habitat for the machines, their pilots and mechanics. In California, it is said, there are three kinds of people—ocean people, mountain people and desert people—and most aircraft men seem drawn emotionally to the desert. The people from the coast come to love the challenge of the climate and the camaraderie of the cut-off community.

Here everyone is dedicated to perfecting the military planes, undisturbed by liberal politicians or social priorities. Brisk young air force officers show off the fine points of the brand-new fighters and bombers basking under the desert sun. There are rows of Northrop Tigers, painted in different colours for their customer-countries. There are F15 Eagles, flown up from McDonnell Douglas in St Louis, with long noses like elegant predators. And in pride of place is the controversial Rockwell B1 bomber. An eager air force spokesman briefed me about its achievements; how it could fly supersonically at 50,000 feet, and then dive down to fly subsonically at one hundred feet, and unload its nuclear bombs in a few seconds. The bombardier, he explained, was called the offensive weapons system operator. Disconcertingly the giant bomber was more beautiful than any civil airliner. With its sleek lines and curvaceous body, its jet engines tucked neatly under its wings, it lay on the tarmac, shimmering in its white paint like a magnificent fish.

The need for the B1 bombers was being questioned by many military experts in the summer of 1976: for nuclear warheads could be delivered far more swiftly and certainly by missiles, and by July 1976 the cost of 244 bombers was reckoned at $88 million apiece. But in this outpost, surrounded by its admirers and dependents, the B1 had generated a whole way of life around it, where its demise was scarcely imaginable. And there was another critical reason for continuing the project, my guide was quick to point out: it would provide at least 20,000 jobs for California. The passionate involvement of the air force seemed to create its own logic in the desert. It was only over in Los Angeles, with all its acute social problems, that the cost seemed prohibitive.

In southern California the equation between arms and jobs seems crude, but it is much more discreet in San Francisco, four hundred miles further north. The suburbs in Santa Clara county, between San Francisco and San Jose, have a sense of peace in keeping with their saintly names, with small ranches on the hillsides with white-painted fences and discreet redwood houses nestling in the woodlands. Stanford University, with its rural campus, seems to have turned its back on commercialism, and in the university town of Palo Alto the trim avenues and sprinkled lawns suggest all the detachment of rich academia.

So the innocent visitor is surprised to discover that here too the arms business lies just under the surface: that Santa Clara county has more defence contracts than any other county in the United States, amounting to around three billion dollars for 1977 or 3.5 percent of the total, and that Stanford has been the hub of a network of plants and laboratories which have helped to revolutionise electronic warfare. The professors of electronics have set up their own lucrative companies in the industrial estates, and big corporations have moved in to make use of the university's brains: the result has been a military-scientific complex which rivals Massachusetts. Along Route 101 out of Stanford the serious business reveals itself in the rows of electronics companies, neat and hygienic, which have given it the name of Silicon Valley. Much of their business is very peaceful, turning out pocket calculators or digital watches. But arms are the backbone of their prosperity. By far the biggest employer in Santa Clara county is Lockheed: in the town of Sunnyvale, just off Route 101, Lockheed employs 15,000 people, many of them making the Trident missiles for nuclear submarines—a contract whose value was estimated at $1.6 billion for 1977.

Radical groups in Santa Clara county have pressed for bold

planning to convert war industries to peaceful purposes. The *Plowshare Press*, a vigorous broadsheet, reports how the valley is being wrecked by the freeways and sprawl, and insists that the money invested in missiles and death-machines must be diverted to mass-transit systems or research into solar energy; and they have been supported by a few Lockheed engineers who have defected, to turn to peaceful research. But the Pentagon still rules as the supreme patron of the valley. It is here, in the suburbs of Sunnyvale or on the campus of Stanford, that a contemporary Andrew Undershaft would find his home, promising full employment and all-enveloping welfare in return for acceptance of the Armourer's Faith: 'to give arms to all men who offer an honest price for them, without respect of persons or principles'.[1]

Every Californian politician knows that arms means jobs. Even the most radical, speaking out against nuclear power-stations, oil companies or industrial pollution, will play down the weapons question: even Tom Hayden, the ultra-radical and unsuccessful candidate for the Senate in 1976. In the political geography the equation between arms districts and defence policies is not necessarily straightforward. There are of course militant hawks in the aerospace strongholds, like Barry Goldwater junior, Clair Burgener, or Bob Wilson in the navy stronghold of San Diego down south. But there are also congressmen for aerospace districts who are sufficiently secure or independent-minded to oppose high defence budgets; like Don Edwards, the Democrat for Santa Clara county, or Yvonne Burke, the Democrat for the Hughes Aircraft district of Culver City. There is also the resilient Robert Leggett, the representative for the Vallejo district which includes the huge Mare Island shipyard in San Francisco bay. As a senior member of the House Armed Services Committee, Leggett has consistently voted against higher defence spending as a waste of taxpayers' money, but has also been so assiduous in obtaining Pentagon contracts for his own shipyard that he could describe it as an 'oasis of employment'. When in July 1976 it was discovered that he had for thirteen years been secretly maintaining a second family with an ex-secretary in Washington, his constituents were reluctant to hold it against him, and re-elected him four months later. He was the guardian of their jobs.

But the views of congressmen are unimportant compared to the labour unions, from whom the aerospace companies can be

[1] Bernard Shaw: *Major Barbara*, Act III.

sure of some vocal support. I talked to the regional director of the United Auto Workers, Gerry Whipple, who is in charge of the six western states, with heavy representation in the aerospace companies. What, I asked, was his attitude to defence spending, and the B1 bomber? He let loose an immediate tirade. 'The B1 is the best deterrent we have, and it's got a helluva lot of plusses: it provides a very necessary job programme and it stimulates the aerospace industry. Remember, in times of national crisis the aerospace companies are pressed into service with all kinds of nice promises; but when the crisis passes they're thrown on the heap. California has been built on food, defence and oil: you can't expect us to convert into industries for garbage disposal or cheap houses. There are some super-liberal congressmen with their heads in the clouds who dream of building houses instead of bombers: but workers can't have pride in making low-cost housing, when the low-income families just use them for putting garbage in the hall. You can't convert workers into leaf-raking jobs, keeping them pushing a broom. The people making the B1 bomber think they're working for the good of the community, and people have pride in it. This used to be the aerospace capital of the world, and now I reckon there's as much as fifty percent unemployment in part of the industry: the Pentagon are squeezing every dollar, and the companies are moving to Texas or Georgia. If the B1 bomber is not consummated there'll be real problems with employment and capital investment. As for exporting arms, if we didn't do it, someone else would: and without arms those countries would be totally defenceless.'

With this kind of support, the companies do not need to spend much time directly lobbying the congressmen: they leave the unions to do it for them. A liberal politician in Los Angeles explained sadly: 'We get shit from the companies about defence, but they didn't come up with money for campaigns. They don't need to: they can rely on the flag-waving business, and the unions. The unions don't need to have secret discussions with us: they have public meetings, where they pound the table about jobs—the real muscular approach. There's not much we can say against *that*.'

THE SLUMP

The dependence on arms has been both a fact of Californian life and a source of economic insecurity for the past fifty years.

From the time when the shipyards and little airfields first boomed in the First World War, to the abrupt slump in 1919, to the vast expansion in the Second World War, to the depression of 1946, the workers were accustomed to all the anxieties of boom-or-bust. After the Korean war and the massive build-up of defence spending, the industry appeared to be permanently established, with its contribution to the security of the nation recognised beyond doubt. But California was still not secure, still dependent on the changeable policies and decisions in Washington three thousand miles away. The companies, for all their profits and size, were each at the mercy of the even bigger monopoly, or monopsony, of the Pentagon. And thus arose the paradox which has puzzled so many visitors: while Californians like to present themselves as the champions of extreme free enterprise and the rugged pioneer spirit, they have been more dependent than any other state on federal spending. The greater the dependence, the more defiant the postures of right-wing politicians, whether Nixonites, Birchites or Reaganites, promising to rid their people of the domination of Washington.

The master-keys to the prosperity of California were to be found, not in Burbank or Sacramento, but within the embattled fortress on the Potomac. Yet the Pentagon, on their side, were constantly aware of the rival pressures, the demands for jobs and the political leverage, whether of California, Missouri or Long Island: however ruthless a secretary of defence, he could not afford to let whole communities crumble or production-lines disappear. The aerospace tycoons like Dan Haughton of Lockheed or Tom Jones of Northrop were men with heavy political clout, who could hold their own between the two sides. They were much more than plane-makers: they were political operators battling (as they saw it) for the livelihoods of tens of thousands of workers.

In the long years of the great aerospace boom, through the 'fifties and 'sixties, the situation of the companies was often precarious, but the total business in terms of jobs and sales was always expanding. The development of jet fighters and bombers, missiles, spacecraft, electronic warfare; the huge increase in commercial air travel, in jets, super jets or jumbo jets—all these brought new challenges and opportunities. There were a few bad years of downturn, like 1958, before the Sputnik was launched, or 1964 before the Vietnam war intensified. In that year

the management consultants Arthur D. Little pronounced that
the aerospace industry was no longer a growing market. But with
the stepping-up of the Vietnam war the next year, the companies
had a new rush of orders from the Pentagon, and a new opportunity to test the weapons that had been made for hypothetical
wars. In the next two years the number of jobs went up and up
until by 1968, the wonder-year of the industry, total aerospace
employment in the United States had reached a peak never
attained in the Second World War—of 1.5 million, of which
600,000 was in California. The aerospace industry, embracing
aircraft, missiles and electronics, accounted for as much as thirty-
seven percent of all manufacture in the state.

The captains of industry reassured themselves that the boom
would be sustained. Tom Jones, writing in July 1967, explained
that California would welcome an end to the Vietnam war:
'Time has outmoded the notion that war's end means the onset
of recession. . . . Our industry deserves to see an end of the
"boom-or-bust" myth which has persisted since the Second
World War.' He pointed out that half the prime contracts for
the space programme, which was spending more than seven
billion dollars a year, were now going to California; and that the
American presence in South East Asia was contributing to a long-
term Pacific boom. 'Those who have recently been there to see
the situation first hand are greatly encouraged by evidence of
progress and know that this is only the beginning.'[1]

But 1968 proved to be the high peak. The Vietnam boom was
subsiding, the space programme was being cut back, the Pacific
boom did not materialise. There were big orders from airlines
for the new wide-bodied jets, but the most successful company
was Boeing, producing its jumbos up in the state of Washington. The long-term prospects for airliners were not hopeful; like
the railroads in the eighteen-eighties, the airlines were competing
desperately for diminishing profits. The prospects of a new boom
in supersonic airliners were now slender, and the golden age of
aerospace seemed to be passing, or (in engineers' language) to be
reaching an asymptote. For the four years after 1968 the total jobs
and sales in the industry went steadily and ominously downward,
as they had not done for twenty years. By 1971 aerospace jobs
were reduced to 440,000, down 157,000 from three years before.

Already in 1967 two of the great aerospace companies had faced

[1] Tom Jones: 'The Virtues of Diversity' in the *Los Angeles Times*, July 9, 1967.

catastrophes. The Douglas company, with its long tradition of famous airliners, was desperately behind schedule with its new DC9 airliners, partly as a result of the shortages and delays from the Vietnam war. For Donald Douglas, the ageing founder of the company, the future was once again as dark as the inside of a boot, but he could not face up to it; he carried on as chief executive, coming into the midday meetings with his young wife and his big dog Wunderbar, and still dominating his son Donald junior, who was president of the company. After frantic evasions, the great company faced bankruptcy, and was forced to sell at a knock-down price to McDonnell of St Louis, which had been making handsome profits out of its Phantom fighters, supplied to the air force in Vietnam. It was a searing humiliation for the Douglas executives; the profits from war had proved safer than the gambles of peace, and in the new merged company it was Jim McDonnell, 'Mister Mac' down in Missouri, who was the undisputed boss of the California plant.

Another pioneer Californian company, North American, faced a similar calamity. During the Second World War the company had produced more planes than the whole of Britain, and under its founder 'Dutch' Kindelberger it had expanded into electronics and missiles and made equipment for the Apollo moonshots. But after Kindelberger died in 1962 it lost much of its momentum, and faced cash problems with the decline in the space race. Eventually in 1967 it merged with the Rockwell Corporation, the aggressive conglomerate in Pittsburgh which was looking for new sources of research and development. Rockwell's mixed bag of industries, like that of General Dynamics or General Electric, was part of the tendency for arms factories to become interlocked with all kinds of other technologies, and Willard Rockwell made no bones about his ambition: 'By 1980, it has been estimated that only two hundred companies will control sixty percent to seventy-five percent of the world's gross national products, and we intend to be one of them.'[1]

The slump was felt all along the West Coast. Boeing, which employed over 100,000 people in 1968, had a succession of setbacks, including the cancellation of their supersonic project. Their employment fell to 38,000 and Seattle faced the prospects of becoming a ghost city. Like other aerospace companies, Boeing tried to switch plants and workers to other products: they began

[1] *The Magazine of Wall Street*, September 10, 1968.

building a mass-transit system in West Virginia, and a desalination project in the Virgin Islands. In San Diego, the Rohr Corporation began making railroad cars for the new subway system in San Francisco. But the cost of these peaceful projects proved far higher than was expected; and as so often before, the companies accustomed to extravagant defence projects found it hard to adjust to the demands of the commercial market-place. Boeing's fortunes eventually revived, with the help of the jumbo, the Boeing 747. But the investment in that single new plane amounted to almost the total of the company's assets, and the moral was clear: they could not again risk such a venture, without a collaborator.

The most spectacular crisis of all came with Lockheed. Throughout most of the 'sixties the company had been the biggest arms company in the nation, the leading 'prime contractor' to the Pentagon. The export of the Starfighter, the steady sales abroad of Hercules and Orions, had added to the profits, but it was the Pentagon which was its mainstay, with such valuable contracts as the Polaris missiles at Sunnyvale. The intensifying of the Vietnam war brought record new sales, and in the fiscal year ending June 1965 Lockheed received $1.7 billion in orders, twice as much as its closest competitor General Dynamics. The Hercules transport, the 'Herky-Bird', became the chief cargo-carrier inside South Vietnam, and the Lockheed jet transport, the Starlifter or C141, flew half the American servicemen to the war. The prospects for giant transports seemed still more promising, for in 1964 Lockheed, undercutting Boeing, had won a contract from the Pentagon to develop the biggest transport of all—the C5A Galaxy. It would be four times as big as the Hercules, able to carry seven hundred troops or six Greyhound buses inside its belly; and it held the promise of being later converted into an airliner which would, said Lockheed, be 'an ocean liner of the air'. It would provide an assured future for the 20,000 Lockheed workers in Georgia, and it brought double pleasure to Senator Russell of Georgia, presiding over the Armed Services Committee and looking after the interests of his state.

But Lockheed's position was dangerously dependent on the Pentagon, when the latter began cutting back its patronage; and for all the strength of the military-industrial complex, the Pentagon could still assert itself against companies. The Lockheed Cheyenne helicopter, which became an extravagant fiasco, was abruptly cancelled, and down in Georgia the Galaxy transport became far more expensive, and took far longer than Lockheed had promised; after five years the extra cost was over a billion dollars. In the old days, as Lockheed people now lament, this might not have mattered: the basic decisions in Congress and the Pentagon were taken by a handful of men (like Senator Russell) who understood that aircraft were always more expensive and more complex than had been expected. But now under the austere regime of McNamara, and the fierce discipline of Total Package Procurement, the extra cost was much more serious, and the Pentagon was actually demanding that Lockheed pay a penalty of $16,000 for each day the planes were late.

In March 1969 Dan Haughton was brazenly asking the Pentagon for $640 million in advance payments, without which (he said) Lockheed could not continue its money-losing defence programmes. By 1970 Lockheed was in serious difficulties. Haughton explained that the government was inflexible: 'the gold of good intention,' he said, 'has turned into the sand of reality.' The arguments about the cost of the Galaxy had now grown into a major scandal, opened up by a dissident Pentagon official, Ernest Fitzgerald, and pursued by Senator Proxmire in Washington, who was determined to stop government help. As the Vietnam war raged, Lockheed became the focus for all the hatred of the military-industrial complex, the scapegoat for all the arms companies who were both asserting their defiant independence, and demanding help from the Pentagon. Lockheed's links with the Pentagon became notorious: in 1968, it transpired, Lockheed employed 210 retired military officers of the rank of colonel or above.[1] But behind all the polemic there was a fundamental dilemma. The costs and risks of major defence contracts were becoming greater than any company could realistically bear on its own; yet competition, whether between companies or between the services, was still at the root of the system, and only a few critics (like Professor Kenneth Galbraith) seriously advocated nationalisation. Thus the companies went on playing 'Pentagon games'—first bidding much too low for the contract, then trapping the Pentagon people into a position where they had to bail them out.[2]

[1] Congressional Record, March 24, 1969.

[2] For a detailed account of the nature of the games, see Ernest Fitzgerald: *The High Priests of Waste*, New York, W. W. Norton, 1972. Also Richard J. Barnet: *The Economy of Death*, New York, Atheneum, 1969. I am indebted to both.

Lockheed had tried to diminish their dependence on arms. By 1967, while Vietnam raged, they were building ships, dams and computers, and Dan Haughton was projecting a new image as head of the diversified company: in the words of the *Los Angeles Times*, 'Mother Hen to an Exotic, Growing Brood'. It was as part of this policy that Haughton wanted to get back into building commercial airliners, and began developing a wide-bodied plane, later called the TriStar. It was a brave venture, for Boeing and Douglas were ahead of Lockheed in the airliner business and could develop their designs from military transports, whereas the TriStar was 'clean', being conceived as a commercial plane from the beginning. Moreover the engines were to be supplied by Rolls-Royce of Britain, who regarded this contract as a historic break-through into the American market, and the collaboration was proclaimed as marking a new stage in Anglo-American inter-dependence. But Lockheed soon found the TriStar far more expensive and long-delayed than they had reckoned, and Rolls-Royce on their side were soon suffering unprecedented losses in developing their engine: they lacked the long experience in military engines of General Electric (who were making the Douglas engines), and the terms of their contract with Lockheed were harsh. (When the British company Hawker-Siddeley heard the terms, they took the precaution of insuring themselves against Rolls-Royce's bankruptcy). The lame were leading the lame.

In January 1971 came a new disaster for Lockheed: Rolls-Royce was declared bankrupt. The British Conservative govern-ment had gone to a point of ruthlessness to which Washington could not go; it decided to nationalise the defence part of the Rolls-Royce business, and let the rest collapse—which meant that it could not honour its obligations with Lockheed, and was absolved from the penalties of bankruptcy. For Lockheed, the Rolls-Royce collapse seemed to foretell theirs too; Haughton flew to and fro across the Atlantic, cajoling and threatening, while the governments on both sides were alarmed at the prospects of mass unemployment of skilled engineers. After bitter wrangles the British agreed to continue to finance the engine development on condition that Washington guaranteed the future of Lockheed.

In Washington, the Nixon administration was now under heavy pressure to support Lockheed; a group of banks agreed to lend the company $250 million, only on condition that the government guaranteed its survival, and in May 1971 John Connally, the secretary of the treasury, formally announced that he would ask Congress to approve a federal loan guarantee for the quarter-billion. There followed historic hearings about the bail-out, which raised the fundamental questions about the government's responsibility for arms companies, and corporations in general. Senator Proxmire, again leading the attack, protested that this was the 'beginning of a welfare programme for large corporations'. Connally stressed the need to keep 31,000 jobs; but David Packard, the deputy under-secretary of defence, was lukewarm in his support. Admiral Rickover, from the sidelines, complained about the tendency to 'state socialism' and quoted Herbert Spencer's dictum: 'To protect men from the results of their folly is to fill the world with fools'.[1] But the pressure from Lockheed, and from Nixon in the White House, was strong, and Senator Cranston from California tirelessly lobbied colleagues to save Lockheed. Eventually in August 1971 the Senate approved the loan, by only one vote.

But Lockheed's bankruptcy was still only just round the corner. They were now living, as Senator Percy reminded them, 'by the grace of Congress';[2] and in the meantime they had incurred still greater political odium. They were still the nation's biggest arms company, but now doubly dependent on the taxpayer; and the perils of the past years had left them with a still greater sense of insecurity and aggression. It was their commercial airliner which had precipitated the immediate crisis, but it was the Galaxy and the whole relationship with the Pentagon that had hardened their unlovable character, alternately pushing and pleading. Whatever the shortcomings of many of the Lockheed executives—their greed, recklessness and mendacity—it is only fair to say that the Pentagon had contrived a system designed to bring out the worst in the companies: like cocks in a cockfight they had been spurred to gore each other and drive themselves on. It was this frenzy that had encouraged the Lockheed men, as it encouraged the other companies, in their exploits abroad, to suborn and bribe to ensure their critical contracts, to pay Prince Bernhard, Khashoggi, or the Widows' and Orphans' Fund, without much thought for the consequences. With their insecurity heightened, they were now more reckless than ever.

[1] Fitzgerald, p. 311.
[2] *Multinational Hearings*, part 12, p. 344.

13

Japan: Behind the Black Curtain

In Japan there is no such thing as truth.
Lockheed executive

IN AUGUST 1972, when Lockheed was still reeling from its financial crisis and desperately short of orders, the president of the company, Carl Kotchian, flew from Los Angeles to Tokyo for a visit which, as he saw it, could make or break the future of both Lockheed and Rolls-Royce. It was this journey which, more than any other of Lockheed's adventures abroad, would eventually illuminate the darkest places between business and government, providing a uniquely detailed narrative of the process of bribery; and which led to a political upheaval unparalleled in Japan's post-war history.[1]

For the past five years Kotchian had been the man most directly responsible for authorising Lockheed's bribes. Since 1967, when he had become president under Dan Haughton's chairmanship, he had been virtually foreign minister of the Lockheed

[1] In this chapter I have made use of the documents and testimony provided by the Church Committee (Multinational Hearings, part 14) and of Carl Kotchian's interviews in the *Asahi Evening News*, August 21-27, 1976, later expanded in his memoirs published by Asahi Shimbun in Tokyo in 1976: Kotchian's account is substantially corroborated and augmented by the prosecutor's statements in the Tanaka trial (January 27, 1977). But I have also benefited from my own discussions with Mr Kotchian in Los Angeles, and with several sources in Tokyo.

empire, for Haughton normally travelled abroad only to Britain and Canada. The two men kept frequently in touch, with endless long-distance telephone calls, and in Burbank Kotchian was usually seen as Haughton's side-kick. But Kotchian held his own definite political views; he had graduated at Stanford University in management and economics, and he often liked to reflect upon international affairs, and on world communism. He was constantly concerned with the battle against communists, and when he wavered his wife Lucy would reinforce him. On his travels he kept the CIA informed of his movements: they knew what he was doing, and 'if they wanted to they could have stopped it'.

There was nothing sheepish or reptilian in Kotchian's view of bribery: to him, payments to foreigners were business costs, or an insurance policy, as he put it, like fire risks or life insurance, which any prudent man would pay. The only criterion was the return on investment: thus in Indonesia, he had disagreed with Dan Haughton when he had tried to cut down the 'hanky-panky' (see chapter 10). Such payments were part of the great battle for business, and for the free world: he saw nothing wrong with what he was doing, and still does not. He believed that the British had lost out in their exports by refusing to bribe.

Kotchian took responsibility for the company decisions and while many other Lockheed men were involved in single sectors, only Kotchian had the overview of the whole. He tried to delegate to the representatives abroad, but there was often local bickering, which compelled him to deal directly with secret agents. It was a lonely responsibility, involving clandestine assignments with inscrutable characters, about which he could not tell the others. But it was dramatic and exciting compared to the workaday negotiating and administration; and he later used to enjoy reading spy stories which reminded him of it. Kotchian identified with Nixon during the Watergate scandals; he was an admirer of Nixon and knew what it was like to go through such an isolated ordeal. Perhaps, like some earlier arms dealers, Kotchian began to enjoy the secrecy for its own sake.

By the late 'sixties, when Lockheed was first faced with possible bankruptcy, Japan loomed largest in Kotchian's operations: for it was now (before the boom in Iran) the richest single overseas market for aerospace. Like Germany, Japan had no major arms industry of its own, and hence no big aerospace companies, so that the government and airlines were compelled to look abroad for their aircraft.

Japan was a country where the connection between money and politics could not be ignored, for money *was* politics: it was like a caricature of a Washington scandal, with the major politicians indebted to corporations and financiers for their support, and with money exerting influence on every deal and every appointment. Operating behind the ordered world of managerial corporations there were a few very rich financial manipulators, like throwbacks to nineteenth-century America. Corruption in Japan had always been specially associated with deals with arms companies: before the First World War Vickers had bribed a Japanese admiral to get an order for a battleship—a scandal which had toppled the prime minister.[1] But normally the nature of the deals and the power of the brokers were concealed by what the Japanese called the *kuromaku*, the black curtain—a metaphor derived from the Japanese theatre.

THE SECRET AGENT

Kotchian saw Japan as the key to Lockheed's salvation, and he made clear to his colleagues in California that it was his special province. To achieve his aims, he soon slipped behind the black curtain. In the Lockheed network in Japan, much the most important figure was Yoshio Kodama, who had been their secret agent for the past seventeen years. Kodama was far more melodramatic than Lockheed's other arms dealers—than Prince Bernhard, Fred Meuser or even Khashoggi. With his narrow eyes and expressionless mouth he looked like a punch-drunk boxer, and he was known to the Japanese left as 'the monster': he had been a shadowy manipulator in right-wing politics for two decades. His flamboyant career had survived each Japanese upheaval. As a boy in the 'twenties he had become a nationalist politician, dedicated to attacking both communism and political corruption, and advocating direct rule by the emperor. By the time of Pearl Harbor, at the age of only thirty, he was put in charge of procuring war material in China, and at the end of the war his agency had a huge hoard of diamonds, platinum and cash; half of it was seized by the American occupation forces but half was said to have remained hidden. On the day that Japan surrendered in August 1945 Kodama watched his hero Admiral Onishi, who

[1] See chapter 2.

had organised the Japanese kamikaze pilots, put his sword through his stomach. 'I clasped his blood-covered hands tightly,' he said later in his memoirs, 'but I could not stop the hot tears that fell from my eyes.'

Soon afterwards Kodama was jailed for three years, awaiting trial as a Class A war criminal, together with other Japanese leaders, including the wartime premier General Tojo. But by 1948, with the onset of the cold war, the Americans were relenting towards suspects who were effective anti-communists, and on the same day that Tojo was executed, Kodama was released, together with other prominent future politicians. Kodama was still only thirty-seven, and he quickly re-established his power behind the black curtain. While in jail he had made influential right-wing friends, and he still apparently controlled some hidden treasures of platinum and diamonds. Whether there was really such a hoard, or whether money was provided by the American intelligence services, remains a matter of speculation; but in any case Kodama gave much of it, according to his own account, to the founder of the new Liberal Party, Ichiro Hatoyama, who later became prime minister; and he also financed other future prime ministers, including Nobusuke Kishi, with whom he had been in jail.

It might seem remarkable that a suspected war criminal with a fortune derived from arms-selling should have moved so quickly into this central position: but Japan's break with the past was in some ways less drastic than Germany's. Kodama had money in an impoverished country, and his intense and mystical conservatism still had a magic both for his contemporaries and for the young. To General MacArthur's occupation forces, faced with the threat of the Korean war, Kodama and his anti-communist friends became valuable allies. When the war broke out, Kodama was actually in Seoul with the American forces, and it was often suspected that the CIA used him as a funnel to subsidise pro-American Japanese politicians.

By 1958 Kodama was already one of the most powerful men in Japan. He had made a new fortune through his agency, run from a small office in the Ginza district of Tokyo, and he had a gang of young supporters who, it was thought, could make life very difficult for his opponents. One of his protégés, Nobusuke Kishi, was now prime minister, presiding over a phenomenal boom, which had originated with American purchases for the

Korean war. Kishi and many of his business supporters, including Kodama, were in favour of extending Japan's military role, as Strauss was in Germany. The ex-enemies were both emerging as critical allies, to be re-armed urgently against the communists. But in Japan the public antipathy to armaments after the experience of Hiroshima (see chapter 18) provided a special political tension.

It was at this formative time that Lockheed mounted their first major campaign in Japan, to sell their Starfighters, simultaneously with their European campaign. Both efforts were masterminded by Ken Hull, who was running Lockheed's international division under Bob Gross, and who was adept at high-pressure salesmanship. Hull already knew post-war Japan quite well, with its combination of poverty and greed, and he realised that the Japanese wanted the American know-how, but not their ethics; he was determined to establish a private route to the Japanese power-structure. He first engaged an American-Japanese public relations man, Taro Fukuda, to advise him on government contacts. Born in Salt Lake City, Fukuda had been an interpreter with the American forces, and became friendly with Kodama when Kodama was in jail, so that later Kodama helped to set up Fukuda in public relations, maintaining a close contact with him. Fukuda thus naturally introduced Lockheed to Kodama (who spoke no English).

Ken Hull was tremendously impressed by Kodama's contacts, and saw him as a great Japanese patriot. He did not know whether Kodama was connected with intelligence, but he knew that he had very important friends in the American occupation. Kodama suggested that Lockheed should openly deal with one of the trading companies, the Marubeni Corporation, whose slogan was 'Man, Materials and Money'. Marubeni was relatively an upstart company, but it was beginning to rival the established trading giants Mitsubishi and Mitsui (the company that had once been so crucial to Vickers, and that had been Lockheed's agents up till now). Kodama however also offered to exercise his own leverage behind the scenes as Lockheed's secret agent, without Marubeni's knowledge. Like all the great arms dealers from Zaharoff to Khashoggi, Kodama thrived on a reputation as a man of mystery: to each side he could suggest a hinterland of untold influence on the other.

Lockheed had a difficult challenge, for their American rivals,

Grumman, had promoted their fighter the Super Tiger (F11F)[1] with much more success in Japan than in Europe; and by late 1958 the Japanese Defence Council had tentatively decided to buy the Grumman plane. But the Grumman salesmen were much less experienced than Lockheed in international adventures outside their base on Long Island, and for the salesmen on both sides Japan, with its amazing language and customs, was even more baffling than Germany or Holland: the temptation to take short cuts was very strong. As one of these salesmen described to me his recollection of that time: 'You're sitting in your hotel room, thinking that you've done everything right, with all the technical details, you haven't farted in the general's face, and you're still waiting and waiting, thinking "What have I forgotten?" Then some middleman comes along and says he thinks some politician's on the take. Really you're *relieved* to be able to pay out something to the middleman; it gives you something to do, and makes you feel safer. It's a question of belts and suspenders.'

Both sides were groping in the dark. The Grumman people first learnt that the decision to buy their plane had been postponed, and then noticed that all kinds of voices were now speaking out in favour of the Starfighter: aviation experts were coming out of the woodwork. They suspected a sinister force, but they did not know who. Behind the black curtain, Kodama was now very well placed, for he had unusual leverage on prime minister Kishi, his old protégé. The newspaper *Yomiuri Shimbun*, owned by a friend of Kodama, launched a crusade in favour of the Starfighter and the deputy chief of the air staff, General Minoru Genda, spoke publicly in favour of the Lockheed plane. Genda was the commander who had led the Japanese attack on Pearl Harbor, and was another wartime friend of Kodama; by July 1959 he had been promoted to chief of the air staff, and he went over to California and personally flew the Starfighter. Genda's approval, like that of the German pilots, may well have reflected his genuine fascination with such a sophisticated plane; but he was also a very political general, and three years later became a member of the Diet or parliament (which he still is).

Whatever the reason, the lobby for the Starfighter was soon effective: the Grumman plane was dropped, and eventually Japan ordered 230 Starfighters—nearly all of them made under licence by Mitsubishi in Japan. Lockheed was estimated later to

[1] Not to be confused with the Northrop Tiger.

have paid bribes of about $1.5 million to Japanese officials, and a
fee of $750,000 to Kodama for his services. The details of the
bribes were evidently passed on to the CIA, and a former American intelligence official later confirmed that every move made
was approved by Washington.[1] The CIA's interest, together with
Kodama's complex relationships, raises further doubts as to how
far Lockheed was conducting its own foreign policy, or a deeper
layer of Washington policy.

Throughout the 'sixties Kodama continued secretly to look
after Lockheed's interests; but there was no opportunity comparable to the first Starfighter sales. In 1968 McDonnell Douglas
won a contract for Phantoms for the Japanese air force, with the
help of their agents, which aroused Lockheed's suspicions about
bribery. Already in crisis in California, Lockheed was now
determined to make a comeback into the Japanese market with
two planes. One was the Orion (P3) anti-submarine plane, which
was already being promoted through Europe with the help of
such agents as Prince Bernhard and Ovidio Lefebvre (see chapter
6): in Japan Kodama was now offered a commission of $8.5 mil-
lion for an expected first contract for fifty Orions, which would
be worth half a billion dollars to Lockheed.

The other was the airliner, the TriStar, whose prospects were
gloomy. At the Paris air show in June 1968, while Kotchian was
giving a lunch for high dignitaries including Prince Bernhard, the
news came through that a consortium of four European airlines
had turned down the Lockheed plane. The last big chance was now
Japan, and in 1969 Kotchian launched a sales campaign of mounting intensity to persuade the Japanese to buy their airliner.
Lockheed's two main rivals were both well established with their
commercial airliners, with extensive maintenance networks, and
with agencies with intimate political connections. McDonnell
Douglas civil aircraft were represented by Mitsui, whose influence
over the president of All Nippon Airlines, Tetsua Oba, was so
blatant that he eventually had to resign; while Boeing was looked
after by the Nissho-Iwai trading company, to which Boeing was
later found to have made large 'improper payments'. For Lockheed and Rolls-Royce to break into such a well-defended territory might seem a hopeless task: but if Kotchian could get the deal
it would not only be worth a billion dollars to Lockheed and
ensure its immediate survival; it might also open the way to the

[1] *International Herald Tribune*, April 3, 1976.

rest of the Far East. Kotchian was persuaded it could be done (he says) by Kodama: but there were many who suspected that his real source of confidence was his fellow-Californian Richard Nixon.

To supervise Lockheed's campaign Kotchian had appointed John Clutter, a much less genial and communicative man than his predecessor Ken Hull. Clutter was always having trouble with Kodama, who kept asking for more money than Clutter thought he was worth; and Clutter had his own Japanese staff, which was soon augmented by a special sales team for the TriStar, including a gregarious public relations man, Al Elliot, who had been in Japan since the American occupation. But Kotchian preferred the back route. He put great trust in Taro Fukuda, the Japanese PR man who became his chief mentor and guide to Tokyo, and it was in Fukuda's car that Kotchian in 1971 was first taken to see Kodama, in a mysterious meeting-place out of town. Kotchian was fascinated by this stocky man with short hair and a soft voice who seemed so unlike a man of great power, but knew so much about Japanese politics,[1] and he insisted, against Clutter's advice, that Kodama's fee as a 'marketing consultant' should be increased. Kotchian was determined, the other Lockheedians realised, to handle the Japanese campaign his own way.

Kotchian was not much concerned about Kodama's political ideas or behaviour. He knew that Kodama had been classified as a war criminal, but noted that he had never actually been convicted; and he had read Kodama's own book *Sugamo Diary* which described his influential friendships in jail. From this first meeting, Kotchian saw Kodama each time he flew into Tokyo. The spell of Kodama resided not only in his mystery but also in his impression of positive energy: 'In Japan, it's easy to be a spoiler, and hard to be constructive,' one Lockheed man explained to me, 'Kodama really would *move*.'

TWO MONTHS THAT CHANGED JAPAN

On August 20, 1972, Kotchian arrived in Tokyo with his wife Lucy for his fourth visit in that year. They checked in at Room 1070 of the hotel Okura, the best suite in the best hotel in Tokyo, with deep armchairs and a sofa; the suite in which Kissinger had just been staying. The political atmosphere in Tokyo was now

[1] Kotchian: *Lockheed Sales Mission*, chapter 3.

highly charged. A new prime minister, Kakuei Tanaka, had come to office the previous month, with the reputation of having shadier financial friends than most of his predecessors: every leader of a faction in Japan needs large funds for election expenses and favours, but Tanaka, as a self-made man, had used some dubious sources of funds to push his way to the top. The son of a horse-dealer, he became a labourer at the age of fifteen, and worked his way up to be head of a construction company. In 1948 he had been convicted for bribery, but was later acquitted and soon became prominent in politics and big business, rising to be minister of finance, minister for international trade and industry, and then prime minister. His election caused murmurs, but he had public appeal as a man of the people; he was only fifty-two, with a thrusting and extrovert style compared to his elders, with their law-school tradition and links with the establishment of old corporations; and he was now presiding over a spectacular boom.

There was also now tense diplomatic activity between Japan and the United States. President Nixon had recently delivered a succession of rude shocks to Japan, with the restrictions on Japanese textiles, the dollar-yen battle, and his visit to Peking without warning Tokyo. Nixon was now pressing Tanaka to import more American goods to redress the huge surplus, and a week after Kotchian's arrival he was due to meet the Japanese prime minister for talks in Honolulu; many Japanese were dreading a new 'Nixon shock'. All this, Kotchian reckoned (by his account), could be turned to Lockheed's advantage; he would circulate rumours, which were not difficult to foster, that Nixon was specially close to Lockheed, which would impress the Japanese: for Nixon was a Californian, and a year earlier he had rescued Lockheed by approving the $250 million loan. (It might seem rash for Kotchian thus to encourage notions of conspiracy, but this was before Watergate.) So Kotchian made use of Al Elliot, who was always at parties with journalists; and as Kotchian reckoned, nothing is easier than to convince journalists of something they want to believe. Elliot let out that Kotchian was a friend of Nixon who had contributed to his last election campaign, and that Nixon was pressing Tanaka to buy the Lockheed planes; Elliot was so successful that American as well as Japanese papers published the stories. Some Japanese sources believe that Nixon *had*, in fact, urged Tanaka to buy Lockheed at an earlier meeting at San Clemente in January 1972, when Tanaka was minister of trade and industry. But Nixon's true involvement remains unresolved.

(Certainly Nixon's staff were well able to relate the needs of the aerospace companies to the needs of the Nixon campaign fund. The former president of Grumman International, Dr Thomas Cheatham, had a talk with a White House aide, Richard Allen, just before the same Honolulu meeting between Nixon and Tanaka. Cheatham later testified that he had asked Allen whether Nixon could encourage Tanaka to buy a Grumman plane, the E2C radar aircraft, and that on the way out Allen had suggested a contribution of a million dollars to the Nixon campaign fund.[1] But no such bargain with Lockheed has yet been revealed.)

Kotchian had worked out a careful strategy to sell the TriStars. Both the two big Japanese airlines, All Nippon Airlines (ANA) and Japanese Air Lines (JAL), were planning to order big wide-bodied planes, and Boeing and McDonnell Douglas were competing heavily, with the short-range version of the Boeing 747 and the DC10. ANA had already tentatively decided to take the DC10, but Kotchian had persuaded them to delay their choice until the TriStar was ready. Lockheed wanted to get that ANA contract, while leaving JAL to order Boeing 747s for domestic routes and Douglas DC10s for its shorter international routes. It could, Kotchian reckoned, be made to *look* fair, but in fact the ANA order was much the most valuable.

Kotchian was convinced that the keys to the contract lay not so much with the airlines as with the government and politicians. This was true in most countries outside the United States, but specially true of Japan. The injection of three ruthless American companies all competing for the same government's custom was in itself a formula for corruption, but Kotchian soon raised the stakes; for he was in a hurry and obsessed by the need for political influence. On his first three days he saw his three principal agents. Each of them, three years later, was to be ruined by that contact.

The first was Hiro Hiyama, the president of the Marubeni Corporation which had been formally representing Lockheed for the past fifteen years: Hiyama had built it up into Japan's third biggest trading company with extensive interests, including electronics and chemicals, and useful political connections.

[1] Multinational Hearings, part 15. Cheatham's statement was denied by Grumman but he was testifying under oath.

Kotchian had lunch with Hiyama on the sixteenth floor of the
Marubeni building, and asked him to talk to the new prime
minister, to explain the good points of the TriStar. There was
some difficulty in communication: Hiyama spoke faulty English
which Kotchian did not want to admit that he could not understand. But Hiyama appeared to get the message.[1] The next day
Kotchian went to see the senior managing director of Marubeni,
Toshiharu Okubo, to make the same point. Okubo came out
with a simple proposal: to pledge money to the prime minister.
He then explained that the customary amount for such a major
transaction was 500 million yen, or about $1.7 million: the money
must be paid by Lockheed in cash, when the signal came. Kotchian
agreed, though it was the first time (he insists) that he had bribed
a Japanese official. But he was sure that his rivals must have done
likewise. The pledge, as he saw it, was like a fee for participating
in a game, a defensive rather than an offensive move.

On that same day Kotchian also went to see Kodama—whose
involvement he kept carefully concealed from his official agents
Marubeni. He went at night, again in Fukuda's car, parking
it underground and walking through the subway passage to
Kodama's discreet office. Kodama was not as close to Tanaka as
to earlier prime ministers but he did have a strong link through
another crony behind the black curtain, the billionaire financier
Kenji Osano. This formidable tycoon, with the style of a restless
gorilla, was not easy to do business with, but he was now doubly
influential: he was a key financial supporter of Tanaka and he was
also the biggest single private shareholder in *both* the Japanese
airlines. Osano's beginnings, like Kodama's, were shady: he had
been jailed by the Americans for illegal dealings in gasoline and
had begun his career as a car-parts dealer. He had then built up a
monopoly in transportation for American soldiers in the Korean
war; he had moved from cars to airlines and a chain of hotels
through Asia and Hawaii. Many members of the Diet were
indebted to him, and unlike Kodama he did not try to conceal his
power: he enjoyed making business appointments in the night
clubs of the Ginza district. In Lockheed cables he was called
'Curly' because he was almost bald.

Kodama was soon able to convince Kotchian that he must
have his friend Osano's support, and Kotchian had already met
Osano on a previous visit, when he had called on him to try to

[1] Kotchian, chapter 4.

interest him in Lockheed. But Kodama now made clear that there was only one way to interest this billionaire: to pay him 500 million yen. It was the same figure that Kochian had already pledged to Tanaka. Kotchian again agreed. In one day he had already committed Lockheed to pay $3.4 million in bribes. Part of this huge payment may well have been also to encourage the sale of the Orion anti-submarine planes, which was also critical to Lockheed: but that side of the deal remains buried.

In the following week the wheels began turning. Hiyama of Marubeni called on prime minister Tanaka on August 23 at his private residence, to convey the promise of Lockheed money in return for his help in getting ANA to order the TriStars. Tanaka agreed, saying 'Yosha, yosha' (All right, all right).[1] A few days later, on about August 28, Hiyama met the prime minister again, this time at a party of top businessmen, just before Tanaka was due to meet Nixon in Honolulu. Hiyama now pointed out to Tanaka (in a very significant conversation) that the British prime minister, Edward Heath, was also about to visit Japan, to try to find means to redress the adverse trade balance with Britain. While the TriStar airliner was made in the United States (Hiyama stressed), the engines were made by Rolls-Royce in Britain; so that if Japan would buy the TriStar it would help the British balance of payments as well as the American; it would thus kill two birds with one stone.[2] Tanaka appeared sympathetic to Hiyama's approach, and the nest day the news of his goodwill was duly relayed to Kotchian,[3] just as Tanaka was setting off for his critical meeting with Nixon.

Exactly what was said at that meeting will probably never be known; the official communiqué only mentioned that the Japanese would be buying American planes, without specifying which. But soon after the meeting Tanaka told his billionaire friend Osano that Nixon had mentioned that he would be grateful if a Japanese airline could buy some Lockheed TriStars—with the clear implication that Osano should pass on the message to ANA.[4] Tanaka also himself telephoned the president of ANA, Tokuji Wakasa, to urge him to buy Lockheed while leaving JAL to buy McDonnell Douglas DC10s—which was just the division

[1] According to the prosecutor's statement, Tanaka trial, January 27, 1977.
[2] Ibid.
[3] Kotchian, chapter 2.
[4] Prosecutor's statement, January 27, 1977.

that Kotchian wanted. Whether Nixon had really thus served as Lockheed's salesman, or whether Tanaka was using Nixon as an excuse for exerting pressure in return for his bribe, is still obscure.

Kotchian in the meantime was unaware of this pressure. He had a difficult interview with Wakasa of ANA, who asked searching questions about engine troubles and the financial stability of Rolls-Royce, which Kotchian then referred to the Rolls-Royce sales manager, Dennis Jackson. Kotchian had now learnt the Japanese word for worry, *shimpai*, which he kept repeating to his friends. Two weeks after the Honolulu meeting Kotchian managed to get to see the alarming Osano at his office behind Tokyo Central railway station, full of crowded ante-rooms and telephones. The bald figure of 'Curly' was rushing between them, apparently doing hundreds of things at the same time: he showed Kotchian the name-cards of representatives of Boeing and McDonnell Douglas who had already been to see him; but he promised Kotchian he would check with the chief cabinet secretary to see what was happening.

On the same day a new actor arrived on the Tokyo scene: Ted Heath, the prime minister of Britain, was paying his official visit to Japan, including long talks with Tanaka. The British were worried about the rising Japanese imports of cars and electronics, with no comparable increase in British exports, and there was already some pressure for protective measures. In this context the prospect of selling the TriStar to Japan, equipped with British engines, was much more important to Britain than to America. At the British embassy there seemed at least a fifty-fifty chance of pulling it off; for the British reckoned that the Japanese resented Boeing's domination, and distrusted Douglas. The British diplomats had the impression that Kotchian, holed up in his hotel suite, was blundering about, way out of his depth in the deep Japanese waters.

Heath's actual decision with Tanaka, like Nixon's, was in private: the communiqué referred vaguely to agreeing on an orderly balance of trade, and technical collaboration in civil aviation. But British diplomats assumed that Heath raised the TriStar issue, and Tanaka already knew its importance for Britain: there was nothing improper about Heath promoting Rolls-Royce, as there would be about Nixon promoting Lockheed, since Rolls-Royce had no British competitor. Heath was certainly much encouraged by his talks with Tanaka, whom he liked and later invited to Britain, and he was now convinced that Britain should not restrict Japanese imports. He even made plans for a British trade centre in Tokyo, which today stands as a monument to his optimism. It is very possible that Heath's visit to Tokyo was more important to Lockheed in clinching the TriStar deal than any of Kotchian's large bribes.

Kotchian was still waiting with increasing *shimpai* for his bribes to bear fruit. At last, three weeks after his visit to Osano, he was rung up excitedly by his interpreter, Fukuda, with the news: Lockheed would get an order from Japan Air Lines. But Kotchian was appalled, for it was the opposite of what he had plotted: the order would be small compared to All Nippon's, and JAL, being in no hurry to order, could well change their minds. This must be a conspiracy by his rivals, Kotchian thought, to keep Lockheed out. They had turned his own plot on its head. He had fallen into a trap. He was now (he claims) thoroughly unnerved—surprisingly for such a phlegmatic man—and he even lost his appetite. He went to see the dread Osano again, wishing that Clutter was there to bolster him against 'Japan's most influential man'. Kotchian complained about the JAL order but Osano was angry, for Kotchian had not previously been candid in describing his strategy: he called Kotchian 'an odd person' and broke off the meeting to fly to Hawaii.[1]

Kotchian now turned again to his secret agent and eventually got to meet Kodama at eight in the evening, climbing up the emergency staircase in the darkened building. Kotchian explained his *shimpai* that his plot had been reversed, and Osano's annoyance. Kodama explained that some top people might not have grasped the whole situation: and then in Kotchian's presence boldly rang up the minister for international trade and industry Mr Nakasone, and talked for fifteen minutes, after which he assured Kotchian that the minister would take up the issue the next morning. Kotchian went back to his hotel and rang up Dan Haughton in California (who had just reached his office at six a.m.). It was, Kotchian thought, the most painful day in his long Lockheed career.

Next day Kotchian went early to the Marubeni Corporation, to report the bad news and how he was trying to reverse it. Okubo, the managing director, evidently now suspected that

[1] *Asahi Evening News*, August 24, 1976.

Kotchian was using Kodama as his secret agent, but he did not seem to object, and later Okubo confirmed that there *had* been a plot against Lockheed, which had now successfully been reversed. Eight days later the awesome Osano came back from Hawaii and received Kotchian again: this time he was in a very good humour, which Kotchian thought must be due to Kodama's intervention. On the same day Hiyama of Marubeni reported that the prime minister had assured him that everything was going all right.

Kotchian now saw himself attacking on five fronts. The first route went through the official agents, the Marubeni Corporation, to the prime minister; and the other four routes all went through the secret agent, Kodama. The insurance policies were now thorough and Kotchian had little doubt that Kodama was the key: in talking to him he felt that his expectations were 'being pushed to the core of the government'.[1] But giving this impression was (as with Prince Bernhard) the essence of Kodama's business success.

Kotchian was feeling the strain: after another three weeks he woke up with a high fever and a pain in the stomach. He felt suicidal, and a doctor diagnosed prostatitis: he spent three days in bed in his hotel room. At last, watching the television set in his pyjamas, he heard the news that All Nippon Airlines would buy the Lockheed TriStars. He could not believe that it was in the bag, and indeed it was not. In the evening Okubo from Marubeni rang him up to explain that Lockheed would only get the contract on condition (among others) that they provided another 120 million yen in cash as soon as possible. Kotchian, still shaky, was confused by all the millions of yen and asked Okubo to come round at midnight to explain the position, which he did. $300,000 should be given to the president of ANA, Mr Wakasa— $50,000 for each of the first six planes ordered. And $100,000 should be shared between six politicians, including Mr Hashimoto the former transport minister who had, it was said, helped to delay the choice of plane to give Lockheed their chance.[2] If Kotchian could fix these the next morning, Lockheed would get the contract tomorrow without fail.

It was a tall order, even for Lockheed. The next morning at six a.m. Kotchian woke up Jack Clutter, his close-mouthed

[1] Ibid., August 27, 1976.
[2] Prosecutor's statement: Hashimoto trial, January 31, 1976.

representative, and called him straight round to the hotel. Kotchian asked him to raise $100,000 by ten a.m. and a further $300,000 later; Clutter agreed and the first instalment was delivered. In the afternoon Kotchian was invited round to ANA, where the top executives were all assembled in the conference room. With deadpan formality, he was told: 'Congratulations, Mr Kotchian, your company has got our contract.'

The next day was Halloween and Kotchian was exultant over his victory. In spite of all the shady manoeuvres, he saw it in terms of a military triumph: it had been the most intensive sales campaign of his life, he recorded, 'after seventy straight days of battle, at the head of the Lockheed forces, literally running about in the great city of Tokyo'.[1] In the evening he threw a party in his suite to celebrate: all the Lockheed team were invited, and so were the Rolls-Royce representatives and Kotchian's loyal interpreter Fukuda; but it was a comic façade, for none of the men who had actually pulled the strings were there. The Lockheed PR man Al Elliot unwrapped a big package which revealed a Japanese *Daruma*, a papier-mâché figure of a famous Buddhist monk; and he explained the legend about it: to make a wish, one must paint the left eye of the *Daruma*; and then when the wish is fulfilled paint the right eye; and then burn the whole figure. Kotchian took a black brush and painted the left eye, and the party went on with champagne.

Two days later, the formal letter of intent arrived from All Nippon Airlines, ordering the first six Lockheed planes. Kotchian put it in his briefcase, and flew back to Los Angeles. He was met at the airport by Dan Haughton and an array of Lockheed executives, who gave a party for the Kotchians that evening. The company had been saved. Kotchian blacked out the other eye of the *Daruma* after his wish had been granted, but he never burnt the effigy; perhaps, he reflects now, Buddha later took his revenge.

THE TWELVE MILLION DOLLAR BILL

Kotchian left behind him in Tokyo a staggering commitment, in four separate categories. The first was to Marubeni, the official agents, who were entitled to a formal commission of $160,000 for each TriStar that was sold. Their commission for the eventual

[1] *Asahi Evening News*, August 25, 1976.

twenty-one planes amounted to about $3.4 million, later reduced by negotiation to about $2.9 million.

The second and far the biggest was to the secret agent Kodama, who was paid for several different services. His agent's contract entitled him to one million dollars between 1969 and 1972, and another half-million dollars in the next two years. His commission for the sale of the first six TriStars was $1.7 million, and for the next eight planes another $960,000. Another $150,000 was due to him, to be passed on to Fukuda, the PR man and interpreter. And another whopping $1.7 million (or 500 million yen) was to be passed on to 'Curly', the billionaire Osano, as he had proposed in his first talk with Kotchian. Kotchian, it seems, had no means of knowing whether all that money was actually passed on: all he knew was that Kodama had received around $6.3 million over six years.

The problem of delivering the money was difficult, for Kodama always insisted on receiving the payments in cash. Lockheed therefore had to make use of the New York firm of Deak and Company, which specialised in discreetly transmitting currencies abroad; it had been set up by Nicholas Deak, a former Hungarian who had been an officer of the OSS (the forerunner of the CIA) and now had twenty subsidiary offices overseas. Deak was believed to have been sometimes used by the CIA (for instance, to finance the coup against Mossadeq in 1953) and Lockheed's use of Deak revived old suspicions about their links with the CIA. Through Deak, Lockheed could provide cash for Kodama without their auditors knowing; for Deak, unlike Lockheed's usual Bank of America, was not inspected by the comptroller of currency. Deak's Los Angeles office sent the money to Hong Kong, from where it was hand-carried to Tokyo by a former priest called José Aramiya, acting as Deak's secret agent: the cash was thus available to one of the Lockheed men, Clutter or Elliot.[1] The seven million dollars was eventually paid to Kodama in this way, and just after Kotchian had left Tokyo, Kodama had already signed receipts in his own neat hand for 330 million yen or one million dollars.

The third commitment was to Okubo, the managing director of Marubeni, through whom Kotchian had secretly pledged $1.7 million to the prime minister. This money was arranged by Jack Clutter, brought in cash from Deak's office in Hong Kong,

[1] See Tad Szulc in *New Republic* magazine, April 10, 1976.

and neatly stuffed into cardboard orange-boxes. There was also the $400,000 that Okubo had asked for at midnight on October 29, just before the deal was clinched, part of it for the politicians but most of it for the airline. The airline money was duly paid after the sale of the first six planes; but when the next order came, for eight further planes, Lockheed discovered they had to pay *another* $50,000 per plane. And the airline received yet another discreet pay-off: for when Lockheed later sought to borrow a TriStar for a demonstration flight to Australia, they were asked for extra charges amounting to $180,000—which had to be paid in cash.

These last sums to Okubo and the airline had to be carefully concealed, for they were not provided for in any Lockheed contract; and so at this point Kotchian resorted to another remarkable undercover organisation, the ID Corporation. It had been set up in the Cayman Islands, the Caribbean tax haven, by a resourceful American-Japanese businessman called Shig Katayama, who had begun his career as an intelligence officer with the American occupation forces in Japan. Ostensibly, a scrap-iron dealer, he continued to work in intelligence, his special field being narcotics. Smooth, assured and bilingual, he had a long association with Lockheed: in the early 'sixties, when Lockheed had been pushing arms in Indonesia, he had secretly planned the sale of Armalite rifles from Japan, until the deal collapsed when President Sukarno fell.

Katayama had become a friend of both Jack Clutter and Al Elliot, and when Lockheed needed to transmit their secret cash, they asked their invaluable friend to fly to Hong Kong and simply sign some receipts amounting to 600 million yen, or about $2 million; in return for which he was given altogether $75,000. 'I guess the ethics of the thing leave much to be desired,' he admitted later when asked whether he thought his signature was worth so much.[1] The money, thus receipted, was then sent on to Okubo and the airline, and Okubo in turn provided receipts for Lockheed in a childish code: one of his colleagues at Marubeni, Hiroshi Itoh, put his signature under the words 'I have received a hundred peanuts.' A peanut was a million yen.

Through all these circuitous routes Kotchian had caused over twelve million dollars to be paid for the contract—most of it in bribes rather than legitimate commissions. It was, Kotchian

[1] *Japan Times Weekly*, June 26, 1976.

reckoned, quite a reasonable figure in proportion to the sale—less than three percent of the total value of the fourteen airliners sold, modest compared to the ten percent commission in some countries like Saudi Arabia. And Kotchian was convinced, with some justification, that his rival aircraft companies were also paying large bribes.

But what was striking about Lockheed's payoffs was their sheer recklessness and lack of reference to the local scene. In his desperation to break into the market, Kotchian had raised the stakes without really appearing to understand the game. Impressed by Kodama's record of twelve years earlier, and fascinated by this man of mystery, Kotchian was paying out his huge sums with no assurance as to their destination. To this day, Kotchian does not know which of his routes was the one that did the trick; but at the time of writing (in Tokyo in February 1977) the prosecutor's statement against Tanaka suggests that the route through Lockheed's official agents, Marubeni, working through Osano and the prime minister Tanaka, was the decisive one. The two visiting leaders, Nixon and Heath, might well have achieved it anyway, and it seems clear that the secret agent pocketed huge sums for his own purposes. It was in the best traditions of the trade.

When the Lockheed contract was announced, there was some astonishment and speculation among their rivals, and among officials of the two airlines. Lockheed explained that they had been chosen partly because of the special silence of the TriStar and the convenient seating arrangements, but there were sceptical comments: *Time* magazine printed a piece headed: 'Somebody Up There Likes Lockheed', and *Fortune* magazine even hinted at corruption. But the questions, like so many Japanese business questions, were soon hidden behind the black curtain. The three main actors, Tanaka, Kodama and Osano, continued their intricate careers undisturbed. It was only an extraordinary sequence of accidents that would suddenly pull the curtain away, three and a half years later.

14

The Arming of the Shah

Is the government dog wagging the tail of the aircraft companies,
or the aircraft companies' tail wagging the government dog? It is not
an easy question to answer.

Senator Frank Church, September 1976

WHILE Kotchian had been thus desperately selling Lockheed airliners to Japan, the aerospace industry was recovering from its nadir. By 1972, the year of Watergate, of Tom Jones' secret payments to Nixon, and of Kotchian's bribes in Japan, the falling graph of American sales (as shown on p. 242) was already levelling off. But the reprieve did not come from the Pentagon: it came from abroad.

In the first place the biggest companies, particularly Boeing, were now receiving huge orders from foreign airlines buying the new wide-bodied jets: between 1972 and 1973 civil aircraft exports went up from $1.6 billion to $2.3 billion, and in 1974 up to $3.4 billion. But more unexpected and more encouraging to most companies, including Lockheed, was a huge increase in arms orders from abroad. Between 1972 and 1973 military aerospace exports went up from $840 million to $1.4 billion; the next year to $1.8 billion; the next year to $2.5 billion.[1] These booming arms sales were to prove more long-lasting and profitable than the airliner exports, and were changing the whole balance of the business: the American arms industry was now

[1] Aerospace Industries Association of America: Aerospace Facts and Figures, 1975–6.

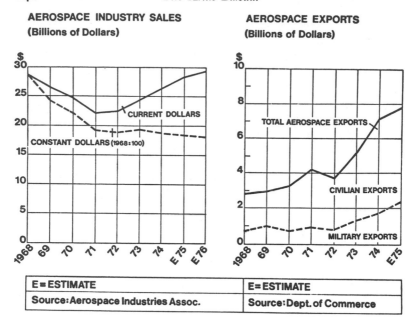

AEROSPACE INDUSTRY SALES
(Billions of Dollars)

AEROSPACE EXPORTS
(Billions of Dollars)

E = ESTIMATE	E = ESTIMATE
Source: Aerospace Industries Assoc.	Source: Dept. of Commerce

becoming seriously dependent for its survival on foreign sales—
and particularly sales to the Third World. It was a situation
familiar enough in Europe, but for the United States it was unprecedented, with far wider consequences.

The roots of this change went back several years. Already by the
time of President Nixon's inauguration in 1969 developments
in both the Middle East and the Far East were preparing the way.
In Britain the prime minister Harold Wilson, after the economic
crisis and devaluation of the pound in 1967, had speeded up
Britain's withdrawal of forces from East of Suez, including the
Persian (or Arabian) Gulf; and Washington thus regarded this
region as providing a dangerous vacuum, which must be filled
either by an American presence or by a powerful ally. At the
same time, as a result of American casualties in Vietnam, Nixon
and Kissinger expounded the 'Nixon doctrine', by which the
United States would supply arms rather than troops, equipping
their reliable allies with large arsenals in crucial areas. As the
doctrine was explained in 1970 by David Packard, the deputy
secretary of defence: 'The best hope of reducing our overseas
involvements and expenditures lies in getting allied and friendly
nations to do even more in their own defence. To realise that
hope, however, requires that we must continue, if requested, to

give or sell them the tools they need for this bigger load we are urging them to assume.'[1]

Thus the American arms industry, with declining orders from the Pentagon, could already expect some relief through orders from other countries. At the time the Nixon doctrine was welcomed with relief by most politicians as the means of extricating American troops from South-East Asia. But it was really a gamble of extraordinary rashness, for it assumed that allies who had this new freedom to buy arms, whether in Asia or beyond, would use them wisely, in the Western interest. And the stakes in the gamble were soon to be abruptly raised.

In 1971 the United States foreign trade balance showed a deficit for the first time since 1893. The need for exports was now far more urgent than ten years before, when McNamara and Henry Kuss had first unleashed the Pentagon's salesmen, and the aerospace slump and unemployment added to the crisis. In the White House, Nixon discussed how to redress the trade balance, and was pressed, for both political and economic reasons, to relax restrictions on arms sales. As the slump in railroad-building in the 1880s had led Vickers and Carnegie into making guns, so the aerospace crisis of the late 1960s helped to encourage the government and companies to sell more weapons abroad.

Nixon and Kissinger both tended to regard arms selling as an extension of diplomacy, in the nineteenth-century tradition, and neither had serious inhibitions about their means. The humiliations of Vietnam, and America's weakened economy, had engendered more sceptical and short-term diplomatic attitudes, treating arms as counters in the world's game with which to bargain for settlement or placate client-states. It was a prevailing cynicism: 'Now that we have no moral influence,' one senior diplomat suggested to me in 1976, 'perhaps selling arms is the only kind of influence we have left.' But certainly Nixon and Kissinger encouraged it, and the pursuit of the 'quick fix' and shuttle diplomacy increased the temptation to use arms as diplomatic bribes. This use of weapons to achieve settlements really doubled the danger: for it encouraged the build-up in just those regions where arms were most likely to be used.

The recovery of the arms industry was thus already under way in 1972, which culminated in Nixon's re-election and the emphatic rejection of McGovern's proposals for defence cuts. But

[1] See Michael T. Klare in *Society*, Sept-Oct 1974

the real take-off began a year later, with the fourth Arab-Israeli
war. In the first place the aftermath of war provided a rush of
orders from both sides, to replace the wrecked equipment with
new systems—particularly air defence systems. But, more important, the quadrupling of the oil-price brought a surge of wealth to
the states of the Persian Gulf, led by Iran and Saudi Arabia. For
any nation faced with sudden wealth, arms provided the easiest
and quickest way to spend money, bringing prestige and new
authority to the rulers. Hospitals, schools or welfare provided
huge problems of administration and social disruption, but arms
companies brought their own infrastructure and training, making
the links with high technology which rulers longed for. And
commissions or bribes increased the incentives, while redistribut-
ing part of the wealth on the way.

In Washington the increase in the oil-price had induced a
sense of near-panic about the effects on the international economy
and America's balance of payments, and William Simon at the
treasury was not inclined to discourage orders for arms. The
quickest way to recycle oil money or to 'sop up the surplus', it
was said, was to sell arms in exchange—much safer and stabler
than having the surplus oil-money 'sloshing around the short-
term capital markets of the world'.[1] In this topsy-turvy world,
arms were now being touted as the means to make the world safer.

Only gradually did the extent of this trend dawn on American
politicians and the public; with the oil crisis and the impending
impeachment of a president there were too many other worries.
But by the summer of 1974 the statistics were making the point:
in one year the Pentagon had more than doubled their total
foreign sales, from $3.9 billion in 1973 to $8.3 billion in 1974.
The world arms trade had been transformed beyond recognition.

THE MAKING OF A WARLORD

Of those total sales in 1974, nearly half—or $3.9 billion—were
going to a single nation. The Shah of Iran, who twelve years
earlier had been regarded as a mere pawn of Western diplomacy,
was soon the commander of the most extensive armoury of
weapons outside America, Russia and Europe. The making of

---

[1] S. Stanley Katz (Assistant Secretary for Economic Policy and Research in the Department of Commerce), writing in *National Defence*, May-June 1976.

this warlord demonstrated both the impact of a single personality and the limitations of Western arms control.

The Shah's determination had been forged by harsh experience. When he had first been put on the throne by the British in 1941, to replace his father whom they exiled, he was regarded as a puppet by the British government and the British oil company, Anglo Iranian (later BP): as Churchill explained, 'We have chased a dictator into exile, and installed a constitutional sovereign . . .' He watched his country being invaded by the Russians, and used as a base by the Allies, and after the war he saw that his subjects were just 'clicking their heels to the orders of the oil company'.[1] His resentments and ambitions smouldered, and his relations with the West became still more tricky after the coming to power in 1951 of the fiery Dr Mossadeq, who nationalised the oil company and eventually exiled the Shah. He was only reinstated with the help of a coup instigated by the CIA and the British secret service, and while this painful incident underlined his dependence, he did not wish to be reminded of it, or to risk being again outbid by an extreme nationalist leader.

He had already developed a passion for armaments. He had his own pilot's licence, he subscribed to *Aviation Week*, and he followed every development of aircraft, missiles or warships, which gave him a cutting edge when arguing with less militaristic Western diplomats. Throughout the 'fifties and early 'sixties he depended on British and American grants for military equipment, which were justified by his common frontier with Russia, but he obtained much more than his obvious needs. As President Kennedy's special counsel Theodore Sorensen complained: 'The Shah insisted on our supporting an expensive army too large for border incidents and internal security and of no use in all-out war.' His army, Sorensen was advised, 'resembled the proverbial man who was too heavy to do any light work and too light to do any heavy work'. The Russians professed themselves outraged by the American support for such a reactionary regime; and Khrushchev complained to Kennedy in 1961 about the Shah's insistence that his power was given to him by God: 'Everybody knew how this power was seized by the Shah's father, who was not God but a sergeant in the Iranian army.'[2]

[1] See Anthony Sampson: *The Seven Sisters*, New York, Viking 1975, p. 116–7.

[2] Theodore C. Sorensen: *Kennedy*, London, Hodder & Stoughton, 1965, pp. 547, 628. See also Arthur M. Schlesinger: *A Thousand Days*, London, André Deutsch, 1965, p. 329.

The Shah's self-confidence was very uncertain: his own auto-biography, published in 1961, gives the impression of an un-formed and insecure character:[1] as a frail young man he had been overawed by his huge father who had climbed the throne. But he was borrowing the mystique of the peacock throne, which could dazzle both his own people and the Western leaders, and his combination of authority and charm had a strange capacity to reassure presidents and prime ministers: Kennedy was not impressed but Lyndon Johnson was very vulnerable, as was Nixon. The State Department were fearful of offending this awesome ruler and in the meantime, as his oil revenues increased, the Shah was becoming an increasingly important customer for arms. The Shah's ambitions for weaponry were insatiable: as he talks nowadays about planes he sounds, as Sam Cummings does, like a schoolboy whose dreams have been fulfilled, surveying the world as his toyshop.

It was a thrilling prospect for the arms companies, for the Shah not only had the money to spend, but could appreciate the finer points of 'the state of the art'. Already in 1962 the Shah had visited California, where he met Tom Jones of Northrop, when the Tiger fighter was first going into production: as a result Iran was the first foreign government to buy Tigers, which began flying in Iran in 1965. Tom Jones forged a personal friendship with the Shah, as with Prince Bernhard; he flew in and out of Teheran in his own jet. The two men, the king and the arms-king, shared the same passion for planes and the same playboy style, concealing their single-minded ambition.

Tom Jones cemented his Iranian alliance by appointing as his agent Kermit Roosevelt, whose efforts in Saudi Arabia we have already noted.[2] Roosevelt is one of the more engaging characters to pass through the arms-dealing scene. As the grandson of Theodore Roosevelt, he had inherited both an aristocratic confidence and a buccaneering streak: he has a slow charm to conceal his basic toughness. He had served in the OSS in the war, when he first encountered King Feisal, and then with the CIA; like so many other arms agents he was deep in the world of intelligence, but on a very high plane, and it was he who organised the coup which overthrew Mossadeq and restored the Shah to the throne in 1953. Remarkably, although the Shah preferred to

[1] *Mission for My Country*, Hutchinson, London, 1961.
[2] See chapters 8 and 11.

forget his dependence on the CIA, Roosevelt retained his friendship and confidence, with occasional ups and downs.

Roosevelt's success with the CIA in Iran led to further clandestine operations for which he was responsible, including the
Guatemalan coup: but he found himself getting pushed into situations he did not really believe in, including an attempted Syrian
coup, and he resigned in 1957.[1] He had a very special prestige: he
worked for a time for Gulf Oil, but was asked to resign in 1963
just when (it turned out) Gulf were embarking on their career of
bribery abroad. He then set up his own company dealing with
the Middle East: pictures of the Shah and King Feisal as well
as Teddy Roosevelt adorned his Washington office. His firm,
Kermit Roosevelt and Associates, signed a contract with Northrop in January 1965, under which they were to be paid $15,000 a
year (later rising to $75,000 a year) to 'monitor all activities in the
Middle East', and to establish Northrop's contacts 'with the
highest levels of government in the Middle East'.[2]

Kim Roosevelt was Northrop's ambassador to Iran. Already
in April 1965 he was in Teheran, talking to his old friend General
Khatami of the air force, pressing him to take more squadrons
of fighters; the next day he saw the Shah, to try to sell more
Tigers, as opposed to more F111s (made by General Dynamics),
which the Shah thought had a longer range ('I don't know enough
to argue about this,' admitted Roosevelt). The Shah was very
cordial, and invited Roosevelt to bring his wife for a holiday
with him; though two days after their talk there was an attempt
on the Shah's life which made Roosevelt very aware of the fact
that 'Iranian stability rests on the life of one man'. Roosevelt was
back six months later, to discuss training in electronics, both for
the air force and for Savak, the Iranian secret police.[3]

But the Shah was buying from arms companies everywhere,
and by the next year, 1966, he was allowed by the Pentagon to
acquire the latest version of the McDonnell Phantom fighter, the
F4D. It was still four years behind the US air force, but the Shah
had now established priority among foreign customers. He was
still anxious not to depend on any one country, and he loved to
play nations against each other. He bought extensively from
Britain and France, and just after the Phantom deal he played his

[1] Interview on 'World in Action', Granada Television, June 23, 1975.
[2] Multinational Hearings, part 12, p. 696.
[3] Ibid., pp. 694–9.

boldest hand. He flew to Moscow and in February 1967 announced an arms deal involving $110 million of military equipment, including armoured troop carriers, trucks and anti-aircraft guns. The Soviets had never before sold arms to a country within the Western alliance, and the US Congress, suitably shocked, convened special hearings (see chapter 10). But the hearings suggested that the Shah's approaches to Russia would encourage Washington to sell all the more arms: the trick of blackmail was soon shown to be effective.[1]

There was never much serious danger of the Shah being lured into the communist camp; on the contrary, the companies were able to play on the Shah's anti-communist fears while building on his relationship with LBJ. In September 1968 we find Tom Jones of Northrop, in an ingenious letter, advising Kim Roosevelt to persuade the Shah to support his projected new Northrop plane, the P530 (later the Cobra), which was planned to replace the Tiger. Jones stressed the advantage of the Shah's closeness to LBJ, and emphasised to Roosevelt that 'in any discussions with the Shah, it is important that they be kept on the basis of fundamental national objectives, rather than allow it to take the appearance of a sales plan'. Northrop were then trying to frustrate the rival multi-combat plane which was being planned by the German, Italian and British governments (which eventually went ahead as the MRCA or Tornado). Tom Jones knew that the Shah would soon be meeting the German chancellor, Kurt Kiesinger, and urged the Shah to tell Kiesinger that the Northrop plane, which represented a 'common interest in freedom', was far preferable. Jones was now turning to use the Shah as his own super-salesman, to ginger up the rest of the Western alliance.[2]

Whether Roosevelt and Jones were really convinced that their fighters in Iran were saving the free world may be doubted. Kim Roosevelt, in the course of trying to persuade King Feisal of Saudi Arabia to buy Tigers, stressed the importance of having proper ground control, and pointed to the warning of 'one of his neighbours' who was himself an expert flier, and who had picked the best plane, but 'who was totally lacking in ground

[1] Henry Kuss from the Pentagon explained that the Shah 'has made it abundantly clear that if the United States is unwilling or unable to meet his major military requirements he is determined to go elsewhere to acquire what he needs'. (Senate Foreign Relations Committee: Near East and South Asia Hearings, March 1967.)

[2] Multinational Hearings, part 12, pp. 721-31.

environment, and who was therefore as good as blind'.[1]

As the Shah's income and orders increased, so all the major arms companies, including Lockheed, Boeing and McDonnell Douglas, were cashing in with the help of their own agents (Boeing took the precaution of appointing the Empress' uncle as their agent). Much of this new business went to the West Coast, but the most spectacular beneficiary was the Grumman corporation, based on Lond Island, only forty miles out of New York City near the drab suburb of Hicksville. The relationship between Grumman and the Shah was to become the most controversial of all new alliances between companies and countries.

Grumman had never been a very outward-looking company. They had grown up with the United States navy, ever since their founder LeRoy Grumman had built his first naval plane, a small bi-wing fighter, in 1931. In the Second World War they employed 25,000 people and built 17,000 combat planes, including two famous fighters, the Wildcat and the Hellcat. With peace they diversified into other products, including aluminium canoes, metal boats, a crop-duster and an executive jet (the Gulfstream). After 1960 they won important space contracts, to build satellites and lunar modules, but they had lost out to Lockheed, as we saw in the last chapter, in the battles to sell fighters to Japan and Europe. Grumman remained dependent on the Pentagon, and particularly on the navy: seven different Grumman planes flew over Vietnam.

Then in 1969 Grumman won a contract to build a new fighter for the navy, which seemed a brilliant prize. The F14, or the Tomcat as it came to be called, had sweep-wings which enabled it both to shoot up like a rocket at a speed of over Mach 2, and to turn and manoeuvre for dog-fights. It could carry a multi-barrel gun and could launch four Phoenix missiles simultaneously against four targets. It contained an intricate tangle of electronics including a computer to control the wings; it claimed to be the first 'flying computer'. It was planned to be a 'MiG-killer'—against the new MiG 25 or 'Foxbat'—and to ensure American air superiority for the 'eighties. It was the first entirely new American fighter to be designed for a decade, and its chief rival, the Eagle

[1] Ibid., p. 714.

or F15A, designed by McDonnell Douglas for the air force, was a year behind.

The Tomcat first flew in December 1970; an ungainly plane, with a long pointed nose and clean lines at the front, and a clutch of missiles and two dirty black holes at the back. Its performance was breathtaking, and by late 1971 seven Tomcats were flying. But making them had almost bankrupted Grumman. The contract was one of the last to be based on McNamara's principle of Total Package Procurement, which had nearly ruined Lockheed over the Galaxy, and once more the cost had zoomed up. In 1971 the project lost $18 million, the next year $70 million; and meanwhile Grumman was losing other orders in the prevailing cutback, which made it harder to charge the development costs on to other projects. The price of each Tomcat went up from $7.3 million to $11 million—the most expensive fighter ever built. And Grumman's board were in disarray with the death of their young president, Llewellyn Evans.

A new president, John Bierwirth, took over to rescue it: he came from National Distillers, with a much more cosmopolitan background, and saw no basic difference between liquor and arms. He was dismayed by Grumman's dependence on the navy ('an overwhelming realisation when it finally sinks home'[1]). He first persuaded the navy to pay more and to lend Grumman money, and then looked around for foreign customers to buy Grumman planes, and particularly the Tomcat. The navy by this time shared the anxiety: they had first planned the plane only for themselves, but now they had a vested interest in protecting Grumman's future. Some navy men were worried about allowing foreigners to buy a plane that was still at the development stage and was still having serious problems. But the need to share the costs was very pressing.

Grumman were already looking towards the Shah long before the Pentagon were involved, and their ingenious salesmanship reveals a basic flaw in the system of arms control. It showed how a company can whet the appetite of a sovereign nation, which the American government cannot easily turn down.

Grumman had one very versatile salesman: Colin Jupp, a former Australian with intelligence connections, who had just happened, remarkably enough, to be in Iran in 1953, the year of the coup which reinstated the Shah. Jupp was there (he later explained to the senators) as a student on an archaeological expedition, in the course of which he conveniently became acquainted with many influential Iranians, including the Shah, who came to visit the diggings. Jupp was also a friend of the American military attaché in Moscow, Colonel Mansfield; and Mansfield in turn knew the Iranian attaché in Moscow, General N. Payrow, who was very influential with the Shah.

Thus by 1971 Colin Jupp was very well placed: he invited Colonel Mansfield to the Grumman headquarters at Long Island, to show him the Tomcat as the answer to the Soviet air threat, and Mansfield in turn briefed the Iranians. Jupp had a further opportunity in October 1971, when the Shah was celebrating the 2,500th anniversary of the Persian empire. Spiro Agnew was leading the American delegation and Jupp was also invited; he gave General Khatami a model of the Tomcat, and tried to persuade Agnew's staff to press its claims. By March 1972 General Howard Fish at the Pentagon (see chapter 18) was asking permission for the navy to give classified briefings to the Shah's military adviser General Hassan Toufanian. In Washington, Grumman also had a very useful ally in the shape of Charles Colson, who had served as their counsel and adviser and who was now an influential aide at the White House. In April 1972 Jupp called at the White House to talk to Colson and Bob Haldeman, to try to obtain the president's support for selling the Tomcat to the Shah.[1]

In the meantime the Shah was still craving for more arms. In November 1971 he had occupied two islands in the Strait of Hormuz, provoking new fears among his Arab neighbours, and he began building a big new naval base on the island of Kharg, very close to Iraq. By early 1972, when the British had finally left the Persian Gulf, he already had an armoury which amazed military visitors and journalists. But he was soon insisting that he must have the Tomcat or its equivalent in the new generation of American fighters. Early in 1972, while Nixon's election campaign was gathering weight, a succession of Washington leaders arrived in Teheran: first John Chaffee, Nixon's secretary for the navy; then Robert Seamans, secretary for the air force, and finally in May the top men themselves. Nixon and Kissinger had been in Moscow to discuss the SALT disarmament plans, and on their way back they stopped to talk to the Shah.

[1] Multinational Hearings, testimony of Colin Jupp, September 13, 1976.

They talked alone: Joseph Sisco, the under-secretary for the Middle East, was left in his hotel room, uninformed about the outcome. It was not until much later that the full significance became clear. The Shah stressed to Nixon that Russian Foxbats (MiG 25s) had been flying over Iranian soil, and insisted he must have the most up-to-date fighters. Nixon agreed to sell Iran 'virtually any conventional arms it wanted', supported by unlimited American technicians in Iran: and he personally told the Shah that he could choose between the two new-generation planes, the Tomcat and the Eagle.[1]

It was the first time that any non-industrial country had been allowed to reach the same level as the United States in the 'state of the art'. There had been no major review beforehand and Nixon's decision was passed to the Pentagon with no chance to revise it. It opened the way for the Shah's next massive expansion and thereafter (as one Pentagon official explained to me) the Pentagon had difficulty in maintaining any logical policy towards Iran: for Nixon's decision was based not on what the United States thought best, but on what the Shah wanted. There was little evidence (as Senator Hubert Humphrey complained, introducing a Senate Report four years afterwards) that Nixon had recognised the far-reaching foreign policy implications.[2] One well-placed State Department official told me in 1976 that he had been trying to find out for two years why the deal was made: 'Perhaps the answer will only be found on Nixon's tapes.'

How far was Nixon influenced by the plight of the aerospace companies? Might the Shah himself—as some conspiratorial critics have suspected—have promised support for Nixon's campaign?[3] Was Nixon genuinely convinced by the Shah's account of Soviet dangers? Or was he mesmerised by the personality of the Shah, and fearful of offending him? The answer may never emerge. But what is clear is that the decision soon caused a surge of activity in the aerospace business.

In February 1973 the Pentagon revealed that Iran had contracted to buy $2 billion worth of weapons from the United States—the biggest single deal ever negotiated: it would include 175 jet fighters, five hundred helicopters, and numbers of air-to-surface missiles. By June *Aviation Week* was reporting that the

[1] Senate Report: US Military Sales to Iran, Washington, July 1976, p. 41.

[2] *Washington Post*, August 2, 1976.

[3] Ibid., September 14, 1976.

American government had 'loosened the wraps on what can be sold abroad'. The two rival arms companies, McDonnell Douglas and Grumman, began feverishly promoting their rival planes, the Eagle and the Tomcat. Grumman stressed to the Pentagon that if the Tomcat were sold to the Shah it would diminish the huge cost to the navy; and they spent $250,000 in promoting the Tomcat at the Paris air show in June, where Iranian officers were watching. The Shah saw the two planes together at the Andrews air force base outside Washington. The Grumman salesmen brought a special flightsuit for the Shah, decorated with his crest, and an air-conditioned trailer where he could change. The Eagle was not ready for a proper demonstration, but the Tomcat performed amazing aerobatics, touching down in front of the Shah and then shooting up like a rocket. The Grumman men observed the Shah's delight as he illustrated the swoop with his hands.

Grumman were desperate to get the order, and to help them they hired an Iranian-American arms lobbyist called Houshang Lavi, who lived in Long Island where he operated with his two brothers a company called Starlight International. Lavi was a controversial figure in Iran: he had been under fire from General Toufanian over a huge previous commission from an Italian helicopter deal; but he was a friend of General Khatami, the chief of the Iranian air force (who later died in a glider accident), who was a brother-in-law of the Shah. The Grumman contract promised to pay him $89 million (which was later reduced to $28 million), if the sale of the Tomcats went through.

By August 1973 the Shah had decided to order the Tomcat. Two months later came the Arab-Israeli war, the embargo, and the doubling of the oil price. The Shah's diplomatic support was now suddenly crucial, to prevent the price going still higher; but Kissinger decided that to bring pressure on him might be counter-productive, leading him to find weapons elsewhere. In December the Shah pressed for a further doubling of the oil price, and succeeded. He would thus receive still greater oil revenues, to allow him to buy still more arms.

The transmuting of oil into arms was now quickening, until by the end of 1974 the Pentagon were selling nearly half their world exports to Iran. The orders included helicopters and machine-guns, hovercraft and missiles. But the most controversial was still the Tomcat, and by June 1974 the Shah increased his order to eighty, which would cost nearly $2 billion. About half the sum would go to the engines and weaponry, including the Phoenix missiles made by Hughes Aircraft; the other half would go to Grumman.

The Grumman crisis was not yet over: indeed at first it got worse with the shortage of credit to carry out the new orders. In August 1974 Congress unexpectedly voted to cut off the navy loan which had helped finance Grumman, who now had to find $200 million in six weeks. On Long Island it looked as if the whole Tomcat project would have to be scrapped: you could literally hear the loss of morale, as one executive described it to me, in the hangar where the Tomcats were being built; the shriek of drilling, the hammering and clattering, had become fitful and desultory. The president John Bierwirth looked once again to the Shah. The government-owned bank, the Bank Melli Iran, agreed to lend Grumman $75 million, to help ensure the delivery of the planes: and this encouraged the American banks. Within six weeks a consortium of banks had provided credits. The Long Island community were now doubly indebted to the Shah, both their customer and banker.

The navy too were relieved that their favourite plane would go ahead, with its costs shared by a foreign power, but some admirals were not without misgivings, for the real price of the rescue was very high: they no longer had a technological lead over every other country. It was the old dilemma of the admirals in Victorian Britain who had been glad to let the shipyards of Armstrong's and Vickers export abroad, to pay the costs of the technology; the export trade could quickly deprive them of their technical lead, and speed up the arms race still further.

Grumman's fortunes were soon transformed, and the drilling and hammering resumed their full volume as the workers pieced together the flying computers. Walking through the hangar, it was hard not to marvel at the dedication and the precision, and all the complex technologies devoted to these small lethal objects, each one costing as much as a small hospital. A label was stuck on each plane with a cartoon of a stripy Tomcat, smoking a cigar and holding a gun in one hand: it symbolised well enough the strange atmosphere of the place—half toyshop, half death-factory.

Some planes had an extra label with the words 'Imperial Iranian Air Force', and by January 1976 the first Tomcat, ahead of schedule, had been delivered to Iran. Soon the Iranian connection was changing the whole perspective of the company, who were sending not only planes but engineers, administrators and instructors to train the Iranian pilots. By 1976 eight hundred Grumman expatriates (including their families) had gone to live in Iran, while Iranian officers were frequently visiting Long Island. Both sides were locked into the Grumman-Iranian alliance, linking Long Island to the shaky peacock throne five thousand miles away.

By the time of the annual meeting in May 1976 the mood of Grumman was jubilant, and a thousand shareholders gathered on the airstrip to look at the Tomcat. John Bierwirth described how, thanks to the navy and Iran, Grumman had shown the biggest sales in its history, of $1.3 billion for 1975; and they now hoped to sell Tomcats to many other foreign clients, including Saudi Arabia, Japan, Canada and Australia. He looked to a target for exports of thirty percent of total production.

Iran was now already setting a pace for other arms-buying countries, through her exchange of oil for weapons. 'We can see the effects of two elements,' said Senator Church, introducing hearings on the Grumman sales in September 1976, 'which have done so much to make the US government the leading arms merchants of the world. First, the promotional push of US arms companies undeterred by effective US government supervision. Second, the embryonic beginning of the vicious circle in which we are now caught—the appetite for sophisticated weapons feeds the needs of revenues to pay for the arms, which leads to more pressure for oil price increases.'[1]

The Grumman-Iranian alliance was not without tensions. In April 1975 the deputy minister for war, General Toufanian, had been warned by an American friend that the Lavi brothers had been appointed Grumman's agents: the general (according to his own account) complained to the Pentagon and to Grumman, and was assured there was no such agent. But later it emerged that Grumman had paid $28 million to agents, and the general burst into public protest: at a press conference he told reporters, 'This shows that the foreign companies want to loot us. We will not allow this and we will pull the extra money out of their throats.'[2] Houshang Lavi retorted by accusing the general of himself

[1] Multinational Hearings, September 10, 1976.
[2] *New York Times*, February 15 and February 23, 1976.

benefiting from kick-backs, but Toufanian continued to insist that the $28 million be repaid.[1]

Grumman were not alone in their embarrassment over agents. Northrop, true to form, had not been content to hire Roosevelt as their representative, but had paid out large sums, particularly for a telecommunications project which they shared with three other companies, Siemens, Nippon Electric and General Telephone and Electronics. For this they had paid several hundred thousand dollars to Prince Chahram, a nephew of the Shah, and they had also established a $600,000 slush fund in Switzerland, part of which was thought to have gone to Iranian officials. The Iranian government later demanded that Northrop should pay them $8 million as a penalty for having made pay-offs, and Northrop eventually agreed to pay a two million dollar rebate.[2]

By now the Shah's total military build-up was setting new records. In 1975 his arsenal included 300 Chieftain tanks, with another 1,680 on order, 860 medium tanks, with another 250 Scorpion tanks on order, three destroyers, with six more destroyers and three submarines on order, and a total of 238 combat aircraft, with 349 fighters, including the Tomcats, on order. His total defence expenditure for 1975-6 was estimated at $10,405 million, or nearly a third of the total Gross National Product of Iran, and slightly more than the defence expenditure of Britain ($9,974 million), which had more than five times Iran's GNP.[3]

I asked the Shah about his rate of spending in an interview with him in February 1975, and he replied: 'I hope my good friends in Europe and the United States and elsewhere will finally understand that there is absolutely no difference between Iran and France, Britain and Germany. Why should you find it absolutely normal that France will spend that much money on her army, and not my country?' He insisted that 'the more powerful we get, the more responsible we feel,' and he added: 'We don't want the land of others, we don't need the wealth of others, we have enough: furthermore, we could have crushed all those nuisance people much more: we never did it . . . the strength that we have now in the Persian Gulf is ten times, twenty times more than the British ever had.'[4]

[1] *Washington Post*, September 30, 1976.
[2] *New York Times*, February 23, 1976.
[3] *The Military Balance 1975-76*, The International Institute for Strategic Studies, London.
[4] Interview with the author, St Moritz, February 1975.

THE CALIFORNIA ALLIANCE

The flow of arms to Iran continued unabated. In August 1976 the Senate Foreign Relations Committee published a well-documented report on the Iranian build-up, showing how Nixon's agreement had caused a loss of control and a bonanza for the arms industry, while the presence of so many Americans in Iran would create hostages who could be exploited in a crisis. But the State Department promptly contradicted it, explaining that the sales were a natural outgrowth from the Nixon doctrine. Just when the Senate Report was published Kissinger was again visiting Iran, promising the Shah even more up-to-date weapons. At a press conference the Shah insisted that Iran must be the only judge of what she needed, and threatened once more to buy his arms elsewhere. 'If you do not pursue a policy of standing by your friends, who are spending their own money and are ready to spend their own blood, the alternative is nuclear holocaust or more Vietnams.'[1] Soon after Kissinger's visit, the Shah was allowed to buy 160 General Dynamics F16 fighters (which had just been ordered by NATO[2]) at a cost of about $3.4 billion, together with missiles worth another $600 million.[3]

Tom Jones was now exploiting his friendship to the full. He flew out to Teheran for an audience with the Shah in September 1976, to persuade him to ask for some F18 planes—the new version of the Cobra which was being jointly developed by Northrop and McDonnell Douglas for the US navy. Soon afterwards the Shah wrote a letter to the Pentagon requesting the plane: several Pentagon officials strongly suspected that the letter had been written by Tom Jones himself. The Shah was in effect serving as a Northrop agent, of a kind that was hard to refuse.

Nearly every arms company now looked towards the Shah. When I visited California in the summer of 1976 the Shah seemed to be lurking everywhere, under every balance sheet, inside every projection of future earnings. 'Everywhere you turn in Iran today,' said the magazine *California Business*, 'you're likely to run into someone associated with a California-based company ... Lonely? How about a trip to Iran?' Northrop declared record earnings with the help of their exports of 140 Tiger fighters to

[1] *Washington Post*, August 7, 1976.
[2] See next chapter.
[3] *New York Times*, August 30, 1976.

Iran, a half-share in Iran Aircraft Industries, and their share in the telecommunications consortium: and there were the prospects of F18s to come. Lockheed had not only sold sixty-four Hercules transports to the Shah and six Orion reconnaissance planes; they had also won a contract for a costly inventory system, called Peacelog, to keep track of all his military supplies, which had become a minor industry in itself.

Iranian contracts had spun a whole web of new relationships, some of them very discreet. At the Hilton Hotel at Anaheim, near Disneyland, I observed a bus delivering a whole load of young Iranians, who then disappeared into a private lunch-room serving special Iranian food: they occupied, it turned out, a whole wing of the hotel, piped with Iranian music, where they were carefully segregated from other Iranians, while their teachers were sworn to secrecy about their activities. I learnt that they were working on a top-secret intelligence project called Ibex (named after the mountain goat), run by the Rockwell Corporation at Anaheim, at an estimated cost of over $500 million. The project had already aroused some concern in Washington, for Rockwell had recruited former officers of the National Security Agency to train the Iranians. Ibex was described as a sophisticated electronic intelligence system to be placed along Iran's frontiers as a protection against impending aggressors: but there were suspicions among some Iranians that it also involved an extensive bugging system, which could be used to pick up conversation of Iranians inside the country—which might help to explain the elaborate secrecy.

Whatever the full scope of the Ibex, its execution soon began to run into trouble. Rockwell, in their anxiety to get the contract, had resorted, like Grumman, Northrop and the others, to secret agents; and they had promised payments to—among others—a secret agent called Abolfath Mahvi with a postal address in Bermuda, whose appointment enraged General Toufanian. But there were far worse problems. At the Anaheim hotel, the young trainees began having serious psychological disorders as they reached the climax of their course; eventually a psychiatric specialist from the State Department was secretly sent over to advise. In Iran, as the equipment began to be installed, there were doubts as to whether it could be made to work at all. The ambassador, Richard Helms, tried to wash his hands of the project, and the CIA, who had been much involved in its preparation, found themselves much more heavily committed.

The Shah suspected that he had been sold a dud system, and bitterly complained about the chicanery of Pentagon officials. The American Rockwell executives, with their aura of secrecy, were increasingly unpopular and exposed. In August 1976 three of them were driving together in Teheran. A red Volkswagen pulled in front of them. A minibus rammed them behind. A gang of terrorists appeared, armed with Polish machine-guns, and shot the three Americans dead.[1]

The Ibex murders caused horror among other American employees in Iran, some of whom hastily left the country. The whole development exemplified many of the problems of the new commitment to Iran, and the real consequences of the Nixon doctrine. The Pentagon and the CIA had hoped that they could achieve their defence objectives while leaving the Shah to pay for them, and to supply most of the personnel. But the Shah's eagerness to buy, and the company's eagerness to sell, had gone too far. The Iranians were too inexperienced, the real usefulness of the equipment had never been worked out, and the mistakes called for an increasing commitment of Americans, whose presence was now all too visible. The idea of the Nixon doctrine, of arms without troops, was turning itself round. The weapons were making their own demands in terms of 'white collar mercenaries', and were creating their own kind of neo-colonialism, while the Shah was determined to assert his own authority. It was an explosive combination.

---

[1] See Bob Woodward in the *Washington Post*, January 2, 1977.

15

The Deal of the Century

The real stakes are whether Europe will have an aircraft industry or
whether it will be a captive market for America.

General Hugues de l'Estoile, 1973[1]

FROM California Tom Jones of Northrop, while he was exploiting markets in the Middle East, was constantly keeping his eye
on Europe, which was still the front line for the most advanced
weapons outside America. And by the late 'sixties the prospect of
another huge European prize was coming up again. The ageing
Starfighters, untested in combat, were soon due to be replaced
by a new generation of lightweight fighters in the smaller nations
of Europe, whose lead might be followed by others. The aerospace companies were limbering up for another Battle for Europe
which would be, as the Belgians first called it, *le marché du siècle*,
the deal of the century.

The same issues arose as a decade earlier: the nature of the
Atlantic alliance, the need for a common European technology,
the problem of standardisation. But in the intervening years the
stakes had become higher, and the role of the governments more
active: the pressures and lobbying came as much from diplomatic
and defence officials as from the companies. Both Paris and
Washington had taken to heart the lessons of the Starfighter
battle: the choice would affect not only the future of the aerospace

[1] *Le Monde*, May 5, 1973. See also chapter 17.

industry, but the political character and development of Europe. The battle was too important to be left to the aerospace tycoons.

Tom Jones had for a long time been looking to Europe as a market for his new lightweight fighter, the Cobra or F17, which Northrop had first begun designing in 1966 (when it was known as the P530). As the prospect of the NATO fighter approached, Jones brought into play his secret network, to prepare for the contest. His agent in Washington, Frank De Francis, with his special links with West Germany, had spent much time trying to undermine the Anglo-German multi-combat plane, the MRCA, later called the Tornado: 'I attacked the MRCA with every fibre of my being, knowing that except for two nations, nobody would support it.'[1] Tom Jones had also tried to use the Shah, as we have seen in the last chapter, to impress the advantages of the Cobra on Dr Kiesinger, then Chancellor of West Germany. He also brought Prince Bernhard into play, after his vigorous support of the Northrop Tiger, and early in 1971 there is a glimpse of Bernhard's efforts in Germany: he talked in Bonn to Helmut Schmidt, then minister of defence, about the merits of the Cobra, while Tom Jones himself visited Schmidt's secretary of state, Dr Mommsen. Schmidt wrote to the Dutch defence minister, Willem den Toom, about the Cobra, but later insisted that he had no intention to buy it.[2]

Tom Jones could also rely on his secret representative in Paris, the redoubtable General Paul Stehlin. The retired general, as we saw earlier, had been receiving his payments of $5,000 a year since 1964, later going up to $6,000 a year,[3] but he scarcely needed this modest fee to commit him to the Atlantic alliance, for he was passionately pro-American and opposed to French Gaullist policies, and he pursued this *idée fixe* to the detriment of his own career. He had been the open representative of Hughes Aircraft, another Los Angeles company, until 1968; in that year he became a deputy in the French parliament, where he was later elected vice-president. At the end of 1972 he published an outspoken book called *La Force d'Illusion*, describing the dangerous decline of NATO, the mounting communist threat, and the absurdity of France's attempts at independence.

But in the meantime, in return for his fee, Stehlin was privately

[1] Multinational Hearings, part 12, p. 591.

[2] *The Times*, London, September 3, 1976 and *Newsweek*, September 13, 1976.

[3] Multinational Hearings, part 12, p. 671. See also Chapter 7.

advising Tom Jones with regular letters. In January 1973 he sent
one of his 'highly perceptive analyses' (as Jones called them) to
Los Angeles, mentioning in passing that he had just moved into
a new apartment in the rue de Cirque, 'very close to the Elysée
palace' (though he was hardly very close politically to President
Pompidou). Stehlin, writing just before the parliamentary
elections, accurately assessed the predicament of the European
aircraft industry:

> Due to the high cost of aircraft produced in small quantities, the air forces
> concerned—British, German, French—complain about their rapid decline in
> strength. In France, for example, Dassault has been in a position, to a certain
> point, to build larger series as long as the company has possibilities of export.
> This seems now, anyway for the time being, to have come to an end.
> Dassault is threatening to close part of his plants if the government does not
> increase its orders.

Stehlin urged Jones to engage in a press campaign which would
point out that the Northrop Cobra could provide a cheap
tactical plane for all NATO countries, at far less cost than the
various national projects.[1]

It was true, as Stehlin reported, that the European aircraft
industry was very fragmented. But there were nevertheless two
serious European contenders for the deal of the century. Britain
was right out of the running, for neither of her two companies,
BAC and Hawker Siddeley, had a suitable lightweight fighter to
offer. Why or how the British government had failed to finance
one remains something of a puzzle. Britain was collaborating with
the French to produce the Jaguar light support plane, but this
had not inhibited Dassault from going ahead with their own
advanced plane, the Mirage F1, which they promoted to the
exclusion of almost everything else. And the Anglo-German
project, the MRCA or Tornado, was too heavy and long-range
to be a candidate for the NATO fighter. In the aerospace industry
there is some suspicion that the British promised the Americans
to stand off from the contest; but whatever benefit Britain got in
return is obscure.

The Swedes, on the other hand, with a population a seventh of
Britain's and an aircraft industry one-twentieth in size, were
offering a quite promising candidate. The Swedish Saab company,
making cars and aircraft and run by a very cosmopolitan techno-
crat Curt Mileikowsky, was more compact and well-integrated

[1] Northrop Papers: Stehlin to Tom Jones, January 23, 1973.

than its British counterparts; and the Swedish air force was much more decisive about its needs. Three days after the British government had cancelled its TSR2 fighter-bomber in 1965, the Swedish government presented a bill to parliament for developing the new Saab plane, called the Viggen or Thunderbolt, to be delivered by 1971.[1] It was, it later turned out, probably Sweden's last throw for survival as an independent aircraft producer: for the cost of making planes for such a small market was becoming prohibitive. But by 1969 six prototype Viggens were flying, and the plane was sufficiently successful to be a candidate for other European countries: 'I reckoned we had only an eight percent chance,' Mileikowsky told me, 'but it was a challenge worth taking.'

The Swedes, being neutral, may have underestimated the political element in the choice. They saw their plane being welcomed by their neighbours, Norway and Denmark, as a means to Scandinavian industrial co-operation; and they promised very generous offset or 'backscratching' agreements, by which they would buy other goods in return for the planes. But they did not fully appreciate their neighbours' NATO loyalties, and the fear of being left out of America's protection.

From France, Dassault was determined once again to challenge the Americans, and to devise a plane to appeal to all NATO countries—even though France's own membership of NATO was half-hearted. Dassault had already developed, as a private venture, their new lightweight Mirage F1, which first flew in 1969; it was far more manoeuvrable than the Mirage III, with a longer range. The French government salesmen, in the Délégation Ministérielle pour l'Armament, asked Dassault to develop, as a candidate for NATO, a multi-mission version of the plane to be called the F1E ('E' for Europe). The French realised that the choice would be highly political, and they began to lobby vigorously among the four nations who would be their customers, putting their greatest hopes in their near neighbours Belgium and Holland. The Dassault representative in Holland, Jan Botterman, was very active among the Dutch members of parliament, including one Socialist, Piet Dankert, who later complained (with another member) that he had been offered a large bribe. In the subsequent trial, the prosecutor concluded that although Botterman had gone too far, Dankert had 'allowed an atmosphere to be created in which, in terms of corruption, anything was possible';

Ingemar Dörfer: *System 37 Viggen.* Oslo, Universitetsforlaget, 1973, pp. 77, 143.

and Botterman was acquitted.[1] But Dassault's pressures were certainly persistent, both in Holland and Belgium.

Northrop, Dassault and Saab were at first the only contenders, and in the capitals of Europe the pressure and lobbying were building up to a climax. The four small nations of the 'northern tier' of NATO—Holland, Belgium, Norway and Denmark— all agreed to choose the same plane, advised by a committee of experts. The French presented the choice as a battle for the very identity of Europe; the Mirage, though conceived as essentially French, was now portrayed as a European enterprise. The French prime minister Jacques Chirac, visiting Denmark in August 1974, proclaimed that the decision would be 'a test of the political will for a united Europe'; the choice of an American plane would be a defeat for European technology. Newspaper articles studiously reminded the public of the Starfighter disasters.

Holland was regarded as being Northrop territory, partly because of its special NATO loyalties, partly because of Northrop's holding in the Fokker company (though Prince Bernhard's very special relationship was not then public). When the deputy Piet Dankert came out with his allegations about Dassault's bribes in October 1974, the Dutch press let loose attacks on Dassault's unprincipled methods, and Marcel Dassault complained about the 'campaign of calumnies' and 'low manoeuvres'. In fact there was a strong faction inside the Dutch cabinet who would have preferred not to buy American, including the voluble minister of defence Henk Vredeling; but the Dassault pressure had become counter-productive. 'You French fools!' one minister protested later to a French diplomat. 'We wanted to choose you, but you went too far!'

Belgium was Dassault's great hope, for the French-speaking population were loyal to France and Belgium had already bought seventy-two earlier Mirages for their air force. The minister of defence, Paul Vanden Boeynants, was an admirer of Dassault's planes, and had previously been the administrator of the Belgian Philips company, which had been involved in making the Mirages under licence in Belgium. Brussels was full of rumours that Belgian deputies were being bribed by one side or the other. Northrop, too, were stepping up their pressure as the deadline came closer, and from Paris General Stehlin was now stirred to a rash intervention. In September 1974 he wrote a letter to the

[1] *Le Monde*, February 14, 1976.

new president, Giscard d'Estaing, insisting that the European air forces and aircraft industries would gain much more from co-operation with America. 'The choice of a French plane,' he said, 'will be a great commercial success for Dassault, but it will once more be at the expense of French public money.'

Stehlin sent copies of his incautious letter to senior officials in the four NATO countries, one of which soon came into the possession of General de Bénouville, Dassault's chief executive, who was also a French deputy: he received it from a senior Belgian officer who, although personally in favour of an American aircraft (he explained), was outraged that a senior French officer should defend a non-French plane.[1] De Bénouville promptly took the letter to the prime minister Jacques Chirac, and protested that Stehlin was, 'as the Americans say, talking through his hat'. A bitter debate raged round the two general-deputies, both (as later transpired) employed by aircraft companies, about patriotism and honour. *Le Monde* commented wryly that politicians were now talking about 'military honour' as if France was at war with America: but what had the arms business, either in its aims or its methods, got to do with honour? The real problem, *Le Monde* pointed out, was the confusion of politics and business, on both sides; and it called for Stehlin's resignation—which 'should be followed by some others from the French parliament'.[2]

Marcel Dassault himself entered the fray, writing to the *Figaro* to remind readers that Stehlin had previously represented Hughes Aircraft, and suggesting that Stehlin's intervention was simply a demonstration of gratitude to his former employers. Perhaps, he speculated, the Cobra fighter would eventually be equipped with Hughes weapons? He suggested that there should be a contest between the three main contenders for the NATO plane—the Mirage, the Cobra and the Viggen. Many deputies, in the meantime, called for Stehlin to be dismissed as vice-president of the Assembly, and soon afterwards he did resign, while remaining a deputy, unrepentant in his opposition to Dassault.

But during all this angry lobbying the real pressure was building up from the Pentagon and the United States air force. The secretary of defence, Jim Schlesinger, was determined to have the same plane on both sides of the Atlantic—unlike the Star-

[1] *Le Monde*, November 8, 1974.
[2] Ibid.

fighter, which had never been adopted by the US air force. The Pentagon was resolved to exert all its leverage to persuade the Europeans to buy American, while Congress was also becoming more impatient of the Europeans' unwillingness to pay for their own defence. The air force had already decided that they needed a lightweight fighter, much cheaper and lighter than the navy's Tomcat. Lockheed this time were soon out of the battle, for Kelly Johnson, the master-designer who had produced the U2 and the Starfighter, could not agree to the air force's specifications: and by April 1972 the five candidates among the companies were narrowed down to two—Northrop and General Dynamics. The air force asked Northrop to produce a prototype of the F17 or Cobra: and they asked General Dynamics to produce the F16. If the Europeans had made their choice before the US air force, Northrop would probably have won; but now they were up against Pentagon politics.

General Dynamics had a long history in the arms business, going back to the Electric Boat submarines which had been in partnership with Vickers before the First World War.[1] Electric Boat had merged with other companies in the 'fifties, including Convair aircraft, to make up an ambitious new company called General Dynamics, which was one of the first conglomerates, producing not only arms, including missiles, aircraft and nuclear submarines, but building materials, telecommunications and coal. Their last big aircraft project had been the F111, the swing-wing plane which McNamara had promoted to supply both the navy and air force, and also Britain. But the plane had big cost overruns, the navy did not accept it, and it crashed repeatedly in Vietnam: by 1973 the air force stopped ordering it, in favour of Rockwell's new B1 bomber. General Dynamics thus urgently needed a new contract for their huge aircraft plant at Fort Worth in Texas, and began competing hotly with Northrop. The F16, developing some of the skills of the F111, was a good match for the Cobra, and it suited the air force, complementing their previous plane, the F15 or Eagle. Through 1974 the F16 and the Cobra showed their paces against each other. The F16 flew up to 60,000 feet at Mach 2, dropped ten 2,000 pound bombs, fired 13,000 rounds of 20mm ammunition, flew up to three hours without refuelling; and finally won the air force contract in

[1] See chapter 3.

January 1975, with the eventual prospect of orders for 650 planes.[1]

For General Dynamics it meant not only profits and jobs in Texas but a big chance of getting the NATO contract, too. But their executives, unlike Northrop's, were not very aware of the world outside: from their offices in Texas or Missouri they had few contacts with Europe, and they were not very sure where Holland and Denmark were to be found. In Washington, however, Jim Schlesinger, determined on standardisation, urged them into battle, promising the full weight of the Pentagon behind them. General Dynamics' situation was almost the opposite of Lockheed's fifteen years earlier: they were reluctantly dragged into the fray, and content to 'let Uncle Sam do the lobbying'.[2]

For the first five months of 1975 the contest for the NATO plane was at fever pitch. Northrop were soon rejected by the Europeans, too, who agreed that if an American plane were chosen it must be standardised. (Northrop, in fact, would soon have another chance, for their Cobra was later merged with a McDonnell Douglas project, to produce a new plane, the F18, for the US navy.) But the Swedes still had not given up, offering ever more tempting offset agreements; and Dassault and the French government renewed their offensive against the new American invader. They put forward suggestions for the future integration of the whole European aircraft industry, including the French nationalised company, Aérospatiale; and they assured the other countries that France would be thoroughly integrated with NATO.[3]

By February General Dynamics, urged on by Schlesinger, had put together a marketing team from Texas to tour the European capitals. Dassault brought down the price of the Mirage and offered more tempting 'back-scratching' to the other countries. General Dynamics, like Lockheed before, arranged for all the planes to be built in Europe, but with more attractive inducements to each of the four countries, to prove that it would really be a European plane. And they promised the Europeans a share in the profits and production of any planes sold to the Third World— which they reckoned, with great exaggeration, would amount to two thousand planes.

The Pentagon was now rooting remorselessly for the General Dynamics plane through the European capitals, reminding the

[1] *Jane's All the World's Aircraft*, London, 1975-6, pp. 341-2.

[2] *Business Week*, May 3, 1976.

[3] *Aviation Week*, March 24, 1975.

nervous Norwegians or Dutchmen that NATO must be standardised: if they did not buy American, the whole future of America's
defence of Europe would be in doubt. The pressures that were
always implied in the background of the Starfighter contest were
now very overt. The Belgians still wavered. The Pentagon now
rolled on President Ford, who visited Brussels for a NATO meeting
and made a point of discussing the deal with the Belgian prime
minister, Leo Tindemans. ('Could you imagine us using our
president as a salesman?' a Dassault executive asked me.) The
French counter-wooed the Belgians by offering to buy Belgian
rifles if they bought the Mirage.

The four NATO governments still could not agree, and in April
there was a new crisis when the Dutch social democratic party
congress passed a resolution saying that all three planes were too
expensive and provocative. They advocated a shorter-range plane,
like the Northrop Tiger, which would not encourage an arms
race with Eastern Europe; but the Dutch minister of defence,
Henk Vredeling, himself a social democrat, argued against the
resolution.[1] The four nations met again in May, and again
delayed; it looked as if they might, after all, choose separate
planes.

At last, at the end of May 1975, three governments, without
Belgium, agreed to order the General Dynamics plane; the
Dutch compromised by cutting down their order, hoping that a
European lightweight fighter might later emerge. The Belgians
were still split: many cabinet ministers favoured the Americans,
but Vanden Boeynants still wanted the Mirage; and the coalition
between French-speakers and Flemish seemed threatened. Then
Schlesinger invited Vanden Boeynants to Washington: he pointed
out that the four countries would probably get back their whole
initial investment in the American plane by producing more
planes for the Third World (an expectation which proved quite
false);[2] and he offered to buy $30 million worth of Belgian
machine-guns—which are made in French-speaking Belgium.
The machine-guns clinched the deal. Finally on June 6—just at
the time of the Paris air show—the triumphant outcome was
announced. All four NATO countries would now buy the
American plane.

---

[1] *Aviation Week*, April 7, 1975.
[2] *Newsweek*, June 16, 1975 and *International Herald Tribune*, August 7, 1976.

Sixteen months later, the first production model of the F16 taxied out of the plant in Fort Worth, Texas, and took off into the sky, in front of the officials of five countries. It was a historic moment in the aircraft industry. The plane would replace Starfighters, Tigers and Phantoms with a single standardised fighter. The nations of NATO, said *Aviation Week*, had shown that they do have the spirit and will to defend themselves against Eastern aggressors.[1] The production of the plane in several nations, with all its complexities (said the defence secretary, Donald Rumsfeld) heralded a new stage in international collaboration. Undoubtedly there had been major concessions to the Europeans; there would be production lines in Belgium and Holland and components from all over Europe. But the prospects of an independent European industry were again dashed; and the Europeans were again paying for American technology, contributing as much as half-a-million dollars to the development costs of each plane.[2] The keys to the future of aerospace lay not in Paris or Stockholm, but in Texas, California and Washington.

There was little doubt as to how the sale had been clinched. The technical arguments were important, but not decisive; the basic political choice was unavoidable. The fact that the American air force had chosen the F16 gave a far greater reassurance to the Europeans than Dassault could offer. The Pentagon had been relentless in making the connection between the commercial and diplomatic choices; one American aerospace executive even told me, 'I felt ashamed to be American.' But that pressure only underlined the Europeans' basic weakness: they were not prepared to build up their own independent defence force, and therefore could not generate their own aerospace industry. European unification had not progressed very far since the Starfighter fifteen years earlier.

Behind all the lobbying, leaking and suspicions of bribery, Uncle Sam was always the most powerful manipulator. But the smell of corruption still lingered: much later Marcel Dassault explained that his company had never indulged in bribery, which was probably why they did not win the deal of the century.[3] And on the very day the American victory had first been announced, on June 6, 1975, a sensational revelation emerged from Washing-

[1] *Aviation Week*, October 25, 1976.
[2] *Forbes Magazine*, December 15, 1976.
[3] Commenting on *l'Affaire Dassault* on French television, September 8, 1976.

ton. Senator Church's committee, who had been investigating Northrop and Lockheed, disclosed that General Stehlin had for the last eleven years been secretly paid by Northrop, and published his letter to Tom Jones of two years earlier advocating the press campaign in favour of Northrop's Cobra.

When the news reached Paris, the Associated Press rang up Stehlin at his home to ask for his reaction. Stehlin then went to his office near the Opéra, and soon came out again. He stepped off the pavement in front of a bus, pulled back, and then stepped forward again. He was run over, taken to hospital, and died ten days later.[1] He was the first casualty of the wave of arms scandals that were now suddenly spreading out from Washington, across the world.

---

[1] The French bus system RATP was later held only to be half responsible for this death, on the grounds that the reason why he suddenly stopped in front of the bus could not be determined. His 'aberrant behaviour' allowed his widow only $45,000 in damages. See *Aviation Week*, December 6, 1976.

16

The Scandals

Capitalism is the greatest thing going, but unchecked it is its own undoing.

Stanley Sporkin (Securities and Exchange Commission) 1976[1]

EVER since the Watergate disclosures, the two American arms companies Northrop and Lockheed had been sitting on a time-bomb, and the long fuse was eventually to cause explosions with wider global repercussions than Watergate itself. In uncovering business corruption after Watergate, the Washington investigators could not confine themselves to their own country even if they had wanted to: so much of the evidence led to foreign nations, and the domestic revelations thus rapidly extended to international scandals. There was some resemblance to the arms scandals of the mid-'thirties, when Senator Nye's crusade against the Merchants of Death likewise reverberated abroad. But the American reaction this time was unlikely to turn to isolationism, for in the intervening four decades American interests had become more closely knit with other nations, as the Lockheed story itself would reveal. The affairs of a single American corporation were to cause shudders in a dozen capitals at opposite ends of the world.

The first clues to the scandal came not from Lockheed but from Northrop, which had aroused the interest of the Watergate committee under Senator Sam Ervin, when it turned from the

---

[1] *New York Times Magazine*, September 26, 1976.

Watergate burglars to the campaign contributors. Herbert Kalmbach, Nixon's chief fund-raiser, told the committee how he had called on Tom Jones in his office in Los Angeles in August 1972, and how Jones had taken from his desk a package containing $75,000 in hundred-dollar bills, ostensibly for Nixon's campaign fund, but actually for the secret fund for the defence of the Watergate burglars.[1] This revelation led naturally to the question: how had Jones obtained this hoard of cash? The following year—in May 1974—the Watergate Special Prosecutor charged both Northrop and Tom Jones with making unlawful contributions amounting to $150,000, for which they were fined the modest sum of $5,000 each.

But in the meantime the Watergate revelations had attracted the intense interest of Stanley Sporkin, head of the enforcement division of the Securities and Exchange Commission. Listening to the evidence on secret cash payments to Nixon's fund, Sporkin realised that a whole new field of illegal company behaviour was being uncovered: 'When you see such bold and brazen conduct,' he said later, 'you can't ignore it.'[2] Sporkin was a frenetic investigator, the son of a judge, a Yale law school graduate; and he was determined to clean up the corporate slush funds. His own staff was too small to cover the huge territory, so he warned companies that, unless they investigated themselves, they would be sued and investigated by outside auditors. Thus a succession of big corporations, including Exxon and Gulf, felt compelled to look into their accounts, and came up with sensational 'voluntary disclosures' about improper payments. But the case of Northrop was more deeply significant.

After the first disclosures, the Northrop directors commissioned the Los Angeles auditors, Ernst and Ernst, with the help of Price Waterhouse, to report on 'the extent of the misconduct'. This report, delivered in November 1974, revealed in copious detail the arrangements for secret cash from William Savy in Paris and the payments made to agents across the world (see chapters 7 and 11). The Northrop directors (strengthened by three new members appointed as a result of shareholders' lawsuits) then prepared their own special report, published in July 1975. It provided, in restrained language, a devastating indictment of the personal rule

[1] Select Committee on Presidential Campaign Activities of 1972 (Ervin Committee) Hearings, Book 5, p. 2125.

[2] *New York Times Magazine*, September 26, 1976.

of Tom Jones. Surveying his secret arrangements with De Francis, Savy, Khashoggi and others, the directors repeatedly accused their chairman of 'poor business judgment', 'disregard for sound corporate procedure', or 'the appearance of impropriety'. They chose to ignore the corrupt implications of the secret funds, like the EDC, and they did not enquire into the relationship with Bernhard. But they concluded that Tom Jones 'must bear a heavy share of the responsibility for the irregularities and improprieties noted in this report', and they were not convinced that he had communicated openly with the auditors. They recommended therefore that while continuing for the time being as chief executive officer, he should be succeeded by a new chairman.

The new chairman, Richard Millar, a director of Northrop for the past thirty years, was not inclined to reform the company, and his fellow directors preferred to forget their complaints about Jones. Even some of the new directors were impressed by his high-level contacts abroad—particularly with the Shah of Iran, Northrop's biggest single customer. By February 1976 Tom Jones could announce the company's best performance in its history, with net income up by thirty-seven percent to $25 million, and sales up to nearly a billion dollars. Tigers were roaring out at the rate of eighteen a month, and the new navy fighter, the F18, now being jointly developed with McDonnell Douglas, was expected to continue in production until the 1980s. The directors were in no mood to maintain their misgivings, and the man who had misled and deceived his colleagues was reinstated as chairman.

The Securities and Exchange Commission (SEC) had access, in the meantime, to the report of Northrop's auditors, Ernst and Ernst, but they did not publish the section which gave details of the overseas payments, to avoid embarrassing the state department. The international scandal thus remained buried. Other Washington investigators however were now also following the trail of corruption. The Senate Subcommittee on Multinational Corporations, under the chairmanship of Senator Frank Church, had already become something of a bogy to big business: it had been set up in 1972, after the first disclosures about ITT's interventions in Chile, to investigate how far big companies were influencing or forming foreign policy. Church and his chief counsel, Jerome Levinson, were prepared to confront the strongholds of big business, and they had acquired a staff adept at extracting corporate documents and secrets, armed with powers of subpoena.

It was the conviction of Church and Levinson that foreign policy was inseparable from economic policy and the commercial decisions of corporations. They had already produced a unique body of evidence about the foreign policies of companies including ITT and the oil companies, and their curiosity was naturally aroused by Northrop with its apparently intimate relations with foreign governments. They subpoenaed the secret section of the auditors' report and went through the Northrop files in California to extract secret documents. The senators on the subcommittee voted for maximum disclosure, and then instituted public hearings in June 1975.

Senator Church opened with a righteous tirade: 'The documents lay out in excruciating detail a sordid tale of bribery . . . a cast of characters out of a novel of international intrigue . . .' The competition in the arms race, he warned, was out of control. The Church committee revealed the full Northrop documents, giving details and names of the secret agents in Europe and the Middle East: among them General Paul Stehlin, who on the same day walked in front of the bus in Paris.

Tom Jones testified the next day, polished and articulate. He regretted and apologised for his mistakes and promised they would not be repeated, but he explained how his Tigers had been an effective instrument of US foreign policy over the past twenty years, and had brought credit to American industry. He also seized an opportunity to shift the blame: he coolly explained to the senators that Northrop, in setting up their secret agents, had only followed the example of Lockheed. There was some hint of this in the documents, but Jones (as we have seen) did not need Lockheed to teach him about corruption; he carefully exaggerated the precedent, knowing that Lockheed was not only a much bigger fish, but a far more unpopular one. Tom Jones later rang up Dan Haughton to explain that he never intended to incriminate him: but in the meantime he had neatly passed on the blame. Lockheed was already the favourite scapegoat of Congress and the press, after the bail-out and the Galaxy scandal, and other aerospace companies were not sorry to see them pilloried. Northrop was much less notorious (it was often mis-spelt Northrup) and had a more gallant image, as a David battling with Goliath.

Both the Church committee and the SEC were already accumulating evidence about Lockheed. At first Lockheed stubbornly denied any wrongdoing, but in August 1975 a bare but sensational press release emerged from Burbank, admitting that Lockheed had spent at least $22 million since 1970 on payments which they believed went to officials and political organisations in foreign countries. Two months later, in September 1975, Church opened the first Lockheed hearings. The Church committee released a new pile of documents which revealed Lockheed kickbacks and bribes ranging from Indonesia and Iran to Saudi Arabia and the Philippines: it was a pattern, said Church, which made crookedness in politics look like a Sunday school. Dan Haughton, now a man of sixty-four and close to retirement, appeared to testify. He pleaded that Lockheed had not contributed money to American political campaigns (Kotchian had been pressed to contribute after Tom Jones' generosity, but had not made a corporate contribution); and he stressed that 15,000 Lockheed jobs depended on exports. Lockheed, he admitted, had paid $106 million in commissions to Khashoggi alone, but these practices were widespread; he submitted an article from the London *Sunday Telegraph*, describing the French 'Ministry of Bribes'.[1]

Haughton was under fire from conservatives as well as radicals. Senator Percy of Illinois, the ranking Republican on the committee, was a former president of Bell and Howell, married to a Rockefeller and normally loyal to big corporations; but some of his Chicago banker friends who had underpinned Lockheed now believed that Haughton should go, to enable the company to be restructured. Percy was indignant that Lockheed, having been saved from bankruptcy by the grace of Congress, should be subverting its own government's objectives by its bribery and pay-offs.

But this onslaught on Haughton proved only the prelude. Five months later the Church committee had assembled much more incriminating documents, and in February 1976 they convened further hearings. In the committee-room foreign journalists were waiting expectantly. A sheaf of documents was dumped on the press table, but they were cryptic and allusive, involving political situations in Japan, Holland, Germany or Italy, with handwritten letters, bank statements, and coded receipts. One of them was a bare page from Tokyo with the words: 'I have received one hundred peanuts.' Slowly in the evidence that followed the allusions and implications became clear.

[1] *Sunday Telegraph*, London, September 7, 1975.

By the end of the week the committee-room was besieged by foreign journalists, led by scores of Japanese, who flew over in task-forces from Tokyo, occupying the whole committee-room until they were removed by the police and the tables carefully allocated. Japanese, Dutch and Italian journalists pursued the Senate staff and the Lockheed executives, waiting at their houses and jamming their telephones.

It was not surprising, for the future of prime ministers and governments now rested on disclosures from Washington. The state department was already acutely embarrassed. Lockheed had been confident that their government would protect their agents and highly-placed friends, and they had retained the services of William Rogers, the former secretary of state, now back in law practice. Rogers had written to Kissinger to ask him to stop the names of Lockheed agents from being published. Kissinger duly wrote to the attorney-general, Edward H. Levi, protesting that the Lockheed documents contained 'uncorroborated, sensational and potentially damaging information' which would damage foreign relations.[1] But the appeal was rejected, and the Church committee then voted to reveal the full facts. They foresaw upheavals abroad, but not quite the extent of them.

THE LOCKHEED ELECTIONS

It was the evidence about Holland that was most immediately shocking, involving a country not normally associated with corruption (at least outside aerospace circles). The first clues to Dutch bribes had come through a persistent character, the former Lockheed executive in Germany, Ernest Hauser, the man who had been employed by Lockheed in the early 'sixties, at the time of the Starfighter deals.[2] Hauser, now living in Arizona, was determined to denigrate his old employers and had given sensational information to the Church committee, and also to the *Wall Street Journal*, alleging among many other things that Lockheed had paid huge sums to Prince Bernhard of the Netherlands. Much of his evidence proved very unreliable, but it provided the critical catalyst.

The Church committee in secret session asked Dan Haughton

---

[1] Letter from Henry Kissinger to the attorney-general, November 28, 1975.
[2] See chapter 6.

whether Lockheed had paid anything to Prince Bernhard. Haughton replied: 'I wish you hadn't asked that question.' The senators were stunned, while Haughton revealed that Lockheed had in fact paid a million dollars to the Prince. The next day in the public hearings Carl Kotchian testified more discreetly that the million dollars had been paid to a 'high Dutch official'; but there were soon leaks that the man was in fact Prince Bernhard.

The Dutch press was ablaze, but incredulous. Three days later the Dutch prime minister appointed a committee of three wise men, headed by A. M. Donner, a judge in the European court of justice. For the next six months they pursued their painful enquiries from Burbank to The Hague: the Prince pleaded loss of memory and Fred Meuser refused to co-operate, protected by the Swiss government. At first the Lockheedians all held together in protecting the Prince, as they protected all their agents. Then, on the last visit of the Dutchmen to Burbank, one Lockheed official finally broke the discretion, protesting that the Prince had extorted the payments, and produced the two incriminating letters from Bernhard, demanding money. Eventually the Donner Report confirmed and extended the charges against Bernhard so that he was forced to resign all his public positions. Lockheed had come close to shattering the Dutch monarchy.

In Italy the reaction to the Lockheed revelations was predictably less shocked and more devious. The rash letter from Lockheed's lawyer Roger Bixby Smith in 1969, which now came to light with other documents, clearly indicated that two Italian ministers of defence had been collecting bribes, together with 'Antelope Cobbler', translated as the Italian premier (see chapter 6): and this appeared to implicate several leading politicians in Rome including the former defence ministers, Luigi Gui and Mario Tanassi. As soon as the news from Washington broke, the Lockheed agent Ovidio Lefebvre, with his associates, disappeared from Italy. A parliamentary commission of twenty was appointed to investigate, but moved very slowly; and Italy was soon in the midst of an election campaign in which the communists made great play with the scandal, and probably gained some votes from it. After the election the new government, under Giulio Andreotti, appointed another slow-motion commission, which seemed to be quietly forgetting the charges; but after the bold response in Holland and Japan it was less easy to ignore Lockheed, and the communist members were in full pursuit. Eventually in

March 1977 the Italian parliament reached a decision unprecedented in thirty years: to indict the two former ministers, Gui
and Tanassi, so that they would stand trial before the Constitutional Court—thus creating a new political crisis. The Washington clean-up was spreading abroad with a vengeance.

In Germany, Lockheed likewise became an issue in a general
election. Here the evidence of corruption was much less definite
than in Italy and Holland, but the suspicions were pervasive. The
chief allegations came from the unpredictable Ernest Hauser
whose testimony and diaries had mentioned payments not only
to Bernhard but to Franz-Josef Strauss, Hauser's former friend,
who as minister of defence in 1959 had first bought the Lockheed
Starfighters. Hauser insisted that twelve million dollars had been
paid to Strauss' party in Bavaria, which in the light of the original
doubts about the deal and Lockheed tactics elsewhere was not
incredible. In Germany the question became explosive in the
midst of an election campaign in which Strauss was hoping to get
back into office, and old Starfighter scandals were quickly raked
up. Strauss issued writs, and accused Hauser of working for the
KGB. Hauser's evidence was questionable, and in Washington
Church refused to publish it, while in Germany the key Starfighter documents had been removed by Strauss when he left the
ministry of defence. The truth never emerged.

But it was in Japan, where the bribes were biggest and where
corruption was widely condoned, that the reaction was most
far-reaching and unexpected. The committee's evidence strongly
indicated that Lockheed had paid $12 million to Japanese officials
for the TriStar deal three years earlier, and that the premier,
Tanaka, was involved. But since then Tanaka had resigned after
other alleged murky financial dealings, and he had been succeeded
in 1974 by Takeo Miki, who had an unusual reputation as 'Mr
Clean': he was the leader of a much smaller faction within the
Liberal party, who thus needed less money for politics, and his
background was prosperous and international. He had been
selected as premier as a compromise caretaker before the next
manoeuvrings, and at the beginning of 1976 there was talk of
Tanaka making a comeback. But now the Lockheed scandal
provided Miki with a platform which, however resented by his
political rivals, soon gave him enthusiastic public support. In the
following months the Japanese press and public found to their
astonishment the black curtain being drawn apart. The inscrut-

able East was suddenly becoming more scrutable than the West.

The Lockheed documents that had been dumped on the table in Washington caused a political earthquake in Tokyo far more devastating than the shudders in Washington. The government announced that the expected purchase of Lockheed Orion patrol planes, worth over a billion dollars, would be reconsidered. The general election planned for the spring was hurriedly postponed. The offices of Lockheed agents, including Kodama and the Marubeni Corporation, were exhaustively searched. Lockheed immediately became the target for every kind of conspiratorial theory about Nixon, Tanaka and Watergate—still further encouraged by the coincidence that the current American ambassador, Jim Hodgson, was a former Lockheed employee appointed by Nixon.

The character of Kodama, who had worked so long in the shadows, was now suddenly exposed to view, but he himself retired to bed, supposedly with a stroke. A young actor, flying a small plane and dressed as a wartime kamikaze pilot, dived his plane into Kodama's villa where the old man lay in bed, shouting over the radio the old kamikaze cry: 'Long live the Emperor!' The actor was instantly killed, but Kodama was carried out of the burning house unhurt. Some of his money was seized, in payment of taxes, and police persistently questioned him at his bedside.

To many observers it seemed that the furore would soon spend itself, for corporation scandals in Japan were frequent and easily buried. But Miki was persistent, with public opinion still behind him; and the Lockheed scandal proved a very special case. The corruption had been exposed to the world through the workings of Washington, causing serious loss of face. It was now Japan's Watergate; the press was unleashed and the Japanese felt themselves challenged to show that their democracy worked. Gradually most of the men whom Kotchian had dealt with—and many others—were indicted: the directors of Marubeni, including the former president Hiyama, officials of All Nippon Airlines and politicians. Taro Fukuda, Kotchian's loyal interpreter, retreated to hospital and died of cirrhosis of the liver. In July 1976 the unimaginable happened, which had never happened to Nixon: the former prime minister Tanaka was arrested and taken to jail, charged with accepting 500 million yen ($1.2 million). He was released three weeks later on record bail of $700,000, pending his trial.

By December 1976 elections could no longer be postponed, and Japan went to the polls under the shadow of the scandal. It was the third of the Lockheed elections. The socialists and communists tried to expose the bribery as a typical capitalist racket; but the electorate were not so extreme. The socialists gained a few seats, but the communists lost some. Tanaka, only five months after his arrest, stood as an independent and romped home in his country constituency. Inflation and the price of rice, not Lockheed, were the chief issues; but Lockheed had had its effects. The liberals had lost their overall majority for the first time in their twenty-five-year reign, losing votes to younger moderates who advocated clean government. Miki himself had lost out, accused of having divided his party, and he was soon afterwards succeeded by a more conservative elder, Takeo Fukuda. But the machinery of justice, in the meantime, was apparently irreversible; in January 1977 Tanaka's trial began and the ex-premier appeared weeping in court to hear the prosecutor's statement and plead his innocence. The trial was quite likely to stretch over several years.

Many different lessons were drawn from Japan's Lockheed scandal, a year after it first broke. To the American ambassador Jim Hodgson, making his farewell speech, it had been beneficial in showing Americans that they should take more note of the customs of the country.[1] To Kotchian and many other Lockheedians, it had only served to encourage the communists. To the younger liberal politicians, it showed that Japan must clean up its whole political system. To Senator Church, it showed that 'we *do* live in an interdependent world. But that is no reason to tread lightly in cleaning up the corrupt practices of multinational corporations. There is every indication that instead of increasing the animosity of other peoples, our investigation, disclosure and enactment of remedial legislation engendered admiration abroad.'[2] Certainly in my own travels, in Japan, Holland or Germany, I was struck by the lack of resentment against Washington. The Lockheed revelations encouraged self-questioning and internal criticism, rather than anti-Americanism: and Lockheed was providing a common problem in the face of which no nation could be complacent.

But while the Lockheed scandals had nearly toppled a monarchy, influenced three elections and caused the arrest and trial of

[1] January 29, 1977.
[2] Speech to Harvard East Asia Conference, October 15, 1976.

a former prime minister, their consequences were much less evident in Washington, in the inscrutable West.

EXIT HAUGHTON

In California, Lockheed was now once again in desperate straits, for not only the Japanese but governments all over the world were wary of dealing with such notorious bribers, who might yet again be exposed. The twenty-four banks who had lent Lockheed $600 million had become more restive ever since Lockheed's first admission in August 1975 that they had paid $22 million to government officials. Some of the bankers, led by Robert Abboud of the First National Bank of Chicago, were demanding the resignation of Dan Haughton. Abboud checked through Senator Percy whether the treasury would now object (as they had earlier objected) to the replacement of Haughton, and was informed that it was not their job to protect management. The bankers reluctantly agreed to another six months' refinancing, but then came the revelations in February 1976 of Lockheed's secret agents, including Bernhard and Kodama. Four banks now insisted on a change of leadership. Dan Haughton called a special board meeting and announced his resignation, but Kotchian still resisted. Some directors said he was an indispensable salesman, others that he was just the company's bagman; eventually Kotchian resigned, bitterly convinced that he was the scapegoat.[1] The board then elected Robert Haack, the director who was closest to the bankers, a former chairman of the New York Stock Exchange, as their interim chairman, to restore the confidence of airlines and bankers.

It was the end of the nine-year wonder of Haughton's regime. For a few months the two men were given generous consultancy agreements, but they were suspended awaiting Lockheed's own full report. Dan Haughton retreated back to Georgia where he suffered in silence, but Kotchian defied his company's discretion and his lawyers' advice, and published his own version of his dealings in Tokyo, unrepentant about his role: 'I did it because I thought it was right', he told me: 'and I still do'.

It was a crisis for Lockheed's identity; for the fierce loyalty to Haughton and Kotchian had kept the company together and secrets

---

[1] For a full account of the bankers' discussions see William M. Carley's article in the *Wall Street Journal*, April 8, 1976.

had strengthened the bonds. Two years earlier one executive had guessed that Prince Bernhard had been in Lockheed's pay: he was worried, but simply asked his boss, 'What do you want me to say?' The company was its own intelligence agency, with its own vows: the lies increased the loyalty. Haughton had held it all together through its setbacks and onslaughts, with his own evangelical confidence, and a toughness that no others possessed. He and Kotchian had driven on their salesmen to their gruelling missions, but there was scarcely a sign in all the Lockheed evidence of any dissidents against their confident command: it was all part of a higher cause, and a continuing cold war. Now Lockheed was just another troubled company, with bankers in charge; and without Haughton the problems still beset the company, insecure and isolated in the Burbank redoubt.

It looked as if those problems might sink it. Congress was warned that Lockheed might not be able to repay its loans in June. The Canadian government cancelled a $750 million order for Orion patrol planes. The TriStar airliners were still not selling well against their competitors. Boeing and McDonnell Douglas made no secret of their belief that there was one big company too many, and waited for Lockheed to be dismembered.

But the Pentagon under Donald Rumsfeld still wanted Lockheed in business and tried to reassure foreign governments. Robert Haack, the new chairman, flew hectically between Washington, Ottawa, London and California, reassuring his customers. By June the twenty-four banks had agreed to convert some of Lockheed's debt into equity; by July Canada had agreed after all to buy the patrol planes; by August British Airways had ordered further TriStars. Once again Lockheed had been pulled back from the brink.

THE CHALETS

At the Farnborough air show in September 1976 the leaders of aerospace assembled for their annual jamboree, celebrated alternately in Paris and Farnborough. They flew over from California, Texas, Seattle or Toulouse, casually oblivious of geography, to occupy their company chalets overlooking the Farnborough airfield where they entertained their friends in the industry. Lockheed was always a big spender, and their style was not seriously cramped by the recent threat of bankruptcy. Outside, their chalet was just a wet tent with its flaps flicking in the wind, with a strict security check. But inside, it was an elaborate pavilion, looking as solid as a boardroom, with a private dining room, a long bar, a row of hot dishes, and attentive English hostesses looking after the Lockheedians and their guests.

Outside the long window the planes were shrieking and roaring but no one had much time to watch them, for this was a Lockheed reunion from all corners of their empire. A cohort had come from Burbank, including Robert Haack and Bill Perreault, the big, slow-speaking chief spokesman who had issued so many stonewalling denials but was now opening up. Another contingent was from Georgia, including the manager of the Marietta plant who had once been a room-mate of Jimmy Carter. Others had come from the firing line, like Bill Conley from the Middle East or Jack Davidson from Tokyo. Old Lockheedians had joined them, including Michael Parker, the former private secretary to Prince Philip, who had once been their man in London and was still enthusiastically loyal to the company.

Within the camaraderie of the chalet there was some sense of relief that the secrets of the company were finally emerging: the Donner Report on Prince Bernhard had just been published, Carl Kotchian had just given interviews in Tokyo, and both stories showed that there had, after all, been extortion as well as bribery. The Lockheedians seemed quite glad to talk about the days of Haughton's dictatorship, how Dan had exploited them, while at the same time dropping hints about the practices of Boeing or Northrop. The news had come through that the British would buy more TriStars and the bank loan be renewed; and there were a number of big new orders for the Middle East. But there was some nostalgia for the old days, when the business was a crusade, full of dangers and secrecy. As one Lockheed executive had remarked to a Senate investigator: 'This was the most exciting job in the world before you guys came along.'

A hundred yards away, the Northrop chalet was smaller and more austere, the food was less lavish and the visitors scruffier. Tom Jones stood out from the crowd, tall and handsome like a battered film star, joking with his colleagues whom he had so misled, watching the Tiger and the Cobra climbing and swooping down. He followed them like a boy—'Wow, there she goes,' 'Look at her!'—while his executives tried to attract his attention. The Northrop scandal, I was assured, was now closed: the company had reformed itself, and everyone in the aerospace industry, after all, knew the facts of life.

Liberals often like to depict the arms makers as inhabiting a separate underworld, like the caves of the Nibelungen dedicated to destruction and greed, which if only it were abolished would leave the body politic safer and healthier. To blame the evils of society on the weapons or the people who make them is comforting, and not without some justification. Certainly many of these genial men seemed to have made a kind of Faustian pact with themselves and their company, not to question the moral issues. They like to cultivate an adolescent enthusiasm, more frenetically as their years advance, which helps to suppress any doubts. If Dan Haughton and his executives had questioned themselves more, many abuses might have been avoided. But to blame it all on them evades the real issue. For they are themselves the consequences of political decisions and choices which have been made by the voters; Lockheed and Northrop are both, in the end, the responsibility of Congress. Whatever the excesses of Haughton and Jones, they are the fruits of a system which might have been designed to produce just such men.

TO BRIBE OR NOT TO BRIBE

The Lockheed and Northrop bribes were only the most flagrant among countless cases that emerged in the wake of Stanley Sporkin's investigations from the SEC: before long a tenth of America's five hundred biggest corporations, including Boeing and McDonnell Douglas, had admitted questionable payments totalling $100 million over five years.[1] In the moral indignation that followed there was much humbug, for up till this surge of 'post-Watergate morality' bribery had been widely and tacitly condoned: American embassies abroad (as Lockheed found in Indonesia) had willingly offered advice about bribes, and the Pentagon had encouraged arms salesmen to adopt 'the custom of the country'.

The frontiers of bribery were always difficult to define: what about the congressman who accepts free hospitality, or the journalist who accepts caviar or free trips abroad? How could such social corruption ever be outlawed in a free society? One vocal apologist for the companies was Professor Peter Nehemkis, a

[1] See Lloyd N. Cutler in *Foreign Policy* magazine, Fall, 1976, p. 162.

lecturer in business law in Los Angeles, who had previously represented multinational corporations in Washington. The incidence
of large bribes in the aerospace industries (he explained to me) was
an inevitable part of the pressure of competition. 'This is an
industry which flourishes in corruption; I have no problems with
payments, only with their concealment.'

In Europe the reaction was more sceptical than in America.
The British were amused rather than shocked, and relieved that
the Lockheed scandals had not touched their own politicians. The
chief secretary of the treasury, Joel Barnett, asked about bribes by
British oil companies, insisted that it was the foreigners' fault,
and that the main responsibility must rest with the host countries.
Soon afterwards it emerged that the British tax authorities (like
the Germans) permitted business bribes to be regarded as tax-
deductible expenses.

French and Italians enjoyed attacking the American bribers,
while not exposing their own: they saw the chance of doing more
business abroad by preserving discretion, compared to the
Americans. A Dassault official expressed amazement to me at the
Americans' insistence on writing things down, and then revealing
them: 'It must be one of those strange emanations from the
puritanism of the Mayflower.' The fact that Americans had first
raised the stakes of the bribes, then passionately denounced them,
made their posture the more dubious to Europeans: they seemed
like those characters in Ibsen's plays who insist on uncovering
the truth and wrecking everyone's lives, only to discover that the
truth is much more complicated. 'If the Americans can now export
more of their investigative enthusiasm and less of their business
morals,' commented the London *Times*, 'so much the better.'

It would certainly be hard to ban bribery in those countries
where it is a way of life, as in Saudi Arabia, where the princes
and Khashoggi seemed closer to seventeenth-century Europe than
to contemporary Washington. How could Western companies
dictate to the Arabs how to buy their arms? If they wished to pay
more for their Phantoms or Hawks, and pass on the extra to some
fun-loving prince, why should anyone—least of all the US
treasury—object? And how much more relaxing for Western
businessmen to do their deals over midnight parties with pretty
girls.

But the size of the arms companies was so overwhelming that
their very arrival in the Third World upset the local equilibrium.

They were themselves major actors in the play of politics; and actors of a very blundering kind, like bulls in china shops. They were not simply following the 'custom of the country'; they were creating new customs. However plausibly Lockheed could maintain that they were victims of extortion, whether in Holland or Saudi Arabia or Japan, they were creating a permissive atmosphere with their largesse, in which extortion became very tempting, if not irresistible.

The problem of controlling bribery was really bound up with the accountability of the corporations. By allowing these giant companies to accumulate international slush funds, the Washington governments were losing control over their own policies. The upper structures of Lockheed and Northrop were designed to maintain secret channels controlled only by one or two men at the top, which could be used both for bribery abroad and corruption closer to home, for the bank accounts in Switzerland or Liechtenstein were beyond the reach of enquiry. The bribes could corrupt the company as much as the recipient. One French diplomat told me how he had investigated a case of bribery by a French arms company in the Middle East which the company readily admitted, only to discover that the bribes were merely an excuse to set up a secret foreign bank account for quite different purposes.

The efficiency and cost-effectiveness of bribes may often seem doubtful. Lockheed appears often to have spent large sums paying men, like Bernhard or Kodama, with uncertain returns, and the big companies have shown themselves very vulnerable to bluff and mystique. The attraction of the 'mystery man' dies hard, and once a company like Lockheed shows that it is in the market for bribes, it becomes an easy prey to grand-sounding con men. Uneasy executives (as Khashoggi plausibly suggests) may often pay bribes to reassure themselves more than anyone else—or to keep part of the bribe on the way. Bribery can easily become an industry of its own, divorced from any measurable results.

In the industrial countries, Lockheed and Northrop appear to have wasted a good deal of their slush funds. But in the Third World, the bribes have been much more important, as the means not only of competing with rivals, but of enlarging the market. Whatever the ethics and problems of bribery in ordinary business, it has always had a special significance in the arms trade to the Third World; and we have seen how since the days of Zaharoff the arms companies have been closely associated with bribes. It was Sir Basil's special skill to use money to create new needs for weapons in the developing world of his time, and this role of bribery has been part of the unique character of the arms companies in which (in the words of the 1936 Royal Commission) 'the success of one firm does not mean the failure of another, but rather increases its chances of doing business'. Thus in Colombia and the Philippines, Lockheed used their bribes to foist arms on their clients; and thus today Lockheed and Northrop can get rich together in the Middle East, even using the same agents, confident that the arms market has plenty of room for them both.

But the real importance of the Lockheed and Northrop revelations lies not so much in the details of payoffs as in the relentless pressures that lay behind them, to sell arms at all costs. The mounting bribes were only the symptoms of the growing frenzy to push weapons into the new markets, in the midst of an arms race without precedent over the past thirty years.

17

The Controllers

The values and principles we live by as a nation will be what history
will remember America for, not the sophistication or quantity of our
weapons.

Senate Report on Arms to Iran, May 14, 1976

FROM his big office in the outer ring of the Pentagon, General
Howard M. Fish radiated confidence and command. He is a
stocky three-star general from Alabama, with a very active career
behind him: he was shot down in a bomber over Europe in the
Second World War and rose to be Director of Tactical Analysis
in the Vietnam war, before taking up his job in 1974 as Director
of the Defence Security Assistance Agency (DSAA) or, in other
words, controller of arms sales. A colonel sat in his anteroom,
and when Fish barked his instructions down the telephone,
uniformed soldiers marched in and out. He rocked up and down
on his chair, pouring out statistics and information, in sentences
of cryptic syntax, his eyes twinkling and his mouth shutting into
a grin of certainty. On his desk were a cluster of very sharp
pencils, like missiles; on his tie was a three-star tie pin; and beside
his desk were two tall flags.

The Pentagon's arms sales organisation had changed since the
days of Henry Kuss, who left in 1969 to set up his own marketing
company in Washington (he did not want to deal in arms, he
explains, because they always involve either governments or

gun-runners). The old International Logistics Negotiations had been reorganised and renamed with the equally euphemistic title of DSAA (the changing of names, as for rat catchers or lavatory attendants, suggests some embarrassment). The director of the DSAA was also a deputy assistant secretary for International Security Affairs, concerned with foreign policy. The two hats were intended to relate arms sales to their diplomatic consequences: it was under both hats that General Fish was now talking.

Fish emphasised to me that his main job was not to encourage sales, but to control them: 'That's why they need a man like me, with both combat experience and fiscal experience: it takes a lot of nervous energy to say no. Instead of being an aggressive sales office, we must be a clearing house, a co-ordinating office. We make sure no one is out peddling arms. People misinterpreted what Kuss was doing. The real purpose of promotion is to persuade countries: "If you're going to buy arms from somewhere, buy them from us." ' The Pentagon, Fish explained, could not be pushed by the arms companies: 'Industry's pretty co-operative; they've got to live with this building.' Towards Europe, the Pentagon was in an aggressive selling mood in the interests of standardisation, while also helping Europeans to sell to the United States. But there was no question of urging companies to sell more arms to the Third World.

I mentioned to Fish that only a few months earlier, in October 1975, his chief salesman, Richard Violette, had attended an annual seminar of the Electronic Industries Association in San Francisco. The company men had presented their ten-year forecast, stressing the scope for new markets in arms sales, and Violette himself had talked chattily about foreign military sales. ('It's nice to see some old grey heads around here who have been in as long as I have.') He described how government arms sales had been averaging 1.5 billion dollars through the 'sixties. 'We were quite proud of that. Then in the 1972-3 period, things started happening . . . In 1973, as I reported last year, we did about $3.8 billion worth of foreign military sales. In 1974 it jumped to roughly $8.5 billion.' He then listed the chief countries buying arms, 'just to show you where the action is', and promised the salesmen that, while arms exports might not stay quite so high, they would not go down to three billion. He was 'less optimistic' than some other forecasters, he explained, because there were limits as to how fast the new customers, the oil-producing countries, could expand their capacity.[1] Optimism meant selling the maximum quantity of arms. I put it to General Fish that Violette was really pressing the salesmen to push arms into the Third World. Not at all, he replied, he was only explaining the facts.

General Fish repeatedly contended that United States exports of arms were designed primarily to deter conflict in each region, to eliminate the need for direct American support, and to meet the Soviet threat. In evidence to the Senate in April 1976 he gave the Pentagon's assessment of Soviet arms exports over the past twenty years. Russia, he said, had extended almost $15 billion in arms to thirty-eight Third World countries, and he was unaware that Russia had ever once turned down a prospective arms client. The Soviet deliveries to all Third World countries jumped to $1.2 billion a year in the late 1970s, and they had contributed to the weakening or elimination of Western influence in many countries, including Afghanistan, Algeria, Egypt, Iraq, Somalia, South Yemen and Syria.[2]

Undoubtedly Soviet arms exports have contributed heavily to the arms race in the Third World, since the first deal with Egypt in 1955. The Soviets have poured arms into Africa and Asia, and their satellites have been glad to earn foreign currency by selling guns to almost anyone, from White South Africans to Lebanese Christians. The battle for Beirut, fought with Soviet arms on both sides, was a memorial to the Eastern arms industry as well as to the Western. But it is hard to believe, as General Fish insists, that the Soviet menace was the chief motive for the sudden build-up of American arms sales in the Middle East. After the 1973 Arab-Israeli war, with Russia in retreat from Egypt and America more influential in Egypt and even Syria, the communist danger was certainly no greater: Saudi Arabia and the sheikhdoms were fiercely anti-communist and under no obvious threat from the Soviets. Iraq was no longer at odds with Iran after her reconciliation in March 1975, but was stealthily moving closer to the Western camp, looking to Europe for trade and even arms.

The arms race in the Middle East was not initiated by any perceived new threat from the East but by the commercial opportunities coinciding with the diplomacy of the Nixon doctrine and the British retreat from the Persian (or Arabian) Gulf, which

---

[1] Electronic Industries Association annual meeting, San Francisco, October 9, 1975.

[2] Statement before Subcommittee on Foreign Assistance, Senate Foreign Relations Committee, April 5, 1976.

had resulted in a general loss of control over arms sales. The system of control looked rigorous enough. Ninety-five percent of the arms deals were negotiated by the Pentagon itself through General Fish, on behalf of the arms companies, in the government-to-government negotiations known as Foreign Military Sales (FMS); while the remaining commercial sales were still subject to Pentagon permission. The Pentagon sales were themselves overseen by the State Department, with its own Office for Munitions Control, and watched by the Arms Control and Disarmament Agency (ACDA). All these safeguards supposedly ensured that arms would only be exported where strictly necessary for the American national interest or international security. But the case of Iran showed how any such calculations could be ignored by the new commercial pragmatism following the Nixon doctrine.

Gradually Congress was waking up to the implications of the sales to Iran, and by June 1975 many congressmen were worried that they were beginning to forge a new kind of commitment to the Persian Gulf. The Pentagon now predicted that by 1980 there would be 150,000 Americans in the whole Persian Gulf, of whom 50,000 would be in Iran. The supply of arms, as the Pentagon admitted, brought with it a whole system of training in industrial skills. It was a kind of responsibility that had never been foreseen when the Nixon doctrine had first been adumbrated: the Shah had succeeded, as one Pentagon official put it, in 'getting us pregnant'.

Congress had received no indication of a policy change. Representative Lee Hamilton questioned Dave Alne, who had recently been director of International Sales at the Pentagon (and who was so impressed by Khashoggi in the Pentagon in 1973) about how sales to Iran had so suddenly increased, and Alne explained: 'First of all they have a lot of money, and second they have the Shah's will, indeed insistence, to establish the kind of defence mechanism in that country that he thinks he needs.'[1]

Many Pentagon officials, too, were worried that the sales to Iran were laying up troubles for the future. The joint chiefs of staff were afraid that the Shah's orders might interfere with their own needs for domestic defence, while officials concerned with the 'nuts-and-bolts' were doubtful whether the huge supplies could really be absorbed. The US navy themselves were already having some difficulties with the Tomcat: how much

[1] House Committee on International Relations, June 24, 1975.

greater would the problems be in Iran? 'I think perhaps we over-
sold the Shah on the Tomcats,' one senior Pentagon official
admitted to me in the spring of 1976. 'It implied an obligation to
make them work.'

The whole Nixon doctrine, with its emphasis on building up
regional powers to support the Western alliance, seemed now in
danger of running away with itself, creating a Frankenstein
monster. Would the Shah be content to be the 'policeman of the
Persian Gulf', or would he extend his interests into the Indian
Ocean, perhaps in alliance with Israel and South Africa? And
where would *that* trio fit into American foreign policy?

The Pentagon offered eloquent justifications. The arms sales,
one official explained to me, were the quickest means of bringing
Iran into the twentieth century, with all kinds of skills and training. The expansion of the military (explained another) was
essentially a democratic force, providing awareness and education
all down the social scale. The arms race (said Amos Jordan) did not
increase the chances of conflict: on the contrary it could well
reduce the dangers as it had in Europe. And by what right,
anyway, could the United States refuse to sell arms to the Shah?
'He's merely mimicking our own noble societies,' said another
official. 'It's been implicit since 1968 that it's up to the Shah to
decide,' said another. 'The age of tutelage is now ended.'

But behind all these explanations lay the obvious fact that the
arms had been allowed and sold in exchange for the oil. It was a
bargain that many officials believed was inevitable—not only
to redress the balance of payments, but to buy the friendship of
the oil states on which the West was now so desperately
dependent.

Congress was not convinced, and by the end of 1975 Senators
Kennedy and Humphrey had initiated a new bill to give greater
control over arms sales. A burst of lobbying followed, and company executives from California, Texas or Missouri flew into
Washington to warn of the dangers. President Ford vetoed the
bill, the senators modified it, and the arms companies lobbied
again. But General Fish advised them that the revised bill would
not seriously injure their trade, and eventually the president
signed the International Security Assistance and Arms Export
Control Act of 1976-7, otherwise known as the Humphrey Bill.

The new bill superseded the Mutual Security Act of a quarter-
century earlier, which had sped the flow of American arms to the

non-communist nations. It would 'shift the policy emphasis from expanding arms exports to strengthening controls', and bring arms sales out into the open. Congress could now veto any arms sale valued at more than 25 million dollars. American military missions and grants would be reduced, and no security assistance would be provided to governments which grossly violated human rights—except under extraordinary circumstances.

The Humphrey Bill achieved something, and it publicised arms deals, forcing Congress to take note. But it hardly affected the volume of sales, and the arms tycoons were right in believing that they 'could live with it', for congressmen were always under strong pressure to let sales go through; even those who strongly opposed arms sales would support contracts for their own states. The stipulation about human rights cut off sales to Chile and Uruguay, but Iran, with its political prisoners and torturers, was an 'extraordinary circumstance'.

The competition to sell arms was as great as ever, both between companies and between countries. The American salesmen were competing not so much with the Russians as with the British and French, and the framers of the Humphrey Bill specifically insisted that it would not 'impair the US competitive position in foreign arms sales'. There was always the old argument that if the Americans did not sell arms, someone else would. In October 1975 a hundred members of Congress, led by Senator John Culver, wrote to Kissinger to protest about 'the anarchic and escalating nature of the worldwide rush to acquire new weapons'; they emphasised that unilateral action could not alone solve it and recommended that the NATO nations most active in the arms trade should convene an international conference to discuss guidelines for arms sales. But Kissinger in his reply was very sceptical about any international conference or agreement. The United States, he explained, had repeatedly raised the problem at Geneva, but the other members had shown little interest, for three main reasons. First, many nations believed that the discussion of conventional arms would distract attention from the more urgent need for nuclear disarmament. Secondly, the developing nations resented measures to limit the conventional arms trade as discriminating against them. And thirdly, arms-selling countries regarded their exports as essential to their own national interest.

Certainly, as the rest of this chapter suggests, there were some grounds for Kissinger's scepticism. But the American responsibility could not so easily be avoided. For the United States was now by herself responsible for half the world's arms trade; and if she did not take an initiative to restrict it, no one else would.

BRITAIN'S NAUGHTY STUFF

Britain was in no mood to restrict her arms sales, for the increased oil-price had coincided with an economic crisis worse than any before, and arms were one of her few growing exports. Her sales were tiny compared to America's, but spectacular in relation to her own economy, and between 1972 and 1975 they went up from £257 million to £600 million. A quarter of Britain's total arms production went into exports, and both Labour and Conservative governments encouraged their official arms salesmen to greater efforts abroad.

Several of the customers for arms were the same as in the nineteenth century. Many countries whose potentates had adorned Lord Armstrong's visitors' book—Persia, Chile or Siam—were still important clients. Newcastle, which had built the world's battleships, was now building tanks for the Middle East. The workers in Barrow-in-Furness still depended on Vickers making warships for Latin Americans, among others. But clean new electronic companies had also grown up, in quiet suburban towns like Stevenage and Chelmsford, which few people associated with arms. In Windsor, Racal Instruments, the company founded by Raymond Brown, was heavily dependent on arms equipment for its spectacular profits: in 1975 fifty-four percent of its production worth £43 million went to arms sales abroad; while Decca, from their electronic warfare division in Walton-on-Thames, exported around £48 million worth.[1] The big corporations with homely images for shoppers or housewives, like EMI, ICI, General Electric or Lucas, had their arms divisions which showed a very different face: 'We can offer not only hardware,' explains Lucas to its arms customers, 'but a total systems design and management capability.'

British arms sales were looming so large that in June 1976 the ministry of defence mounted an exhibition at Aldershot of military equipment—the equivalent of the Farnborough air show—to help push up arms sales to a new target of £750 million a year. It

[1] See Estimates by Greene & Co. in *The Economist,* July 3, 1976.

was a cosy occasion with marquees and plenty of refreshments, like a sports day or a horticultural show. After some modest protests from the Campaign Against the Arms Trade it went ahead peacefully. Chieftain tanks were lined up along the lawn, while wives and children of soldiers clambered over them and popped up in the turret. Mortars and guns were laid out on neat gravel or clipped grass, like sports goods in a shop. A painful new kind of barbed wire called a 'Barbed Tape Concertina' was stretched across a lawn, shining brightly in the sun like gay bunting. Nowhere could I notice the word 'kill'. Stalls were decorated with artists' impressions of battles, in the style of boys' comics. Vosper-Thornycroft showed two monster hovercraft beaching themselves on a marshy shore, with trucks and troops racing out of them: the company hoped to sell some of them to the Shah, who had a passion for hovercraft, explained the Vosper man, and if he agreed the British themselves might buy some. On the lawn was a big black 'Internal Security Vehicle', the AT 104, which had just been designed to disperse rioters, heavily armed with a machine-gun on top. Again the British forces had not yet ordered it (the salesman explained) but they would be encouraged by a foreign sale.

The eagerness for foreign clients was visible everywhere; whole brochures were printed in Arabic, and some waxwork soldiers had a very Iranian appearance. The real climax of the show was the two private days devoted to foreign buyers from seventy countries, with the Middle Eastern states in the forefront. The patter of the salesmen underlined the need to take foreign prospects into account when the weapons were actually being designed. At the ministry of defence, the Defence Sales Office was now given formal representation on the Operational Requirements Committee and the Weapons Development Committee; and the British forces were frequently pressed to accept weapons like the Maritime Harrier, because they would then have an export market.[1] The tail was growing longer, and the dog was smaller.

A few politicians have stood out against the mounting arms sales, including two vocal Labour MPs, Robin Cook and John Roper, and one thoughtful Conservative, Julian Critchley, the member (remarkably enough) for Aldershot. Critchley accepts

[1] See Robin Cook: *Britain and the Arms Trade*, Labour Party International Department, 1976.

that 'what is good for Vickers is good for Britain', but only up to eighty-five percent. He asks: 'Are we not, together with the French and the Americans, making war inevitable by our sales to the oil-rich nations of the gulf?'[1] There is also a singular movement among trade unionists in Lucas Aerospace, led by Mike Cooley, who put forward their own detailed corporate plan to show how skilled engineers could be redeployed after defence cuts, to work on socially useful projects including medical equipment, low energy housing and transport systems—an initiative which had wide response from other arms regions, including California.[2] But most British politicians have been inclined to regard arms sales as a necessary evil, which they prefer not to discuss.

The British Defence Sales Organisation, which mounted the Aldershot exhibition, has extended its scope since Denis Healey set it up ten years earlier. Sir Ray Brown had been succeeded in 1969 by a car salesman, Lester Suffield, who insisted that selling arms was just the same as selling cars; he did not, he explained, give any thought to the moral implications, which were already taken care of by the government, and 'in a way it's much easier than selling cars, because the policy is there'.[3] The arms salesmen were now thoroughly integrated inside the ministry of defence, where the generals and air marshals treated them with grudging respect, as the people who were helping to finance Britain's own forces. I went to see Sir Lester in the summer of 1976, just before he retired (to be succeeded by *another* car salesman, Ronald Ellis). A genial, outspoken man with a long doggy face, he had the usual enthusiasm of a salesman, impatient of government controls and regulations. Inside the stone palace of the ministry of defence in Whitehall, he took me round the permanent exhibition of British weapons for sale, displayed in a big central hall, the black heart of the ministry, where visiting potentates, generals and admirals are tempted with new instruments of warfare.

'This is what I call the naughty stuff,' said Sir Lester with a smile, waving at one corner where small arms, including Sterling sub-machine guns, hand-held missiles and 81mm mortars with 'maximum lethality', were elegantly laid out on gravel, like

[1] House of Commons, July 8, 1975. *The Spectator*, February 5, 1977.

[2] Lucas Aerospace Combine Shop Stewards Committee: Corporate Plan, January 1976. See also *The Engineer*, February 5, 1976.

[3] Interview with BBC television 'Midweek' programme, July 2, 1975.

neo-realist sculpture. An exploding high explosive shell was displayed with armour-plating alongside, pierced with a six-inch hole. A diorama, like an exhibit in a science museum, showed a squadron of British tanks encircling a small native town with model bushes and trees and a bridge which they had just blown up, all controlled by a British radio system, indicated with coloured lights. At one end of the hall were exhibits on internal security, a British speciality since the civil war in Northern Ireland: there were rubber bullets, riot control equipment, and a remote-controlled gun on wheels. Counter-insurgency was now making good business, and Sir Lester explained that he could even supply labrador dogs for export, trained to sniff out explosives.

No one in the ministry will disclose what proportion of British arms sales go to each country, and parliamentary questions are rejected on the grounds of security: all that has been revealed is that total arms sales in 1976 amounted to £700 million, and that about three-quarters are normally air equipment.[1] 'There's nothing to be gained by publicising sales,' said one defence official; 'it's not like other businesses, where you need to advertise to get other people on the bandwagon. We don't want to give ammunition to our critics among the extreme politicians. The French always exaggerate their sales. If the full facts were known, Britain would very likely be seen to be exporting more arms than France.'

But it is very clear that the Middle East is the biggest market for Britain, as for America: 'We prefer to deal with people with money,' as one salesman explained, 'who are not too particular.' Iran is even more crucial for the British arms industry than for the American, providing (according to one source) as much as sixty percent of the market. The Shah has bought more Chieftain tanks than the British army itself, and the government agency that executes arms deals, Millbank Technical Services, told me in 1977 that the 'great majority' of their orders, worth £1,500 million, were destined for Iran. But the British defence officials, like the Iranians, have faced growing troubles over the weapons after they arrive. The Iranians have criticised the cost and ineffectiveness of British weapons, as they have of the American ones, but the flow of arms has continued. The Chieftain tanks, I was told, did not travel further than fifty miles a year, and as for the

[1] Parliamentary Question by Robin Cook, M.P., October 22, 1976.

warships, the Iranian sailors were seasick whenever they put out, and could not use the extravagant equipment: 'But they always say that it is our fault.' As the Shah began to run out of money, he tried to make direct barter deals to buy arms in exchange for oil; having failed in America, he turned to Britain, and in November 1976 the British Aircraft Corporation announced a joint deal with Shell by which they would supply the Rapier ground-to-air missile system, worth $640 million, in exchange for 13,000 barrels of crude oil a day for the next eight years. Thus the nature of the bargain was more nakedly established: we give you oil, if you give us arms.

When I left the ministry, I was weighed down with a heavy box containing three volumes, which are very well known in arms dealing circles, called the *British Defence Equipment Catalogue*. They are masterpieces of the dead-pan style of the trade, like the conversation of Sam Cummings, with no hint that they are selling anything out of the way. The cover is emblazoned with the crests of the three services, and each double page gives photographs and specifications in drab layout, of guns, fighters or warships. The introduction explains that the equipment has been 'tested in nearly all climates, conditions and geographical locations', and advises potential purchasers to contact the local British embassy. The catalogue, I discovered, was the envy of American companies; 'But here they'd call it unethical,' complained Mr Simcox of the Electronic Industries Association in Washington. 'If we produced something like that, we'd be accused of being part of the military-industrial complex.'

It is a widespread grudge among American arms sellers, that their European rivals take advantage of much closer links between government and industry. As General Fish put it: 'Foreign companies dealing in this area can usually deliver their governments, and their governments can usually deliver their industry. The opposite is true with the United States, and I believe properly so.' British and French arms sellers, whether nationalised or not, certainly have a cosier relationship with their governments and embassies than is permitted in Washington. But the American government is not necessarily any less effective in promoting sales: the selling of the F16 in the Deal of the Century revealed the full force of American diplomatic pressure, while the Northrop and Lockheed papers show the extent of embassy support. And there is no real British equivalent to the fierce rivalries between American companies, each abetted by the rival services.

What the British intimacy does ensure is secrecy. The arms sales may be carefully scrutinised by the diplomats and defence officials in private, and may be turned down, in such cases as Chile and South Africa. But the British parliament are not allowed to share in the decisions, or to know how the sales are apportioned; and the British public are never told the extent to which they are arming the world.

THE CONSCIENCE OF A CONTINENT

The European governments all faced the same basic problem: their arms industries were too small and fragmented to provide their own defence needs, so that they had to import advanced weapons from America; while to make their own companies viable and to recoup the cost of their own purchases, they felt impelled to sell to the Third World. The obvious solution lay in the unification of Europe, which could make the arms industries self-sufficient and remove the need to export. There had been attempts in this direction, like the Anglo-French Jaguar, or the Anglo-German Tornado. But the Deal of the Century had shown up once again the political disunity of Europe: and in the meantime the Third World helped to pay the cost.

Each country in Europe has its own traditions of arms sales, often going deep into history, and its own special pressures and conflicts. The most persistent sellers of all are the Belgians, who have been notorious since the Middle Ages, when the city of Liège was the centre of Europe's firearms industry; so notorious that in the fifteenth century Charles the Bold of Burgundy forbade them to make arms, and when they defied him, razed Liège to the ground and slaughtered its inhabitants.[1] In the nineteenth century Liège became still more important as the headquarters of the Belgian company Fabrique Nationale d'Armes de Guerre (FN) which is now one of the most aggressive of all arms exporters, specialising in rifles, machine-guns and Browning pistols. Belgium now exports more than ninety percent of her total arms production, and the government are unusually generous with their licences. FN rifles have mysteriously found their way to many explosive areas: they were the first arms to reach Cuba after Castro came to power, and they appeared on

[1] See George Thayer: *The War Business*, Weidenfeld and Nicolson, 1969, p. 23.

both sides in the Congo civil war, and on the Christian side in the Lebanon.

The two former enemy countries, Germany and Italy, were both strictly restrained from arms production and sales in the post-war years. But they were urged to rearm with the formation of NATO, which produced new pressures to sell arms to pay for their own purchases: the more dependent they were on buying American arms, like the Starfighter, the greater was the temptation to sell their old weapons elsewhere.

In Germany arms exports crept up during the 'sixties, reaching as much as $100 million in 1966: weaponry was given away as part of the military aid programmes, and a third of it was surplus equipment, which was sold off as the German NATO forces were re-equipped. The Social Democrat government coming to power in 1969 was determined to restrict exports, and the defence minister, Helmut Schmidt, insisted that he would 'in no way act as an aide to the sales managers of German industry'.[1] But more recently the Bonn government, even under Schmidt as chancellor, has found it more difficult to stand up to the demands for employment and export markets, backed by trade unionists. An ominous precedent was the announcement of the huge deal to supply eight nuclear power stations for Brazil, with the potential to produce nuclear weapons (see next chapter).

The Italians became more aggressive and unscrupulous arms sellers after their earlier exclusion from the trade. As Italy built up her own defence industry within NATO she sold first ships and then aircraft to the Third World, to make her home industry viable. Like the French, the Italians were prepared to break embargoes to find new markets, and the Italian aircraft companies, including Fiat, Macchi and Piaggio, pressed their government to relax their control of exports. When Britain embargoed Egypt in the early 'fifties, Italy sold British Vampire fighters to Syria who passed them to Egypt. After the embargo of South Africa in 1963 the Italians saw a chance to sell missiles, helicopters and armoured cars, and the Macchi company helped the South Africans to establish their own aircraft industry.

The moral dilemmas of arms sales are most poignant in the neutral countries, who wish to be both self-sufficient in defence and to preserve their sense of morality. Switzerland has been constantly torn between its commercial needs and its humani-

[1] SIPRI: *The Arms Trade with the Third World*, p. 304.

tarian ideals, symbolised by the Red Cross. As the Swiss foreign minister described it in 1969:

> The question is to find a compromise between the partly contradictory interests of our defence and our trade and the demands placed on us by the rules of the neutrality law, and also as a country pledged to the Red Cross and humanitarian actions.[1]

Swiss exports account for thirty percent of their arms industry and the biggest arms company, Oerlikon-Buehrle, produces more weapons in its factories abroad than in Switzerland. The Swiss government have thus been reluctant to embargo their old customers; they continued to supply Indonesia during its confrontation with Malaysia, and they have supplied both India and Pakistan. The pressure of the industry and the feebleness of the controls were vividly illustrated in November 1968, when Oerlikon guns were found to have been illegally exported to Nigeria: the Swiss guns may well have been firing at Red Cross planes flying to Biafra, thus symbolising the split minds of the Swiss. The ensuing scandal and trial eventually revealed that $21 million worth of arms had been illegally exported by Oerlikon-Buehrle, including $12.1 million to South Africa, and other arms to Nigeria, Egypt, Saudi Arabia, Lebanon and Malaysia—all exported through the simple device of forging the 'end-use certificates' which were supposed to guarantee their destination. The Oerlikon scandal led to three prison sentences for company officials, a suspended sentence for the head of the company, and public demands for nationalisation. But a commission of experts, while demanding more effective controls, reported that a ban on exports would put up the costs of many weapons by sixty-five percent, and would endanger the home industry. Oerlikon remained intact, and the exports continued to rise. And in the meantime Switzerland, with its secret bank accounts and protection from investigation, has become the indispensable haven for arms dealers everywhere, from Lockheed and Northrop to shady suppliers and hijackers.

Only the Swedes have succeeded, with occasional lapses, in rigorously controlling their sales. Sweden faced the same dilemma of combining armed neutrality with commercial viability, and was caught between an inventive industry and compassionate ideals. The dichotomy which showed itself so tragically in the

[1] Ibid., p. 347.

brilliant but confused mind of Nobel has run through Swedish history since: Sweden now has two of the most advanced arms companies in the world, Saab and Bofors, and also the most industrious peace lobby, the Stockholm International Peace Research Institute (SIPRI), which provides a unique body of research and documentation (to which this book is heavily indebted). The Swedish arms companies, like all others, have been persistent in pressing the governments, who have sometimes in the past allowed dangerous exports. In the 1956 Suez war the Swedes had helped to arm Egypt with a Bofors AA gun and submachine-guns and rifles, having already sold Mustang fighters to the Israelis; while Saab have sold fighters to many Third World countries, including Haiti and Brazil. The pressures can be expected to become stronger as the cost of self-sufficiency becomes heavier: at the time of writing, the Saab aircraft industry appears to be threatened with extinction by rising costs. But Sweden has been more restrained than other nations, and the arms trade has accounted for only 0.6 percent of Swedish exports, compared to 2.4 percent of British exports, 3.1 percent of French exports, and 3.8 percent of US exports.[1] There is some encouragement in the fact that Sweden has become the most advanced industrial nation in Europe, and one of the world's great traders, with very little help from arms sales.

THE FRENCH CONNECTION

Among the Europeans, the French have stood out over the past two decades as the most aggressive and successful exporters of arms, catching up and perhaps overtaking the British in their time-honoured contest. American companies, as we have seen, have been obsessed by the belief in French cunning and bribery, using it to justify their own corruption. How far the French success has been due to bribery is not known, but what is clear is that it owes much to the very close workings between government and industry. Successive French governments and their senior civil servants have seen the arms industry both as an instrument of diplomacy and as a means of developing engineering skills, as the spearhead of the new technological France.

The effects are very visible in the city of Bordeaux, the noble capital of Aquitaine and the wine trade. Today the proud port,

[1] See Ingemar Dörfer: *System 37 Viggen*, Oslo Universitetsforlaget, 1973, p. 45.

with its faded grey terraces, its long quayside and its second-empire railway station, conjures up vanished glories: since the Second World War its naval shipyards have slumped and unemployment has been rife. But near the airport, the whole scene is transformed. The suburb of Mérignac is a model town with an atmosphere more Californian than French. The white apartment blocks and low houses have coloured blinds shining in the clean air; markets, sports centres and playgrounds are neatly laid out round a compact shopping centre. A prime cause of the prosperity is soon evident, for alongside the airport stands a long cream-coloured building with big letters saying: AVIONS MARCEL DASSAULT. Inside, the rows of neat drawing boards and the clean-cut executives seem a century away from the genial boozers down at the docks.

It has been the showpiece not only of French arms, but of French engineering; from here successive new fighters—Ouragans, Mystères, Mirages—have flown out to all corners of the world. To Western rivals the Dassault traffic might seem unprincipled, but here in Mérignac Marcel Dassault has been not only the bringer of employment to a depressed city; he has been the master-engineer, a key component of the miracle of the French recovery.

French governments have put all their weight behind Dassault and other arms companies. Like most other Western nations, France strengthened its own sales organisation in the wide wake of Henry Kuss in Washington. The Délégation Ministérielle pour l'Armament (DMA) was augmented in 1965 with a special export department, the Direction des Affaires Internationales (DIA), more discreet but more far-reaching than its Anglo-Saxon equivalents. It organises military missions abroad and demonstrations, including the bi-annual Paris air show at Le Bourget and the arms exhibition at Satory, and provides links with a network of quasi-governmental bodies to stimulate exports.[1]

The head of the DIA is much more integrated within the bureaucracy than his foreign counterparts, but he is in effect the chief French arms salesman and a man of decisive influence. The first head, Louis Bonte, was sacked after Israeli torpedo boats, banned by the French government, were allowed to leave Cherbourg for Israel on Christmas Day 1969. Bonte was suc-

[1] See John Stanley and Maurice Pearton: *The International Trade in Arms*, London, Chatto and Windus, 1972, pp. 94–7.

ceeded by General Hugues de l'Estoile, a graduate of the Poly-
technique who brought both aggression and style to his job, and
sold arms with a clear conscience: 'When I am criticised for
being an arms dealer,' he has said, 'I always think that when I sign
a contract I can guarantee for instance 10,000 jobs over three
years. Yes, I am a practising Catholic, and I have never had
problems with my conscience. Have you noticed that in the
Bible the centurion is never put in a bad light?'[1] When the French
Protestant federation attacked arms sales, he counter-attacked by
describing how France had just lost an order for helicopters for
the Lebanon to the American Bell company, whose agent in
Beirut was the papal nuncio: he noted in passing that French
arms sales abroad only accounted for six percent of the deaths
produced by French cars abroad. The Americans, he complained,
were dumping their arms on the world, and were competing
with special aggression towards France.[2] In 1974 de l'Estoile was
succeeded as chief arms salesman by another *polytechnicien*, Paul
Assens, but he retained the responsibility for the sales of the new
Mirage fighter, the F1, and in the contest for Deal of the Century
he was able to pit himself against the American aggressors.

L'AFFAIRE DASSAULT

There has been little effective French criticism of their arms
sales to the Third World. The workers are mindful of the extra
jobs: 270,000 French jobs depend on defence, of which a quarter
are dependent on exports. The unions advocate nationalising the
arms companies and converting some of their factories, but are
cautious in their condemnation.[3] In January 1976 the archbishop
of Paris, Cardinal Marty, preached an eloquent sermon at Notre
Dame denouncing the mounting 'commerce of death' which,
he said, was becoming an institution supported by collective
hypocrisy: the attack was briefly taken up by the left, but the
prime minister Jacques Chirac explained that the jobs provided by
arms sales were particularly helpful at a time of high unemployment.[4] The American arms race provided an excuse and a new

[1] *Vision* magazine, Paris, May 1975.
[2] *Le Monde*, May 5, 1973.
[3] Interview with Michel Marcholac by Christine Ockrent on French television, January
28, 1977.
[4] *New York Times*, January 25, 1976.

challenge to the French salesmen: by late 1976 they had sold
seventy-two Mirage F1s to Iraq, as up-to-date as the French air
force planes. It was a kind of revenge for losing the Deal of the
Century.

The workings of the Dassault empire had remained much more
concealed than those of the Americans. But just when the Lockheed scandals were unfolding across the world an extraordinary
story emerged from Paris, so opposite in its origins from the
American revelations, so Gallic in its mixture of corruption, sex,
adventure and ideology, that it took some time to realise that it
had to do with the same basic problem—the accountability of
arms companies.

It began in July 1976 when a lean, sad-looking man with
haunted eyes walked into a Paris bank, withdrew $1.6 million
from a company account, and then disappeared with the money.
It was Marcel Dassault's personal accountant, Henri de Vathaire,
who had this remarkable access to money, and 'le pauvre
Vathaire', as Dassault called him, had just been through a period
of domestic anguish. He had found his wife dead in the bath, and
in his bewilderment had subsequently taken up with a nightclub
hostess, who in turn was a friend of a celebated French adventurer
called Jean Kay, who had achieved fame five years earlier after
trying to hi-jack a Pakistan Airlines plane, to raise money for
Bangladesh. De Vathaire, the accountant, had been collecting
a dossier about some of the more remarkable operations of the
Dassault company (as some French executives are inclined to do,
to insure themselves against their bosses' caprices). He rashly
showed the dossier to his wild new friend Jean Kay, who kept it,
and evidently used it to extract money from de Vathaire, which
led to his visit to the bank, and subsequent disappearance.

The events remained concealed from the public for two months,
for Dassault had not desired to sue or pursue de Vathaire, and
such a loss could easily be hidden within the ample womb of the
Dassault empire. But in September the story was leaked to
France Soir, who exposed it with full relish, but with no indication of the contents of the dossier. A stir of excitement followed:
a voice purporting to be Jean Kay rang up French television to say
that the money had been given to the Lebanese Christians for
arms. Marcel Dassault himself appeared on television, charming
and unperturbed, to explain that de Vathaire had been in a
depressed state of mind, and that this was not a 'Lockheed type'

scandal: Dassault had never been involved in bribing. Then de Vathaire himself flew into Paris from Athens, and was promptly arrested and jailed, charged with 'abuse of confidence'.

The next month, in another huge leak, the magazine *Le Point* published a sixteen-page resumé of de Vathaire's secret dossier, which made some astonishing allegations about the operations of Dassault's huge empire. It maintained that the aircraft company had been subsidising Dassault's other companies by paying vastly excessive rents and fees for patents to the parent Dassault company; that a marble country house outside Paris, the 'petit Trianon', built at a cost of ten million dollars, had been charged up to the aircraft company as a business expense; that Dassault had a special team of accountants to prepare bogus wage records, to justify higher prices for his planes; that two senior tax officials received regular payments for their connivance; and that secret funds of $6 million a year had been used for Dassault's own election expenses in his constituency near Paris, including building swimming pools and tennis courts in Dassault's own constituency near Paris, and subsidising a newspaper controlled by the former prime minister Jacques Chirac.

The dossier, supported by lavish coverage from left-wing Paris newspapers, appeared to show that Dassault's private military-industrial complex was beyond the control of the state, and it quickly led to insistent demands for the nationalisation of the company. But Dassault himself was still unruffled. He appeared again on television, explained that he had done nothing illegal; as for the 'petit Trianon', he had the right to do what he liked with his own money, and 'everybody does it, notably Rolls-Royce in England'. Tax experts pointed out that the shifting of funds within an industrial empire was quite normal in other French businesses. And Dassault wrote a letter to the magazine *L'Express*, saying that he was quite willing for his aircraft company to be nationalised, with himself continuing as consultant (as had happened forty years earlier, when the previous Dassault company had been nationalised by the French Popular Front government). The French Assembly, after an angry debate, eventually agreed to set up a committee of enquiry, which would investigate not just Dassault, but also (to the anger of the left) the whole of French aerospace industry—including the nationalised Aérospatiale at Toulouse whose loss-making ventures, including Concorde, made Dassault's tax avoidance seem petty.

Dassault and his executives seemed still unperturbed, even pleased, by this outcome. The real truth about the industry would now emerge (one of them told me, just after the news): the committee would realise that the nationalised companies were incompetent and extravagant: they paid their presidents less than their pilots, and 'if we had engineers like theirs, we'd call a doctor'. The decisiveness and enterprise of Dassault depended on its being a private industry. Dassault was prepared to be nationalised, but it was not in the nation's interest.

Certainly if the French wanted to maintain their aggressive arms sales and independent technology they gained many advantages from a free-booting company, discreetly underpinned by governments—like Krupp's at the beginning of the century, or Northrop in California today. A private company was more flexible and more discreet, and could be both protected and when necessary disowned. But there were indications nevertheless that the heyday of Dassault was now over. The old man himself was now eighty-four, and no successor could be so defiant. The cost of maintaining an independent aircraft industry was increasingly heavy, and for commercial projects Dassault was already looking for an American partner. And the French civil service was becoming more worried about the lack of control over its arms industry: in October 1976 a secret report from the finance ministry, partially leaked to the press, indicated concern at the wastefulness, bribes and dubious relationships surrounding the French arms industry and its sales abroad.[1]

THE RECKONING

Paris was the capital of the European arms-dealing world. Lebanese gun-runners as well as Middle Eastern governments looked to France when they wanted weapons in a hurry. Most arms sales depended on the discreet permissiveness of the French government towards free-booting salesmen, and it was never clear how much the government knew about, or endorsed, the shadier deals. In the penumbra of the trade, while the rewards were huge, the dangers remained; for with illicit arms, as with drugs or gambling, the only ultimate sanction was brute force. Already in 1973 one seedy Lebanese arms dealer, Antoine Kamouh, had mysteriously disappeared in Paris—it was thought

[1] *International Herald Tribune*, October 8, 1976.

in connection with his commission on British arms sales to Libya. Early in 1977 one of Khashoggi's aides, Samir Traboulsi, was accosted in the street and shot in the mouth: he survived, but not before he had been robbed. And on Christmas Eve of 1976 there had been the most spectacular revenge: the Prince de Broglie, one of the richest men in France, a deputy and former minister, was waylaid in broad daylight and shot dead. The truth about the Prince remained obscure; but it emerged that behind his august career, his château in Normandy, and his eminent ancestry, he had acquired an obsession with underworld transactions. He had a company in Liechtenstein called Sodatex which arranged, among other murky deals, illegal arms sales to Arab countries; and the encounter on the Paris pavement was apparently some kind of brutal reckoning.

Set against the big deals of the heavy arms industry, the *bagarres* of the Paris arms underworld read like cheap melodrama; but they underlined the point, that those who live by weapons may find that they blow up in their faces. The French, who more than any other nation had sought to exploit arms sales to their diplomatic and commercial advantage, were finding that the weapons, whether Dassault fighters or small arms, provided their own very rough justice.

18

A World at Arms

There must be a way of coming down the hill, of de-escalating. . . .
The only solution is not to give us more arms for our security, but
to give us more security so we can have less arms.

General Moshe Dayan, August 25, 1976

By the end of 1976 Tom Jones, reinstated as chairman of Northrop, was once again a hero of the industry, with the prospect of
still bigger profits from the Middle East. 'You don't worry about
that,' he said about the scandals, 'you get on with the job.'[1] In
December he addressed a group of Californian bankers in his
most statesmanlike style: 'The interests of a vast number of
countries are inextricably linked to the long-term interests of the
United States . . . And the need for those countries to defend
themselves without sending American troops is all too clear. It
is for those reasons that the government and the Congress
recognise the responsibility of the United States to allow certain
countries around the world to purchase from the United States
with their own funds adequate and appropriate defense systems.'[2]
He went on to explain that both political parties agreed about a
high defence budget, and 'the crisis management mentality is no
longer with us'. But defence companies must be properly run and
properly accountable (he continued with a clear dig at Lockheed);
and well-managed arms companies could now produce a return

[1] *Newsweek*, January 31, 1977.
[2] *Aviation Week*, January 3, 1977.

on equity higher than many other industries—like Northrop, which yielded fourteen percent the previous year.

Tom Jones was smoothly expounding the case that what was good for Northrop was good for the United States; the Nixon doctrine chimed perfectly with the interest of the arms sellers, and friendly nations must be permitted to buy what they want. Tom Jones' sentiments were echoed by the outspoken editor of *Aviation Week*, Robert Hotz, who welcomed the end of the boom-bust cycle over the last seventeen years, and the realisation that there must be fewer 'strangling regulatory legalisms'.[1] From California and Washington this hard-headed view looked very convincing. But how did it look at the receiving end of the weapons?

The State Department in Washington had at first insisted that the arming of Iran was a very special case of security needs, but Iran was setting a pace which her Arab neighbours were soon determined to follow. By far the richest potential arms customer was Saudi Arabia, across the Persian Gulf, and even before the oil-price increase the Saudis had been stepping up their orders with Northrop, Lockheed and others. The Saudis did not, like Iran, have a common frontier with Russia, and with their fierce anti-communism they were very unlikely to look to the Soviets to supply their arms; they would not even allow any known communist into their country. But arms spending gathers its own momentum: the Saudis wanted to keep up with Iran in quality, if not in quantity, and they were much richer. In the fiscal year 1976 the American arms sales to Saudi Arabia amounted to $2.5 billion, temporarily overtaking sales to Iran. Prince Sultan, the minister of defence, was the object of intense wooing by Western arms companies and governments. When Sultan visited London in November 1976 he was greeted by a guard of honour and the British minister of defence, Fred Mulley, while the British Aircraft Corporation and Rolls-Royce waited anxiously for a billion-dollar order.

Each batch of weapons generated the need for more. By 1976 the Saudis had already bought 110 Northrop Tigers, and they now wanted 2,000 Sidewinder missiles which could be fired from them, together with sixteen batteries of Raytheon Hawk missiles to provide an air defence system across the nation. The Israelis were now worried about these weapons' eventual destination, and

[1] Ibid., December 6, 1976.

the Arms Control and Disarmament Agency in Washington questioned whether the Saudis really needed a five-fold increase in missiles. But the Pentagon insisted that they were necessary in the event of a war with Iraq; and Congress eventually agreed on the deal. Soon afterwards the Saudis asked for 2,500 Maverick air-to-surface missiles, 1,000 laser-guided bombs and 1,800 wire-guided TOW missiles. The Senate protested, but Kissinger persuaded them to allow 650 missiles, in view of the United States' dependence on Saudi friendship.[1] The oil was still lubricating sales.

The arms companies offered contradictory justifications for their huge sales to Iranians or Arabs; first that they were essential to Western security, secondly that they were not really dangerous, because their customers could not effectively handle them. I spoke to one director of Northrop, Tom Barger, a respected former president of Aramco with wide experience of the Middle East, who explained: 'The Shah likes to be prickly, and then his neighbours decide they want to be prickly too. They don't really want to go to war. But the problem is, when you get a lot of playthings, how long is it before you want to try them out?'

As in Iran, the Saudi arms brought in their trail an auxiliary army of civilian technicians and engineers, demanding a closer American commitment. The Vinnell Corporation in California were hired to train the National Guard, serving much like mercenaries, but treated as normal commercial employees with a civilian contract. As General Fish explained to Congress in his immortal syntax: 'The accent is to try to fix as many as you can so that they don't have to come through the military.'[2] By far the biggest contractor was the United States Corps of Engineers, whose contracts in Saudi Arabia approached a billion dollars in 1976, going far beyond military projects.[3] The presence of so many American technicians was again justified in Washington as a safeguard of American interests, strengthening the Saudi-American relationship. But would the Saudis really continue to buy arms if they could not use them as they wished? While the Saudis were following the Iranians in their arms-buying spree, the tension between the two great oil-producers was mounting—particularly after the rift over the oil-price in December 1976. As the oil turned into arms, the stakes became more dangerous.

[1] *New York Times*, August 1, September 28-9, 1976.
[2] Testimony to House Committee on International Relations, March 20, 1975.
[3] *New York Times*, September 28, 1976.

Saudi money went far beyond the frontiers of the country, and the Saudis were becoming the paymasters of many poorer Arab states. In the Lebanon, as we have seen, the Saudis were paying both sides, thus escalating the destruction, and Beirut revealed all too clearly the growing mobility of arms. Jordan, with its common frontier with Israel, was promised by the Saudis in 1975 an air-defence system including Hawk missiles and Vulcan anti-aircraft guns, costing $350 million. Congress complained that they could be used against Israel, while the companies raised the total price to $800 million, to which the Saudis objected. King Hussein of Jordan then resorted to the customary ritual of a visit to Moscow. Washington duly registered deep concern at this communist danger, the Saudis agreed to pay $540 million, and the missiles were sold on condition that they were fixed so that they could not be moved up to the Israeli frontier.

No oil country could now be seen without modern arms. All down the Persian Gulf the rich sheikhdoms, with Iran facing them and Saudi Arabia surrounding them, were buying fighters, tanks and ships to catch up with their neighbours. The richest of them, Kuwait, was determined to balance its purchases, buying Skyhawk planes from America, Mirage F1s from France, and Chieftain tanks from Britain; but what kind of war they visualised was hard to discover. In Abu Dhabi in December 1976 the United Arab Emirates celebrated their fifth anniversary with a parade of Mirage fighters, missiles and armoured vehicles, while their ruler, Sheikh Zayed, pledged support for the Palestinian cause and called for Arab solidarity against 'the common danger' of Israel.

In Libya Colonel Gaddafi was having difficulty in buying the modern Western arms that he wanted, particularly after he had sent his Mirage fighters to Egypt in the 1973 Arab-Israeli war. In 1975 he made a huge deal for Soviet arms, thought to be worth over $500 million, including 2,000 tanks and two squadrons of MiG 23 jets. There was little sign of this developing into a serious Soviet-Libyan alliance, but the Russians were glad to have the foreign currency. The Libyans could hardly use all the weapons themselves, and the greater danger lay in Gaddafi re-exporting his arms.[1] He continued to get what he could from the West through devious sources and he became known to arms dealers as easy game for huge orders of doubtful value. After the 1973

[1] *Washington Post*, May 26, 1976.

war, when the Israelis had used a new American night-seeing device called Star-Tron, the Libyans ordered 3,000 Star-Trons from a Paris company which had obtained the licence. But the French forbade their export, so the company faked instruments instead at a fraction of the price, and dispatched them through the arms dealing company Atlantico in Madrid. The Libyans were warned, but a Libyan inspector authorised the deal, the money was paid and the inspector then disappeared.[1] It was a comic case of bribes taking control; provided the middlemen were paid, what did it matter if the weapons were not real?

On the front line between Arabs and Israelis the arms were again building up. Egypt, increasingly financed by the Saudis, was determined to keep pace and having ejected the Russians she turned again to the West. When Kissinger persuaded the Egyptians to disengage from Sinai in the summer of 1975 he promised to supply Cairo with arms, and the next year Washington agreed to sell six Lockheed Hercules transports—the first American military planes sold to Egypt. But the Americans preferred to let Europeans be the main sellers, to avoid annoying the Israelis, and the Egyptians went back to their old suppliers Britain and France with big orders for fighters, helicopters, missiles and hovercraft. By October 1976, at the annual parade of the Egyptian armed forces, President Sadat was able to inspect a turn-out of mixed weapons representing a kind of pageant of past Egyptian alliances, including old Stalin tanks and Tupolev bombers, SAM missiles, French Mirage jets, brand-new Anglo-French Gazelle helicopters, and British Swingfire guided missiles.

But the Israelis were buying still more sophisticated weapons, with the help of massive aid from Washington. Israeli arms purchases abroad had gone up from $574 million in 1972 to $1.6 billion in 1975, and the proportion of American assistance was up from twenty-eight percent to forty-two percent.[2] By December 1975 the Pentagon had agreed to sell twenty-five Eagle fighters (the McDonnell Douglas F15s) to Israel, the first foreign country to receive them. In the American election year the Israelis pressed for more weapons. Three weeks before he lost the election, President Ford agreed to sell Israel the controversial

---

[1] *Le Monde*, December 25, 1976.

[2] Statement by David Kochaw, Senior Economic Adviser, Israeli ministry of defence, 1976.

'concussion bombs': they could squirt out a film of inflammable liquid which then detonated, crushing bodies and tearing them apart. 'We think of this not as a weapon,' said the US army film describing it, 'but as a kill mechanism.'[1] By February 1977 President Carter, in his first bold arms-control move, had rescinded the decision and banned the bomb to all foreign nations.

The build-up caused concern even in Israel, lest it set off a race with the Arabs that the Israelis could not eventually win. General Dayan, the former war minister, while insisting that Israel must retain the nuclear option, argued that the escalation of arms could never provide real security. But in the short-term the Israelis felt themselves more secure, and therefore less inclined for a settlement. They were still ahead of the Arabs in arms technology, and much better equipped to handle it: they knew what they wanted, and their funds were less wasted by corruption and middlemen. Their advantages seemed greater as Syria was deflected by her intervention in Lebanon, as Egypt came closer to the United States and as the Soviet influence became weaker. But the piling-up of weapons in surrounding Arab nations was acquiring its own momentum, putting an extra strain on the American support that paid for much of the Israeli arsenal.

The oil money was thus causing a long chain-reaction. Iran was herself friendly to Israel, but was setting a new pace in arms-buying among her neighbours; and the oil-producing countries, led by Saudi Arabia, had almost unlimited funds, and growing diplomatic leverage with Washington to insist on more lethal weapons. Diplomats and arms-makers still argued that the Arabs could not really use the weapons, or present a serious threat to the Israelis. The arsenals in the desert could be seen as another solution to unemployment and over-production in the West: their rapid obsolescence and deterioration might keep Western workers happily employed for decades ahead. But even accepting the rash premise that they would not be used, the arms could easily lead to a war of economic attrition which Israel could not win. The Lebanese civil war, even if it offered some short-term security to Israel, provided a warning of how a local shooting-match could be blown up into a holocaust by the inrush of arms from all sides, with arms supplied to one country being transferred to another.

[1] *International Herald Tribune*, October 14, 1976.

THE COLONIALISM OF WEAPONS

The arms boom was not confined to the oil-producing nations, and the relaxing of controls had encouraged sales to countries that could ill afford to buy weapons. It seemed almost like a reversion to the nineteenth-century trade. In Europe two of the oldest rivals of all, Greece and Turkey, were providing new opportunities, as they had to Sir Basil Zaharoff when he had first begun to make his fortune by selling to both sides. Lockheed had been active in both countries, and in Greece they employed as their agent a retired air marshal, Constantine Exarhakos, who negotiated the sale of twelve Hercules transports.[1] The Greek Junta bought many American arms after 1967, with much corruption: after the Turks had invaded Cyprus in 1974 the Junta planned a counter-invasion, but when they came to unpack their military stores, crates of M16 rifles turned out to be filled with stones.[2] The guns were later believed to have been sold by army officers to Black Africa, and the military fiasco contributed to the Junta's collapse.

In Turkey, Lockheed were more deeply involved, paying commissions of $876,000 over a few years. In 1973 their agent in Ankara, Nezih M. Dural, asked for his fee to be increased to $5,000 a month, but Lockheed insisted that in future he must 'buy real influence, not just intelligence'.[3] Dural's great opportunity came after the Turks invaded Cyprus, when the United States imposed an embargo on arms to Turkey. It was circumvented with the secret approval of the state department, when Turkey bought two squadrons of Starfighters produced in Italy: for one squadron Dural received a commission of $240,000. Three years later he was arrested on charges of currency fraud.[4]

Turkey bought arms wherever she could, including Northrop Tigers, via Libya and Iran, and submarines and torpedo boats from West Germany; by 1976 the Turks were spending more than two billion dollars a year on defence, or more than thirty percent of their budget. Greece was receiving a mass of French arms, including 120 AMX tanks and forty Mirage F1s (negotiated

---

[1] See David Tonge in *The Guardian*, London, October 27, 1976. Ernest Hauser alleged in his diary that Lockheed paid half-a-million dollars to a Greek general during the regime of the Junta, but this was not corroborated by a Greek judicial report in October 1976.

[2] *Washington Post*, August 28, 1974.

[3] Multinational Hearings, part 14, pp. 384-7, 87-97.

[4] *The Times*, London, January 12, 1977.

by the shady Prince de Broglie). The Greeks also negotiated with their old friends Vickers, whom Zaharoff had represented, to buy an entire tank factory, to 'balance' another proposed tank factory to be built by the West Germans in Turkey.[1] It was the old game, with much bigger stakes.

But the most depressing arms race was between the countries of the Third World who could least afford it, who were buying weapons instead of food or welfare; among the developing countries without oil to sell, orders for American arms had gone up from $240 million in 1972 to $2.3 billion in 1976—a nearly tenfold increase.[2] Latin America was again a free-for-all for arms salesmen after Nixon had relaxed the embargo. Brazil was now arming herself more heavily, not only against insurgents, but against neighbours, and Boeing, Lockheed, Hughes and Bell Helicopters were all profiting. The Peru-Chile rivalry was again hotting up: after Peru had been refused Tiger fighters, she accepted an offer of thirty-six Soviet fighters on much more favourable terms, and Washington felt unable to make any serious protest to Moscow in view of the extent of other American arms sales close to the Soviet frontiers, particularly in Iran.[3] Thus the Middle East build-up helped to justify the build-up elsewhere.

Black Africa was also presenting a promising new sales territory. Nigeria, with big oil exports, was becoming an important new buyer, and in East Africa the infection was spreading. Uganda, under the mad dictatorship of Idi Amin, was the protégé of Gaddafi in Libya, and after the Israeli raid on Entebbe Libya agreed to lend Uganda twenty Mirage fighters. But Amin could also obtain some supplies from Britain, including special counter-insurgency equipment flown out in September 1976 with devices for tracing secret radio transmissions.[4] Kenya in turn was worried by Uganda on one side, and by Russian arms in Somalia on the other, and in June 1976 she turned to America for arms, buying ten Northrop Tigers; while Zaire and Ethiopia, both impoverished countries, followed the arms-buying spree. American sales to Black Africa—nearly all to Zaire, Kenya and Ethiopia—went up by eight hundred percent in one year. The chart on the following pages shows the extent of the increase in American arms sales

[1] See David Tonge in *The Observer*, October 12, 1976.
[2] See Emma Rothschild in *New York Review of Books*, January 20, 1977.
[3] See Juan de Dris in the *New York Times*, October 14, 1976.
[4] *The Guardian*, London, September 27, 1976.

US FOREIGN MILITARY SALES AGREEMENTS 1970-6
(Value in Thousands of Dollars)

	FY 1970	FY 1971	FY 1972	FY 1973	FY 1974	FY 1975	FY 1976
Worldwide	945,547	1,568,802	3,297,421	5,772,189	10,562,412	9,862,811	8,368,527
Argentina	10,827	12,496	15,056	16,445	8,421	15,689	12,093
Australia	53,784	57,884	117,210	25,948	31,759	166,697	411,854
Austria	1,324	3,739	2,398	2,453	4,456	7,587	8,781
Bahrain	—	—	—	—	—	18	—
Belgium	4,345	2,993	4,514	6,167	11,082	738,077	6,522
Bolivia	—	44	5	37	122	795	1,134
Brazil	2,458	17,845	32,575	14,962	71,288	27,090	10,610
Burma	7	86	268	223	118	21	82
Canada	52,167	28,617	37,248	90,353	106,985	96,839	65,752
Chile	7,523	2,898	6,252	14,977	76,001	49,324	12
China (Taiwan)	35,118	65,043	75,419	202,439	87,846	144,385	193,012
Colombia	158	2,168	5,397	1,247	1,083	992	1,370
Costa Rica	—	—	34	—	—	237	*
Denmark	6,596	15,928	13,381	10,964	21,325	367,783	23,602
Dominican Republic	—	31	16	82	31	2	39
Ecuador	20	315	4	—	—	14,960	2,099
Egypt	—	—	—	—	—	—	67,271
El Salvador	—	11	*	52	388	418	728
Ethiopia	6	—	10	—	7,426	22,100	118,840
Fiji	—	—	—	—	—	—	160
Finland	—	1	63	—	12	1	1
France	3,402	5,979	7,455	8,543	22,504	6,131	4,429
Gabon	—	—	—	—	—	211	—
Germany	245,022	176,908	875,751	220,285	231,436	299,682	194,221
Ghana	51	*	—	—	187	16	1
Greece	29,171	24,535	180,176	56,825	458,121	214,595	82,981
Guatemala	464	7,586	2,057	3,359	854	909	3,621
Haiti	—	—	—	—	291	84	441
Honduras	—	—	27	5,269	681	291	732
Iceland	—	*	436	46	—	—	—
India	2,094	856	46	*	2,617	8,142	3,266
Indonesia	*	18	*	148	148	48,955	3,101
Iran	113,081	397,563	522,128	2,138,143	4,280,652	2,570,296	1,301,287
Ireland	*	12	228	197	16	21	32
Israel	44,416	413,518	409,871	196,102	2,468,340	863,061	919,478
Italy	36,142	23,441	76,569	64,421	47,847	44,885	24,680
Jamaica	8	9	3	7	42	74	6
Japan	21,222	10,607	42,223	51,459	58,749	29,353	34,642
Jordan	28,826	16,282	18,863	6,096	61,538	80,923	434,145
Korea	—	393	8,764	1,592	98,840	228,932	625,877
Kuwait	—	—	*	53	29,001	377,812	130,617
Lebanon	1,177	187	194	5,210	9,747	295	315
Liberia	—	—	—	1,315	370	449	145

US FOREIGN MILITARY SALES AGREEMENTS 1970-6. *Continued*
(Value in Thousands of Dollars)

	FY 1970	FY 1971	FY 1972	FY 1973	FY 1974	FY 1975	FY 1976
Libya	5,282	632	2,672	130	12	—	—
Luxembourg	101	85	11	638	21	25	—
Malaysia	1,837	98	40,473	1,457	1,414	4,363	2,940
Mali	5	—	48	—	—	176	—
Mexico	12	437	175	693	411	153	2,053
Morocco	2,439	2,272	7,527	2,441	8,355	299,888	120,820
Nepal	—	11	—	60	2	—	—
Netherlands	7,465	7,038	29,214	35,522	18,986	638,904	19,639
New Zealand	5,294	7,293	3,290	3,279	5,401	4,409	6,004
Nicaragua	82	674	63	134	388	607	518
Niger	—	—	—	—	8	—	—
Nigeria	—	—	2,409	696	4,403	2,771	1,803
Norway	9,652	25,522	21,173	13,297	51,285	458,953	34,868
Oman	—	—	—	—	—	1,613	229
Pakistan	4,423	22,490	5	18,652	11,203	37,368	38,620
Panama	14	9	6	1,615	1,867	258	1,266
Paraguay	*	—	—	26	12	37	—
Peru	2,153	1,479	882	24,816	43,332	27,279	24,024
Philippines	843	1,107	468	1,159	4,889	31,809	28,371
Portugal	1,055	1,011	2,565	382	1,677	2,263	1,705
Saudi Arabia	44,854	14,980	459,347	1,993,537	1,906,499	1,549,944	2,502,454
Senegal	—	—	4	—	—	—	—
Singapore	2,472	1,958	5,504	7,638	12,748	1,422	5,093
South Africa	1			1	2	1	—
Spain	25,872	108,452	22,742	60,774	151,735	57,652	79,357
Sri Lanka	—	—	*	—	—	—	—
Sweden	265	885	1,496	2,012	6,972	782	24,356
Switzerland	4,435	450	11,252	2,412	8,634	49,512	454,735
Thailand	21,146	48	16,978	1,907	20,603	14,768	89,608
Trinidad/Tobago	85	—	—	—	—	—	—
Tunisia	—	—	—	2,137	737	382	1,673
Turkey	2,590	1,141	5,099	212,740	19,056	78,461	—
United Kingdom	63,749	45,560	124,511	109,496	53,150	31,999	46,532
Uruguay	241	1,631	1,588	1,493	1,207	8,258	1,997
Venezuela	738	1,636	43,047	25,341	4,838	45,557	6,920
Vietnam	—	—	2	1,155	4	—	—
Yemen	—	—	—	—	2,634	372	138,479
Yugoslavia	41	2	104	1,218	6	262	631
Zaire	54	16,111	286	700	1,383	1,723	8,781
International Organisations	38,928	17,717	39,839	99,218	18,215	32,711	35,071

The lists of figures are the value of foreign military sales agreements by fiscal year. Annual totals are adjusted for amendments, price increases, cancellation of orders or other changes as of the year the case was originally recorded.

NOTE: Totals may not add due to rounding.

Source: Defence Security Assistance Agency, September 1976.

across the world over six years: but no comparable figures are available for Britain and France.

It was tragic (commented Senator Dick Clark) that while both Kenya and Zaire were desperately short of food, their governments were nevertheless increasingly preoccupied with buying arms.[1] The weapons to the Third World were forging their own kind of colonialism, exploiting the poorer countries without the need of foreign armies or empires. While appearing to fortify sovereignty, they were creating new patterns of dependence: and some new nations were coming to realise it. In the past most developing countries have complained, when the major powers have tried to restrict arms sales, that this was a plot to keep them weak and defenceless, as the pawns of the superpowers. But by the autumn of 1976 there were some signs of a new mood at the United Nations. In the general debate, several nations protested about the exploitation through arms sales. Ambassador Dumas from Trinidad complained that the flow of arms was subsidising the industrial countries. The Philippine foreign minister, Carlos Romulo, described how the major powers were competing as arms salesmen. The foreign minister of Singapore (itself a heavy arms buyer), Sinathamdy Rajaratnam, complained with special animosity: 'The massive flow of arms to the Third World confronts it with a new danger. It is, first of all, a drain on their economies; but even more important is the fact that it creates a new form of dependence on the Great Powers.'[2] A subsequent resolution by Japan, to institute a study of arms sales, was frustrated by India and other nations which did not wish their arms buying investigated. But the Third World were at least becoming more aware of the real cost of the arms race.

THE SORCERERS' APPRENTICES

The arms buyers wanted not only the most sophisticated weapons, but a guarantee of their future supply. The producing governments had always tried to reserve control over future shipments, so that they could exercise 'spare parts diplomacy' in the event of a war. But the earlier embargoes, such as America's against Pakistan, or France's against Israel, had made the buyers all the more determined to preserve their independence of action.

[1] *Washington Post*, September 13, 1976.
[2] See *New York Times*, October 5, 1976, and United Nations debate.

Their ultimate ambition was to make their own weapons and for this they offered the most tempting contracts to Western companies. Over the previous century only a handful of major industrial countries had been able to make advanced warships, fighters or tanks: first Britain, Germany and France; then the United States and Russia, with a few countries like Czechoslovakia and Belgium exporting specialised weapons. The smallness of this exporters' club offered some hope of eventual control. But the more ambitious nations were determined to obtain the secrets and the resources, and arms companies began to export their technology as well as their weapons—thus ultimately threatening their own future.

The major Middle Eastern buyers all wanted their own arms factories. Iran made agreements with several companies, including Vickers and Northrop, to assemble planes and tanks as a half-way house towards full production. Egypt negotiated with Britain and France for arms factories. But Israel was forging much further ahead than any nation with her own dynamic arms industry, to make her self-sufficient in weapons. After 1967 the Israelis, having first been helped by Dassault, designed their own modification of the Mirage called the Kfir, or 'young lion', and within seven years they were offering Kfirs for export: Israeli Aircraft Industries (IAI) were by 1976 one of the country's biggest companies, employing 18,000 skilled workers. In Israel they refused to discuss their exports with me, but in June 1976 a special Israeli supplement appeared in *Aviation Week*, offering a wide range of arms for sale, including the Shafrir air-to-air missile (with 'extensive battle experience with overall kill ratio of about sixty percent'), bombs, rockets, submachine-guns, anti-tank guns and assault rifles. The Kfir fighter was available, equipped with General Electric engines, at a very competitive price ($4 million). By 1977 Israeli arms sales were expected by the Pentagon experts to reach a billion dollars a year—coming close to the total arms exports of Britain or France.[1]

The Western arms companies were now becoming uneasy about this aggressive new rival, but the arms control experts were more disturbed. For the Israelis had a much more powerful incentive to sell arms than Britain and France: they desperately needed exports to subsidise their domestic industry, and they were prepared to sell to countries like South Africa or Chile which

[1] *Aviation Week*, December 13, 1976.

came under Western embargoes. By late 1976 Pentagon officials were becoming seriously worried that the Israelis could acquire American technology and then quickly re-export it to other nations, circumventing the restrictions imposed by Congress;[1] while Israel's industry was a challenge to other Middle Eastern countries to imitate them. The sorcerers' apprentices were taking over from the sorcerers.

In the meantime a more terrifying risk was emerging in the export of nuclear reactors, where peaceful and warlike intentions were interlocked. The complex nuclear problems are beyond the scope of this book, but they cannot be altogether separated from conventional arms. The secrets of making nuclear power stations, like making advanced weapons, at first belonged to only a few Western nations, who might thus have reached some agreement, but the industrialists played down the warnings that reactors could provide the means to explode nuclear bombs. It was the Canadians' building of a research reactor for India which first showed how easily peaceful uses could be turned to war, when in May 1974 the Indians, using plutonium made by the reactor, exploded their first nuclear bomb in the Rajasthan desert.

The Western companies, frustrated by their lack of home orders, were still determined to export nuclear reactors. West Germany made an unprecedented deal with Brazil, to supply eight nuclear reactors, an enrichment plant and a processing plant. The United States agreed to supply both Israel and Egypt with nuclear power stations. France signed contracts with South Africa, Iran, South Korea and Libya. Canada sold reactors to South Korea and Argentina, and the Canadian state corporation (it emerged in November 1976) had handed out 'expenses' of ten million dollars in connection with these nuclear sales, part of them paid into bank accounts in Switzerland and Liechtenstein.[2] There were clearly prospects for bribery in boosting nuclear sales.

The Middle East was again the most dangerous laboratory. The Israelis were already thought to have their own nuclear bombs, and both the Iranians and the Egyptians were likely to acquire the means to make them in the next decade. Some experts believed that a nuclear balance, like the balance in Europe, could achieve a safe peace; that, as Nobel or Armstrong had forecast, war would

[1] Ibid.
[2] *The Times*, London, November 30, 1976.

at last become so terrible that ultimate peace must follow. But there had been little sign from the superpowers' behaviour in the rest of the world—in Korea, Vietnam or Cambodia—that the possession of nuclear weapons on both sides would diminish the scale of conventional wars. And the very attempts to prevent nuclear proliferation could well boost conventional arms; for often the easiest way to persuade a country to abandon a nuclear project was to bargain with conventional arms sales, or to promise to increase them. Thus Kissinger threatened to cut off South Korea's credit arms sales and promised attack bombers to Pakistan in return for abandoning their nuclear plans. But this bargaining opens up opportunities for blackmail; for countries can threaten to buy nuclear plants, to get permission for more arms; and the greater danger is only averted by spreading the lesser.[1]

THE JAPANESE ALLERGY

In January 1977 the British ministry of defence was arranging to send a 16,000-ton support ship, the *Lyness*, on a cruise through East Asia, equipped as a floating exhibition of missiles, guns and other weapons—a favourite device of the Defence Sales Organisation to boost exports. The climax of the voyage of the *Lyness* was to be a visit to Tokyo harbour, to advertise its weapons. But the mayor of Tokyo, a prominent socialist and pacifist, was outraged. The application was leaked to the press, the mayor refused to allow the ship in the port, and diplomats explained that to receive it was contrary to Japanese principles about arms sales. The British embassy expressed their disappointment, and the *Lyness* set sail for Malaysia, the Philippines and Thailand, where weapons were more obviously welcome, without stopping in Japan. It was a long way from the days when British shipyards built the Japanese navy, or when the Japanese themselves, in the 'thirties, built the world's third biggest navy.

But it was an outcome that might have been predicted, for the Japanese opposition to arms sales is well known, and among industrial nations Japan is a unique case. The post-war constitution lays down that 'the Japanese people forever renounce war as a sovereign right of the nation and the threat or use of force as a means of settling international disputes'; and while first imposed by the Allies, the renunciation has been accepted by most Japanese

[1] Leslie Gelb: 'Arms Sales' in *Foreign Policy* magazine, Winter 1976-7.

people and politicians ever since. The chief cause of this special allergy, as the Japanese call it, is not difficult to detect: the Japanese alone have been the victims of a nuclear war.

Thirty-two years after the dropping of the first atom bomb, the thriving city of Hiroshima shows no obvious scars: it is newer and cleaner, with wider streets than other cities. Only one ruin remains from the era before 1945—the shell of the old industrial exhibition hall, with its gutted dome of bare girders silhouetted in front of the bright shops and shiny offices. The Peace Park, below where the bomb exploded, looks like any other municipal park, except for a simple mound which covers a mass grave. In the Atomic Museum, an austere low building on stilts, the exhibits speak for themselves. A circular model shows the whole city just after the raid, flattened except for a few empty shells. A waxwork scene depicts burnt children running from the flames; the showcases contain girders, pediments and safes blown apart by the blast, and photographs of the hairless, deformed children who escaped the flames. The commentary is quiet and dead-pan, assigning no blame, except to the evils of war. Half the population of Japan now has no personal memory of the day the bomb dropped; but every child is brought up on the facts of the fearful legend—the black rain of death, the maimed bodies in the river. Coming out of this memorial, it is not difficult to believe that the Japanese have an allergy to war.

Hiroshima, once a great military base and builder of warships, is now much more prosperous as the Mazda company town, exporting cars round the world. The continuing Japanese economic miracle, without recourse to armaments, has apparently disproved the old belief that capitalist nations need war production to maintain their economies. While California or north-east England remained dependent on arms spending, the cars and transistors of Toyota or Sony provided a more spectacular expansion, and Japanese electronics could develop without a major aerospace industry. The Pentagon's favourite theory, that defence spending produced a spin-off which was invaluable to the consumer, looked much less convincing to the Japanese as they became less dependent on foreign technology and licences.

It was true that the Japanese economy had been boosted by other people's wars: first the Korean war and then the Vietnam war brought huge infusions of American money. Like Germany, Japan could feel secure under the American nuclear umbrella;

but unlike Germany, Japan was not up against the front line of the cold war. In their position of offshore security, and with their new horror of war, the Japanese dynamism and military discipline could be sublimated into brilliant commercial organisation. It was an escape from death-dealing that would have made Andrew Undershaft despair.

But after the oil shock of 1973 and the boom in arms sales the Japanese felt less confident of their trading future. They were soon able to balance the huge extra costs of their oil with a new export drive to the West; the Mitsui shipyards, hit by the shipping slump, turned to building pre-fabricated houses for Iran. But could Japan hold her own with the Middle East oil producers without exporting arms? I put the question to the new Japanese prime minister, Takeo Fukuda, in February 1977, just after he had succeeded Miki. He replied that the economy was quite sound without a defence industry, and that the Japanese were still firmly opposed to the export of arms, which could always lead to future military action. But Japan's trading relations with the Middle East countries were very difficult, with a deficit of $10 billion. 'To resolve this imbalance some nations have resorted to the export of arms, but we in Japan are trying to export industrial plants and the facilities for construction developments.'[1] To many Japanese it was ironic that while the West justified their arms sales as a valuable recycling of petrodollars, Japan's peaceful exports of cars or cassettes were regarded as a threat to the Western economies: 'If we had joined the arms race in the Middle East,' one Japanese diplomat remarked to me, 'no one would have complained.'

But the arms race was still more worrying to the Japanese in the Far East itself, where the Nixon doctrine had originated. The fall of Saigon and the impending American withdrawal from South Korea had caused a rush of buying: Singapore, the Philippines, Malaysia and Thailand—spurred on by her new military rulers—were all asking for bigger arsenals, usually beginning with Northrop Tigers: and all except the Philippines were paying for them.[2] South Korea aimed to be self-sufficient in arms, which was doubly disturbing for the Japanese; for to subsidise their arms industry the Koreans would want to export. The Japanese heavy

[1] Interview with prime minister; see *Japan Times*, February 3, 1977.
[2] *Japan Times*, January 29, 1977.

industries, including Mitsubishi and Mitsui, were constantly pressing to build warships, large aircraft or military electronics, and already the distinction was fine, between exporting heavy trucks and sea-rescue ships, or military vehicles and patrol boats. Aerospace was specially tempting to the Japanese, as for Britain and France, as a means to deploy their skills to pay for raw materials; they resented having to import all their commercial airliners from America (the extortion of bribes may have been partly an index of that resentment—a kind of extra tax on foreigners): but no thriving aerospace industry could be built without a defence base. The most alarming future scenario would show the Japanese finally being impelled to join in the arms sales race, becoming the most formidable of all the sorcerers' apprentices. The Chinese mainland once again, as fifty years earlier, would be a stamping-ground for arms salesmen.

But for the present, the Japanese allergy remains a powerful inhibition, which might be expected to give Japan a unique authority and opportunity to take a lead in arms control: she alone is in a moral position to ask others to refrain, and her commercial interest is to restrict a trade from which she cannot benefit. Japan in the past has been very diffident about her diplomatic initiatives, with the traditional inwardness and insulation of her culture, the demoralisation of wartime defeat, and the extreme sense of dependence on America. 'Never in modern history,' Frank Gibney has written, 'has a country with such wealth and breadth of relationships, a major power by any consideration, projected such a squeaky international voice.'[1] But by late 1976 Japan showed signs of being more actively concerned with arms control; she became more outspoken at the United Nations, supporting the speeches from the Third World leaders, and in December the Japanese ambassador Motoo Ogiso urged the necessity 'of not waiting for agreement on nuclear disarmament, before tackling the enormous leviathan of armaments which is casting dark shadows on the world'.

In the global arms contest each nation has its own justifications and recriminations against others, and to allocate blame is not simple or helpful: the fact that the Europeans and Japanese in different ways depend for their defence on America complicates any neat equation. Every country can point to the Soviet Union waiting to move in if they withdraw. The American companies

[1] Frank Gibney: *Japan, the Fragile Superpower*, Tokyo, Charles E. Tuttle, 1975, p. 323.

blame the French for their unprincipled salesmanship; France blames the Americans for the commercial domination of Europe, while Britain resents the French and American invasion of their traditional markets. Germany and Japan observe the hypocrisy of the other powers who expect them to renounce the trade they are so avidly pursuing; and the countries of the Third World, listening to the chorus of humbug, complain about being exploited but buy whatever they can.

Whatever initiative Japan or others may take, the only effective agreements must be led by the two superpowers, and originated by the United States, which is responsible for half the world's arms trade. Of course the Soviet Union is essential to any lasting agreement; but the current build-up of Western arms sales has not primarily been in response to a Soviet threat, and the Russians have themselves shown some signs of unease about the escalating arms race from which (as in Egypt or Lebanon) they have derived little diplomatic benefit. Some Russians are openly admitting that they, like the Americans, face the problem of controlling their own military: 'Unless the military-industrial beast is tamed,' said a member of their UN delegation, Stanislav Menshikov, in August 1976, 'the reduction of armaments and military spending will remain a utopia.'[1]

For the past century it has always been Europe, with its desperate dependence on exports, which has led the arms sales race. But in the past three years the United States has become far more reliant on selling weapons abroad. Compared to this great American sales machine, backed by more advanced and organised technology, the European efforts look increasingly puny, and whatever the cynicism and misdeeds of the Europeans, the first moves towards effective restraint can only come from America.

[1] Interview on BBC Radio 3, May 7, 1976.

19

The Challenge

What makes the arms race a global folly is that all countries are now
buying greater and greater insecurity at higher and higher costs.
                                                    Alva Myrdal, 1976[1]

THE most popular of all the magnificent museums of Washington
is now the National Air and Space Museum which was opened
in Bicentennial Year. Behind its austere stone walls along the
Mall is a single vast hall with planes hanging in a great slice of
sky, from the Spirit of St Louis to the Lockheed Starfighter and
the Northrop Tiger. Schoolchildren, grannies and tourists stream
up and down the escalators, gaping from all angles at this pageant
of frozen aerobatics. From the floor to the ceiling the great
missiles, the Minutemen and Vikings, rise up as the totems of the
space age. At one end the great metal spider of a space module
stands with the Capitol framed in the window behind it; and in
pride of place hangs the Apollo linked to the Soyuz, looking
unmistakably Russian with its green onion shape. The whole
scene suggests ecstatic liberation from the forces of gravity or
enclosure, the spirit of American inventiveness facing the challenge of space. It would be churlish to complain that most of the
objects are dedicated to destruction.

The aerospace industry has always had an influence beyond its
size, as the spearhead of industrial development, the vanguard on

---

[1] Alva Myrdal: *The Game of Disarmament*, New York, Pantheon Books, 1976, p. 7.

the road to the future. From their beginnings the aerospace companies had a special panache. The heroic pioneers like Lockheed or Northrop gave way to teams and bureaucracies, but the thrust still remained; with all the ups and downs of the industry, there have always been new worlds to conquer, and new records to break.

But in the past five years, since the establishment of wide-bodied jets and the costly fiasco of the Concorde, the civil aircraft industry has faced a much less promising future. The pace of inventiveness which constantly produced bigger, faster and cheaper planes, and which brought continents within hours of each other, has settled down: so that many experts assume that air travel in thirty years' time, though perhaps quieter, safer and cheaper, may not be very different from what it is now. The great adventure of landing on the moon has now passed into history, and Man is forced back to the problems of earth. So it is perhaps appropriate that the aerospace industry should now be so splendidly celebrated in a museum: for it is in the nature of museums that they commemorate arts and sciences which are past their greatest days.

The precedent of the railroads a century ago is still relevant, if ominous. The great railroad companies were in the forefront of all industry, opening up the continents and speeding up all communications, bringing other technologies in their track. But the companies soon cut each other's throats in their ferocious competition, the construction boom collapsed as the networks covered the industrial nations, and the passengers settled down to a comfortable acceptance of reasonable speed and safety. With the end of the railroad boom the steelmasters like Krupp, Vickers and Carnegie, who had built up whole cities in Essen, Sheffield and Pittsburgh, looked elsewhere to fill their order books; and they looked to the industry which was most profitable and which was also in the vanguard of invention—to arms.

The end of the American aerospace boom has also coincided with the huge expansion of arms sales abroad, prompted by the withdrawal of American and British forces, the flow of oil money into the Middle East and the recession in the West. It is a tragedy of history that these fundamental changes should have come at a time when statesmanship in Washington was at its weakest. Both Americans and Europeans were content to take the most cynical and dangerous solution: to sell arms in the wake of their withdrawal, and to pay for their oil with the new arms sales, with little attempt to restrict them. While commercial aerospace had passed its peak of innovation, military aerospace was offering thrilling opportunities for development, including cruise missiles, laser bombers and electronic battlefields.

The arms trade has always had its own imperatives, and the gospel of all arms dealers must be, like Andrew Undershaft's, to sell arms to anyone who will buy them. The extension of un-controlled free trade, then and now, puts a premium on arms as the most liberated trade of all; for it remains the unique characteristic of the arms traffic that it can expand its market rapidly and almost indefinitely by playing one side against the other—Saudis against Iranians, Israelis against Egyptians, Greeks against Turks. With this special scope, it is no accident that the arms dealers, from Zaharoff to Kodama to Khashoggi to Prince Bernhard, have always had similar traits, thriving on the tradi-tional secrecy and bribery, cultivating the reputations of Men of Mystery; and it is not surprising that so many of the companies' agents are former intelligence agents. Their trade is always a kind of espionage and subterranean warfare, calling for subter-fuge, high-level contacts and Swiss bank accounts.

The consequences of unleashing these forces without effective controls have, I hope, emerged in chapters of this book. It took some time for the full extent of the arms sales, and the loss of control, to become clear to the West: but gradually, through hearings, protests and scandals, the story began to unfold. Two years after the oil crisis the supply of arms had become—at least in the United States—a political issue; and by the time of the inauguration of President Carter there was a much wider aware-ness that the export of arms had got out of hand.

ENTER CARTER

Carter's administration moved into Washington with hopeful credentials. Carter himself had made an issue of limiting arms sales, insisting that America must be the world's granary rather than its armourer. Vice-President Mondale had protested that 'America is no longer an arsenal of democracy; it is quite simply an arsenal'. And just after the election a trenchant report on the conventional arms race was published in New York by the United Nations Association, produced by a panel whose chairman was

Thornton Bradshaw of Atlantic Richfield and whose vice-chairman was Cyrus Vance, now secretary of state. They maintained that arms exports had been of very doubtful advantage in achieving political influence in the Third World, and were bound to increase the insecurity between rival nations, that their economic benefits at home were very questionable, and that dependence on export markets could be detrimental to America's own defence interests. The panel recommended that the economic motives for arms sales must be subordinated to foreign policy and national security, and that America should unilaterally restrict sales to the Third World.[1]

A more emphatic commitment to a new policy came with the appointment of Paul Warnke to be director of the Arms Control and Disarmament Agency, and also chief SALT negotiator with the Russians. Warnke had been influential on the UNA panel, and in talks with me before his nomination he made no secret of his radical views. He is a soft-voiced lawyer with a teddy-bear face, and he expounds the case for arms control with a clarity and wit which make it sound almost too easy; but he has had a testing experience of the realities of politics. In the Pentagon from 1966 to 1969 he had played a crucial role in pressing for extrication from Vietnam: he had seen the power of the military-industrial complex but refused to be awed by it.

Warnke was appalled by the loss of control over arms sales, and increasingly sceptical of the foreign policy advantages. Selling arms to both sides, he insisted, gave no effective control; and America should not give in to blackmail from countries who threatened to buy arms from the Russians. The Nixon doctrine was fundamentally dangerous: where the United States did not supply forces abroad she should not supply arms. The boom in arms sales had created a new constituency in America, which was now becoming harder to control. But Warnke insisted that the Federal government has the power to restrict the industry, provided it has the will; and it must face the task of converting industries: 'it is never impossible to say No.' The essential goal for Warnke was to reverse the existing assumptions about arms sales: they must be regarded as unnecessary and undesirable, unless proved otherwise; and only when there was a clear advantage to American national security should they be allowed.

[1] UNA-USA National Policy Panel on Conventional Arms Control: *Controlling the Conventional Arms Race*, New York, 1976.

The United States must take the first steps, both in controlling arms sales and in limiting the central arms race with Russia; if America insists on obvious superiority against the Soviets she will only keep up the race 'like apes on a treadmill'.

With these views it was hardly surprising that Warnke's nomination should be vigorously opposed; the arms control directorship had previously not been a very influential post, but Warnke's prestige and outspokenness would give it an independent public voice. He was at first vigorously criticised by such senators as 'Scoop' Jackson, 'the senator for Boeing', and Sam Nunn, the senator for the Lockheed stronghold of Georgia; and by more formidable intellects such as Paul Nitze, his former colleague at the Pentagon, who was leading a lobby for a bigger defence budget. But Carter stood firm on Warnke's appointment, which he insisted was crucial for his administration. Eventually in March 1977 he was confirmed by the Senate.

The administration thus had an unambiguous commitment to control arms sales; but the political battle would be long and arduous, for it involved confronting one of the most powerful of all industrial lobbies. And the problem of arms sales was interlocked with the central problem of the nation's own defence.

For the past century the European powers have encouraged their companies to export in order to help maintain their own industry in peacetime. Since Krupp and Armstrong first began to arm the world, European governments have argued that only by exporting weapons can they develop their own technology, and thus retain their own potential for war: and this argument re-echoes through this book, whether from Armstrong's agent Lord Rendel in 1866, from the Kaiser's war minister in 1913, from Bernard Baruch in 1935, or from European defence salesmen in the 1970s. Since the Second World War it has been the central confrontation of the superpowers and the nuclear balance which has been the preoccupation of Washington, and conventional arms sales have made up only a small fraction of total arms production. But in the past few years, in the course of the oil crisis and the arms boom, American companies like Grumman and Lockheed have come to depend much more heavily on sales abroad for their survival, and nearly every arms company has found its proportion of exports rising. The United States has thus found itself coming closer to the traditional situation of Britain and France: to afford to arm themselves they must arm the world.

But this dependence does not lead to any simple argument between hawks and doves: it does not follow that anyone who supports a strong defence posture towards the Soviet Union must therefore be in favour of maintaining extensive arms sales. For once a nation finds itself exporting its most up-to-date weapons, even if it stops short of selling them to the enemy, it is in danger of undermining its own security: the threat of war is just as likely to come from the outlying danger areas, particularly in the Middle East, as from the central frontier of the superpowers. Some of the most forceful opposition to sophisticated arms sales has come, not from Congress or the State Department, but from the Pentagon officials who saw their most advanced weapons being sold to the Middle East, producing new commitments and new dangers.

The control of arms sales is always complicated by the close and individual relations between states. Thus Leslie Gelb, writing shortly before joining the State Department, explained that 'sales are so intertwined with other matters that they have to be treated on a country-by-country basis with decisions based on pragmatic trade-offs'.[1] The arguments of diplomats cannot be ignored: the problem of maintaining a balance in the Middle East, and ensuring Western influence among the oil-producers, would call for the supply of some weapons even if there were no pressure at all from the industry. But the most recent explosion of arms sales cannot—as many Pentagon officials privately admit—be ascribed to any rational calculation of America's own security interest, let alone Europe's. It can only be explained by a succession of *ad hoc* decisions, including Nixon's visit to the Shah and Kissinger's bargains, and by the overwhelming pressure from the arms industry.

The companies have always had a powerful influence over the Pentagon, as the Northrop documents show. But now they have frequently succeeded in forging their own direct connections with foreign powers: Grumman or Northrop have established their own alliances with Iran or Saudi Arabia, making it much harder for the Pentagon to control them, if they wish to. The foreign policy of the arms companies has acquired its own momentum. The first object of control, as Warnke insists, must be to prevent weapons being sold unless they are strictly necessary: but this reform can only be achieved through a drastic reform of the government's relationship with the companies.

It can never be safely assumed that the company's interest is the

[1] *Foreign Policy* magazine, Winter, 1976-7.

same as the nation's, and the salesmen's morality is always suspended. So long as the hucksters are competing abroad there can be no prospect of a sane policy, as some will even admit: 'You can't expect *us* to control ourselves,' one company executive told me: 'It's only the governments that can prevent the world becoming an International Dodge City.' One disillusioned former arms salesman put the problem to me in more positive terms: 'The merchants of death are no different in their methods from salesmen of washing machines: they don't moralise, they just sell their machines, with whatever methods they can. If the Pentagon wants to control arms sales, it must prevent the competition of arms salesmen abroad. When a foreign country applies for a weapon, the decision should be made by the Pentagon, after a competition inside the United States—in the same way as they choose their own weapons. In that way they would avoid the corruption and funny business in foreign capitals—and they would prevent a lot of broken marriages, drunkenness and breakdowns among the salesmen.'

But even with such a restriction, the companies' pressures cannot, I believe, be neutralised so long as they remain subject to the incentives of private enterprise; and the connection between arms sales and profits will always distort foreign policy. The competition between American companies, spurred on by the Pentagon, may well have provided a more dynamic and inventive arms industry at home—even though at an extravagant price, with cost-overruns, bail-outs, and wasteful rivalries between companies and services. But the profit motive once unleashed abroad has far wider and more dangerous implications: the huge stakes involved in a deal, with the web of agents, commissions and bribes, can distort a whole nation's economy, all in the name of private shareholders. The Pentagon has continually abdicated its responsibilities to control the companies, whether through MAAGs abroad or through the DSAA in Washington; and it is difficult to be confident of the Pentagon's future abilities without restraining this great head of steam at its source.

The case for nationalising arms companies has always been separate from the general case for nationalisation: ever since the First World War the association of weapons with private profits has been repugnant to many people not otherwise concerned with the ownership of industry. The issue has been more muffled since the governments, whether in Washington, London or Paris, have taken over the responsibility for arms sales, for they have removed the moral problems from the companies and shrouded their operations in secrecy. But both Britain and France now appear to be moving towards nationalising their major arms companies; in France Dassault's private empire has come under heavy political fire, and in Britain the aircraft and shipbuilding companies are due for nationalisation under the Labour government's policy. In the United States the contortions of the Pentagon and Congress towards Lockheed, providing guarantees and bail-outs, show how far American governments will go to avoid nationalisation; but the price of these 'Pentagon games' is the avoidance of ultimate responsibility.

Nationalisation in itself will not provide the solution to arms sales; for, as the companies continually make clear, they contribute not just profits but jobs. They can continually represent themselves as champions of whole communities that would otherwise collapse, and they receive whole-hearted support from many union leaders, including (in Britain and France) some very left-wing ones. When Hawker-Siddeley's aircraft business is nationalised in Britain it may (one director put it to me) remove some of the pressure to export arms for the sake of quick profits; but the aircraft workers themselves will remain the strongest lobby, for their union leaders can exert their influence direct on the government. In Los Angeles or in Bordeaux the unions likewise reinforce a powerful aerospace lobby, and the higher the unemployment, the more effective the argument.

In the present predicament of the aerospace industry it may be politically unrealistic for any government to drastically reduce arms sales without some compensation, by financing new ventures in commercial aerospace; and while the era of spectacular developments may be over, there are still future projects which call for government investment. The development of a wide-bodied supersonic airliner is a project that many aerospace companies hope for in the 'eighties; its financing would be expensive, and its usefulness limited, but such a venture would be a small price to pay in exchange for the reduction of military sales. There are many other peaceful prospects in aerospace, including civil space projects and the development of fuel-saving aircraft, which would require government aid; and even the development of future subsonic airliners is expected to be too costly for any one company or country. Already the three big American companies are looking for European partners to share the costs and the markets for their next project. These collaborations would give governments the opportunities to strike bargains and to rationalise the over-competitive industry; an interdependence across the Atlantic could help to reduce the breakneck rivalries which have led to many of the worst abuses in arms sales. With Dassault linked to McDonnell Douglas, both companies would have less excuse for their ruthless counterselling of arms.

But providing new opportunities in aerospace can only be a partial and short-term solution to the problem of arms; and many engineers agree that aerospace has reached an 'asymptotic' state, with diminishing returns. No policy of arms control can be effective without tackling the underlying problem of economic priorities, and the pressure of companies, whether nationalised or not, will remain dominant unless governments can face up to the need to redirect their industries. The crisis in aerospace is only part of the larger problem, of the failure of the West to redeploy its manpower and resources into constructive and socially profitable channels for the future.

The roots of the problem go deep into history; but the origin of the present imbalance is to be found in the years 1972 and 1973 which marked a watershed for the West. The problem went much further than the shift of wealth to the oil-producing powers, and the world recession; the oil embargo and the subsequent high cost of oil was a warning of the end of the long era of cheap energy, on which much of the basis of Western industry had been built. Of course there could be no quick response to such a fundamental shock, and the first priority for America had to be the reinforcement of alliances with the oil producers on whom she had become so dependent. But the long-term problems were almost ignored. President Nixon made his stirring speech about 'Project Independence' and promised a new kind of Manhattan project to explore alternative energy sources. But the crisis was quickly forgotten when the embargo was lifted. No more was heard of the great Project. Instead, the Western nations soon realised that they could help to pay for the oil with weapons.

The result was the beginning of a change in the priorities of the whole world. The oil-producing nations, thus urged on by the West, provided an ugly new model for developing countries: the weapons streamed in, clogging the airfields and ports, while ships rode at anchor for months waiting to unload supplies;

hospitals, schools and roads remained hopelessly inadequate and disorganised. A single Chieftain tank, priced at $400,000, costs more than twenty tractors; the current price of a Tomcat fighter, $20 million, could pay for a thousand. By 1975 the total world expenditure on arms was approaching $300 billion a year, and the developing world was spending more on arms than on health and education together.[1]

The Western predicament remains, and the energy crisis will not go away; the economic security of America can never be achieved by arming rival nations at the other end of the world. California, as in so many other fields, symbolises the predicament of the future: a society which, more than any other, has been built on the assumption of unending cheap oil, with its far-flung suburbs linked only by the automobile and its old mass-transit systems abandoned or destroyed. But the Californians, in spite of some past brave attempts, have failed to escape from their energy-trap. Their nightmare of the future remains, of crumbling free-ways and isolated suburbs made unviable by the shortage of oil; and in the meantime they find themselves more than ever depend-ent on the arms industry which has been such a perilous source of prosperity.

The problem of changing priorities and converting industries can never be seen in purely rational terms, and arms and aerospace have always had their special magic. As a means of providing employment, arms are in fact unusually extravagant in relation to investment; both health and education provide more jobs with the same outlay.[2] But the special excitement of the arms industry and its appeal to *machismo* has always given it a clout far beyond its usefulness: the workers on the B1, the labour unions insist, regard their job as more worthwhile and noble than 'leaf-raking' jobs like building houses.

No politician can altogether afford to ignore the atavistic appeal of arms to the male psyche. The word weapon was up till the fourteenth century synonymous with penis;[3] the missiles and machine-guns, and the sexy roar of the Tigers, still hold their phallic spell whether in Iran or Los Angeles. It is no accident that many of the most effective crusaders against arms have been

[1] World Military and Social Expenditures 1976. Leesburg, Virginia, WMSE Publi-cations, 1976, p. 5–6.

[2] *Controlling the Conventional Arms Race*, p. 74.

[3] 'While thou art young and thy weapon keen, wreak thee with wiving.' William Langland, *Piers Plowman*, 1377. See the *Oxford English Dictionary*, Vol XII, p. 224.

women, who are not vulnerable to this primitive thrill, from Berthe von Suttner to Alva Myrdal and the many active young women now involved in the movement for arms control; there are even some men who insist that only a government of women can really be trusted with diplomacy.[1] But until that time, the *machismo* factor cannot be completely excluded. Lockheed and Boeing will continue to have a special leverage with their employees and their voters, and the Shah and the sheikhs will continue to be excited by their products.

It would be absurd for the Western leaders to surrender to these primitive priorities, or to accept them as inevitable: the arms trade feeds on itself, and weapons breed more aggression, heading back towards international anarchy and poverty. But the emotional appeal of the aerospace companies does call for special boldness and leadership in presenting the alternative policy; it must be projected not as a retreat into 'leaf-raking' but as a major challenge to the nation, to open up a future which can offer real security in a civilised environment.

The challenge is there, calling out for strong policies; the industrialised countries will have to face up, sooner or later, to a world in which not only oil reserves are dwindling, but all resources are being tragically wasted, most of all land, leaving a wretched inheritance for future generations. The city-centres of the Eastern United States, the car-clogged roads of Japan, the polluted rivers of Europe, are all warnings that the long consumer boom of the West is reaching a dead end; and the solutions to these problems call for far greater enterprise and high technology than ever went into the arms industry. The idea of Project Independence, if it had been seriously conceived and carried through, had all the makings of a real change of direction, and the goal of national self-sufficiency can generate popular appeal. There may be some encouragement in the fact that a former secretary of defence, James Schlesinger, is now redirected to the problem of energy in Washington. But the real leadership can only come from the top, and the scale of the problem calls for a redeployment on the scale of Roosevelt's New Deal.

---

[1] 'Today our phallic toys have become too dangerous to be tolerated. I see little hope for a peaceful world until men are excluded from the realm of foreign policy altogether and all decisions concerning international relations are reserved for women, preferably married ones.' W. H. Auden: *A Certain World*. London, Faber, 1971, p. 299.

THE PROSPECT

Whatever the United States may attempt or achieve, the long-term limitation of arms sales must depend in the end on international agreement; and the prospects do not at first sight seem encouraging. More nations are joining the competitive free-for-all, young countries like Israel are acquiring their own arms industry, and attempts at embargoes are continually frustrated by other countries. The refrain repeats itself like a dirge: 'If we don't sell arms, someone else will.'

But this excuse, as has often been said, was made for the slave trade; and the parallel between the slave trade and the arms trade may give grounds for hope. In the early nineteenth century the apologists for slavery regarded it as essential to the free-trade system and the economies of Europe and America; but Britain, which had once been enriched by it, persisted in the long and arduous blockade of the trade, and she alone, as the dominant world power, could achieve its international abolition. The Brussels Act of 1890 for the Repression of the African Slave Trade was not only a victory against slavery, but against the arms trade in Africa too. Like Britain then, the United States is today the only power that can take an effective lead; she cannot, as the chief participant, take refuge in the fact that other nations will still do it.

It is true that Britain and France are aggressive arms sellers, with their economies still more dependent on exports than America's; and they will not readily relinquish their trade. But American arms technology, particularly in aerospace, has become increasingly overwhelming, and even Dassault is now having more difficulty in competing; much of the British and French business has been achieved only with the tacit support or agreement of Washington. In the Middle East the United States has become the dominant supplier; and the European opportunities in Egypt, for instance, only occur because the Americans wish to keep out for their own diplomatic reasons. The United States retains considerable leverage over her allies.

Ever since the early 'sixties, when McNamara and Henry Kuss set up their Pentagon sales-machine, the United States has set a brisk pace for arms selling, which other nations felt impelled to follow with their own government sales organisations. In Western Europe the high cost of buying American arms has been the incentive and excuse for selling arms to developing nations, which have thus helped to pay for NATO. For much of this, Europeans have only themselves to blame: the solution to their predicament can ultimately only be found in effective unity between the nations, to produce their own viable industry. But in the meantime the United States—as the UNA report stresses—can help to alleviate the situation by allowing a more genuine 'two-way street' for NATO arms. At present, as Sir Ray Brown complains, 'it's ten lanes one way, and one lane the other way'. But the granting of fairer opportunities for European exports to America could be accompanied by much firmer constraints on Europe's exports to the Third World. The cost of arming NATO must be settled firmly within NATO, and should never have been allowed to spill over into the Third World.

Of course no lasting restraint can be achieved without agreement between the superpowers; for whether in Europe or elsewhere, a great deal of the arms trade and arms aid to the Third World has been a by-product of the central confrontation. But the assumption that providing arms will also provide diplomatic influence has become far less confident than in the 'fifties, and both superpowers have found their arms sales rebounding on them, like Russia in Egypt or the United States in India. The more both sides have turned to selling arms rather than giving them away, the less certain they have been about their political objectives: coups, revolutions or re-exports can always reverse the original purpose. The Soviet satellites are pressed to sell arms, whether to Christians in the Lebanon or to white South Africans, to help pay for their own arms from Russia, but the consequences are the opposite of Soviet policy. The arsenals in the Lebanon, or the armouries of Sam Cummings, bear testimony to the treachery of weapons.

In this general loss of control, this International Dodge City, no major power can really win. As in the years before the First World War, the central balance is constantly endangered by the sales of arms elsewhere. which have been made to pay for it. The economic advantages of the exports are tiny compared to the cost of a Third World War.

Arms salesmen have always thrived on the most pessimistic view of human nature. 'You will never control the trade unless you can change the minds of men,' one Lockheed executive explained to me; and Sam Cummings enjoys the role of a gloomy prophet, surveying the world's folly. But this Manichean view is not really supported by the history of the business. The great surges in arms sales, culminating in the current boom, cannot be ascribed to any sudden new warmongering mood: it was primarily economic pressures that dictated the rush of American weapons into the Middle East, and the scale of the arms race could have been very different if Nixon had said no to the Shah. The minds of men were not really consulted: the decisions were taken by very few people, and only emerged publicly much later—when they aroused great public concern.

The arms business has always insisted that it is like any other business, with no special moral responsibility, and the complexity of modern weapons makes it all the easier to forget their ultimate purpose. The involvement of governments has encouraged arms salesmen to delegate any misgivings; but the governments deliberately conceal the full extent and implications of the trade, for fear of arousing public opinion and 'left-wing extremists'. Yet informed public opinion, in spite of the old spell of weapons, can often be wiser and more moral than governments operating in secrecy.

The problems of arms may be more complex, and their control more difficult, than the layman might at first imagine; but the ordinary citizen is right in thinking that the arms trade, like narcotics or slavery, is different from other trades. The more the public is informed and involved, the more prospect there will be of achieving a saner world.

Index

compiled by Robert Urwin